Competing Fundamentalisms and Egyptian Women's Family Rights

Brill's Arab and Islamic Laws Series

VOLUME 4

Competing Fundamentalisms and Egyptian Women's Family Rights

International Law and the Reform of *Sharīʿa*-Derived Legislation

By

Jasmine Moussa

BRILL

LEIDEN • BOSTON
2011

This book is printed on acid-free paper.

Library of Congress Cataloging-in-Publication Data

Moussa, Jasmine.
Competing fundamentalisms and Egyptian women's family rights : international law and the reform of Shari'a-derived legislation / by Jasmine Moussa.
p. cm. – (Brill's Arab and Islamic laws series)
Includes bibliographical references and index.
ISBN 978-90-04-20309-9 (hardcover : alk. paper)
1. Women–Legal status, laws, etc.–Egypt. 2. Women (Islamic law) I. Title.

KRM517.5.M68 2011
342.6208'78–dc22

2011011913

The views expressed in this book are the author's own and do not reflect the policies of any of the institutions to which she is affiliated.

ISSN 1871-2894
ISBN 978 90 04 20309 9

For my parents, and my brother

"And He it is Who hath produced you from a single being,
and (hath given you) a habitation and a repository."
– Quran (6:98)

"He it is Who did create you from a single soul, and therefrom
did make his mate that he might take rest in her."
– Quran (7:189)

CONTENTS

ACKNOWLEDGEMENTS

The idea behind this book was inspired by a lecture by Dr. Jean Allain (Queen's University, Belfast) on the subject of reservations to international human rights treaties, given at the American University in Cairo over eight years ago. Many years later, I owe him much gratitude, not only for introducing me to the subject of international human rights law, but also for his incessant encouragement and support for my work, without which I would never have survived the challenge of writing on this controversial and often frustrating subject.

I owe a lot to Dr. Nathalie Bernard-Maugiron, who supervised the MA Thesis that later developed into this book, for her methodological precision and scrupulous attention to detail. The rigour and patience with which she went through my work, complemented by her invaluable field experience and insights, appreciably enhanced my understanding of the dynamics of personal status law reform. Dr. Amr Shalakany of the American University in Cairo is credited with drawing my attention to the most challenging questions regarding the development of Islamic family law and its encounter with modernity, forcing me to question many of the prevailing assumptions on this subject. Ms. Naz K. Modirzadeh has also contributed to this work through several valuable discussions and feedback.

Many of my friends and colleagues, too numerous to mention here, have contributed to this work both personally and professionally. I would like to take this opportunity to thank them all.

Finally, I have my parents and my brother to thank for their unfailing support in all my endeavours. My father's idea to produce a book on this subject was followed up with a quest to provide me with access the most credible sources, both in print, and in person. I cannot thank him enough for making this project as much a personal endeavour of his as it is of mine.

PREFACE

Soon after this book had been submitted for publication, a popular revolution toppled Egypt's long-time dictator Hosni Mubarak, on January 25th, 2011, ending his three decades of repressive rule. The revolution, driven by Egypt's youth who mobilised the nation through blogs and social networking sites such as Facebook, was both classless and genderless; it united men and women, young and old, religious and secular, raising the banner of liberty, democracy and social justice. Almost 850 Egyptians died during the eighteen days of protests that ultimately brought down the ruling regime.

Awakening Egypt from the lethargy that had beset the country for more than half a century of bad governance, the revolution promises to usher in a new era of freedom and democratic rule. For the first time in many decades, Egyptians voted in a referendum that was free and fair, in favour of constitutional amendments which lifted previous restrictions on Presidential nominees, largely thought to have been engineered to favour President Mubarak's son, Gamal. The former President and his family, as well as members of the previous ruling regime, were indicted for corruption-related charges, while a spate of legal and social reforms was introduced to allow for greater civil and political rights, as well as to address poverty and meet demands for higher wages.

For all the changes brought about by the revolution, one area in much need of reform has been largely overlooked: Egyptian women and their rights. Although the images broadcasted from *Tahrir* (liberation) square, the seat of the revolution, showed women as leaders and agents of change, reporting, mobilising, assisting with security and communication, even hurling stones at pro-government thugs, a few months after the revolution it seems that Egyptian women have decidedly put their own demands on the back burner.

There was an outcry amongst intellectuals when the ruler *ad interim*, the Supreme Council of the Armed Forces, set up a Committee of experts to draft the proposed constitutional amendments; not one of these experts was a woman. Another blow arrived when the text of the amendments was revealed. Although they opened the door for independents as well as party candidates to nominate themself for the Presidency, the language used to describe the criteria for nomination was exclusively masculine, with a specific phrase excluding from candidature any Egyptian married to a non-Egyptian woman. In spite of claims to the contrary, this language implicitly excludes women from running for the Presidency. When a new 'caretaker' Cabinet was appointed, it included only one woman (as compared to three under the previous regime). Women were similarly under-represented in the newly-established 'National Dialogue' which brings together representatives of civil society and diverse political groups to make policy recommendations for the transition period, and for restructuring the country's institutions.

The aftermath of the revolution witnessed another threat to Egyptian women; the resurgence of political Islam, as restrictions on the participation of the Muslim Brotherhood and the more radical *Jamāʿa Islāmiyya* and *Salafi* movement disintegrated. Public attacks against the emancipation of women started proliferating in the media. Heated debates erupted regarding article 2 of the 1971 Constitution (which stipulates that the Islamic *Sharīʿa* is the primary source of law) with thousands of people taking to the streets to protest any amendment of the provision. The debate lead to trepidation amongst many observers wary of an impending sectarian conflict between Egypt's Muslims and Coptic Christians, and fearing a regression from the Supreme Constitutional Court's interpretations of article 2, which had previously guaranteed legislative gains made by feminists.

In spite of open criticism by a number of intellectuals and feminists in the press (one commentator warned against the return of the age of the *Ḥarem*), to date, there have been no serious attempts to include women in the process of rebuilding Egypt. In the critical weeks and months ahead, it can only be hoped that the spirit of *Tahrir* Square will finally prevail, bringing diverse groups of women to the forefront of the new democratic process. History has shown that feminism and nationalism go hand in hand, that once nationalist demands have been met, women have proceeded with determination to demand their own rights. Just as they have liberated their own society from dictatorship, this new generation of Egyptian women is well-placed to liberate themselves from the chains of patriarchy, according to their own priorities and needs, and without the need to conform to anyone else's ideal of the emancipated woman.

Jasmine Moussa
25th April 2011

LIST OF CASES

International Case Law

Aumeeruddy-Cziffra et al. vs. Mauritius (Communication No. 35/1978), Committee on Civil and Political Rights.
Avellanal v. Peru (Communication No. 202/1986), Committee on Civil and Political Rights.
Belgian Linguistics, Eur.Ct.HR. (decision of 23 July 1968).
Belilos vs. Switzerland, Eur.Ct.HR. (decision of 29 April 1988).
Broeks v. the Netherlands, (Communication No. 172/1984), Committee on Civil and Political Rights.
The Effect of Reservations on the Entry into Force of the American Convention, Advisory Opinion OC-2/82, Inter-Am.Ct.HR. (Ser. A) No. 2 (1982).
Gordon C. van Duzen v. Canada, (Communication No. 50/1979), CCPR, U.N. Doc. CCPR/C/OP/1 at 118 (1985).
Lovelace vs. Canada, (Communication No. 24/1977), Committee on Civil and Political Rights.
Military and Paramilitary Activities in and against Nicaragua (Nicaragua vs. U.S.), ICJ Rep. (1984), 392.
Opuz v. Turkey (*Application no. 33401/02*), Eur.Ct.HR (judgment of 9 June 2009).
Orr v. Orr, Supreme Court of the United States of America, 440 US 268 (1979).
Reservations to the Convention on the Prevention and Punishment of the Crime of Genocide, Advisory Opinion, ICJ Rep. (1951), 15.
US Diplomatic and Consular Staff in Tehran (United States v. Iran), ICJ Rep. (1980), 3.
Velasquez Rodriguez v. Honduras, Inter-American court of Human Rights (judgment of 29 July 1988).
Yilmaz-Dogan v. the Netherlands (Communication No. 1/1984), Committee on the Elimination of Racial Discrimination.

Egyptian Case Law

Court of Appeals, Case no. 432, 1964
Court of Appeals, Case No. 89, 11/12/1965
Court of Cassation, Case No. 28, 18/4/1962
Supreme Constitutional Court, Case no. 28, 2nd Judicial year (4 May 1985)
Supreme Constitutional Court, Case no. 7, 8th Judicial year (15 May 1993)
Supreme Constitutional Court, Case no. 35, 9th Judicial year, (14 Aug 1994)

Supreme Constitutional Court, Case no. 23, 16th Judicial Year, (18 March 1995), Official Gazette no. 14, (6 April 1995)
Supreme Constitutional Court, Case No. 8, 18th Judicial Year, (18 May 1996)
Supreme Constitutional Court, Case no. 74, 17th Judicial year (1 March 1997)
Supreme Constitutional Court, Case no. 18, 14th Judicial year, Official Gazette, Issue 20, (15 May 1997).
Supreme Constitutional Court, Case no. 82, 17th Judicial year, (5 July 1997).
Supreme Constitutional Court, Case no. 144, 18th Judicial year, (1 Sept 1997).
Supreme Constitutional Court, Case no. 164, 19th Judicial year, (3 July 1999).
Supreme Constitutional Court, Case no. 243, 21st Judicial year, (4 Nov 2000), Official Gazette, Issue 46 (16 Nov 2000).
Supreme Constitutional Court, Case no. 201, 23rd Judicial year, (15 Dec. 2002), *Official Gazette*, Issue 52 (26 December 2002).

LIST OF TREATIES AND DECLARATIONS

Charter of the United Nations (1945)
Universal Declaration of Human Rights (1948).
Convention on Consent to Marriage, Minimum Age for Marriage and Registration of Marriages (1964).
International Convention on the Elimination of All Forms of Racial Discrimination (1965), 660 UNTS 195.
International Covenant on Civil and Political Rights (1966), 999 UNTS 171.
International Covenant on Economic Social and Cultural Rights (1966), 993 UNTS 3.
Convention on the Elimination of all forms of Discrimination against Women (1981), 1249 UNTS 13.
Optional Protocol to the Convention on the Elimination of Discrimination Against Women (1999), UNGA Res. 54/4,6 (Oct. 1999).
Convention against Torture and Other Cruel, Inhuman or Degrading Treatment or Punishment (1984), 1465 UNTS 85.
Convention on the Rights of the Child (1989), 1577 UNTS 3.
International Convention on the Protection of the Rights of All Migrant Workers and their Families (1990), UNGA Res 45/158 (18 Dec. 1990).
European Convention for the Protection of Human Rights and Fundamental Freedoms (1950), ETS No. 5, 213 U.N.T.S. 222, entered into force Sept. 3, 1953.
American Convention on Human Rights (1969), OAS. Treaty Series no. 36, 1144 UNTS. 123, entered into force July 18, 1978
African Charter on Human and People's Rights (1981), 1520 UNTS No. 26, 363 OAU Doc. CAB/LEG/67/3 rev 5; 21 ILM 58 (1982).
Protocol to the African Charter on Human and People's Rights on the Rights of Women in Africa (adopted July 11th, 2003).
Declaration on the Elimination of Discrimination against Women, UNGA 22nd Session, (7 Nov. 1967), UN Doc A/RES/2263
UN Declaration on the Elimination of Violence against Women, UNGA, 85th plenary meeting, (20 December 1993), UN Doc A/RES/48/104.
Vienna Declaration and Programme of Action, UNGA, World Conference on Human Rights (12 July 1993), UN Doc A/CONF.157/23.
International Conference on Population and Development, Programme of Action, (1994) UN Doc A/CONF.171/13
Beijing Declaration and Platform of Action (15 Sept 1995) UN Doc A/CONF. 177/20 (1995) and A/CONF.177/20/Add.1 (1995).

LIST OF EGYPTIAN LEGISLATION

Constitution of the Arab Republic of Egypt, adopted 11 Sept 1971, amended 22 May 1980, 25 May 2005, 26 March 2007.
Decree Law No. 25 of 1920 Concerning Maintenance and some Provisions in Personal Status, *Official Gazette*, Issue 61 (15 July 1920).
Law No. 56 of 1923 on Marriage Age
Decree Law No. 25 of 1929 Concerning Provisions in Personal Status, *Official Gazette*, Issue 27 (25 March 1929).
Shari'a Court Regulations (*Decree Law No. 78 of 1931*) *Official Gazette*, Extraordinary Issue No. 53 (30 May 1931)
Law no. 58 of 1937, Egyptian Penal Code
Law No. 77 1943 on Inheritance
Law No. 71 of 1946 on Testamentary Bequests
Law No. 118 of 1952 on Rules of Guardianship over Self
Law No. 119 of 1952 on Rules of Guardianship over Money
Law no. 103 of 1961 (Islamic Research Academy)
Law No. 62 of 1976 Modifying Some Rulings on Maintenance
Decree-Law No. 44 of 1979
Law No. 100 of 1985 Amending Certain Rulings of the Laws of Personal Status, Official Gazette, Issue 27 (4 July 1985).
Law No. 6 of 1998, regarding the criminalisation of the threat or use of violence against wives, offspring and ascendants.
Civil Status Act No. 143 of 1994
Law no. 1 of 2000, Regarding the Promulgation of a Law to Organize Certain Conditions and Procedures in Matters of Personal Status, Official Gazette, Issue 4*Bis*; (29 Jan 2000).
Law no. 91 of 2000 amending Law no. 1 of 2000, Official Gazette, Issue 21 (a) (18 May 2000.)
Procedural Personal Status Law (No. 10 of 2004).
Law No. 11 of 2004 on the establishment of the Family Courts.
Law No. 4 of 2005 amending Article 20 of Decree-Law No. 25 of 1920 (raising the age of custody)
Law No. 126 of 2008 amending the provisions of the Child Act (No. 12 of 1996); Penal Code (No. 58 of 1937); and the Code on Civil Affairs (No. 143 of 1994), *Official Gazette*, Issue 24*Bis* (15 June 2008).
Edict of the Minister of Justice on the Regulation of Marriage Registrars (4 Jan 1955), Official Gazette, Issue 3*Bis*, (10 Jan 1955).
Edict No. 113, 1994, on Islamic attire
Edict No. 208 of 1994, on Islamic attire
Edict No. 1727 of 2000 of the Minister of Justice on the amendment of the 1955 Regulation of Marriage Registrars, Official Gazette, Issue 184 (15 Aug. 2000)

Qadri Pasha's Collection of Sharī'a Rules on Personal Status According to the Ḥanafi Doctrine, in Bek, Ahmed Ibrahim and Wassel Ibrahim, *Aḥkām al-'aḥwāl al-shakhsiyya fil shari'a al-islāmiyya walqanūn* (Cairo, 2003).

INTRODUCTION

As a Muslim woman, I have often pondered the limits placed by my religion on my own rights and choices. Many women living in majority Muslim societies have faced obstacles to their empowerment that are widely justified on the basis of religion. This trump-card has always been convenient to conservatives, as it renders the limitations potentially unquestionable and reform attempts largely unthinkable. The question that arises, however, is whether such obstacles are truly ordained by religion or are the result of diverse social, economic, cultural and even political factors. There is no straightforward answer to this question, in part because the human rights of Muslim women have long been taken to symbolise the cultural standoff between the 'liberated West' and seemingly more 'conservative East'.

Women in predominantly Muslim societies "have been the subject of images and generalisations, romantic Orientalist tales and feminist exposé, Muslim reformers and apologetic tracts."[1] Negative perceptions of Muslim women, which are in many instances stereotypical and far from accurate, abound in the so-called 'West'. Although, many Muslims and non-Muslims have countered such views by arguing that Islam, when it descended hundreds of years ago, actually liberated women, the ideal they often present fails to account for the various forms of discrimination confronting Muslim women in their contemporary societies.[2] The fact remains that women living in majority Muslim societies, such as Egypt, face many forms of discrimination. Popular perceptions of women as irrational beings with lesser mental faculties prevail, advancing the view that women are vulnerable beings in constant need of protection and guardianship by a male relative. The effect of such perceptions is significant, particularly in the area of family relations, which is at the very heart of every woman's existence.

Social attitudes that discriminate against women are not, however, unique to Egypt or other majority-Muslim societies. One only needs to read about the chilling accounts of rape and violence in the United

[1] John L. Esposito, *Women in Muslim Family Law* (1982), 3–10.
[2] Ibid.

States,[3] girl-child infanticide in parts of Asia, trafficking in women and sexual slavery in Asia, Europe and Africa to realise that Egyptian women are often better off than their counterparts in other parts of the world. The fact that gender discrimination exists elsewhere, however, is not an acceptable justification for the toleration of discriminatory laws, policies or practices in Egypt.

In spite of a long history of feminist struggle, women in Egypt have been most successful in advancing their human rights in the public domain. The first achievement was acknowledging women's right to education by establishing the first government school for women as far back as 1873. Writing in 1899, *Qassem Amin*, in his seminal book "The Liberation of Women" lamented the backward social and political status of Egyptian women, calling for their participation in public life. Over the next two decades, the Egyptian feminist movement grew in tandem with the nationalist movement and continued to evolve. In 1923 the first Egyptian feminist federation was established by *Hoda Sha'rawi*, and played a leading role in the struggle against British occupation. The formation of feminist political parties in the 1920's 30's and 40's further propelled the drive for women's political emancipation, and in 1956, Egyptian women earned the right to vote and to nominate themselves for membership of the National Assembly.[4] Women's participation in public life continued to grow in the 1960's and 70's.

However, in recent years, the position of Egyptian women has been threatened by a number of setbacks. In 2008, Egypt remained amongst the three lowest performing countries in the global Gender Empowerment Measure (GEM)—an index which gauges the empowerment of women in public life using data pertaining to the number of women in parliament, in the technical workforce and in senior management postions, falling behind Iran, Oman, and the United Arab Emirates. The trend is disturbing, not only for Egypt's poor performance as compared to other Arab and majority Muslim countries, but because its rank actu-

---

[3] According to Amnesty International, a woman is raped every six minutes in the United States, and battered every 15 seconds 'Violence Against Women: A Factsheet' available at http://www.amnestyusa.org/violence-against-women/violence-against-women-a-fact-sheet/page.do?id=1108440 (accessed Dec. 3rd, 2010).

[4] However, it is argued the initial success of the women's movement in the public domain has not had a lasting effect. Today, women comprise only a quarter of Egypt's workforce, mostly occupying unskilled work mainly in agriculture. However, the government employed an equal number of women and men. See Maria Golia, 'Egyptian Women: Waiting for the Gender Renaissance', *The Middle East* (Feb. 1st, 2007).

ally slipped from seventy-fifth in 2004 to ninety-first.[5] Neither has Egypt fared much better in the Gender-Related Development Index (GDI); there is a significant gender gap in the areas of adult literacy (59% for women as compared to 83% for men), estimated earned income (USD 1635 per annum for women as compared to USD 7,024 for men), as well as economic activity and employment. The only area where the gender gap was not substantial was in the field of education.[6] Although the adoption in 2009 of a law granting women a quota of 76 seats in the 454 member People's Assembly promises to assuage the gender gap in one aspect of public life, there are other areas which require immediate attention if women are to be fully empowered politically, economically and socially.

In the personal or private sphere, both *de jure* and *de facto* achievements have been rather modest. In spite of decades of legislative reform, cultural practices and traditions make it more difficult for a woman to freely choose a spouse, to dissolve an unhappy marriage, or to leave a polygamous or abusive husband. Early marriage may cut a girl's childhood short, and force upon her a spouse she does not desire. A wife may be forced to remain in the matrimonial home for fear of losing her maintenance, or worse still, may wake up to find herself divorced without any prior notice.

Such forms of discrimination are often erroneously justified in the name of Islam. As a Muslim, first and foremost, and then as a woman, I find it difficult to accept that injustice against women is ordained by Islam, a religion that has at its heart the principles of human dignity, equality, full participation, consultation, and social justice. Without claiming to advance an interpretation of what Islam truly does or does not ordain, my belief is that this religion's strong egalitarian message should not be overshadowed by those that advance a distorted understanding of its scriptures. In spite of this personal conviction, however, the aim of this book is not to draw conclusions about women's rights according to some particular interpretation of the scriptures, or to make generalisations about the whole so-called 'Islamic World'. Rather than

[5] *Egypt Human Development Report 2004: Choosing Decentralisation for Good Governance*. United Nations Development Program 24. Available at http://www.undp.org.eg/publications/HDP-2004-E%20.pdf.

[6] *2007/2008 Human Development Report: Egypt* (2005 figures). United Nations Development Program. Available at http://hdrstats.undp.org/countries/data_sheets/cty_ds_EGY.html. Egypt didn't appear in the final global ranking because of the absence of essential data.

engaging in such a debate, I have found it more effective to focus on the area of rights most greatly affected by the Islamic *Sharīʿa*, namely personal status law in one Muslim-majority country, Egypt. The book examines whether the provisions of this body of positive, man-made law is compatible with Egypt's international obligations under treaty law and customary international law establishing standards for the protection of women, and addresses ways in which the law can, and has been reformed, without prejudice to its religious nature. Addressing this question requires a multidisciplinary study of the relevant domestic legislation, and complex law-making processes, as well as the precise scope of existing international obligations and the role of domestic and international enforcement mechanisms. The book focuses on the interplay between domestic reform processes, on the one hand, and relevant international enforcement mechanisms, on the other. In pointing out the shortcomings of Egypt's domestic law, but also highlighting how unidimensional readings of international human rights law fail to foster dialogue that is conducive to reform, this book attempts to draw conclusions regarding the prospects for reconciliation between the domestic and international planes, starting with a detailed and thorough analysis of the contents of each.

Defining Personal Status Law

Personal status law, also known as family law (both terms are used interchangeably throughout the text) is the law that governs family relations including marriage, divorce, child custody and successions. But what makes the study of this body of law particularly significant? First and foremost, family law is an area of law that most directly affects women by defining their rights and status within the family. Since the family is, in turn, the building block of society, hierarchical family structures determine and are simultaneously determined by women's status in society. Understanding the sources of discrimination within the family, as an institution, is thus essential to empowering women. Personal status legislation that discriminates against women may be considered the "primary location of women's oppression" for its "tremendous impact on gender and power hierarchies within the family."[7] Arguably, without equality

[7] Nemat Guenena and Nadia Wassef, *Unfulfilled Promises. Women's Rights in Egypt* (1999), 20. Available at http://www.popcouncil.org/pdfs/unfulfilled_promises.pdf (last visited Dec. 20th, 2004).

in family relations, there cannot be equality in any other area of social organisation. Second, as mentioned earlier, personal status law is the only body of law in Egypt that has not been secularised, resisting various attempts at displacement and modification. The development of family law has therefore been heavily affected by ideological power-struggles since the nineteenth century, rendering it the area of law where Egyptian feminists have achieved most modest results and repeatedly lost ground to conservative forces that have impeded the full empowerment of women.

In order to realise any further advancement for women in Egypt, it is essential to start with the family, where gender hierarchies and stereotypes are most clearly articulated and most forcefully adhered to. Guaranteeing greater rights for women in this area is no easy task, yet neither is it a complete impossibility. Patriarchy and discrimination, whose roots are in reality to be found in culture and tradition, are often erroneously expressed and justified in Islamic terms, rendering attempts to change such attitudes a thorny task, and discouraging women from taking up the challenge for their own rights. The *Sharīʿa* itself leaves much room for the reform of existing personal status laws. Garnering support for such reforms, however, necessitates an informed debate that distinguishes between religiously-ordained rules, and inherited traditions that have been intertwined with interpretations of the text over many centuries.

Reformers have, for decades, maintained that it is not Islam that impedes the empowerment of women, but rather deep-rooted traditions handed down throughout the generations of a patriarchal society. Although the merit of this argument is widely recognised, in practice the dynamics of male-dominance in the family have been difficult to challenge. Even more arduous is the attempt to discredit harmful traditions and oppressive cultural practices, even when they are clearly not grounded in religion.

In spite of the enormity of the task, Egyptian feminists have achieved important reforms through defying interpretations of the religious scriptures which they deemed discriminatory. This process is analysed in detail in Chapters 5 and 6 of this book, which addresses indigenous methods, grounded in the *Shari'a* for reforming family law, as well as the role of Egypt's Supreme Constitutional Court in advancing this process. All references made to the *Quran* rely on the authoritative translation of M. Pikthal, unless otherwise indicated (in which case reference is made to the translations of Yusuf Ali). Relevant prophetic traditions (*aḥadīth*) are extracted from the Compendia of *Al-Bukhari*, *Al-Nisāiʿi*, and *Abu Dawud*. All these sources were accessed through the online database of the University of South Carolina's Centre for Muslim-Jewish Engagement.[8]

In spite of a century of legal reform, crowned by important steps described in Chapter 8, there is still more to be desired in terms of further developing the substance of Egypt's family laws and enforcing the reforms already achieved. The obstacles to this process are addressed in Chapter 9, which relies on field studies and reports of non-governmental organisations to assess the extent of judicial conservatism and the prevalence of conservative social attitudes that impede the reform process. A limited number of interviews with lawyers and judges have been included by way of illustration, but not as a comprehensive field study of judicial attitudes, an enormous and highly sensitive subject that I hope will attract more scholarly attention in the future. A theme that appears throughout the book is the interaction between domestic and international institutions and mechanisms, with a view to 'indigenising' international standards such that they may be translated into further empowerment of women on the ground.

Defining Women's International Human Rights Law

The body of law that can be referred to as "women's international human rights law", consists of international treaties, custom, and 'soft law' instruments, whether they exclusively address the human rights of women, or contain specific provisions relating to this area. At the apex of this legal regime is the 1981 Convention on the Elimination of All Forms of Discrimination Against Women (CEDAW),[9] which Egypt ratified on September 18th, 1981.[10] As the most comprehensive treaty addressing women's human rights, it will form the focus of this book's examination of Egypt's international obligations, in Chapters 2 and 3. Other instruments of relevance include the UN Charter,[11] the Universal Declara-

[8] Available at http://www.usc.edu/schools/college/crcc/engagement/resources/texts/ (last accessed Dec. 12th, 2010).

[9] Convention on the Elimination of All Forms of Discrimination Against Women, *opened for signature* Dec. 18th, 1979.

[10] See *Egypt. Treaties: Ratifications and Reservations*, For the Record 2003: The United Nations Human Rights System [Hereinafter Ratification and Reservations] (Human Rights Internet, 2003) http://www.hri.ca/fortherecord2003/vol2/egyptrr.htm.

[11] The Preamble of the UN Charter stipulates that "the People of the United Nations determined to reaffirm faith in fundamental human rights, in the dignity and worth of

tion of Human Rights (UDHR),[12] the International Covenant on Civil and Political Rights (ICCPR),[13] the International Covenant on Economic Social and Cultural Rights (ICESCR),[14] in addition to regional human right treaties to which Egypt is a party.[15] The provisions relating to equality between the spouses in family relations are mainly articles 16 of the CEDAW and the UDHR and article 23 of the ICCPR.[16] An analysis of these instruments—including through the application of the rules of international law relevant to treaty interpretation—is essential to elucidate the scope of Egypt's international obligations in the area of eliminating gender discrimination.

Customary rules of international law are of equal relevance, as well as the body of 'soft law' that reinforces the principle of non-discrimination on the basis of gender, including non-binding resolutions of the United Nations General Assembly, Economic and Social Council and relevant subsidiary organs, in addition to outcome documents adopted by States at international conferences. Although 'soft-law' is not, as such, legally binding, it clarifies areas where there is a degree of consensus on women's human rights and may sometimes indicate the emergence of customary norms of international law. Finally, the general recommendations of the Committee on the Elimination of Discrimination against Women (CEDAW Committee), established to monitor compliance with the CEDAW, as well as the general comments of other UN treaty-monitoring bodies, are central to this analysis for their authoritative interpretative value.

---

the human person, in the equal rights of men and women ..." Article 1 also stipulates that States are to "promote universal respect for and observance of human rights and fundamental freedoms for all without distinction as to ... sex."

[12] Universal Declaration on Human Rights, *adopted* 10th Dec. 1948. Article 1 of the UDHR stipulates that "all human beings are born free and equal in dignity and rights."

[13] International Covenant on Civil and Political Rights, *opened for signature* Dec. 16th, 1966. Article 2 of the ICCPR stipulates that all civil and political rights detailed in the Covenant are to be guaranteed to men and women equally, without distinction.

[14] International Covenant on Economic, Social and Cultural Rights, *opened for signature* 16th Dec. 1966, article 2 of which states that the rights enunciated in the Covenant "will be exercised without discrimination of any kind as to race, colour, or sex ...." Article 3 further provides that all States party undertake to ensure the equal rights of men and women with regards to the enjoyment of all economic, social, and cultural rights.

[15] Egypt is a party to the African Charter on Human and People's Rights, which prohibits discrimination on the basis of gender in article 18, to which Egypt has entered a reservation.

[16] Egypt ratified the ICCPR and ICESCR on January 14th, 1982. See *Ratification and Reservations*.

The examination of Egypt's international obligations also necessitates a thorough consideration of Egypt's reservations to human rights treaties inasmuch as they affect the family rights of women. The general rules of public international law relevant to the treatment of reservations and objections are constantly evolving, particularly in the area of international human rights law, and are examined in Chapter 4 of this book. The aim is to assess the extent to which such reservations may be said to modify Egypt's obligations under the CEDAW and other relevant human rights treaties.

Whereas initially the women's rights discourse focused on the concept of non-discrimination on the basis of sex (a biological distinction), eventually, the notion of sex was replaced with that of gender (which includes both the biological aspect as well as socially constructed roles for women and men).[17] Setting aside debates regarding the appropriateness of using either term, both will be used interchangeably throughout this book to describe the phenomenon of discrimination against women.

Whereas much of the scholarly work on the human rights of women living in Muslim-majority countries attempts to answer the question of whether the *Sharīʿa*, as such, is compatible with international law, such writings not only assume the superiority of international standards, but are also impervious to the fact that in the Muslim world, the question is consistently being framed in the exact opposite terms. It is thus easy for both sides of the debate to reach conclusions that highlight their mutual exclusiveness, even to the point of reciprocal contempt, as each one is portrayed as the antithesis of the other. To break away from this cycle, it is crucial to start by asking the right questions, questions that do not make value-laden assumptions about the *Sharīʿa* in general, treating it as an 'alien' system that arouses fear and distrust. A useful starting point would be to frame the debate in terms of how international human rights law can contribute to advancing the rights of women living in Muslim-majority societies, without impinging on their unique identities. Simultaneously, examining how 'Islamic' values[18] can contribute to international

[17] *What do we mean by "sex" and "gender"?* World Health Organisation available at http://www.who.int/gender/whatisgender/en/index.html.

[18] Prince Charles, for example, is credited for promoting a better understanding of the many historical and contemporary contributions of Islamic values see, for example, *HRH Prince Charles speaks on Islam and the Environment* Foreign and Commonwealth Office, available at http://www.fco.gov.uk/en/news/latest-news/?view=News&id=22350511, and the full text of his speeches at http://www.exploreislaam.com/index.php?option=com_content&view=section&id=16&layout=blog&Itemid=14.

debates and norm-setting, including in the area of women's human rights, can enrich the debate and help achieve a truly pluralistic global society.

No single society or worldview can claim to monopolise the true meaning of human dignity and empowerment. International mechanisms of enforcement of women's human rights have a tendency to seek to replicate the realities of women living in the West in every other society. They seek to construct all women as identical and promote a form of homogenisation that is not only divorced from the social realities in diverse economic, political and cultural settings, but that also threatens to foster resistance to the whole idea of advancing women's rights. This book attempts to uncover a view of women's human rights that takes into consideration the richness of cultural diversity on the one hand, and the universality of human rights standards on the other, thus avoiding the trap of "comparing one's ideal to someone else's reality."[19] It is noteworthy that religious minorities living in majority Muslim societies, including Egypt, have the right to apply their own personal status laws, distinct from the Islamic *Sharīʿa*, which attests to Islam's toleration of religious and cultural autonomy. Such is the case with Egypt's sizeable Christian minority. Although Christian women in Egypt also suffer from various forms of discrimination, the challenges that they face do not fall within the scope of this study.

This book also seeks to better understand the complex sources of discrimination against women in the area of family relations, as well as avoid prevailing generalisations that plague a great deal of the literature on the rights of Muslim women. By removing the debate from the realm of theory and focusing on a particular area of law in one Muslim-majority country, Egypt, it attempts to eschew such generalisations and suggest practical tools to advance the family rights of Egyptian women. The book departs from the premise that Muslim scholars have, and should continue to develop a jurisprudence that is embedded in the rules of the *Sharīʿa*, yet relevant in a modern context. Such efforts, which are underway not only in Egypt, but also in a number of other Muslim-majority countries, and are founded on a great deal of serious and critical reflection, have the potential to bridge the gap between local tradition and international standards, but only insofar as the latter proves sufficiently flexible and pluralistic to accommodate divergent worldviews, and rid itself of any seemingly inherent 'Western' liberal bias.

[19] Esposito (1982).

I hope this book can contribute, in small part, to the mammoth effort being undertaken by many Egyptians in their search for effective and pragmatic methods to uphold the rights and dignity of Egyptian women, while allowing them to stay true to their identity and their ideals. It is as much a testament to the importance of international standards of human rights, and their potential to empower and inform domestic debates, as a celebration of diversity, that eschews the deterministic urge to do away with belief systems that have alternative conceptions of women's rights, and replace them with a 'Western' liberal notion of formal equality.

CHAPTER ONE

THE HUMAN RIGHTS OF WOMEN IN A SPECIFIC CULTURAL CONTEXT

Violations of the human rights of women are an unmistakable reality of all modern-day societies, albeit to different extents. The fundamental components of patriarchy do not differ between Muslim and other societies; women's subordination is a reality everywhere and exists at multiple levels. Discrimination against women is discernible in "the immediate structures of family and kinship,"[1] at the level of state policies, within the decision-making structures of private-sector corporations, and even in international policy-making; and such is the case whether religion is a factor or not. Global statistics regarding literacy rates, school enrolment, employment and remuneration, poverty and access to basic services, show that women all over the world are at an obvious disadvantage when compared to men. Notwithstanding this reality, the so-called 'Islamic world' is frequently singled out—erroneously—as a region that is unique in discriminating against women.

Many writers have blamed Islam "for the accumulated ills of Muslim women",[2] and accused it of acting as a vehicle for the subjugation of women. Such reductionism abounds in the literature on this sensitive issue, sending the wrong message that 'Islam' alone is responsible for the inferior status of women in most Muslim societies. However, these writings commit the twin error of ignoring the myriad factors, other than religion, that affect women's empowerment, as well as inaccurately assuming the homogeneity of the so-called 'Islamic world' and the uniformity of *Sharīʿa*-derived legislation.[3] Although "the impact of *Sharīʿa*-based

---

[1] Farida Shaheed, 'Dossier 23–24: Constructing Identities—Culture, Women's Agency and the Muslim World', *Women Under Muslim Laws (WUML)* http://www.wluml.org/english/pubsfulltxt.shtml?cmd[87]=i-87-2788 (July 2001).

[2] See Heba Raouf Ezzat, 'The Silent Ayesha: An Egyptian Narrative', in Jane H. Bayes and Nayereh Tohidi (eds.), *Globalization, Gender and Religion: The Politics of Women's Rights in Catholic and Muslim Contexts* (2001) at 232.

[3] See Shaheed (2001). For an example of such generalisations, see for instance, Linda Cipriani, 'Gender and Persecution: Protecting Women Under International Refugee Law', 7 *Geo. Immigr. L.J.* 511 (October 1993) who advocates granting refugee status to Muslim

legislation and customary law on women's status is by no means minimized," it is a fallacy to attribute to Islam "the sole influence in explaining the ways of life of Muslim women."[4]

Existing literature is replete with references to "women's rights in Islam," or "women in Islamic societies" which mistakenly assume a unipolar relationship between Islam, on the one hand, and the status and rights of women, on the other. Such works also suggest that in all matters relating to women there exists "a qualitative difference predicated on the presence or absence of Islam"[5] which automatically separates Muslim women from all others. Such generalisations are, however, misleading. They imply a false universality and uniformity throughout the so-called 'Islamic world' and perpetuate the inaccurate view that Muslims live in a world that is defined exclusively by their religious identity, and that is somehow insulated from all other significant social, political and cultural influences.[6] In *Covering Islam*, Edward Said aptly demonstrates that:

> The term 'Islam' as it is used today seems to mean one simple thing, but is in fact part fiction, part ideological label, part designation of a religion called Islam. In no really significant way is there a direct correspondence between the 'Islam' in common Western usage and the enormously varied life that goes on within the world of Islam, with its more than 800,000,000 people, its millions of square miles of territory principally in Africa and Asia, its dozens of societies, states, histories, geographies, cultures.[7]

Although Islam's formative influence on the roles of men and women cannot be ignored,[8] women living in Muslim societies enjoy different degrees of protection and benefit from different rights; a consequence of variations in culture, political and historical circumstances, social realities, economic conditions, as well as numerous other complex factors.[9] The rights of women are also determined by "the history and politics of

---

women who are "victimised" by their societies; and Manoucher Parvin, 'On the Synergism of Gender and Class Exploitation: Theory and Practice Under Islamic Rule', 51 *Rev. Soc. Econ.* 201 (1993) who draws parallels between the 'economic exploitation' of women in Islam and racial apartheid in South Africa.

[4] Camillia Fawzi El-Solh and Judy Mabro, 'Introduction: Islam and Muslim Women', in Camillia Fawzi El-Solh and Judy Mabro (eds.), *Muslim Women's Choices. Religious Belief and Social Reality* (1994) at 20.

[5] Shaheed (2001).

[6] Ibid.

[7] Edward Said, *Covering Islam* (1997) at 1.

[8] Esposito (1982) at xii.

[9] See Helie-Lucas, 'What is your tribe? Women's Struggles and the Construction of Muslimness', in Courtney Howland (ed.), *Religious Fundamentalisms and the Human Rights of Women* (1999) at 23–24.

the State—that is, the specific experiences and legacies of colonial rule, and the trajectories of national independence, integration and development."[10]

For more than a thousand four hundred years, the sources of Islamic law have been subjected to a perpetual process of interpretation and reinterpretation, not to mention the influence of interaction between Islam and other diverse cultures and religions throughout history. In fact, Islamic law or *Sharīʿa* is an aggregation of individual opinions and juristic interpretations, which differ not only from one school to another, but also between distinct opinions within each of the jurisprudential schools. As such, *Sharīʿa*-derived laws are not the same in all countries that apply them. In codifying personal status matters into modern laws, contemporary legislators have selected from among these opinions and interpretations, giving rise to laws that differ markedly in the extent of rights and degree of protection afforded to women. This subjective law-making process has been affected by political struggles, cultural attitudes and social traditions. Evidence of this lies in the large disparity between the Tunisian, Egyptian, and Saudi Arabian personal status laws, although all three of these countries derive such laws from the *Sharīʿa*.

In other words, discrimination against women applying such laws is not divinely-ordained; it is without doubt man-made, yet insulated through the guise of religious sanction. Parochial and reductionist analyses that deny this reality fail to both identify the complex sources of discrimination against women, as well as to propose a pragmatic approach to counter discriminatory attitudes against women living in Muslim societies. They simultaneously serve the agendas of conservative groups that seek to insulate their societies from change by contending that the values of Islam may not be reconciled with international standards of protection for the human rights of women.

In matters of personal status and religious affairs, Egypt's legal system adheres to the principle of the 'personality of laws,' by virtue of which non-Muslims are granted relative legislative and judicial autonomy. Egypt's personal status law is thus a plurality of laws: no uniform personal status code exists for all Egyptians, but "a separate code for almost every one of the fifteen religious communities within Egypt."[11]

---

[10] Lisa Hajjar, 'Domestic Violence and Shari'a: A Comparative Study of Muslim Societies in the Middle East, Africa and Asia,' *Islamic Family Law Project*, at http://www.law.emory.edu/IFL/index2.html (last accessed 15 March 2005).

[11] Maurits Berger, 'Conflicts Law and Public Policy in Egyptian Family Law: Islamic Law Through the Backdoor,' 50 *Am. J. Comp. L.* 555, 558 (Summer 2002). See discussion *infra* at p. 119.

The personal status law for Egypt's *Sunni* Muslim majority is based on the Islamic *Sharīʿa*, and is the only one promulgated by the Egyptian legislature. Non-Muslims are subject to *Sharīʿa* law only in three circumstances, which have been justified by reference to the principle of *ordre publique*. The first case is when either of the spouses is Muslim (which naturally means the husband, since a Muslim woman's marriage to a non-Muslim man is not recognised by law), and the second occurs when both spouses are non-Muslim but they each belong to a different non-Muslim religious sect. Finally, Islamic *Sharīʿa* law is applied generally with respect to the law of successions.[12]

Family relations is the area of human relations that has been most meticulously regulated by the *Quran*, codified in a series of personal status laws dating back to the 1920's. Efforts to address discrimination in this area have proven arduous. Reforms are thus sporadic and often hampered by negative social attitudes and beliefs. As a corollary to its inspiration from interpretations of the religious scriptures, personal status law is strongly entrenched, almost to the point of sanctification. The result is that gender hierarchies and inequalities established under these laws are widely accepted.[13]

Muslim family law is the main aspect of the *Sharīʿa* that was carried on to modern times in Egypt, resisting displacement by European codes during the colonial era, and surviving attempts at secularization in the post-colonial period.[14] As such, the protection and preservation of *Sharīʿa*-derived personal status codes has become intricately tied with attempts to preserve culture and identity, prompting a defensive reaction to any international instruments that seek to modify or challenge the principal tenets of such legislation. The issue of women's rights has thus fuelled much public debate, couched in the rhetoric of foreign influence versus cultural authenticity, rendering women a charged symbol of cultural conflict.[15] In this conflict, it has often been the most conservative of voices that have found resonance and following, as "attachment to medieval patriarchy came to mean attachment to the Islamic."[16] There can be no doubt that

---

[12] Ibid. at 562.

[13] Hajjar (2005).

[14] Ibid.

[15] See Tove Stang Dahl, *The Muslim Family. A Study of Women's Rights in Islam* (1997) at 62.

[16] Lama Abu Odeh, 'Modernising Muslim Family Law: The Case of Egypt', 37 *Vand. J. Transnat'l L. 1043* (October 2004) at 1047.

Sharīʿa derived personal status law has proven central to the identity of Muslims even in a formally secular state structure.[17] Although reforms in the area of personal status law, over the last century, have overcome the most egregious gender inequalities in the areas of marriage, divorce, child custody and successions, discrimination in the area of family relations still persists in a number of areas and is often justified in religious and cultural terms.

Any serious approach to improving the human rights of women living in majority Muslim societies must avoid the so-called 'Orientalist trap' which divides the world into two poles: the progressive 'West' and the backward 'East'. It must avoid the unnecessarily pejorative view of the *Sharīʿa* as a cause for the subordination of women, while simultaneously evading the apologetic counter-argument that Muslim women are not in need of universal human rights norms, which are allegedly based on an individualism rejected by Islam's elevation of family values.

Having said that, it must be emphasized that Islamic religious scriptures do, indeed, sanctify the institution of the family, granting it considerable protection as a unit. This notion, however, is neither alien to international human rights law, nor the world's principal legal systems.[18] The value placed on the family, as a unit, should not be used to overstate the irreconcilability of laws based on the *Sharīʿa* with international standards of non-discrimination. Neither should they be manipulated in such a way as to justify the subordination of women. After all, there is nothing in the Islamic religious scriptures that suggests that the rights of women, equally sanctified by Islam, are secondary to the rights of the family. What is required is the balancing of these various rights in a way that fulfils the Islamic ideal of social justice and human dignity.

---

[17] See, in general, Andra Nahal Behrouz, 'Transforming Islamic Family Law: State Responsibility and the Role of Internal Initiative', 103 *Colum. L. Rev.* 1136 (June 2003).

[18] The UDHR establishes the right to found a family in article 16, and protects the family from arbitrary interference in article 12, while the ICCPR stipulates in article 23 that "the family is the natural and fundamental group unit of society and is entitled to protection by society and the State". The same is true of the vast majority of domestic legal systems, which often endow the family with a special status and protections including through constitutional provisions. For instance, the Basic Law of the Federal Republic of Germany stipulates in article 6 that "marriage and the family shall enjoy the special protection of the State", whereas the 1978 Spanish Constitution states in article 39 that "the public authorities shall assure the social, economic, and legal protection of the family". Article 22 of the Belgian Constitution guarantees everyone's "right to the respect of his private and family life".

Admittedly, it is very difficult for someone with a 'liberal Western' mindset to understand many of the precepts on which *Sharīʿa*-derived family-law is based. Feminists and human rights activists are therefore divided on how to address such laws, which deal with marriage as a large scheme of reciprocal rights and duties. The *Sharīʿa* treats marriage as a contract, by virtue of which both spouses have certain rights and duties. The first right, is the exercise of 'conjugal' or sexual relations; such relations are not tolerated outside the institution of marriage. This must be understood clearly when addressing issues related to positive law, such as the minimum marriage age, registration of marriage, and polygamous unions. Whereas the typical 'Western liberal' approach would view sexual conduct as something separate from marriage, such that there can be a separate minimum age for consensual sexual relations which is much younger than the minimum age for marriage,[19] such a distinction is not perceived by the *Sharīʿa*. Under the latter, sexual relations outside a marital relationship are not condoned, which may explain the existence of considerable resistance to raising the minimum marriage age. Similarly, some Islamic scholars lament attempts to prohibit or limit polygamy, which they compare to what they consider morally inferior practices of 'fornication', 'adultery' and 'promiscuity' that are not outlawed or restricted by law in Western legal systems.[20] The 'Western liberal' outlook may also fail to comprehend the centrality of the dowry to an Islamic marriage, or the husband's maintenance obligations, although such practices have the effect of transmitting property from the husband to the wife, in a way that balances the effect of inheritance laws[21] and grants the wife financial security. Custody rights are also predicated on a the distinction between the roles and inherent natures of the husband and wife. Younger children are considered as requiring the emotional nurturing that only a mother is perceived to be capable of providing, and hence the law favours the mother, in this area. Whereas this broad scheme of rights and responsibilities must be understood in order to avoid superficial assessments of what is adequate for women living under

[19] The age of consent in European States ranges from 13 to 16. And in some states of the USA it's as low as 12. See Kate Sutherland, 'Form Jailbird to Jailbait: Age of Consent Laws and the Construction of Teenage Sexualities', 9 *William and Mary J. of Women and the Law* 313 (2003) at 314.

[20] Yusuf Al Qaradawy, *The Status of Women in Islam* (1997).

[21] See Pascale Fournier, *Muslim Marriage in Western Courts* (2010) at 17.

Sharīʿa-derived laws, it should not be used to justify rigidity in reforming such laws when possible.

In light of the above, it is prejudicial to examine family laws based on the *Sharīʿa* from the narrow lens of the formal non-discrimination provisions of the CEDAW. International human rights law, which comprises a set of universal standards articulated and agreed upon by the international community as a whole, including States with majority Muslim populations, may, however, be interpreted in a way that allows for a greater rapprochement with diverse legal systems. The essence of international human rights law is to guarantee the dignity of women and promote and protect their rights as human beings regardless of their religion or creed. To do so, it is necessary to highlight the convergence between international standards and Islamic notions of justice, dignity, and equality through adopting a more nuanced view of non-discrimination, one which is not simply based on comparison with a male model, but which takes into consideration different cultural and religious contexts. International practice, however, does not indicate the necessary tolerance for such convergence.

The constant interplay between international and domestic institutions in the legal and social reform process is thus essential; neither must seek to render the other obsolete. Whereas domestic processes are likely to inform international debates of local needs and desires, international mechanisms can help empower local voices to overcome barriers to equality, through providing a platform to voice concerns, as well as necessary resources and networks. It is only through simultaneously employing domestic and international tools and mechanisms that women in Egypt can hope to accelerate legal reforms that aim to eliminate discrimination, while employing methods that are suitable to their own social, economic and political realities.

Theoretical Framework: Situating the Study in the Wider Debate

The two theories that currently constitute the most formidable challenge to the international women's rights discourse are cultural relativism and Feminist legal theory; both argue that their voices have not been recognised in the contemporary human rights paradigm.[22] The codification

[22] Radhika Coomaraswamy, 'Different but Free: Cultural Relativism and Women's

of universally-recognised human rights standards into binding international instruments dates back to the adoption of the Universal Declaration of Human Rights in 1948. The movement gained momentum in the decade of the 1960's, which heralded the two international Human Rights Covenants. Together, these three documents are referred to as the International Bill of Rights, and have been supplemented by a number of instruments dealing with specific human rights issues.

For over half a century, treaties establishing binding international human rights standards have been the subject of a fierce debate between proponents of universalism, who advocate the equal application of international human rights standards to all human beings, regardless of cultural, religious and other particularities and proponents of cultural relativism, who contend that human rights standards differ from one group to another and are thus culturally qualified. Cultural relativists maintain that there is an inevitable conflict between universal human rights standards and deeply entrenched cultural and religious beliefs and practices, which should be resolved in favour of the latter. In other words, the contents of human rights law should be understood through the lens of the cultural setting in question. Universalists, on the other hand believe that human rights should not vary in their application, regardless of the country or culture in which they are applied.[23]

Nowhere has the debate between these two competing doctrines been as intense and ideologically-charged as in the fierce battleground for the human rights of women. Similarly, Feminist legal theory is critical of the body of international legal instruments that purportedly guarantees respect for the human rights of women. Proponents of this theory argue that the formulation of international law has been monopolised by men, who have disregarded the true needs and concerns of women, particularly women from the Third World. Both these critiques will be addressed in the following subsections.

Rights as Human Rights', in Courtney Howland (ed.), *Religious Fundamentalisms and the Human Rights of Women* (1999).

[23] Jo Lynn Southard, 'Protection of Women's Human Rights Under the Convention on the Elimination of Discrimination Against Women', 8 *Pace Int'l L. Rev.* 1 (Winter 1996) at 6.

The Human Rights of Women: The Polemics of Universalism and Cultural Relativism

The discourse on women's human rights has long been trapped in the seemingly impenetrable polemics of the universalist-cultural relativist divide. Both of these analytical approaches, however, suffer from fundamental flaws. The universalist strategy over-emphasises the importance of international laws and standards in "giving women a voice in society's institutions,"[24] often ignoring domestic pressures and processes. Such a strategy cannot succeed on its own for a number of reasons. First and foremost, the international regime protecting women's human rights is plagued with ambiguity, and replete with loopholes that allow States to evade their international obligations. The absence of an effective international enforcement mechanism has also led to non-adherence and impunity by States. That is not to mention the leeway they have in interpreting their international obligations, which, although practical in granting States a "margin of appreciation," may also lead to the manipulation of international legal instruments. In fact,

> the Universalist approach encourages individual states to adopt international human rights laws as models for domestic legislation. Deeper investigation, however, reveals that many states ratify this legislation for political reasons, intending to interpret the legislation in ways much different than was originally intended.[25]

Imposing alien standards on societies with diverse beliefs, however, will most probably result in a backlash, thus diluting the value of the international treaty in question. According to proponents of universalism, "culture" is simply a pretext used to justify the continued subjugation of women. However, such a dismissal of culture as an organising factor in society overlooks the extremely important reality that

> women all over the world believe in and perpetuate the roles that culture, tradition, and religion demand that they play. Moreover, given the choice, many women would decide not to abandon the traditions that they were socialized to accept.[26]

[24] Elene G. Mountis, 'Cultural Relativity and Universalism: Re-evaluating Gender Rights in a Multicultural Context', 15 *Dick. J. Int'l L.* 113 (Fall 1996) at 115.
[25] Ibid.
[26] Shaheed (2001).

Universalism is thus largely an academic debate, divorced from the realities that affect the lives of women and their ability to act as agents of change in conservative societies. In other words, universalism does not recognise the enormous impact of culture and tradition, which may dampen the effectiveness of international human rights law, if not totally extinguishing it altogether.[27] On the other hand, however, cultural relativism threatens to shield discriminatory laws and practices from international scrutiny. Since the social and cultural institutions in many countries have patriarchal ideologies as their foundation, they provide no adequate vehicles for social change. Relying on cultural qualifications thus means that "women become powerless to challenge oppressive traditions" that affect them.[28]

Advancing the human rights of women therefore necessitates an approach that avoids the inadequacies of both conceptual approaches, recognising that universal standards are insufficient in and of themselves particularly if they ignore practical realities on the ground, while simultaneously rejecting a strict cultural relativist approach that defends discriminatory practices. International standards must therefore be tolerant of a certain degree of cultural sensitivity, without acting as a haven for cultural relativists. There is no doubt that international law requires a genuine effort to discredit those cultural values that are manifestly harmful and discriminatory. Although this leads the debate in the direction of further murky grounds, particularly since there is no authoritative body to define what constitutes a manifestly harmful law or practice, the degree of cultural sensitivity proposed in this context is one that is very narrow in scope and hence does not allow for an interpretation of treaty obligations in a way that strips them of their legal value. In fact, the term cultural sensitivity is defined here to mean the elaboration of reform procedures based on indigenous or local tools and methods and grounded in socially-acceptable values, with the objective of gradually achieving the goals set out in international instruments for the protection of women's human rights.

This concept, which attempts to reach a middle-ground between two competing discourses, is not an innovation. It has often been referred to by commentators as 'indigenisation' or 'vernacularisation' of international standards. It is however, understood that this process, in which international standards are given localised meanings may result in the

[27] Mountis (1996) at 115.
[28] Shaheed (2001).

modification of the contents of these standards, making them less 'revolutionary' or far-reaching in their effect and scope, but at the same time more effective, lasting and acceptable to the people they address.[29]

Gender definitions form a fundamental component of cultural consciousness and thus constitute "essential ingredients of the collective identity of any group."[30] It follows that re-definitions of gender relations inevitably demand a "readjustment of the broader culture and collectivity concerned."[31] The result is that in the struggle to demand their rights and re-define the traditional roles ascribed to them, women defy far more than the contours of their own individual lives. For this reason, it is impractical to ignore the significant effect of culture on the human rights of women, or to overlook the importance of giving meaning to universal human rights norms in the indigenous context if they are to take root in culturally diverse societies. In order for international human rights standards to be effective "they have to go beyond the normative, textual essence and become part of the legal culture of a given society."[32]

The result of this analysis is, however, to raise more questions than answers, particularly regarding the socialising role of law and its power to transform society. The most perplexing question is whether legal reforms dictated from above can succeed in changing cultural attitudes, or whether, on the other hand, societal transformation must precede any legal reforms in order for the latter to have their desired effect. Whereas there seems to be no easy answer to this question, the logical course of action is to move simultaneously along both paths. In other words, legislative reforms that seek to address *de jure* discrimination must be accompanied by attempts to change discriminatory cultural perspectives and values, if they are to have an actual impact on the *de facto* status of women. It is only through combining legislative reform with cultural adaptation, at any particular historical moment, that the desired advancement in the position of women can materialise.[33] Such is the case "irrespective of whether the society in question is dynamic

---

[29] See for example Sally Engle Merry, 'Vernacularization in Action: Using Global Women's Human Rights Locally', in Sally Engle Merry and Peggy Levitt (eds.), *Special Issue of Global Networks* 9 (4), 2009.

[30] Shaheed (2001).

[31] Ibid.

[32] Rhadika Coomaraswamy, 'To Bellow Like a Cow: Women, Ethnicity and the Discourse of Rights', in Rebecca J. Cook (ed.), *Human Rights of Women, National and International Perspectives* (1994), 39–57.

[33] Ibid. at 45.

or stagnant, ancient or contemporary, atheist or religious, and of course, Muslim or non-Muslim."[34]

Any practical and workable approach to the advancement of women's rights in the controversial area of family law necessitates the utilisation of indigenous reform tools, grounded in the *Sharīʿa*, coupled with the promotion of gradual social change. It is only through the employment of such a strategy that reform initiatives will be seen as genuinely domestic, enabling them to overcome the detrimental accusation of being a 'Western' imposition. Coulson aptly describes the virtues of this approach as follows:

> Radical though the break with past tradition which such an approach involves might be, it is nevertheless a break with a particular construction of the religious law and not with its essence. This, at any rate, would seem to be the only realistic basis for future development and the only alternative to the complete abandonment of the notion of a law based on religion. Law to be a living force, must reflect the soul of a society; and the soul of present Muslim society is reflected neither in any form of outright secularism nor in the doctrine of the mediaeval text books.[35]

The use of such tools, which are grounded in the *Sharīʿa*, and hence culturally accepted and more likely to be effective, have allowed Egypt to advance women's equality rights within the family without displacing religious law altogether. This approach recognizes that freedom of religion is an equally valid human right deserving of universal protection. Just as it is oppressive to manipulate religion in order to discriminate against women, it is equally oppressive to impose on women standards, values and lifestyles they neither demand nor accept. The affected women must be at the center of the process, and their needs and desires must be the driving force behind any call for reform. According to Falk,

> Without mediating international human rights through the web of cultural circumstances, it will be impossible for human rights norms and practices to take deep hold in non-Western societies except to the partial, and often distorting, degree that these societies—or, more likely, their governing elites—have been to some extent Westernized. At the same time, without cultural practices and traditions being tested against the norms of international human rights, there will be a regressive disposition toward the retention of cruel, brutal, and exploitative aspects of religious and cultural tradition.[36]

---

[34] Shaheed (2001).
[35] Noel Coulson, *A History of Islamic Law* (1968) at 225.
[36] Richard Falk, 'Cultural Foundations for the International Protection of Human

Feminist Theory and Women's International Human Rights Law

Another major influence on the international discourse on women's human rights is feminist legal theory, which highlights the systemic injustice suffered by women worldwide. Feminist theory has generated several separate approaches and diverse schools of doctrine, which may be grouped into four main strands: liberal or Western feminism, cultural feminism, radical feminism, and post-modern feminism. Although these strands take different and even radically opposing positions in the pursuit of women's human rights, they converge in the belief that it is essential to give voice to women's unique experiences and propose distinctive solutions to women's disadvantages.[37] Similarly, they contend that the law has traditionally been insensitive to the needs of women; that it is essentially biased and androcentric, privileging a masculine worldview that has failed to address the specific needs of women. However, many feminists also recognize the significance and potential power of international human rights law in promoting full and equal rights for women. By introducing empowering and norm-transforming principles, it has succeeded in challenging "traditional conceptions of women's roles by applying standards that hold societies accountable."[38] It has also acted "as a catalyst for mobilizing local communities to effectuate normative change through institutionalized means."[39]

Different strands of feminism diverge markedly in their assessment of international women's rights standards. Liberal feminism identifies gender equality with equal treatment between men and women, arguing that the law should reject any formal distinctions between the genders. Most of their efforts have concentrated on eliminating legal barriers to women's full equality in the public sphere. It is this approach which is most prevalent in the existing international law instruments related to women's human rights, and has been widely criticised by other feminist strands for giving women access to "a world already constituted" and for defining women in terms of men.[40]

Rights', in Abdullahi Ahmed An-Na'im (ed.), *Human Rights in Cross Cultural Perspectives: A Quest for Consensus* 44 (1992) at 45–46.

[37] Rebecca J. Cook, 'State Responsibility for Violations of Women's Human Rights', 7 *Harv. Hum. Rts. J.* 125 (1994) at 133.

[38] Laboni Amena Hoq, 'The Women's Convention and its Optional Protocol: Empowering Women to Claim their Internationally Protected Rights', 32 *Colum. Hum. Rts. L. Rev.* 677 (Summer 2001) at 724.

[39] Ibid.

[40] Claire Dalton, 'Where We Stand: Observations on the Situation of Feminist Legal

On the other hand, cultural feminism takes a different approach, identifying a distinctive "women's voice" which has been effectively excluded from current formulations of national and international law. According to this approach, differences between the feminine and masculine modes of reasoning must be celebrated and a specific category of women's rights can hence be articulated. Cultural feminism, however, is not without its critics; it has been accused of adopting a male yardstick in defining the so-called 'feminine' mode of reasoning as compassionate, emotional and subjective as opposed to the rational and objective mode of reasoning, which is the domain of men.[41]

The third strand of feminist legal theory, radical feminism, identifies women's subordination as "the product of domination of women by men."[42] This approach proposes that the masculine world of rights be completely transformed so as to protect women from systematic subordination because of gender, rather than simply settling with the right to be treated without regard to sex. In other words, all policies and practices that contribute to women's subordination must be identified; the role of human rights law is to protect against these structures.[43] The radical feminist critique of existing power structures motivates the need to address new areas such as the 'private sphere' which has traditionally been disregarded by international human rights law.

Finally, post-modern feminism rejects the view that there are universal standards of women's human rights. This approach, which merits much consideration, acknowledges that different conceptions of equality exist in different cultures, and that it is ethically problematic to impose a Western-liberal definition of equality on women of different cultures.[44] There is an apparent convergence between this strand of feminism and the widely criticised cultural relativist approach to international human rights law. However, the two schools of thought are distinguishable in that post-modern feminism doesn't use culture as a pretext to shield discriminatory laws and practices, but rather to underscore the complex realities that confront women and that motivate their needs and lifestyles, rejecting the imposition of any standard model of women's human rights.

Thought', 3 *Berkley Women's L.J.* 1, 5 (1987–1988) quoted in Hilary Charlseworth, 'What are "Women's International Human Rights"?', in Rebecca J. Cook (ed.), *Human Rights of Women, National and International Perspectives* (1994) at 65.

41 Charlseworth (1994) at 65.

42 Ibid.

43 Ibid. at 61–62.

44 Ibid.

Post-modern feminism rejects the essentialism inherent in all feminist analyses; that women worldwide share similar experiences and attributes. It advocates a greater degree of cultural sensitivity in defining equality, a necessary prerequisite for international standards to take root in different societies. It offers a way out of the existing monolithic view of gender non-discrimination.

According to both feminist and cultural relativist critiques, international human rights law, in its current 'Western liberal' formulation doesn't necessarily represent the highest possible attainable standard for women's human rights. In Egypt, the women's rights movement has called for rights that go beyond those envisioned by international standards of equality, such as guaranteeing the financial security of the wife, including through enhancing maintenance rights and property rights, and improving the position of women in child custody battles after divorce. Whereas such rights find no equivalent in international human rights instruments, they are well grounded in the *Sharīʿa* and are not predicated on the principle of formal equality between the spouses. Within these two doctrines, the *Sharīʿa*-inspired notion of complementary roles for men and women, which doesn't necessarily translate into formal equality in the 'Western liberal' sense of the word, may find recognition.

Different Feminisms and the Promotion of Egyptian Women's Equality Rights

Different strands of feminism, which encompass "diverse priorities, fields of power and influence, and consequent activisms, are bound to have an impact on the development and implementation of local and international laws or covenants on women's rights."[45] The four above-mentioned strands of feminist legal theory have all manifested themselves in the demand for Egyptian women's human rights, affecting the discourse to different extents and at different moments in time. They all converge in their belief that Egypt's personal status law is in need of significant reform, yet they differ in the methods they wish to employ to effect that change, and in the way they rationalise the employment of such methods.

[45] Azza M. Karam, 'Women, Islamisms and State: Dynamics of Power and Contemporary Feminisms in Egypt', in Mahnaz Afkhami and Erika Friedl (eds.), *Muslim Women and the Politics of Participation. Implementing the Beijing Platform* (1997) at 24.

The 'liberal feminist' approach, reflected in the CEDAW's definition of non-discrimination, has been advocated by Egyptian secular feminists, who reject any formal distinction based on gender. Secular feminists base their discourse mainly on the grounds of universal standards and human rights principles, relegating religion to a private matter and rejecting it as a potential tool for women's emancipation.[46] They are profoundly critical of Egypt's reservations to the CEDAW.

Secular feminism was the predominant trend in both Egypt and the Arab world until the final two decades of the twentieth century, and succeeding in achieving broad political and economic rights for women. Recently, however, when other types of feminism, most prominently 'Islamic' feminism and 'pragmatic' feminism, which combines aspects of both the secular and 'Islamic' approaches have played a larger role.[47] With the increased influence of political Islam, it has been argued that secular feminism lost much of its resonance in mainstream Egyptian society. In fact, figures of the secular feminist strand, such as the prominent feminist *Nawal el-Sa'dawi* have often been portrayed as Westernised, and their ideas criticised as unusual. In contemporary Egyptian society,

> feminists or activists who would like to operate within a secular framework cannot do so because they would be ignored. A secular approach is not widely shared or appreciated by the society at large. Thus if one hopes to open a dialogue with people, identifying oneself as a secular feminist or activist is a poor entry point.[48]

In spite of resistance to secular, or what is often labelled 'Western', feminism, women's rights activists have managed to articulate indigenous alternatives within the context of their own cultural and political realities.[49] Ever since modernisers took up the question of women's emancipation, a struggle has ensued between conservatives that portray the question of women's rights, particularly as advanced by secular feminists, as an alien, inappropriate 'Western' imposition, on the one hand, and those who assert that women's empowerment knows no religious boundaries, and is indispensable to national development. According to one commentator,

---

[46] Karam (1997) at 21.

[47] Soroya Duval, 'New Veils and New Voices. Islamist Women's Groups in Egypt', in Karin Ask and Marit Tjomsland (eds.), *Women and Islamization* (1998) at 67.

[48] Nemat Guenena and Nadia Wassef, *Unfulfilled Promises. Women's Rights in Egypt* (1999), available at http://www.popcouncil.org/pdfs/unfulfilled_promises.pdf (last accessed 20 Dec. 2004) at 5.

[49] Amarita Basu, *The Challenge of Local Feminisms: Women's Movements in Global Perspective* (1995).

> the specific laws governing personal and family matters delineate the boundaries within which a Muslim woman can hope to define her own identity. Precisely because personal/family laws are so consistently labelled 'Muslim' and justified with reference to Islamic doctrine or culture, in each particular—and often very varied—cultural context, the identity/space defined for women is put forward as that of a 'Muslim woman'. A person who challenges any aspect of law relating to family or personal matters is therefore deemed to be refuting—or at the very least challenging—the very definition of Muslim womanhood in her own setting.[50]

The more external attempts there are to challenge the status of women, in general, and the family law, in particular, the more resistance there is from those who contend that the concept of gender equality is completely inapplicable to 'Muslim culture', and threatens to destroy family relations and disrupt the fabric of society.[51] The unfortunate result is that as human rights issues become a growing global concern, women in their localities are being intimidated through labelling them as secularist, Westernised, or even heretic. Many women are thus discouraged from challenging their position both within the family and in society at large.

Nonetheless, legal reformers and Muslim feminists have persistently argued that Islam has not placed women in a perpetual state of submission to men, but that the prevailing patriarchal interpretations of the sources of Islamic law are the true culprit. They advocate a return to the *Quran* and *Sunnah*, underlining the egalitarian principles inherent in them, to inspire further reforms of family law that would make it more suitable to the social realities of the twenty-first century. Through this process, they assert that women's rights derived from Islamic law can be fully reconciled with universal standards of women's human rights.

In the area of personal status law, Egyptian reformers have, to a certain extent, predicated their arguments on a definition of non-discrimination that takes into consideration the unique cultural and religious setting in which Muslim women find themselves, refusing an imposed model of non-discrimination. They have thus mostly acted within the boundaries of the *Sharīʿa* in pursuing their agendas. According to Badran, "from the colonial era to the present day, women across the spectrum from right to left have continued to ground their feminism in Islam and

---

[50] Ibid.

[51] In 2010, a group of prominent Egyptian religious scholars, including one woman, authored a joint paper in which they argued that the CEDAW, in its entirety, was opposed to Islamic values. The paper was distributed to relevant government ministries and departments (on file with author).

nationalism."[52] In the process, they have affirmed that it is patriarchy, and not Islam that has disempowered women in Egypt, and have thus used 'Islamic' arguments to "end patriarchal tyranny in the private sphere and to legitimize their full entry into the public sphere."[53] Egyptian feminists have also advanced a separate category of women's family rights, distinct from those of men and surpassing them in some areas, taking into consideration the unique nature of women. Finally, they have looked beyond simple legal reforms and addressed the structures, attitudes and realities that hamper women's enjoyment of their formal, legal rights.

It is possible to distinguish, within Egyptian feminism, between two different strands that stand apart from 'secular' feminism, namely 'Islamic' feminism and 'pragmatic' feminism. Islamist feminists, as the term suggests, seek to reform legislation through recourse to Islamic principles. Rejecting 'liberal feminism' and its insistence on absolute equality between the genders, as well as the CEDAW's equality provisions, they emphasize the complementary rather than equal roles for men and women.[54] The Islamist feminist trend in Egypt increased markedly in the 1970's with the rise of political Islam. The most important Islamist women's organisations were the Society of Muslim Sisters (*al-akhawat al-Muslimat*) an offshoot of the Muslim Brotherhood (whose founder *Hassan El Banna* often emphasized the important role of women in the Islamic reformation) and the Muslim Women's Association, established by *Zeinab al-Ghazali*. The main premise of Islamist feminism is the belief that:

> Islam does not forbid women to actively participate in public life. It does not prevent her from working, entering into politics, and expressing her opinion, or from being anything as long as that does not interfere with her first duty as a mother, the one who first trains her children in the Islamic call.[55]

Islamist feminists, in general, ardently reject what they label as 'Western' notions of women's human rights, and emphasize the primary duty of the woman towards the family. They have singled out elements from Islamic history to promote a different view of the 'true' rights that women enjoy in Islam, "challeng[ing] the androcentric dominant culture of established

[52] Margot Badran, 'Independent Women. More Than a Century of Feminism in Egypt', in Judith E. Tucker (ed.), *Arab Women: Old Boundaries, New Frontiers* 129 (1993).
[53] Ibid.
[54] Karam (1997) at 22.
[55] Duval (1998) at 54.

Islam that is hostile to women"[56] They believe that Islam conceives of a different form of gender equality: equality in religious duties and dignity. Worldly responsibilities are, by nature, different between the genders and are based on the principles of complementarity of gender roles and reciprocity. Whereas this analysis merits respect, it may fall into the trap of the cultural relativist argument that completely dismisses international standards, while taking for granted the immutable and ingrained nature of local realities, traditions, and practices, and their incompatibility with any notion of universal rights.

Pragmatic feminism,[57] is similar to 'Islamist feminism' in some respects, but also differs markedly in some important aspects; it is both more inclusive and more pluralistic. Sometimes referred to as 'new secular feminism'[58] it brings together women's rights activists of both genders and all religions who recognise the important role religion plays in Egyptian society and the centrality of that role in legislative reform. This group maintains that reform of personal status legislation should occur through the reinterpretation of religious texts in light of modern exigencies. The main premise of their argument is the validity of the discourse of equality between the genders in Islam; they contend that the CEDAW is "Islamically harmonious."[59] Not only do they analyse the different international human rights treaties and instruments in such a way as to make them applicable to different cultural contexts, but they simultaneously emphasize the need to reform existing laws that are based on the *Sharīʿa*.

In seeking to propose an alternative, authentic feminist discourse in Egypt, such groups have argued that the only way to advance women's human rights is to build a "solid Muslim feminist jurisprudential basis which clearly shows that Islam not only does not deprive women of their rights but in fact demands these rights for them."[60] A large body of their literature has ascribed women's inferior status to what they argue are patriarchal interpretations of the Islamic religious scriptures,[61]

---

56 Ibid. at 64.

57 Karam refers to this strand of feminism as 'Muslim' feminism, which should not be confused with 'Islamic feminism'.

58 H. Esfandiari and M. Badran, 'Islamic Feminism and Beyond: The New Frontier', *Occasional Paper Series, Woodrow Wilson Centre, Middle East Program* (Fall 2010).

59 Karam (1997) at 22–23.

60 Ibid.

61 See, for example, Azizah Al-Hibri, 'Islam, Law and Custom: Redifining Muslim Women's Rights', 12 *Am U.J. Int'l L. & Pol'y* 1 (1997); Badran (1993) at 129, Joelle Entelis, 'International Human Rights: Islam's Friend or Foe? Algeria as an Example of the

contending that there is an obvious gap between what the *Quran* and *Sunnah* stipulate, and how they are put into practice by a conservative society that is historically inimical to the rights of women. They contend that for centuries, reasoning (*Ijtihād*) has been avoided as a jurisprudential tool, and criticize the state-inclined male clergy's monopoly over interpretations of the *Quran*. As such, they have "successfully initiated a dialogue on *Ijtihād* (reinterpretation), which was dormant for centuries," arguing that it is necessary to engage in a modern reinterpretation of domestic laws based on the *Sharīʿa* in order to reconcile them with international legal principles.[62] They agree with the 'Islamist feminist' premise that *Ijtihād* is necessary to reform existing legislation and agree that women are capable of taking on tasks involving interpretation of religious scriptures.

Imbuing their demands for legislative reform with 'Islamic legitimacy' has served the personal convictions of many activists, while allowing them to build a wider support base for their claims. In so doing, they have succeeded in promoting international standards through a process of 'internal validation,' which serves to legitimise and 'anchor' such norms within the cultural traditions of society.[63] In spite of resistance to what is often labelled a 'Western' project, reformers in Egypt have managed to articulate indigenous alternatives within the context of their own cultural and political realities. This approach, arguably indispensable for the legitimization of personal status law reform, was successfully employed to introduce no-fault divorce in 2000 and is currently being utilised to introduce a new draft of the personal status law.[64] A similar approach led to the abolition of polygamy in the Tunisian Personal Status Code, and its restriction in several other personal status codes throughout the Arab-Muslim world.

Although such interpretations don't enjoy as wide a support-base as would be desired, the pragmatic feminist debate clearly provides "an

Compatibility of International Human Rights Regarding Women's Equality and Islamic Law', 20 *Fordham Int'l L.J.* 1252–1305 (1997).

[62] Helie-Lucas (1999) at 25. Proponents of this view include Venkatraman, Hajjar, Chaudry, Ali, and Entelis. See also Al-Hibri (1997), and Leila Sayeh and Adriaen P. Morse, 'Islam and the Treatment of Women: An Incomplete Understanding of Gradualism', *Tex. Int'l L. J.* (Spring 1995).

[63] Abdullahi An-Naim, 'State Responsibility Under Human Rights Law to Change Religious and Customary Laws', in Rebecca J. Cook (ed.), *Human Rights of Women. National and International Perspectives* (1994), 167–188.

[64] See Al-Hibri (1997) at 25–26.

interpretative answer to the challenge of the fundamentalist view of women's rights."[65] Through their efforts, pragmatic feminists have profoundly modified the field of Islamic theological research, with the potential to lead to more extensive reforms in the future. The success of such endeavours is contingent upon the continued support and collaboration of the State and the religious establishment, as well as successful mobilisation at the grassroots level. It is only through such collaboration that feminist groups in Egypt can ever hope to counter the rising trend of religious and ideological conservatism and the prevalence of entrenched patriarchal social attitudes.

[65] Kathleen Suneja, 'The Empowerment of Women Through International Law', in Rekha Datta and Judith Kornberg (eds.), *Women in Developing Countries. Assessing Strategies for Empowerment* (2002) at 41.

CHAPTER TWO

THE SOURCES OF INTERNATIONAL WOMEN'S RIGHTS LAW AND INTERNATIONAL ENFORCEMENT MECHANISMS

The CEDAW Committee has repeatedly held that "neither traditional, religious or cultural practices nor incompatible domestic laws and policies can justify violations of the Convention."[1] The CEDAW Convention clearly places obligations on States to modify family laws that discriminate against women, as well as to eliminate stereotypical attitudes and discriminatory cultural practices. It is a well-recognised principle of international law, reaffirmed in article 27 of the Vienna Convention on the Law of Treaties, that a State may not invoke its internal law to justify violations of its international obligations. States therefore must remove any inconsistency between international human rights law obligations, on the one hand, and "religious and customary laws operating within the territories of the State on the other."[2] Binding international obligations include both a State's contractual obligations under treaty law as well as customary international law.

The framework for the international protection of women's human rights is founded in both the binding sources of international law (namely treaties, custom and general principles of law), as well as in non-binding, soft-law instruments. The treaty regime prohibiting discrimination against women has been in constant development since the very early years of the United Nations' establishment, and culminated in the broad prohibition of all forms of discrimination against women in the CEDAW. This latter Convention has provided a clear and detailed prescription for States to follow in order to 'pursue a policy' of eliminating discrimination against women, including in the area of family relations. It is further supplemented by principles of customary international law, as well as numerous soft-law instruments.

---

[1] Yogesh, 'The Conflict of Law and Policy on Reservations to Human Rights Treaties', *Brit. Y.B. Int'l L.* 240 (2001).

[2] An-Naim, 'State Responsibility Under Human Rights Law to Change Religious and Customary Laws', at 167.

International Treaties

The current regime protecting the human rights of women dates back to the early years of the United Nations system, even before the adoption of the UDHR. The Commission on the Status of Women (CSW), established in 1946, was the first body with a mandate to conduct studies on matters of direct relevance to women, and to promote the protection of women's human rights.[3] The Commission was instrumental in the development of international treaties addressing the human rights of women including the Convention on the Nationality of Married Women, adopted in 1947, followed by the Convention on the Political Rights of Women in 1953, and the Convention on Consent, Minimum Age and Registration of Marriages in 1962. Both the 1947 and the 1962 Conventions deal with issues that arise due to the marital status of women, departing from the Commission's belief, at the time, that "the major issue facing women was that of their marital status."[4] It was believed that women were most vulnerable in that particular area; other areas of concern to them could be promoted and protected through the general human rights treaties.[5]

In the early 1960's, the Commission on the Status of Women was instructed by the General Assembly to prepare a draft international declaration, outlining universal standards of women's human rights and non-discrimination on the basis of gender. The effort culminated in the adoption in 1967 of the Declaration on the Elimination of Discrimination Against Women, which represented a broad, non-binding, statement of principle. Although the Declaration didn't enjoy the binding force of a treaty, it provided a foundation for the subsequent elaboration of a legally-binding international instrument.[6] The CSW's efforts were crowned with the adoption of the CEDAW on December 18th, 1979.

Although the UN Charter, the UDHR, and both human rights Covenants had all guaranteed the human rights of women, on a basis of equality with men, it is the CEDAW that is widely considered as the 'international charter' on women's human rights. Before it came into force, the existing regime functioned in a fragmentary way, failing to deal with gender

---

[3] *Short History of the CEDAW Convention*, Division for the Advancement of Women, UN Department of Economic and Social Affairs, at http://www.un.org/womenwatch/daw/cedaw/history.htm (accessed Dec. 2004).

[4] Margaret Plattner, 'The Status of Women Under International Human Rights Law and the 1995 UN World Conference on Women, Beijing, China', 84 *Ky. L.J.* 1249 (Summer 1995/1996) at 1254.

[5] *Short History of the CEDAW Convention*.

[6] Plattner (1995/1996) at 1254.

discrimination in a comprehensive manner.[7] The CEDAW sought to overcome these shortcomings, and to create a binding framework to monitor violations of the Convention. It has since been considered the most comprehensive international treaty pertaining to the protection of the rights of women.

Although the international prohibition of discrimination predates CEDAW, the latter stipulates in its Preamble that "despite these various instruments, extensive discrimination against women continues to exist." Women's equality rights, particularly their family rights, were frequently subject to qualifications on the basis of culture and religion. Violations of these rights were not considered with the same gravity as other breaches of the principle of non-discrimination, or other systematic human rights violations. The CEDAW thus attempted to provide a more comprehensive definition of gender discrimination and to devise effective means to combat it. The principle of non-discrimination on the basis of gender is the "thread that runs through the Convention's substantive provisions."[8]

The CEDAW is unprecedented in scope; it covers both *de jure* and *de facto* discrimination against women (thus addressing the concerns of both liberal and radical feminists). Not only does it seek to regulate State activities, which is the case with most human rights treaties, but it also places limits on private and non-governmental action. The preamble of the CEDAW acknowledges that "a change in the traditional role of men as well as the role of women in society and in the family is needed to achieve full equality between men and women." It thus concedes that culture and tradition may hamper women's full enjoyment of their rights, emphasising that "the role of women in procreation should not be a basis for discrimination, but that the upbringing of children requires a sharing of responsibilities between men and women and society as a whole." By targeting stereotypes and attitudes, the CEDAW attempts to guarantee both formal and substantive equality to all women.

Article 2 of the CEDAW elucidates specific measures and policies that parties 'shall' undertake in order to achieve the goal of eliminating discrimination, including the adoption of constitutional and legislative provisions, and the institution of legal remedies. Article 4 calls for the provision of temporary special measures, also known as positive discrimination, in order to right the historical wrongs against women and to grant

[7] Ibid.

[8] Andrew Byrnes, 'The Convention on the Elimination of All Forms of Discrimination Against Women', in Wolfgang Benedek et al. (eds.), *Human Rights of Women. International Instruments and African Experiences* 122 (2002) at 124.

them equal access to centres of political and economic power. Article 5 is particularly significant in that it calls for the eradication of stereotypes and cultural practices discriminatory to women. Articles 6 to 16 specify the fields in which governments must act to eliminate discrimination, namely government, law, education, health care, business, reproductivity, and family life, detailing the specific measure required. By demanding that States also intervene to prevent discrimination in the 'private sphere', the CEDAW transcended the scope of all other human rights conventions.

Customary International Law

Commentators have been divided on whether the principle of non-discrimination on the basis of gender constitutes customary international law. Although most of the literature is "absolute and insistent about the customary nature of systematic racial discrimination under customary law" this does not seem to be the case with regards to the status of systematic gender discrimination.[9] It has been asserted that there is no norm of customary international law that prohibits gender discrimination, "although a substantial body of treaty law exists against it."[10] On the other hand, others have held that non-discrimination between men and women is among the cardinal principles of international human rights law.[11]

The objective of customary international law is to "determine the consensus in which sovereign States join and by which they consider themselves bound."[12] To identify the existence of such a rule, its two constituent elements must be apparent, namely the general practice of States and *opinio juris* (the determination that States perceive themselves, when engaging in such practice, as acting under a legal obligation).[13] In order for a principle to be recognised as a new rule of customary international

[9] Courtney Howland, 'The Challenge of Religious Fundamentalism to the Liberty and Equality Rights of Women: An Analysis under the United Nations Charter', 35 *Colum. J. Transnt'l L.* 271 (1997) at 335.

[10] Barbara Stark, 'Bottom Line Feminist Theory: The Dream of A Common Language', 23 *Harv. Women's L. J.* 233 (Spring 2000) at 238.

[11] Sara Hossain, 'Women's Rights and Personal Laws in South Asia', in Rebecca J. Cook (ed.), *Human Rights of Women, National and International Perspectives* (1994) at 467.

[12] Stark (2000) at 233.

[13] Howland (1997) at 334.

law, it is necessary to establish "evidence of a general practice accepted as law."[14] Deducing that a certain principle amounts to a customary norm of international law requires both 'consistency' and 'generality' of practice by a significant number of States; it does not require absolute or universal practice.[15]

Evidence of State practice can be found in the text of international treaties, which may provide "a snapshot of custom at the time of the treaty's drafting."[16] Treaties may also give rise to a rule which later passes into custom. Although, the mere conclusion of a treaty does not necessarily establish its provisions as norms of customary international law, wide adherence to the treaty may be considered as evidence of custom.[17] Since the adoption of the UN Charter, a number of general human rights treaties have incorporated the principle of gender non-discrimination, mainly in terms of formal non-discrimination between men and women. In its preamble, the UN Charter reaffirms faith in "the equal rights of men and women", and in article 1 it commits States to "promote universal respect for and observance of human rights and fundamental freedoms for all without distinction as to ... sex." Similarly, the UDHR reiterates the same principle in its first article, which states that "all human beings are born free and equal in dignity and rights." Article 7 of the UDHR further stipulates that "all are equal before the law and are entitled to equal protection of the law." Moreover, the ICCPR and ICESCR respectively obligate States "to ensure the equal right of men and women" to the enjoyment of all rights whether they are civil and political rights, or economic, social and cultural rights[18] without distinction "of any kind as to race, colour, sex, language, religion, political or other opinion, national or social origin, property, birth or other status."[19]

State practice with regards to the principle of non-discrimination on the basis of gender thus seems to be both consistent and general. States

---

[14] Military and Para-Military Activities (Nicaragua vs. U.S.), ICJ, (1986), 14 at 88.

[15] Joel R. Paul, 'Cultural Resistance to Global Governance', 22 *Mich. J. Int'l L.* 1 (Fall 2000) at 10.

[16] Arthur M. Weisburd, 'The Significance and Determination of Customary International Human Rights Law: The Effect of Treaties and Other Formal International Acts On the Customary Law of Human Rights', 25 *Ga. J. Int'l & Comp. L.* 99 (Fall 1995/Winter 1996) at 111.

[17] Ibid.

[18] Article 3 of the ICCPR and ICESCR.

[19] Article 2 of the ICCPR and ICESCR.

generally consider most of the rights laid down in the UDHR—which the International Court of Justice has treated as a binding source of law[20]—and the Covenants as universal and binding.[21] In addition, the principle of non-discrimination has been adopted in the vast majority of domestic legal systems, appearing in many national constitutions and domestic statutes. It is thus evident that State practice supports the existence of a general customary international rule that prohibits gender discrimination.

Howland and Fairweather both assert that, coupled with this widespread practice, there is also relevant *opinio juris* to suggest that the prohibition of State-condoned gender discrimination constitutes a principle of customary international law.[22] Although they refer to the same sources of State practice as evidence of the existence of such *opinio juris*, they also mention States' consistent affirmation of their unequivocal commitment to gender equality. They also contend that, although the principle of gender equality is widely breached, the criteria established by the ICJ in the *Nicaragua Case* to deduce the existence of customary rules seem to allow for the inclusion of gender non-discrimination. According to the Court it is sufficient that:

> the conduct of States should, in general, be consistent with such rules, and that instances of State conduct inconsistent with a given rule, should generally have been treated as breaches of that rule, not as indications of the recognition of a new rule. If a State acts in a way *prima facie* incompatible with a recognised rule, but defends its conduct by appealing to exceptions or justifications contained within the rule itself, then whether or not the State's conduct is in fact justifiable on that basis, the significance of that attitude is to confirm rather than to weaken the rule.[23]

In other words, it can be argued that, according to the test established by the ICJ, the 'cultural' exception to the norm of gender non-discrimination confirms rather than negates the existence of a customary rule in this regard.

---

[20] See, United States v. Iran, United States Diplomatic and Consular Staff in Tehran, ICJ (1980) at para 91.

[21] See Paul (2000) at 10 and Howland (1997) at note 281 and note 290.

[22] Howland (1997) at 236. See also Cynthia R.L. Fairweather, 'Obstacles to Enforcing International Human Rights Law in Domestic Courts', 4 *U.C. Davis J. Int'l L. & Pol'y* 119 (Spring 1998).

[23] See Military and Para-Military Activities, at para 186.

On the other hand, it seems that the treatment of gender non-discrimination by States indicates the existence of gaps in *opinio juris* that cannot simply be dismissed as exceptions that confirm the rule. For this reason, commentators are divided on whether the question of gender equality, particularly in the area of family relations, can be considered a customary norm of international law. Although "most States agree that men and women should enjoy formal equality under the law," it has simultaneously been argued that "the international community generally accepts the idea that the norm of gender equality implicates culture."[24] As such, the international community has been "willing to consider cultural exceptions to the international norm of gender equality."[25] This is evident in the 1994 International Conference on Population and Development Program of Action, for example, which contains a 'chapeau' article providing that the implementation of all recommendations is subject to "the sovereign right of each country, consistent with its national laws and development priorities, with full respect for the various religious and ethical values and cultural backgrounds of its people."[26] A number of individual provisions, such as Chapter VII (E), which addresses reproductive health of adolescents, contain further claw-back clauses, which guarantee respect for "cultural values and religious beliefs as well as the rights, duties and responsibilities of parents."

A similar tension surfaced in the Fourth World Conference on Women, held in Beijing in 1995, which witnessed considerable negotiation among State representatives in order to incorporate language concerning cultural particularities.[27] Eventually, the Beijing Platform for Action was adopted with the following text:

> While the significance of national and regional particularities and various historical, cultural and religious backgrounds must be borne in mind, it is the duty of States, regardless of their political, economic and cultural systems, to promote and protect all human rights and fundamental freedoms. The implementation of this Platform, including through national laws and the formulation of strategies, policies, programmes and development priorities, is the sovereign responsibility of each State, in

---

[24] Ibid.

[25] Joel R. Paul, 'Resisting Culture', 16 *Leiden J. Int'l L.* 919 (2003).

[26] 'Chapter 2: Principles', ICPD Program of Action, available at http://www.un.org/ecosocdev/geninfo/populatin/icpd.htm#chapter2.

[27] See Paul (2003) at 922.

> conformity with all human rights and fundamental freedoms, and the significance of and full respect for various religious and ethical values, cultural backgrounds and philosophical convictions of individuals and their communities should contribute to the full enjoyment by women of their human rights in order to achieve equality, development and peace.[28]

Although the Beijing Platform for Action emphasises the principle that religious and cultural values should not hamper the full enjoyment by women of their rights, it confirms the view that "it is nearly impossible to engage in a discussion of women's rights under international law without having to address cultural claims."[29] The tension between cultural and religious particularities, on the one hand, and the rights of women, on the other, indicates that women's rights are influenced by the cultural context. This is in stark contrast to other human rights norms, such as the right to freedom from torture and other cruel, inhumane and degrading treatment, as well as the right to a fair trial and to freedom from arbitrary detention, which may not, under any circumstance, be qualified by cultural exceptions.[30]

At another level, reservations to multilateral treaties, even impermissible ones, are arguably "useful for determining the content of customary law."[31] The large number of reservations formulated in response to various substantive provisions of the CEDAW, particularly article 16 on equality in family relations, is often considered a strong indication that States have not accepted these provisions as forming a part of customary international law. Proponents of this view further find support in the paucity of objections articulated in response to such reservations. It is thus evident that State practice relevant to prohibiting discrimination in the 'private sphere' of family relations is not as consistent as in the 'public sphere.' Although most domestic systems prohibit gender discrimination, in general, many national constitutions and legislative provisions make exceptions regarding the applicability of equal rights to women in family relations. There are also evident gaps in *opinio juris*, as the 'cultural exception' has been more widely tolerated by the international

[28] *Beijing Declaration and Platform for Action*, Fourth World Conference on Women, Adopted at the 16th plenary meeting (15 September 1995), para 9. Similar language is incorporated in para 5 of the Vienna Declaration and Program of Action, World Conference on Human Rights, Vienna (14–25 June 1993) UN Doc A/CONF.157/23.

[29] See Paul (2003) at 922.

[30] See Ibid and Paul (2000) at 19.

[31] Weisburd (1995/1996) at 127.

community in the area of family relations. In other words, the principle of non-discrimination on the basis of gender in family relations is, at best, *de lege ferenda*, not yet constituting a clear rule of customary international law.

Soft Law

In the area of gender non-discrimination, as with other areas of human rights law, a body of so-called "soft-law", or non-binding resolutions, recommendations, declarations and "final acts" of international conferences has emerged to supplement relevant treaty provisions. Soft-law generally creates aspirational goals to be achieved in the future rather than strict obligations.[32] Although soft-law is not legally binding, it may serve a number of important functions. Primarily, it reinforces the principles and values incorporated in human rights treaties, and highlights emerging concerns that are unique to women.[33] Repetition also plays an important part in this process, as cross referencing of resolutions and declarations which invoke the same principles all serve to develop a common international understanding.[34]

Several questions have arisen regarding the binding nature of soft law and its influence on the content of international legal norms. In some situations, soft-law instruments use language that could essentially be used in a binding treaty, which may suggest that the intention of the drafters was to create binding obligations. Such is the case with a number of provisions included in the Beijing Platform for Action. It has also been argued that resolutions and declarations adopted at the conclusion of international conferences serve as an indication of the emergence and gradual consolidation of customary norms of international law. They can simultaneously be said to reflect State practice, and their unanimous endorsement may indicate the existence of *opinio juris*. The Office of Legal Affairs of the UN has found that a declaration "may be considered to impart ... a strong expectation that Members of the International community will abide by it" and "in so far as the expectation is gradually justified by State practice, a declaration may by

[32] P.-M. Dupuy, 'The Challenge of Soft Law and the International Law of the Environment', 12 *Mich. J. of Int'l L.* 420 (1991) at 428.

[33] Plattner (1995/1996) at 1236.

[34] Dupuy (1991) at 424–425.

custom become recognized as laying down rules binding upon States."[35] What is most interesting is that some of the commitments articulated in the so-called soft law instruments go beyond what was originally conceived by international treaties and impose further obligations on States.

On the other hand, it has been argued, and rightly so, that soft law cannot be regarded, *per se*, as customary international law. Evidence of the emergence of norms of customary international law must be measured against strict criteria. In order to establish the existence of State practice, it must be shown that an instrument of soft law has in fact been acted upon, whereas proving the existence of *opinio juris* faces the "conceptual problem as to whether action taken in compliance with an instrument specifically denied to be legally binding and asserted to be voluntary can be evidence of *opinio juris*."[36] This does not mean, however, that soft law cannot develop into customary international law; in many cases it can constitute *de lege ferenda*, acting as a pre-cursor to the emergence of 'hard' law in the form of custom or treaties.

Soft law, although formally non-binding, has a moral authority that States can no longer deny. The Beijing Platform for Action, for example, has been followed up by a number of subsequent meetings known as Beijing + 5, Beijing + 10 and Beijing + 15 with the aim of ensuring that States are fulfilling the non-binding commitments embodied in the Beijing Declaration and Platform for Action. In preparation for these meetings, concerned States often meet in their regional groups to articulate common positions, take stock of the progress made in the previous five years, and complete questionnaires designed to scrutinize State compliance. They also often take steps in preparation for such conferences to demonstrate their commitment to their goals. For example, observers have attributed the speed with which Egypt's Law no. 1 of 2000 was adopted to the desire to introduce reforms before the Beijing +5 Conference. The authority of soft law instruments is particularly evident when one considers the exceptions, akin to reservations, which States often articulate when they do not wish to be bound by

[35] Memorandum of the Office of Legal Affairs of the Secretariat, U.N. Doc. E/CN.4/L.610, para. 4 quoted in Louis Sohn, ''Generally Accepted' International Rules', 61 *Wash. L. Rev.* 1073, 1080.

[36] C. Chinkin, 'The Challenge of Soft Law: Development and Change in International Law', 38 *ICLQ* 850 (1989) at 857.

particular soft law instruments. However, it is unlikely that the international responsibility of a State may be invoked for violation of soft law obligations.

Special Issues Arising from the Prohibition of Gender Discrimination

The international legal regime governing the prohibition of gender discrimination includes specific instruments and provisions addressing the issue of equality in family relations, as well as related issues such as violence against women. Although these two areas are articulated in a number of treaties, customary rules and soft law instruments, the level of protection they afford to women who are victims of discrimination leaves much to be desired.

Non-Discrimination in Family Relations

The principle of non-discrimination in family relations is well-founded under treaty law; however, the general human rights instruments failed to elucidate the necessary steps to bring that principle into effect. Article 23 of the ICCPR generally states that "no marriage shall be entered into without the free and full consent of the intending spouses" and obliges States to "take appropriate steps to ensure equality of rights and responsibilities of spouses as to marriage, during marriage and at its dissolution." Article 16 (1) of the CEDAW takes this a step further by providing a comprehensive formulation of the notion of non-discrimination between spouses. It stipulates that States will take "all appropriate measures to end discrimination against women in all matters relating to marriage and family" and further requires States to ensure equality in entering into marriage with free and full consent, choosing a spouse, equal rights during marriage and at its dissolution, equal rights and responsibilities as parents, including with regard to guardianship, wardship and custody, the same personal rights as husband and wife, and equal rights in respect of property.

Paragraph (2) of article 16 of CEDAW prohibits child marriages and makes the establishment of a minimum age for marriage, as well as the registration of marriages compulsory. Article 16 of the UDHR stipulates that "men and women *of full age* … have the right to marry and found a family," while article 23 of the ICCPR and the Convention on Consent to Marriage, Minimum Age for Marriage and Registration of Marriage (1964),[37] contain similar provisions. Although these instruments do not specifically stipulate what age should be considered a 'minimum' age, they clearly do not tolerate child marriages.

Elaborating on this point, General Comment 28 of the Committee on Civil and Political Rights, stipulates that the State is obligated to set a minimum age for marriage "on the basis of equal criteria for men and women" in order to ensure "women's capacity to make an informed and un-coerced decision."[38] In its General Recommendation 21, the CEDAW Committee read the provisions of article 16(2) in conjunction with the provisions of the Convention on the Rights of the Child (CRC),[39] asserting that States may not grant validity to a marriage between individuals who have not yet attained majority. It further required that legal provisions providing for a different age for marriage for men and women be abolished, as they "assume incorrectly that women have a different rate of intellectual development from men, or that their stage of physical and intellectual development at marriage is immaterial."[40] Relying on the CRC definition of a child as a person below eighteen years of age, the CEDAW Committee found that

---

[37] Egypt has not ratified the Convention on Consent to Marriage, Minimum Age for Marriage and Registration of Marriage, opened for signature on 7 Nov. 1962. The Convention was accompanied by a non-binding recommendation that stipulated that the minimum age was 15 years old for both men and women. This standard, however, has clearly changed over the past half century; the Convention on the Rights of the Child defines majority as 18 years of age.

[38] *General Comment no. 28*, Committee on Civil and Political Rights, U.N. Doc. CCPR/C/21/Rev.1/Add10 (29/03/2000). The CCPR asserted that the State has a positive obligation to protect the right of spouses to enter into marriage with their free and full consent and identified a number of factors, including age, which may affect the ability of women to enter into marriage freely.

[39] *Convention on the Rights of the Child*, opened for signature 20 Nov. 1989. Egypt ratified the Convention on 2 Sept. 1990.

[40] Ibid. The African Protocol on the Rights and Welfare of the Child, which Egypt has signed but not ratified, similarly stipulates in article 21(2) that the minimum age for marriage is eighteen years. Although, Egypt has not ratified the Protocol, according to article 18 of the Vienna Convention on the Law of Treaties:

A State is obliged to refrain from acts which would defeat the object and purpose of a treaty when:

(a) it has signed the treaty or has exchanged instruments constituting the treaty subject to ratification, acceptance or approval, until it shall have made its intention clear not to become a party to the treaty.

"the minimum age for marriage should be 18 years for both man and woman."[41]

These comprehensive provisions grant women equality in all aspects of family relations. The CEDAW further imposes upon States the obligation to regulate the private sphere and to influence entrenched cultural attitudes that adversely affect women within the family. However, article 16 of the CEDAW is amongst the provisions that attracted a large number of reservations, precisely because of its comprehensive nature. As mentioned previously, it is generally understood that the equality rights of women may come into conflict with cultural particularities. Because customary international law remains unclear in this area, it is difficult to hold States liable to a strict non-discrimination standard.

Non-Discrimination and Domestic Violence

Freedom from violence is widely recognised as a fundamental human right for women, although it does not appear expressly in any of the CEDAW's provisions. Violence against women takes a variety of shapes and forms in most modern societies, cutting across religious, social and cultural divides. Intervention to eliminate discrimination in the "private sphere" logically obliges States to act against domestic violence. In its General Recommendation 19, the CEDAW Committee asserted that "family violence is one of the most insidious forms of violence against women."[42] It depicted domestic violence in an all-encompassing manner, as an issue that plagues all societies and affects all aspects of a woman's life, asserting that:

> Within family relationships women of all ages are subjected to violence of all kinds, including battering, rape, other forms of sexual assault, mental and other forms of violence, which are perpetuated by traditional attitudes. Lack of economic independence forces many women to stay in violent relationships. The abrogation of their family responsibilities by men can be a form of violence, and coercion. These forms of violence put women's health at risk and impair their ability to participate in family life and public life on a basis of equality.[43]

---

[41] *General Recommendation no. 21*, Equality in Marriage and Family Relations, CEDAW, 13th Session (1994).

[42] *General Recommendation no. 19*, Violence Against Women, CEDAW, 19th Session (1992).

[43] Ibid.

In its General Recommendation 12, the CEDAW Committee considered that articles 2, 5, 11,[44] 12[45] and 16 of CEDAW required States to protect women against any form of violence, whether within the family, the workplace or elsewhere.[46] Violence against women is also prohibited through soft law instruments, most notably the 1993 UN Declaration on the Elimination of Violence Against Women. In its first article, the Declaration defines violence against women as "any act of gender-based violence that results in, or is likely to result in, physical, sexual or psychological harm or suffering to women, including threats of such acts, coercion or arbitrary deprivation of liberty, whether occurring in public or in private life."[47] The definition thus comprises violence occurring in the family, and the community, as well as violence condoned by the State.

---

[44] Article 11 of the CEDAW stipulates that

1. States Parties shall take all appropriate measures to eliminate discrimination against women in the field of employment in order to ensure, on a basis of equality of men and women, the same rights, in particular:

(a) The right to work as an inalienable right of all human beings;
(b) The right to the same employment opportunities, including the application of the same criteria for selection in matters of employment;
(c) The right to free choice of profession and employment, the right to promotion, job security and all benefits and conditions of service and the right to receive vocational training and retraining, including apprenticeships, advanced vocational training and recurrent training;
(d) The right to equal remuneration, including benefits, and to equal treatment in respect of work of equal value, as well as equality of treatment in the evaluation of the quality of work;
(e) The right to social security, particularly in cases of retirement, unemployment, sickness, invalidity and old age and other incapacity to work, as well as the right to paid leave;
(f) The right to protection of health and to safety in working conditions, including the safeguarding of the function of reproduction …

[45] Article 12 of the CEDAW states that

1. States Parties shall take all appropriate measures to eliminate discrimination against women in the field of health care in order to ensure, on a basis of equality of men and women, access to health care services, including those related to family planning.
2. Notwithstanding the provisions of paragraph I of this article, States Parties shall ensure to women appropriate services in connection with pregnancy, confinement and the post-natal period, granting free services where necessary, as well as adequate nutrition during pregnancy and lactation.

[46] *General Recommendation no. 12, Violence Against Women*, CEDAW 8th session (1989).

[47] *UN Declaration on the Elimination of Violence Against Women*, GA Res. 48/104 of 20 December 1993, U.N.T.S. A/RES/48/104, (23 February 1994), art. 2.

The first aspect, namely family or domestic violence, was elaborated on by the UN Special Rapporteur on Domestic Violence in her 1996 Report as:

> All acts of gender-based physical, psychological and sexual abuse by a family member against women in the family, ranging from simple assaults to aggravated physical battery, kidnapping, threats, intimidation, coercion, stalking, humiliating verbal abuse, forcible or unlawful entry, arson, destruction of property, sexual violence, marital rape, dowry or bride-price related violence, female genital mutilation, violence related to exploitation through prostitution, violence against household workers and attempts to commit such acts ...[48]

Article 3 of the Declaration on the Elimination of Violence proceeded to link the right to be free from violence with the right to equality, the right to liberty and security of person, the right to the highest attainable standard of mental and physical health, the right to equal protection of the law, the right to be free from torture or other cruel, inhumane or degrading treatment, and the right to be free from all forms of discrimination.[49] In other words, violence against women was construed as a violation of a combination of human rights that the State is required to protect and to ensure by virtue of international customary and treaty law, including the CEDAW, the ICCPR, the ICESCR and the Convention Against Torture (CAT).[50]

According to the Declaration, States are required to take certain measures to eliminate violence against women, including to "exercise due diligence to prevent, investigate and, in accordance with national legislation, punish acts of violence against women, whether those acts are perpetrated by the State or by private persons."[51] The Declaration was adopted unanimously by the General Assembly and coincided with the "proliferation of domestic legislation, executive action, and national judicial decisions" prohibiting violence against women.[52]

---

[48] *Report of the Special Rapporteur on violence against women, its causes and consequence*, UN Commission on Human Rights, 52nd session, Item 9 (a) of the provisional agenda, E/CN.4/1996/53/Add.2, (2 February 1996).

[49] *Declaration on the Elimination of Violence*, art. 3.

[50] Barbara Stark, 'Symposium on Integrating Responses to Domestic Violence. Domestic Violence and International Law: Good Bye Earl (Hans, Pedro, Gen, Chou, etc.)', 47 *Loy. L. Rev.* 255 (Spring 2001) at 268.

[51] *Declaration on the Elimination of Violence*, art. 4.

[52] Stark (2001) at 268.

The 1995 Beijing Declaration and Platform for Action further called upon States to "condemn violence against women and refrain from invoking any custom, tradition or religious consideration to avoid their obligations with respect to its elimination as set out in the Declaration on the Elimination of Violence against Women."[53] As such, religious sanction may not be used as a justification for any form of domestic violence. Similarly, the Commission on Human Rights called upon States to "enact and/or reinforce penal, civil, labour and administrative sanctions in domestic legislation to punish and redress the wrongs done to women and girls subjected to any form of violence, whether in the home, the workplace, the community or society."[54] It has been argued that "repeated references to State responsibility for domestic violence in reports of the Human Rights Commission, the Special Rapporteur on Domestic Violence, and other international instruments as well as regional human rights instruments, supports the proposition that States may indeed be held responsible for domestic violence."[55] Recent case-law of the European Court for Human Rights supports this conclusion.[56]

International Enforcement of Women's Equality Rights

International human rights law is often criticised for being largely ineffective in achieving the rights it purports to guarantee. There is a common perception that international treaties, such as the CEDAW, represent "nothing more than empty rhetorical gestures lacking in serious enforcement mechanisms and consequently having no effect on actual practice."[57] Others have argued that the CEDAW is nothing more than

---

[53] *Beijing Declaration and Platform for Action*, Fourth World Conference on Women, 15 September 1995, A/CONF.177/20 (1995) and A/CONF.177/20/Add.1 (1995).

[54] See relevant resolutions of the Commission on Human Rights on *The elimination of violence against women* 51st Session of the Commission on Human Rights (8 March 1995) UN Doc CHR Res. 85 E/CN.4/RES/1995/85, and 52nd Session of the CHR (19 April 1996) UN Doc CHR Res. 49 E/CN.4/RES/1996/49, and 53rd Session of the CHR (11 April 1997) UN Doc CHR Res. 44 E/CN.4/RES/1997/44, and 54th Session of the CHR (17 April 1998) UN Doc CHR Res. 52 E/CN.4/RES/1998/52.

[55] Ibid.

[56] See Opuz v. Turkey, European Court of Human Rights, Final Judgement, Strasbourg (9 June 2009).

[57] Michael Kevane, 'Ratification of the CEDAW' (March 10th, 2003) (unpublished) http://emlab.berkeley.edu/users/webfac/bardhan/e271_sp03/mcvane.pdf.

"a waste of the scarce resources of diplomacy, with possibly perverse effects."[58] This view, however, is overly simplistic and probably inaccurate. At the very least, the CEDAW embodies the clearest articulation of the standards that govern women's human rights under international law. It has undeniably succeeded in recognising many rights that were previously denied to women or neglected, and has departed from stereotypical and traditional views of women. Rather than dismissing the CEDAW as irrelevant, it is important to find ways to effectuate its provisions, which represent a quantum leap for women in terms of recognition and protection of their human rights.

In assessing the utility of international instruments in achieving compliance with human rights standards, Medina distinguishes between the 'promotional' functions of international legal standards, and the 'protective' ones.[59] The promotional role of international human rights law is based on the mere act of drafting international conventions, or standard-setting, which in turn has an effect on legitimising such rights. Its protective role, on the other hand, lies in the creation of mechanisms, both national and international, to protect women against possible violations. Adopting this classification allows for a somewhat accurate qualitative assessment of the CEDAW's effectiveness; at the promotional level, it has unquestionably succeeded in providing an important normative framework for women's equality rights. In terms of its protective function, however, international human rights law, in general, and the CEDAW, in particular, leaves much to be desired.

Capitalising on recent global developments that have placed compliance with universal human rights standards at the apex of accepted State conduct, international mechanisms have relied heavily on what is known as 'naming and shaming' to enforce human rights standards in recalcitrant States. In order to avoid the 'shame' of being singled out and publicised as a violator of human rights, States are often compelled to comply with international human rights law, even in the absence of clear penalties for non-compliance. Although this tool is in essence a diplomatic one with no guaranteed results, it seems to act as an incentive for States, in some cases, to avoid deviation from international human rights standards. However, the utility of 'naming and shaming' must be assessed

58 Ibid.

59 Cecilia Medina, 'Towards a More Effective Guarantee of the Enjoyment of Human Rights by Women in the Inter-American System', in Rebecca J. Cook (ed.), *Human Rights of Women, National and International Perspectives* (1994) at 265.

with a degree of scrutiny, as recent evidence has suggested that 'shaming' may often encourage perpetrators to commit more abuses.[60]

International protection or enforcement of women's human rights occurs at several levels in the UN system. Institutionally, the various human rights treaties, including CEDAW have established 'expert bodies' to monitor compliance and examine individual complaints, while other 'political bodies', composed of member-States, also have the authority to examine women's rights questions, and to establish independent follow-up and quasi-investigative mechanisms. Within the UN Secretariat, there a number of departments and divisions specifically concerned with advancing the human rights of women. In 2006, the UN High Commissioner on Human Rights established the Women's Human Rights and Gender Unit within the UN Secretariat, whose mandate was to "maximize the potential of the human rights mechanisms within the UN system to actively address gender justice".[61] However, such piecemeal reforms were hardly effective in strengthening the institutional capacity of the UN in support of gender equality. As such, in October 2009, after three years of intense lobbying, the UN General Assembly adopted a resolution establishing a new, consolidated 'Composite Gender Entity' that would bring together a number of departments, namely the Office of the Special Advisor on Gender Issues and Advancement of Women, the Division on the Advancement of Women, the United Nations Development Fund for Women (UNIFEM) and the United Nations Training and Research Institute for the Advancement of Women.[62] It remains to be seen how this nascent entity, which will be headed by an international civil servant with the rank of UN Under-Secretary General, will streamline and advance the UN's efforts in the area of women's rights.

The UN has also been active in convening a number of high-profile international conferences, particularly in conjunction with the rise of the transnational women's movement in the 1970's. Through "the weight of international law, and the strengthening of grass roots movements"[63] these conferences have promoted the progressive development and codification of women's rights-related norms, and strengthened global mon-

---

[60] See Emilie M. Hafner-Burton, 'Sticks and Stones: Naming and Shaming the Human Rights Enforcement Problem', 62 *International Organization* 689–716 (Fall 2008) at 692.

[61] *Office of the UN High Commissioner for Human Rights* http://www2.ohchr.org/english/issues/women/ (accessed Feb 10th, 2009).

[62] *System-Wide Coherence*, Resolution adopted by the General Assembly, 63rd Session, Agenda Item 107, A/Res/63/311 (2 Oct 2009).

[63] Plattner (1995/1996) at 1237.

itoring of compliance. There have been a total of four UN world conferences on women, held in Mexico City (1975), Copenhagen (1980), Nairobi (1985) and Beijing (1995).[64] The first conference culminated in the General Assembly's adoption of the "UN Decade for Women," placing women's rights at the forefront of the UN human rights agenda, and ushering in a period of codification of women's rights (it was during this decade that the CEDAW was drafted). The 1995 Beijing Conference, by far the most significant of the four, sought to build momentum through the wide participation of civil society and to advance the strategies and Plans of Action elaborated in the previous conferences. It has been followed by a series of review conferences every five years to follow-up on the implementation of the Beijing Declaration and Program for Action.

International conferences of a more general nature, focussing on human rights or general socio-economic development issues, have also played an important role in advancing women's rights. The World Conference on Human Rights, held in Vienna in 1993, and the International Conference on Population and Development, convened in Cairo in 1994, drew a great deal of international attention to the challenges confronting women's empowerment, including the previously neglected issue of Female Genital Mutilation. The Vienna Declaration and Programme of Action, adopted at the 1993 conference designated the human rights of women as a top priority for the international community.[65]

International conferences of this kind serve several purposes; they bring together diverse cultures and traditions and work towards achieving consensus on issues of relevance to women. They also provide a forum for the creation of soft-law instruments, for the international scrutiny of domestic legislation and policies, and for the 'naming and shaming' of violators. They allow for the networking of national and international NGOs concerned with the promotion and protection of women's human rights, often pressuring governments to step up the speed of reforms. Apart from implementing measures in preparation for such conferences, the pressure resulting from the interaction between various stakeholders often creates momentum for more effective reforms in their aftermath. It has been argued, for instance, that Egypt's adoption of the amended personal status Law no. 100 of 1985 came as a result of successful lobbying during the 1985 Nairobi Conference.

[64] Ibid. at 1263.

[65] See *Vienna Declaration and Programme of Action*, at para. 18.

International mechanisms, particularly treaty-monitoring bodies, have favoured engagement and constructive dialogue in order to induce compliance by States. Such bodies, which enjoy a considerable degree of credibility and legitimacy due to their perceived independence, have also taken advantage of their technical expertise to assist States and encourage them to meet their international obligations.

Although international human rights law has given individuals previously without access to the international system the opportunity to resort to quasi-adjudicative international bodies, such bodies haven't had a large impact in the area of women's human rights. The Committee of experts established by the CEDAW to monitor compliance with the Convention is the main mechanism entrusted with monitoring enforcement the CEDAW's provisions. The Committee, composed of twenty-three experts representing the world's principal legal and judicial systems, examines periodic reports by States parties and issues General Recommendations, with the intention of shedding light on their obligations under the Convention. Initially, it wasn't envisioned that the CEDAW Committee would have a complaints procedure, considered by some States as applicable only to 'serious' human rights violations.[66] Eventually, however, sufficient momentum was built in the Beijing Conference to establish an individual complaints mechanism for CEDAW, and the Optional Protocol came into force in 2000.

Although other complaints procedures exist, which may potentially also be used to protect the human rights of women, including the mechanisms established under the ICCPR and the CERD, they have rarely heard complaints related to the specific human rights of women.[67] In 2008, an Optional Protocol to the ICESCR was adopted establishing a complaints procedure; however, with only three ratifications to date, it is unclear when this procedure will come into force. Increasingly, the inter-

---

[66] *History of the Optional Protocol*, Division for the Advancement of Women, available online at http://www.un.org/womenwatch/daw/cedaw/protocol/history.htm.

[67] Only three individual complaints related to gender discrimination have been brought before the CCPR, namely *Aumeeruddy-Cziffra et al. vs. Mauritius (also known as the Mauritian Women's Case*— Communication No. 35/1978), *Broeks v. the Netherlands*, (Communication No. 172/1984), and *Avellanal v. Peru* (Communication No. 202/1986). In *Lovelace vs. Canada*, (Communication No. 24/1977), the complainant alleged the existence of gender discrimination in violation of article 23 of the ICCPR, although the Committee dealt with the complaint as a question of minority rights, under article 27 of the Covenant. One complaint regarding gender discrimination, namely the case of *Yilmaz-Dogan v. the Netherlands* (Communication No. 1/1984), has also been brought before the Committee on the Elimination of Racial Discrimination.

national community is witnessing a growing influence of Charter-based mechanisms, particularly of the Human Rights Council and its special procedures, in the protection of women's human rights.

Outside the framework of the UN, international enforcement mechanisms have had little, if any, effect in the enforcement of international obligations in the area of women's rights. One such example is the individual complaints procedure of the African Charter on Human and People's rights, to which Egypt acceded in 1984, and which has not been used, to date, to advance women's rights.[68] As such, UN Charter-based and treaty-based mechanisms remain at the forefront of the effort to enforce women's human rights internationally.

Charter-based Mechanisms and the Protection of Women's Equality Rights

Several bodies established under the UN system, often referred to as the Charter-based mechanisms, have the power to examine human rights situations in member States, including the status of women. These include 'political' bodies, 'expert' bodies and 'thematic' mechanisms. Political bodies are composed of State representatives and provide an important forum through which States may uncover violations in any individual country. They include the Economic and Social Council (ECOSOC), the Human Rights Council (HRC) and its predecessor, the Commission on Human Rights (CHR), as well as the Commission on the Status of Women (CSW). These mechanisms, however, are rarely utilised to enforce women's human rights, partly due to lack of awareness.

Until it was replaced by the Human Rights Council in 2006, the Commission on Human Rights, established in 1946 with a membership of fifty-three States, had the option of resorting to the '1503 procedure' by virtue of ECOSOC Resolution 1503. This procedure was intended to identify gross and reliably attested human rights violations, which could be brought to the attention of ECOSOC. However, in general terms the 1503 procedure was largely ineffective, neither did it make

[68] The African Charter created the African Commission on Human Rights, which is composed of eleven experts acting in individual capacity. The Commission has the mandate to undertake studies on human rights problems in Africa and may receive communications from individuals and States. For a complete analysis of the functions of the Commission and its role with regards to the human rights of women, see Chaloka Beyani, 'Towards a More Effective Guarantee of Women's Rights in the African Human Rights System', in Rebecca J. Cook (ed.), *Human Rights of Women, National and International Perspectives* (1994), 285–306.

any notable contribution to addressing discrimination against women. The procedure, which was revised in 2006, has retained its confidential nature under the Human Rights Council, and is based on the principle of 'complementarity' or the requirement that local remedies be exhausted in order for a communication to be considered.[69]

The establishment of the Human Rights Council ushered in a review process and subsequent revitalisation of all mandates and 'special procedures', including thematic working groups and designated experts (such as Special Rapporteurs and representatives of the Secretary General). The Council renewed the mandate of the Special Rapporteur on Violence Against Women, established by the Commission on Human Rights in 1994.[70] Although there is no Special Rapporteur with a general mandate to examine violations of women's human rights, gender dimensions do arise in the mandates of a number of Special Rapporteurs and individual experts.

The Human Rights Council has also been relatively active in addressing the issue of women's equality before the law, examining proposals for the creation of a new mandate to address this issue. This has understandably proven to be a divisive issue, particularly since the initiative was perceived to focus disproportionately on family laws, particularly as applied in Muslim-majority countries, at the expense of other areas of legal equality. NGO reports, for instance, focused on laws prescribing unequal inheritance shares and polygyny, and were deeply critical of the so-called waiting period or *'iddah* observed by Muslim women after divorce. The debate reflected the politicisation of the Council, and a process of negotiated compromise eventually led, in 2009, to the adoption of a resolution requesting the High Commissioner to prepare a thematic study, rather than establishing a new mandate to address women's equality before the law.[71] The study, which was examined during the Council's fourteenth session, led to a rift between the sponsors of the initiative,[72] on

[69] *Human Rights Council Complaints Procedure* Online Office of the High Commissioner for Human Rights http://www2.ohchr.org/english/bodies/chr/complaints.htm (accessed Nov 10th, 2010).

[70] *Special Procedures Assumed by the Human Rights Council* Online Office of the High Commissioner for Human Rights http://www2.ohchr.org/english/bodies/chr/special/themes.htm (accessed Feb 10th, 2009).

[71] Human Rights Council, Twelfth session, Agenda item 3, UN Doc A/HRC/12/L.3 (Oct 1st, 2009).

[72] Mexico, Norway, Canada, Brazil, USA, the EU, Switzerland, and Lithuania. See *Council Divided on Need For A New Special Procedure Mandate to Address Women's Equality*, International Service for Human Rights, Available at http://www.ishr.ch/council/907-

the one hand, and the Arab and Islamic Groups—wary of being targeted by any new mechanism—on the other.

The Commission on the Status of Women, composed of forty-five member States, has also played a role, albeit a limited one, in enforcing compliance with international obligations related to gender equality. The CSW, which reports to the Economic and Social Council, adopts so-called 'agreed conclusions' on priority areas. Although it may also receive individual communications to identify policies that reveal "a consistent pattern of reliably attested injustice and discriminatory practices,"[73] the procedure doesn't allow the CSW to adjudicate on such matters. It may examine communications only as a 'source of information,' on which it may rely when drafting its recommendations to ECOSOC. As such, the CSW does not have any powers of investigation. Moreover, the communications are examined by a working group of the CSW and remain confidential throughout the whole procedure. In general, this procedure is hardly known and seldom used.

Unlike the aforementioned 'political bodies' composed of member-States, 'expert bodies' are composed of experts acting in an individual capacity, and hence theoretically enjoy a greater degree of independence and credibility (though it should be noted that the experts are nominated and elected by the member-States of the UN). Previously, the Sub-Commission on the Promotion and Protection of Human Rights, which was established in 1947 to assist the Commission on Human Rights, had the authority to examine individual complaints, and raise human rights violations in public debates. The Sub-Commission, which was comprised of twenty-six independent experts elected with due regard to equitable geographical representation, could also resort to special procedures, and hence appointed a Special Rapporteur on Traditional Practices affecting the Health of Women and Children. In 2008, the Sub-Commission was replaced by the Human Rights Council Advisory Committee, which acts as a think tank for the Human Rights Council, and has no mandate to adopt resolutions of its own or to institute independent procedures. Composed of eighteen independent experts, its role is limited to advising the Council on a number of thematic issues, among which is the issue of gender mainstreaming in the UN system.

---

council-divided-on-need-for-a-new-special-procedure-mandate–to-address-womens equality (accessed Nov. 10th, 2010)

[73] Byrnes (2002) at 119.

The CEDAW Committee

Although several treaty-based individual complaints procedures may examine complaints related to violations of the human rights of women, such practice is very rare. Under the individual complaints procedure instituted by the Optional Protocol to the ICCPR, the CCPR has examined four cases related to gender discrimination.[74] Although the CCPR is willing to scrutinize allegations of violations of the CEDAW, as long as the State in question is a party to that Convention, this procedure is seldom used.[75] Moreover, the complaints procedure remains inaccessible to many women as only one hundred and thirteen States have ratified the Optional Protocol establishing it.[76] The same is true for other treaty-based individual complaints procedures; in short, gender plays a relatively insignificant role in all but the CEDAW Committee.[77]

Article 17 of the CEDAW establishes a Committee of experts, acting in a personal capacity, to monitor compliance with the substantive obligations imposed by the CEDAW. The CEDAW Committee has a rather wide mandate; it may examine reports submitted by parties detailing "the legislative, judicial, administrative, or other measures" put in place to implement the provisions of CEDAW.[78] It reports annually to the General Assembly on its activities through the Economic and Social Council. It may also "make suggestions and general recommendations based on the examination of reports and information received from the State-Parties."[79] Although such General Recommendations are not binding sources of law in and of themselves, they constitute authoritative interpretations of the legal obligations articulated in the CEDAW, and are thus akin to advisory opinions of the International Court of Justice. In addition, the Committee may invite the specialised agencies of the United

---

[74] See discussion *supra* at p. 52 and note 67.

[75] Byrnes (2002) at 119.

[76] Status of Ratifications of the Optional Protocol of the ICCPR, UNTC, vol. 999, p. 171. Available at http://treaties.un.org/Pages/ViewDetails.aspx?src=TREATY&mtdsg_no=IV-5&chapter=4&lang=en.

[77] See Andrew Byrnes, 'Toward More Effective Enforcement of Women's Human Rights Through the Use of International Human Rights Law and Procedures', in Rebecca J. Cook (ed.), *Human Rights of Women, National and International Perspectives* (1994), 189–227 for a comprehensive analysis of these mechanisms.

[78] CEDAW art. 18.

[79] CEDAW art. 21.

Nations to submit reports regarding the implementation of the Convention "in areas falling within the scope of their activities."[80]

Although the CEDAW Committee was modelled after other treaty-monitoring bodies established within the UN framework, it was not initially as well-equipped,[81] which resulted in relatively poor adherence by States. Primarily, the CEDAW made no provision for an individual complaints procedure, thereby limiting access by individual women to the Committee when their rights had been violated. A further restriction was the article 20 stipulation that the Committee was to 'normally' meet for a period of no more than two weeks annually. This "put enormous pressure on the Committee as the number of State-parties and reports to be considered increased."[82] This is in addition to the failure of States to meet their reporting obligations on time, the Committee's backlog in considering reports, and the absence of effective follow-up mechanisms.[83] That is not to mention that only one hundred States have ratified the CEDAW's Optional Protocol. Severe financial restrictions, coupled with all the other deficiencies, also had a direct toll on the Committee's effectiveness, threatening—at times to marginalise it completely.

Eventually, State-parties decided to enhance the Committee's role by allowing it to meet for three weeks annually, in 1993. In 1997 this was expanded to two annual sessions of three weeks each, an arrangement that granted the Committee more time to deal with substantive issues. The Committee's location was transferred to New York in 1993, where a women's rights unit was established, increasing access to data[84] and hence putting more tools and resources at the Committee's disposal. Finally, a complaints procedure for individuals and groups (an innovation that doesn't exist under other complaints mechanisms, which are strictly for individuals) was introduced through the First Optional Protocol to the CEDAW, which came into force in December 2000. The first complaint was considered by the Committee in July 2004; since then the Committee has considered a total of 14 complaints.

When considering a complaint, the Committee will typically take a decision on the merits then make recommendations to the State party. The State party is required to report, within six months, on the action

---

[80] CEDAW art. 22.

[81] Elizabeth Evatt, 'Finding a Voice for Women's Rights. The Early Days of CEDAW', 34 *Geo. Wash. Intl L. Rev.* 515 (2002) at 518.

[82] Ibid. at 519.

[83] Ibid. at 532.

[84] Ibid.

taken to implement the Committee's decision.[85] The Optional Protocol also established an inquiry procedure that authorises the Committee to conduct inquiries into situations of 'grave or systematic violations' of women's rights.[86]

Substantively, the Committee's mandate also advanced considerably over the past two decades. Initially, the CEDAW Committee was reluctant to use its authority to interpret the CEDAW and make pronouncements regarding the obligations of States under the Convention, including on the compatibility of domestic laws and policies with the CEDAW.[87] Eventually, however, the Committee started taking a more proactive stance. In 1986 it requested the opinion of the Legal Counsel of the United Nations on the nature of its mandate, who advised that, by virtue of article 21 of the CEDAW, the Committee could:

> Make general recommendations addressed to all States parties about matters raised by a number of State reports. The Committee could also make suggestions to specific countries, which could be based on a consideration of that country's report.[88]

Departing from this advice, it became the practice of the Committee to provide General Recommendations to help interpret State's obligations under the CEDAW, as well as to openly criticise State-parties that failed to meet their obligations. With time, the CEDAW Committee came to play a central role in inducing compliance with the Convention, primarily by rendering the State-reporting mechanism a useful tool to identify areas of strength and weakness, to engage State-parties in constructive dialogue, provide technical advice, and hence encourage States to give effect to their treaty obligations.

The Committee has also effectively utilised its authority to issue General Recommendations elucidating the scope of obligations under the CEDAW, in order to shed light on ambiguous provisions. However, the effectiveness of CEDAW in protecting women's human rights ultimately depends on the commitment of State-parties, and their willingness to fulfil their obligations and give effect to CEDAW's provisions. Such a com-

---

[85] *Fact Sheet No. 7: Complaints Procedure*, Office of the UN High Commissioner on Human Rights, available online, http://www2.ohchr.org/english/law/docs/Part_of_FS.No.7.pdf.

[86] *Optional Protocol to the Convention on the Elimination of Discrimination Against Women*, Division on the Advancement of Women, Department of Economic and Social Affairs, available at http://www.un.org/womenwatch/daw/cedaw/protocol/.

[87] Evatt (2002) at 537.

[88] Ibid.

mitment is all the more important in light of the absence of any sanctions mechanism to deter and punish violators. The value of the interpretations, remarks, and General Recommendations of the CEDAW Committee thus hinges upon the extent to which it can convince States to execute their obligations at the domestic level.

The existence of a robust monitoring mechanism helps ensure that, when the domestic system fails to give effect to obligations under the CEDAW, there is an international 'safety-net' that individual women can resort to in order to enforce their rights. However, the more robust the CEDAW Committee becomes, the less likely are States—particularly those that have reason to believe that their local laws, customs and traditions may be in conflict with the CEDAW—to opt into the Committee's new procedures. It is those States in particular, which are likely to include States that have articulated broad and sweeping reservations to modify the nature of their obligations and safeguard their religious and cultural practices, that remain outside the reach of the individual complaints procedure. States that have reason to fear the CEDAW's activism are not likely to modify or withdraw their reservations, and if they do, such as Morocco, then it is equally improbable that they will join the individual complaints procedure. Paradoxically, therefore, the more effective the CEDAW becomes, the more difficult it becomes to hold recalcitrant States accountable for discriminatory laws and practices at the international level.

International mechanisms, however robust, thus cannot—on their own—adequately enforce women's human rights, or precipitate widescale domestic reforms. Moreover, the persistence of extensive reservations to the CEDAW raises serious questions regarding the adequacy of the existing international legal regime, particularly in the area of family relations where a cultural exception to equality seems to be widely tolerated. The constant interplay, and mutually reinforcing dynamic between internal and international mechanisms and processes, is thus absolutely necessary, as it undoubtedly contributes to expediting and reinforcing the domestic reform process. This positive function of international law and institutions, however, is contingent upon maintaining the legitimacy, credibility and objectivity of these international mechanisms in the eyes of the people they seek to emancipate.

CHAPTER THREE

THE PROHIBITION OF DISCRIMINATION UNDER CEDAW AND THE ROLE OF THE CEDAW COMMITTEE

Multilateral treaties are often subject to different, sometimes even contradictory interpretations, not only because they usually encompass a wide scope of international obligations, but also for the large number of parties with conflicting interests they bring together under a single regime. It is therefore quite likely that different States will interpret their obligations under the treaty differently, a reality that has made the role of the CEDAW Committee central in recognising a departure from the text of the Convention. An objective assessment of States' obligations under the CEDAW thus necessitates a precise and detailed description of the substantive provisions of the CEDAW, including the scope of the definition of non-discrimination under the Convention, and nature of such obligations. It also requires a consideration of the measures envisioned by the CEDAW in order to guarantee the equal rights of women, particularly in the private sphere.

The issue of interpretation arises in particular with respect to ambiguous provisions of international treaties, specifically where no independent third party is mandated to provide an authoritative opinion in cases of conflict. Article 29(1) of the CEDAW stipulates that disputes concerning interpretation are to be settled by negotiation, and if that fails, through arbitration. However, most States have opted out of this provision (through paragraph (2) of the same article) to avoid being bound by an interpretation of the treaty that doesn't serve their interests. By and large, it is up to each State party to interpret the provisions of the Convention independently.

Interpreting Obligations under the CEDAW

Although treaty interpretation is at face-value a subjective exercise, it is subject to international standards, and thus cannot be left to the whims of individual States.[1] The process of interpretation is governed by the

[1] Byrnes (2002) at 122.

rules of customary international law as well as the Vienna Convention on the Law of Treaties (VCLT). It is generally recognised that the rules on treaty interpretation enunciated in articles 31[2] and 32[3] of the VCLT are applicable to the CEDAW, if not by virtue of the Vienna Convention itself, then by virtue of customary international law. The rules of treaty interpretation are to be applied by States in good faith in order to discern the scope of their obligations under international treaties.

According to article 31 of the Vienna Convention, treaties must be interpreted in "good faith." States are obliged to give preference to the "ordinary meaning" of the text, which must be read in relation to its "context" and in light of the "object and purpose" of the treaty. Paragraph 2 specifies that the "context" includes the text, preamble and annexes of the treaty, as well as any agreement or instrument concluded by the parties

---

[2] Article 31 of the Vienna Convention on the Law of Treaties stipulates that:

1. A treaty shall be interpreted in good faith in accordance with the ordinary meaning to be given to the terms of the treaty in their context and in the light of its object and purpose.
2. The context for the interpretation of a treaty shall comprise in addition to the text, including the preamble and annexes:
   (a) any agreement relating to the treaty which was made between all the parties in connection with the conclusion of the treaty;
   (b) any instrument which was made by one or more parties in connection with the conclusion of the treaty and accepted by the other parties as an instrument related to the treaty.
3. There shall be taken into account, together with the context:
   (a) any subsequent agreement between the parties regarding the interpretation of the treaty or the application of its provisions;
   (b) any subsequent practice in the application of the treaty which establishes the agreement of the parties regarding its interpretation;
   (c) any relevant rules of international law applicable in the relations between the parties.
4. A special meaning shall be given to a term if it is established that the parties so intended.

[3] According to Article 32 of the Vienna Convention:

Recourse may be had to supplementary means of interpretation, including the preparatory work of the treaty and the circumstances of its conclusion, in order to confirm the meaning resulting from the application of article 31, or to determine the meaning when the interpretation according to article 31:

(a) leaves the meaning ambiguous or obscure; or
(b) leads to a result which is manifestly absurd or unreasonable.

in relation to that treaty. In addition to the context, consideration may be given to any "subsequent practice" relevant to the treaty and any "relevant rules of international law" that bind States parties. If the measures set out in article 31 still leave the meaning of the text ambiguous, the parties may refer to the *travaux preparatoires*, according to article 32 of the Convention.

The VCLT further stipulates in article 27 that "a party may not invoke the provisions of its internal law as justification for its failure to perform a treaty." This principle has been reiterated by the Committee on Civil and Political Rights (CCPR),[4] established to monitor compliance with the ICCPR, in its decision on the *Van Duzen v. Canada* communication, in which it held that:

> The interpretation and application of the International Covenant on Civil and Political Rights has to be based on the principle that the terms and concepts of the Covenant are independent of any particular national system of law ....[5]

The existence of a treaty-monitoring body, namely the CEDAW Committee renders the interpretation of the CEDAW more complex. In carrying out its functions, the CEDAW Committee provides interpretations of the Convention through examining State reports and issuing concluding observations and general recommendations.[6] These interpretations are not binding as such; however, because they "interpret and elaborate upon the legal obligations set forth in the Convention; their language and message are significant in determining the nature and extent of state responsibility."[7] It follows that they may also be considered as elements of "subsequent practice" since they are accepted by States and considered an authoritative source on the interpretation of the treaty. As such, they constitute a source of interpretation under the general rules on treaty

---

[4] This Committee is also often referred to as the Human Rights Committee (HRC) though CCPR will be used throughout this text to avoid confusion with the Human Rights Council.

[5] Gordon C. Van Duzen v. Canada, Communication no. 50/1979, CCPR, para. 10.2, U.N. Doc. CCPR/C/OP/1 at 118 (1985).

[6] The CEDAW Committee is mandated to examine periodic reports of States parties on measures taken to implement the Convention, as well as issue general recommendations on matters related to eliminating discrimination against women, based on the reports and information received from States. Through these recommendations, the Committee has elaborated on its view concerning obligations assumed by States under the Convention.

[7] Behrouz (2003) at 1143.

interpretation. According to this view, the process of "constructive dialogue" through which the CEDAW Committee engages States parties represents

> a source of State practice in which agreement as to the meaning of the provisions of the Convention—within the meaning of Article 31(3)(b) of the Vienna Convention—might be found. Due to the proliferation of States Parties and reports under the Convention, this material is in practice of limited utility. However, the Committee's collective concluding comments on each State report (together with any response by the State to those observations) make the results of this process more focused and useful for interpreting the Convention, and these can be used to identify the Committee's view of the meaning of many provisions of the Convention.[8]

In other word, where the meaning of the terms of the CEDAW is unclear, recourse may be made to the subsequent practice of States, as demonstrated by the meaning they give to the Convention through their periodic reports and their dialogue with the Committee. The Committee's General Recommendations occupy a similar position, although they do not formally represent binding interpretations of the CEDAW. General Recommendations issued by the Committee are circulated to States parties, which subsequently may comment on them, endorse them or object to their content. It follows that a State's silence in response to the Committee's recommendation "may arguably be considered as acquiescence in the substance of those recommendations, thus constituting State practice that could be viewed as establishing the agreement of the States parties regarding the interpretation of particular provisions."[9] In general, treaty-monitoring bodies have treated human rights treaties as 'living documents' whose interpretation evolves with the passage of time and with changes in circumstances.

The Precise Scope of the Gender Non-Discrimination Norm under CEDAW

The formulation of article 1 of the CEDAW reflects the intention of the drafters, namely to define discrimination against women "for purposes of legal application and enforcement of the Convention."[10] The

---

[8] Byrnes (2002) at 121.

[9] Ibid. at 123.

[10] Rebecca J. Cook, 'State Accountability Under the Women's Convention', in Rebecca J. Cook (ed.), *Human Rights of Women, National and International Perspectives* (1994) at 235.

concept of gender discrimination is thus defined widely to encompass:

> any distinction, exclusion or restriction made on the basis of sex, which has the effect or purpose of impairing or nullifying the recognition, enjoyment, or exercise by women, irrespective of their marital status, on a basis of equality of men and women, of human rights and fundamental freedoms in the political, economic, social, cultural, civil or any other field.

According to the above definition, any distinction between the genders in any field is a form of discrimination. The CEDAW does not provide for an express right to freedom from discriminatory attitudes; the issue is framed as an obligation on the part of the State rather than an individual right to be claimed. As such, one can discern both a positive and a negative obligation. The negative obligation is quite straightforward; it entails that the State must engage in no practice and adopt no law that discriminates against women. The obligation to protect, on the other hand, places a duty on States to prevent "other individuals or groups from violating the human rights of individuals."[11]

At face value, the principle of non-discrimination, as articulated by the CEDAW seems to be a constant measure of women against men, as advocated by Western-liberal feminism. It has thus been criticised for adopting a male standard to determine equality, in other words for rendering women as copies of men.[12] It accepts no distinction between the genders in any field, with the exception of maternity (inasmuch as it relates to labour law) and positive discrimination to address historical grievances. As a result, the CEDAW arguably guarantees women the same rights to which men are entitled under existing androcentric human rights treaties, failing to reflect the particular experiences and

[11] Corrine Packer, *Using Human Rights to Change Tradition. Traditional Practices Harmful to Women's Health in Sub-Saharan Africa* (2002) at 51.

[12] This critique has been advanced by both cultural feminists, who argue that the differences between men and women should be celebrated, and radical feminists. For a critique of the CEDAW's definition of discrimination see Cook, 'State Responsibility for Violations of Women's Human Rights', at 125. Similarly Charlesworth, Chinkin and Wright criticise the definition of discrimination incorporated in the Convention on the grounds of its "underlying assumption that men and women are the same … Equality is defined as being like a man." See Hilary Charlseworth, Christine Chinkin and Shelley Wright, 'Feminist Approaches to International Law' 85 *Am. J. of Int'l L.* 613 (October 1991). Southard also provides a radical feminist critique of the CEDAW, arguing that the text of the CEDAW came into being through the "male-dominated United Nations" and thus "continues the androcentric approach to women's human rights by using a male standard for determining these rights."

perspectives of women in cases where they may be fundamentally different.[13] For instance, the CEDAW does not explicitly prohibit several gender-based abuses, such as rape, domestic violence, and female genital mutilation which occur in the private sphere.[14] Excluding them from the protective provisions of the CEDAW has meant that the State's responsibility to eradicate them is not clearly set forth.

The CEDAW has also been widely criticised as inadequate by radical feminists, because it "begins with the assumption that the institutions and procedures currently practiced in given societies are basically appropriate modes of behaviour [and that] all that is missing is that women are often denied access, or meaningful access, to these institutions and procedures."[15] It thus fails to recognise and address what is known as indirect discrimination, or gender neutral policies that have the effect of discriminating against women because of the underlying structures, such as traditions, lifestyles, attitudes, and educational systems that privilege men. Finally, it has also been argued that the CEDAW's definition of discrimination privileges "the free, independent and empowered woman."[16]

However, subsequent provisions of the CEDAW demonstrate that the intention of the drafters was not simply to achieve formal equality between the genders. In fact, the CEDAW "is based on the understanding that existing international human rights laws were not effectively addressing the specific disadvantages and injustices faced by women."[17] By developing the legal norm of non-discrimination from a "sex-neutrality norm" that demands equal treatment regardless of gender (usually measured against a benchmark of how men are treated) to a new norm of non-discrimination, it recognises "the distinctive characteristics of women and their vulnerabilities to discrimination" while providing a specific legal response.[18] Effectively, the CEDAW thus provides a more purposeful protection of the particular rights and needs of women.

---

[13] Byrnes (2002) at 126. See also R. Christopher Preston and Ronald Z. Ahrens, 'United Nations Convention Documents in Light of Feminist Theory', 8 *Mich J. of I. Law* 1 (2001) at 9.

[14] Laden Askari, 'Girls Rights Under International Law. An Argument for Establishing Gender Equality as a Jus Cogens', 8 *S. Cal. Rev. L. & Women's Stud.* 3 (Fall 1998) at 25–26.

[15] Southard (1996).

[16] Rhadika Coomaraswamy, 'To Bellow Like A Cow: Women, Ethnicity and the Discourse of Rights', in Rebecca J. Cook (ed.), *Human Rights of Women. National and International Perspectives* (1994) at 40.

[17] Laboni Amena Hoq, 'The Women's Convention and its Optional Protocol: Empowering Women to Claim their Internationally Protected Rights', 32 *Colum. Hum. Rts. L. Rev.* 677 (Summer 2001) at 681.

[18] Cook, 'State Responsibility for Violations of Women's Human Rights', at 156.

Moreover, although the CEDAW fails to mention the specific abuses faced by women, the wide definition of discrimination adopted by the Convention seems to include any possible form of violation. The Convention condemns discrimination against women in all its forms and manifestations. As such, although its provisions do not cover each particular form of discrimination independently, it can be deduced from the wide definition incorporated in article 1 that all forms of discrimination are implicitly covered by the Convention. For instance, although violence against women is not mentioned explicitly in any of the articles of the CEDAW, in it General Recommendation no. 19 (1992), the CEDAW Committee stated that such violence constituted a particularly grave form of discrimination, and was thus prohibited by virtue of a number of CEDAW provisions.

The CEDAW's definition of discrimination covers both *de facto* and *de jure* discrimination. According to article 1, discrimination includes any distinction, exclusion or restriction that has the '*purpose*' or '*effect*' of limiting women's free and full participation and development. One interpretation of this definition is that it covers both direct and indirect discrimination, which includes "seemingly neutral policies and practices that have the '*purpose*' or '*effect*' of disproportionately excluding women from the enjoyment of opportunities."[19] However, another reading of the definition is that the law or practice in question, in order to be considered discriminatory, must not only make a distinction between men and women, but should *also* have the 'purpose' or 'effect' of nullifying the rights of women on a basis of equality with men.

This leaves unanswered the question regarding the effect of laws that make no explicit distinction between the sexes, but somehow disadvantage women. A pertinent example is placing employment criteria that have the *effect* of discriminating against women, such as a job that requires a high degree of educational achievement. Although such a criterion isn't discriminatory at face value, it may effectively discriminate against women who may find it more difficult than men to meet the high educational eligibility standards. It seems that such laws and policies are not covered by article 1, because they are not based on any *explicit* "distinction, exclusion or restriction," arguably another weak point in

[19] Byrnes (2002) at 124. See also Cook, 'State Accountability Under the Women's Convention', at 235.

the CEDAW's protection regime. In its General Recommendation 25, however, the CEDAW Committee stated that:

> Indirect discrimination against women may occur when laws, policies and programmes are based on seemingly gender-neutral criteria which in their actual effect have a detrimental impact on women. Gender-neutral laws, policies and programmes unintentionally may perpetuate the consequences of past discrimination. They may be inadvertently modelled on male lifestyles and thus fail to take into account aspects of women's life experiences which may differ from those of men. These differences may exist because of stereotypical expectations, attitudes and behaviour directed towards women, which are based on the biological differences between women and men. They may also exist because of the generally existing subordination of women by men.[20]

According to Cook, it may be argued that such laws fall under the ambit of article 3 of the CEDAW, which requires States parties to "ensure the full development and advancement of women." A wide reading of this provision may suggest that article 3 places a positive obligation on States to prohibit laws that are "detrimental to women as such" although they might not be discriminatory in their actual terms.[21] Although this wide reading of article 3 is theoretically beneficial to women, it seems to go beyond what States have consented to under CEDAW.

The other question seemingly left unanswered by article 1 of CEDAW is whether every distinction based on gender amounts to discrimination, even if it doesn't have the 'purpose' or 'effect' of disadvantaging women. In its General Comment 18, the CCPR answered this question in the negative.[22] The CCPR held that distinctions may be tolerated if they are "reasonable and objective" and if their aim is to "achieve a purpose which is legitimate under the Convention." Allowing States such a margin of discretion is essential for many reasons. It makes it easier for them to assess their own deficiencies, in good faith, and gives different societies and cultures sufficient room to articulate more particular definitions of gender non-discrimination that are compatible with their worldviews and identities. It is also supported by a strict textual reading of article 1.

---

[20] *General Recommendation* 25, Temporary special measures, CEDAW Committee, 13th session, (2004), note 1.

[21] Cook, 'State Accountability Under the Women's Convention', at 236.

[22] General Comment 18, Committee on Civil and Political Rights, Non-discrimination, para. 13 (Thirty-seventh session, 1989), Compilation of General Comments and General Recommendations Adopted by Human Rights Treaty Bodies, U.N. Doc. HRI\GEN\1\Rev.1 at 26 (1994).

In order to avoid manipulation of this discretionary margin by States, however, a very narrow and stringent interpretation of the terms "reasonable and objective", is required, through the "highest degree of judicial scrutiny."[23] In the *Belgian linguistics* case, the European Court of Human Rights stated that any distinction must have "an objective and reasonable justification" or "pursue a legitimate aim." It placed a further limitation by requiring the existence of a "reasonable relationship of proportionality between the means employed and the aim sought to be realised."[24] Establishing that discrimination has occurred "requires a court to draw lines between justified and unjustified distinctions."[25] This balancing act occurs on a case by case basis.

Although this concept has not been elaborated on by the CEDAW Committee, applying it to the CEDAW's definition of discrimination is essential. It allows for a degree of distinction between the genders to accommodate for different domestic factors, while necessitating that such a distinction meet the criteria of objectivity, justifiability, proportionality and legitimacy. The burden of proving that these criteria have been met is left to the domestic courts of each State, regional courts and mechanisms where applicable, and possibly the CEDAW Committee, which is well equipped, given its even geographical representation, to assess which distinctions may be considered legitimate. Adopting this approach would re-characterize the discrimination test under CEDAW from one of "similarity/difference" to one of disadvantage.[26] By allowing "a member of a persistently disadvantaged group to prove that a law is discriminatory if that law, policy, or behaviour continues or worsens that disadvantage", this test is arguably more consistent with the object and purpose of CEDAW.[27]

Both customary international law and the CEDAW seem to tolerate distinctions on the basis of gender that are 'proportionate', 'reasonable' and 'objective' in the strictest terms. It is thus essential to adopt a somewhat nuanced interpretation of the definition of non-discrimination, yet one that is still compatible with international law. Such an approach should not be used to shield discriminatory personal status laws, but

[23] Anne Bayefsky, 'General Approaches to Domestic Application of International Law', in Rebecca J. Cook (ed.), *Human Rights of Women, National and International Perspectives* (1994) at 357.

[24] Belgian Linguistics, 23 Eur. Ct. H.R. (ser A) (1968).

[25] Bayefsky (1994) at 356.

[26] Bharathi Anandhi Venkatraman, 'Islamic States and the UN Convention on the Elimination of All Forms of Discrimination Against Women: Are the Shari'a and the Convention Compatible?', 44 *Am. U.L. Rev.* (Summer 1995) at 2003.

[27] Hoq (2001) at 723.

rather, to allow for the reform of laws that truly disadvantage women, and that cannot be justified through strict criteria. States do not readily concur on the precise definition of discrimination against women. Perceptions of discrimination depend on empirical information and "insights on how women are subordinated within different legal, social and religious traditions."[28] Granting States a narrow but objective margin of discretion, would not only help CEDAW overcome many of the critiques to its approach to non-discrimination, but would also encourage States to withdraw their reservations in the knowledge that they would not be required to repeal personal status legislation based on religious law and secularise it altogether. Simultaneously, such States would have to modify any distinctions that clearly disadvantage women, and may not be justified under the narrow objectivity and proportionality test. Such reforms must be accompanied by a genuine effort by the state to modify negative cultural attitudes and stereotypes that discriminate against women and hamper their full enjoyment of their equality rights.

Measures to Eliminate Discrimination under CEDAW

The "general undertakings" of States under CEDAW, or the policies and measures they are to implement to comply with their obligations, are detailed in articles 2, 3 and 4 of the Convention. The remaining substantive articles, namely articles 5–16, outline the "specific undertakings," or particular rights that women enjoy under the Convention on a basis of equality with men. These must be read in conjunction with the "general undertakings" clauses.

Article 2 of CEDAW, which corresponds to article 2 of the ICCPR and ICESCR, outlines the nature of the general obligations undertaken by States under the Convention. The CEDAW Committee is currently in the process of drafting a General Recommendation to elucidate the nature and scope of obligations under article 2, a process that has been hampered by the widely conflicting views of experts on the Committee. A strict textual reading reveals that obligations under article 2 include both "obligations of conduct" and "obligations of result", otherwise termed "obligations of means" and "obligations of ends."[29] The distinction here is "between the obligations to take specified steps towards aspirational

[28] Cook, 'State Responsibility for Violations of Women's Human Rights', at 133.
[29] Ibid. at 162.

goals" as opposed to "obligations to achieve certain results by any lawful means."[30] The chapeau of article 2 requires that States pursue a policy of "eliminating discrimination against women" in all its "forms and manifestations," which is clearly an obligation of ends, or of result. It requires States to undertake a number of measures in the constitutional, legislative, judicial and social fields intended to establish both *de jure* and *de facto* equality between men and women.

The eight sub-sections of article 2 and the majority of the remaining provisions of the CEDAW outline obligations of means, leaving the precise choice of means up to the respective States parties. Two major challenges confront the implementation of article 2, however. The first is the claim by States that obligations under article 2 are progressive rather than immediate in nature, and hence may be deferred according to the circumstances of each individual State, whereas the second is the large number of reservations that States have articulated with respect to this central provision.

States' General Undertakings: Progressive or Immediate Obligations?

The wording of articles 2 and 3 of CEDAW suggests, at face value, that obligations under the Convention are of a progressive nature. According to article 2 of the CEDAW, "States Parties condemn discrimination against women in all its forms, *agree to pursue by all appropriate means and without delay* a policy of eliminating discrimination against women ..." Article 3 further requires States to take "all appropriate measures, including legislation, to ensure the full development and advancement of women, for the purpose of guaranteeing them the exercise and enjoyment of human rights and fundamental freedoms on a basis of equality with men." Taken together, these two comprehensive articles ensure that States are to guarantee equality between men and women in all fields, employing all appropriate means and measures to reach that goal.

According to article 2, the general undertaking of parties to the CEDAW is to "agree to pursue by all appropriate means" which suggests, at the outset, that no immediate action by the State is required. However, upon closer scrutiny, it is evident that although States have discretion in assessing which means they deem 'appropriate,' they must pursue

[30] Ibid.

these means 'without delay'. Requiring States to pursue particular policies using 'all appropriate means' indicates progressiveness; however, the phrase 'without delay' signifies that States must act immediately.

The undertaking to "agree to pursue by all appropriate means" falls short of the general undertaking under the ICCPR, whose article 2 requires States to "undertake to respect and to ensure ... the rights recognised under the present Covenant." In general, the obligation to "respect" connotes a negative obligation, by virtue of which the State should immediately refrain from committing violations, whereas the obligation to "ensure" is a positive obligation, requiring States to take positive action to implement the provisions of the Covenant, or to prevent third parties from perpetrating violations.[31] In contrast to the ICCPR, the ICESCR requires each State party to "take steps ... to the maximum of its available resources ... with a view to achieving progressively," which implies that the required action is not immediate (at least partially). The qualification to immediate implementation is, in the case of the ICESCR, the scarcity of resources, which is often erroneously construed as a licence to delay implementation of the rights in question. According to General Comment 3 of the CESCR, however, the correct reading of State obligations under article 2 reveals that:

> while the full realization of the relevant rights may be achieved progressively, steps towards that goal must be taken within a reasonably short time after the Covenant's entry into force for the States concerned. Such steps should be deliberate, concrete and targeted as clearly as possible towards meeting the obligations recognized in the Covenant.[32]

Although the CEDAW doesn't adopt the exact progressive wording of the ICESCR, the use of the phrase "agree to pursue by all appropriate means" as opposed to "agree to eliminate discrimination against women" or "agree to respect and ensure equality of women" suggests that States are not required to "eliminate discrimination" as such, but to implement the specific measures outlined in article 2 'without delay' with a view to *eventually* eliminating discrimination against women. Arguably, however, this does not warrant a delay in the enforcement of treaty provisions; it simply recognises the reality that requiring States to eliminate

---

[31] Thomas Buergenthal, 'To Respect and To Ensure: State Obligations and Permissible Derogations', in Louis Henkin (ed.), *The International Bill of Rights: The Covenant on Civil and Political Rights* (1981) at 72.

[32] *General Comment no. 3, The Nature of States Parties Obligations* (art. 2, par. 1) 14/12/90. CESCR General Comment 3, 5th Sess. (1990), para. 4.

discrimination immediately is not practically possible. Instead, States must execute specific policies that are estimated to eventually have the effect of eliminating discrimination, while enjoying a 'grace period' for such policies to take full effect. Arguably, the duty to act 'without delay' implies that "a State party should not wait until prevailing legislation is challenged in the courts, but should move readily to review and change legislation, particularly if a treaty monitoring body has held that similar legislation in another country violates the Convention."[33]

It has been argued that various 'soft law' instruments, including the Beijing Platform for Action, make the obligation to review and revoke discriminatory laws and practices an immediate one. The Beijing Platform requires in paragraph 232 (d) that governments

> *review* national laws, including customary laws and legal practices in the areas of family, civil, penal, labour and commercial law in order to ensure the implementation of the principles and procedures of all relevant international human rights instruments by means of national legislation, *revoke* any remaining laws that discriminate on the basis of sex and remove gender bias in the administration of justice;

Resolutions of the UN Human Rights Council and the Commission on the Status of Women have also arguably supplemented CEDAW's article 2 by inserting an element of immediacy to the obligation to eliminate discrimination against women.[34] By using the imperative in stating obligations, such instruments may be considering as developing CEDAW's provisions, which foresaw the need for a 'grace period' almost thirty years ago. On the other hand, according to some commentators who disregard the value of soft law, article 2 entails that States are not 'absolutely liable' to achieve any particular result; rather they are only obligated to implement treaty provisions with 'due diligence.'[35] In other words, "States can never guarantee that discrimination against women

[33] Cook, 'State Responsibility for Violations of Women's Human Rights', at 164.

[34] See Human Rights Council Resolution A/HRC/12/L.3 which *expresses concern*, in operative paragraph 4 that "despite the pledge made at the Beijing World Conference on Women and the review by the General Assembly at its twenty-third special session to modify or abolish remaining laws that discriminate against women and girls, many of these laws are still in force and continue to be applied, thereby preventing women and girls from enjoying the full realization of their human rights". Operative paragraph 5 further "*Calls upon* States to fulfil their international obligations and commitments to revoke any remaining laws that discriminate on the basis of sex and remove gender bias in the administration of justice, taking into account that those laws violate their human right to be protected against discrimination".

[35] Cook, 'State Responsibility for Violations of Women's Human Rights', at 160.

will not occur and therefore cannot be held absolutely liable for all or any acts of discrimination."[36] This argument, however, is tenuous, since a State's liability clearly arises in the case of a failure to implement the measures specified in article 2 of the CEDAW 'without delay'.

States may also attempt to evade their obligations under the CEDAW by invoking the 'appropriateness' criterion mentioned in article 2. Arguably, this provision grants States complete discretion in determining what means and measures are appropriate given the differences in political, economic, and social circumstances. By acceding to the CEDAW, however, States undertake to abide by international standards of protection of women's human rights, which they must take into consideration when judging the 'appropriateness' of the measures being pursued.[37] Article 2 thus requires States to "develop *appropriate* means with due diligence and apply them without delay" allowing each State to assess its own deficiencies while implementing its obligations under the Covenant.[38] Finally, the determination of whether the particular measures adopted by the State in question are 'appropriate' may be discerned by examining the CEDAW Committee's recommendations, comments and observations on State reports, through which the Committee may point out areas of concern.

The Nature of Egypt's Obligations under CEDAW

In light of the above, Egypt's obligations as a party to CEDAW can be summarised as the obligation to pursue the goal of eliminating discrimination on the basis of gender, without delay, using all appropriate means and measures. In order to comply with its obligations, Egypt should act immediately to bring into effect the specific measures outlined in article 2, leading ultimately to the elimination of all forms of discrimination against women. These comprehensive measures include 'negative obligations', namely refraining from any act or practice of discrimination and 'positive obligations' including legal measures, such as the prohibition of discrimination in the constitution and in legislation, revoking discriminatory penal provisions, and guaranteeing the legal and judicial protection of the rights of women. They also include measures to achieve

[36] Cook, 'State Accountability Under the Women's Convention', at 232.
[37] Cook, 'State Responsibility for Violations of Women's Human Rights', at 162.
[38] Ibid. at 161–162.

the practical realization of equality, through eliminating discrimination by private actors, and abolishing discriminatory customs and practices. In the interest of simplification, obligations under the CEDAW can be divided into a number of categories, namely:

Legislating against Discrimination and Providing Legal Remedies

The critical sphere for the enforcement of women's human rights is the domestic legal system. As such, parties to CEDAW must repeal any legislation that violates the principle of non-discrimination on the basis of gender, and institute legal remedies in the case of violation if they are to give effect to the CEDAW's provisions. Such reform should include both constitutional as well as legislative reform. There is also a need to provide victims of discrimination with adequate legal remedies in the case of violation. Although the CEDAW does not incorporate a specific article on remedies, article 2(b) obliges States to adopt 'appropriate' measures "including sanctions where appropriate" and article 2(c) calls on States "to establish legal protection of the rights of women on an equal basis with men."[39] This provision may also be interpreted to protect women against the discriminatory application of the law. It is thus evident that the CEDAW requires the institution of legal and judicial remedies so as to ensure the effectiveness of protection under the Convention. States are thus required to "prevent and deter private acts of discrimination, to investigate and negate their harmful consequences, and to provide for compensation or sanctions for the performance of such acts, for instance by penalties of a civil or criminal nature."[40]

Preventing Discrimination by Non-State Actors

The CEDAW represents the progressive development of international human rights law to acknowledge "the need to move beyond the 'public sphere' as the only realm of possible State action or international intervention."[41] This transformation is of profound significance: at the core of the 'private sphere' is domestic and family life, an area whose central occupants are women. Public regulation of the private realm is

[39] Kathryn Christine Arnold, 'Are the Perpetrators of Honor Killings Getting Away With Murder? Article 340 of the Jordanian Penal code Analyzed Under the Convention on the Elimination of All Forms of Discrimination Against Women', 16 *Am. U. Int'l L. Rev.* 1343, at 1381.

[40] Cook, 'State Accountability under the Women's Convention', at 236–237.

[41] Hoq (2001) at 713.

extremely limited, which means that women's concerns in this sphere are largely invisible. Until the adoption of the CEDAW, all international human rights instruments maintained the distinction between the 'public sphere,' in which all political and legal acts take place, and the 'private sphere,' which is deemed 'subjective' and is hence sheltered from government regulation.[42]

Article 2(e) of the CEDAW establishes that the private sphere is no longer "off-limits when it comes to State obligations to protect women's rights."[43] By extending the State's obligation to eliminate discrimination to "any person, organisation or enterprise", the family may no longer be shielded from the authority of the State. States are not only under an obligation to prevent discrimination against women by third parties, but they must also provide adequate remedies against such discrimination.

The Obligation to Influence Cultural Attitudes

In addition to the existence of codified laws that may discriminate against women, informal customs and traditions may play an even more significant role in subjugating women. The CEDAW recognises that belief systems sometimes contribute to women's disempowerment, and has subsequently placed an obligation on parties to influence cultural and social values that impose traditional roles and sexual stereotypes for men and women. The obligation embodied in article 2(f) of the CEDAW to "modify or abolish existing laws, regulations, customs and practices which constitute discrimination against women," goes in tandem with the obligation under article 2(e) to regulate the private realm of the family. The CEDAW is unequivocal in its condemnation of discriminatory beliefs and practices and places a clear obligation on States to eliminate them. Article 5(a) further elaborates on this principle by requiring parties to:

> Modify the social and cultural patterns of conduct of men and women, with a view to achieving the elimination of prejudices and customary and all other practices which are based on the idea of the inferiority or the superiority of either of the sexes or on stereotyped roles for men and women.

This principle has also been reaffirmed by the CEDAW Committee in General Recommendation 3, which stipulates that:

---

[42] Ibid.
[43] Ibid.

> although the reports have come from States with different levels of development, they present features in varying degrees showing the existence of stereotyped conceptions of women, owing to socio-cultural factors, that perpetuate discrimination based on sex and hinder the implementation of article 5 of the Convention.[44]

Similarly, General Comment 28 of the Committee on Civil and Political Rights, states that "States parties should ensure that traditional, historical, religious or cultural attitudes are not used to justify violations of women's right to equality before the law and to equal enjoyment of all Covenant rights."[45] The General Comment further holds that the right to freedom of thought, conscience and religion may not be relied upon as a basis for discrimination against women.

Taken together, articles 2(f) and 5 necessitate a commitment by States to transform popular beliefs and attitudes.[46] In spite of the clearly-stated obligations embodied in these two provisions, the practical steps that need to be taken to achieve such results are unclear. It is in this light that the CEDAW Committee 'urged' all parties to implement education and public information programmes that have the effect of eliminating prejudices and practices that hinder women's full enjoyment of their 'social' equality.[47] The magnitude of such a proposed program would obviously need to be very extensive in order to achieve its stated objective, and should include "a comprehensive and intensive program of formal and informal education, supported by social services and other administrative measures".[48] Such a program "must not only discredit the religious or customary law or practice in question, but also provide a viable and legitimate alternative view of the matter".[49]

Some commentators have gone further than requiring public education campaigns and legislative reforms. It has been argued that taken together, articles 2(f) and 5 obligate States to "confront practices, for instance of religious institutions, that while perhaps claiming to regard

---

[44] *General Recommendation no. 3*, Education and Public Information Programmes, CEDAW 6th Sess. (1987).

[45] *General Comment 28*: Equality of Rights Between Men and Women (Article 3), 29/03/2000. CCPR/C/21/Rev.1/Add.10, Adopted by the Committee at its 1834th meeting (68th session).

[46] An-Naim, 'State Responsibility Under Human Rights Law to Change Religious and Customary Laws', at 178.

[47] Ibid.

[48] Ibid.

[49] Ibid.

the sexes as different but equal, in effect preclude women from senior levels of authority and influence."[50]

The ambiguity of obligations under CEDAW, including questions regarding the precise scope of non-discrimination, on the one hand, and the immediacy and precise nature of obligations, on the other, complicates any assessment of the extent of Egypt's compliance with the Convention. This vagueness, and the potentially extensive reach of the CEDAW's provisions have prompted States, including Egypt, to enter reservations to article 2 in an attempt to limit its scope, as well as to other specific provisions. The role of the CEDAW Committee is thus central in uncovering violations of the CEDAW and inducing compliance by States parties, including where reservations have stood in the way of full compliance. In spite of its shortcomings, the CEDAW Committee has played an important role in bridging the gap between Egypt's domestic law and its international obligations. Part of its effectiveness rests on its ability to advance a culturally sensitive reading of the CEDAW that takes into account the different political, historical and social realities in different States. Through the process of constructive dialogue, the Committee has also succeeded in limiting the effect of broad reservations intended to shield discriminatory laws and practices.

The Compliance-Inducing Role of the CEDAW Committee

The CEDAW Committee's increased activism has placed it at the centre of the enforcement of the CEDAW. The Committee's compliance-inducing role vis-à-vis States that apply *Sharīʿa*-derived family laws is two-fold: it has attempted to give States a margin of discretion in interpreting their obligations, while simultaneously resisting attempts to shield discriminatory laws through incompatible reservations. This role has set the stage for a rapprochement between international standards on the one hand, and domestic laws based on religion, on the other. However, the Committee has a mixed record in engaging with States that apply personal status laws based on the *Sharīʿa*. In general, it should be noted that convincing States to modify their domestic legislation, particularly legislation derived from religion, is no easy task. Such a task can only be accomplished through engaging in constructive, rather than antagonistic dia-

[50] Cook, 'State Accountability under the Women's Convention', at 240.

logue, while maintaining impartiality, credibility and legitimacy at all times. The Committee must therefore exhibit a more profound understanding of the issues affecting women in States with different legal systems and interpret the CEDAW in a consistent manner that demonstrates this understanding.

The enormity of this task is particularly evident in the area of *Sharīʿa*-derived law. Whereas the CEDAW Committee, at times, has demonstrated a degree of understanding of the particular domestic factors affecting the compliance by States applying personal status law based on the *Sharīʿa*, at other times it has antagonised such States, engaging in a reductionist and simplistic criticism of such laws that demonstrates unnecessary rigidity in the interpretation and application of the CEDAW. It is only through an incremental approach, one that is simultaneously culturally sensitive while remaining true to the purpose of CEDAW, that the Committee may succeed in advancing the equality rights of women, while allowing them to simultaneously uphold their right to religious and cultural belief and expression.

Initially, many of the Committee's pronouncements on Islamic *Sharīʿa* law were received with a great deal of hostility. In its Commentary to article 16 of the CEDAW, the Committee condemned "arranged marriages involving payment or preferment," an assertion that was rejected by many so-called 'Islamic States'. This rejection was based on an alternative view, which perceived some form of payment to be a right owed to the future wife. Egypt's personal status law for Muslims provides for the payment of *mahr* or a dowry to the wife upon initiation of a marriage. In other countries, the payment of *mahr* is considered customary, even if it isn't prescribed by law. The *mahr* is not intended for the bride's family, but for the bride herself, and is considered a right guaranteed to her by law, and by virtue of the marriage contract. In light of this reality, the pronouncement of the CEDAW Committee on this matter was described as short-sighted, since:

> the payment of *mahr* (dower), which involves payment or preferment, is a central feature of the marriage contract in Islam and, as a measure "intended to safeguard [a woman's] economic position after marriage," it may not be considered anathema to the Women's Convention, if correctly practiced. Given that Islamic law requires *mahr* to be offered to a bride and not to her relations, the practice of *mahr* in Islamic marriages "could not be considered a sale."[51]

---

[51] Venkatraman (1995) at 2002.

The Committee further erred in assuming that arranged marriages in the Islamic context do not involve choice or consent. Whereas marriages are often customarily arranged in so-called 'Islamic' societies, including Egypt, the Egyptian legal system recognises the legal capacity of both men and women to contract their own marriages, and emphasizes the centrality of consent. The law, which is based on the *Sharīʿa*, makes it illegal to force a woman into marriage. Arranged marriages are often the norm in societies where men and women do not often mix, and such marriages do not necessarily involve an element of coercion. In other words, the CEDAW Committee made a broad generalisation regarding the issue of arranged marriages, based on a subjective standard. Condemning such a significant cultural practise without understanding the relevant context threatens to render the Committee's opinions illegitimate in the eyes of many Muslims, and thus potentially irrelevant.

Antagonism towards the Committee reached its peak in 1987, when a number of so-called 'Islamic States' openly criticised it in the Economic and Social Council. The crisis was precipitated when the Committee pointed out, during its examination of the reports submitted by a number of States, that particular violations of women's rights were predicated on "wrong interpretations of Islam."[52] This was in response to an attempt by one government to justify "throwing acid in a woman's face for punishment" under the pretext of 'Islamic law', although such practices were vehemently challenged by other Muslim authorities.[53] The only Muslim expert on the Committee at the time disputed the attribution of these practices to Islam, and questioned the source of such contentions. Eventually, the Committee decided to request ECOSOC to "call for the compilation of women's rights as stipulated in Islamic scriptures ... in cooperation with a renowned Islamic institution such as *Al-Azhar*."[54] However, ECOSOC failed to take action in this regard due to fierce opposition by 'Islamic States,' which criticised it as an attack against Islam. The Committee thus came to be regarded as a tool of Western hegemony, and cultural imperialism.

[52] Mervat Tallawy, 'National Machinery and Foreign Policy', in Camillia Fawzi El-Solh and Judy Mabro (eds.), *Muslim Women's Choices. Religious Belief and Social Reality* (1994) at 136.
[53] Ibid.
[54] Ibid.

The CEDAW Committee persisted in requesting 'Islamic States' to reform their legislation, emphasising that this process could be achieved using indigenous reform tools. At its Sixth Session, the Committee adopted a decision in which it:

> Request[ed] the United Nations system as a whole, in particular the specialised agencies of the United Nations, and the Commission on the Status of Women, to promote or undertake studies on the status of women under Islamic laws and customs and in particular on the status and equality of women in the family on issues such as marriage, divorce, custody and property rights and their participation in public life of the society, taking into consideration the principle of *El-Ijtihād* in Islam.[55]

Eventually, and in light of the fierce reaction by States the Committee began to adapt its approach.[56] In an unprecedented move, the Committee reneged on a previous statement that "any law or custom that grants men a right to a greater share of property … on the death of a relative" was discriminatory.[57] This reversal in attitude occurred after the representative of Libya explained the logic behind reduced inheritance for women, according to the *Sharīʿa*. According to this logic, women acquired their share of the inheritance "without commitments, whereas men had to take over all the concomitant obligations."[58] He justified this reasoning on the basis of the principle of 'complementarity' of rights, by virtue of which men and women may be considered equal in dignity and worth, but distinct with regards to some particular rights and obligations, a reality that arises from the division of labour between men and women. According to this view, whereas men are required to work and maintain the family, women principally look after the household and hence do not need to earn a living or sustain the family. Women are entitled to maintenance from their husbands, this being considered a principal right for the wife. Even if the wife works, and earns her own income, her money may not be used to finance the household; it is hers to keep for personal use.

As the representative of Libya explained to the Committee, such a division of labour necessitated the unequal allotment of inheritance shares between the man and the woman. Subsequently, based on the

[55] *Decision 4*, CEDAW Committee, 6th Sess. in The Work of CEDAW. Reports of the Committee on the Elimination of Discrimination Against Women 296 (Volume II, 1986–1987, New York: United Nations; 1990).

[56] Hoq (2001) at 723.

[57] Report of the CEDAW Committee, U.N. GAOR, 49th Sess., Supp. No. 38, Annex I, U.N. Doc. A/49/38 (1994), at 174, para 44. See Venkatraman at 2004.

[58] Ibid.

above interpretation, the Committee "felt that there was no need to enter a reservation, because, with that interpretation, women were treated equally with men."[59] In other words, the Committee gave effect to the notion that not every distinction on the basis of gender amounts to discrimination.

As this example demonstrates, the CEDAW Committee ventured to interpret the CEDAW in a culturally-sensitive manner, the result being greater acceptance by States parties of its authority and their deference to its opinions and recommendations. A telling example is Egypt's willingness to discuss articles to which it has entered reservations, and to commit to consider withdrawing these reservations. The Committee sought, through this process, to strike a balance between the protection of women's rights, on the one hand, and respect for cultural autonomy, on the other. In other words, the Committee was able to use its powers of interpretation to assess gender discrimination according to a different benchmark, one that takes culture into consideration.

In recent years, however, the Committee seems to have reneged on some of these opinions, once again rejecting some basic tenets of *Sharīʿa*-derived family law, including unequal inheritance shares for women. This is so, partly for a failure on the part of the States concerned to adequately justify such laws, as well as the increased influence of non-governmental organisations and the Committee's reluctance to allow States a margin of discretion in this area. This development is unfortunate, as engaging with States positively through encouraging indigenous reform within the existing framework of the law is both useful and necessary, even if some degree of differential treatment persists, as long as the State can objectively show that such treatment is objective and reasonable, and aims to achieve a purpose that is considered legitimate under the CEDAW.

Legal norms and their application in different societies are necessarily complex and nuanced. Montesqiueu captured this paradox in his seminal treatise *De l'Esprit des Lois*, in which he stated that "les lois politiques et civiles de chaque nation ... doivent être tellement propres au peuple pour lesquelles elles sont faites, que c'est un grand hazard si celles d'une nation peuvent convenir à une autre".[60] The effectiveness of legal reforms depends on their "compatibility with accepted social norms"; it is hence both impractical and naïve to require States to abruptly introduce

---

59 Ibid.

60 Montesquieu, *De l'Esprit des Lois*, Book 1 Ch. 3.

drastic changes in the hope of reshaping society and restructuring gender roles.[61] Imposing a foreign system of law can only be received with scepticism and possibly very negative reactions. It is through this realisation that the CEDAW Committee can hope to effectively contribute to the advancement of women's equality rights on the ground, and in different cultural contexts. Adopting a conciliatory approach grants the Committee the credibility and influence to encourage States to take measures to comply with their Convention obligations through reconsidering and reforming their domestic legislation in a way that engages realistically with embedded institutions and mindsets.

[61] See Shaman (1997) at 228.

CHAPTER FOUR

SHARĪʿA-BASED RESERVATIONS: THE LAW AND POLITICS OF INVALIDITY

One of the major obstacles confronting the effective implementation of CEDAW provisions is the large number and scope of reservations entered to its substantive provisions. In fact, the CEDAW is the multilateral treaty that has been accorded the largest number of reservations.[1] A wealth of literature has been devoted to the study of reservations to the CEDAW, particularly those that are deemed incompatible with the 'object and purpose' of the treaty, and hence invalid. Reservations invoking 'Islamic law' or the *Sharīʿa* have been articulated by a large number of States including Egypt, attracting a great deal of critical scholarly attention. Such reservations are particularly prevalent vis-à-vis article 2 of the CEDAW as well as article 16 which deals with equality in family relations.[2]

Egypt's practice with regards to the principle of non-discrimination in family relations has been to consistently articulate reservations or interpretative declarations to modify its obligations under human rights treaties, or advance a particular interpretation that conforms with Egypt's domestic law. Apart from its reservations to CEDAW, it has articulated *Sharīʿa*-based interpretative declarations to the ICCPR and ICESCR, as well as to article 18 of the African Charter on Human and People's Rights.[3]

---

[1] The majority of reservations to the CEDAW relate to article 29 of the Convention, which provides for a compulsory dispute settlement mechanism. However, states have also entered a large number of reservations to substantive provisions of the treaty. Out of a total of 36 States that have entered reservations to substantive provisions of the CEDAW, 15 are developing countries. Eleven States have made reservations that have the effect of "neutralis[ing] the Convention as a whole by subjecting it to the constitutional law of the state party or to Islamic law." See William Schabas, 'Reservations to the Convention on the Elimination of All Forms of Discrimination Against Women, and the Convention on the Rights of the Child', 3 *Wm. & Mary J. of Women & L.* 79, 85 (Spring 1997).

[2] There are a total of 21 reservations to article 16 of the CEDAW.

[3] Article 18 stipulates that:

1. The family shall be the natural unit and basis of society. It shall be protected by the State which shall take care of its physical health and moral.
2. The State shall have the duty to assist the family which is the custodian of morals and traditional values recognized by the community.

Determining the scope and legal effect of such reservations and interpretative declarations is a very complex question that has drawn widely divergent views. It is argued that by virtue of their nature, human rights treaties create vertical obligations between States and individuals within their jurisdiction, and hence involve no State-to-State obligations. There is no room for the application of the principle of reciprocity, which is the main motivator for States to either accept reservations or object to them if they are deemed incompatible. It follows that States have no interest in objecting to a reservation that will have no bearing on their own relationship with the reserving State, thus explaining the paucity of objections to such reservations.

It is for this reason that the regime created by the Vienna Convention on the Law of Treaties has been widely criticised as inadequate in dealing with impermissible reservations to human rights treaties. Whereas there is a growing trend to consider the special nature of human rights treaties as warranting a distinct approach to reservations, one that departs significantly from the regime governing other multi-lateral conventions, there are still many commentators who remain true to the text of the VCLT, advancing a strict reading of international law that provides no remedy for such reservations.

The International Law Commission has itself struggled with this issue for years, and is currently in the process of articulating a Draft Guide to Practice for States, to fill the lacunae in international law relative to reservations to multilateral treaties, including human rights treaties. The results of this exercise, due to be completed in 2010, will undoubtedly shed important light on the issue and answer many hitherto unanswered questions.

Reservations to the CEDAW

The CEDAW is widely recognised as the human rights treaty with the largest number of reservations, of which many are considered incompatible with its 'object and purpose'. Such reservations "reinforce patterns of cooptation of what is politically expedient and feasible,"[4] diluting the potential effect of the Convention in guaranteeing the rights of

3. The State shall ensure the elimination of every discrimination against women and also ensure the protection of the rights of the woman and the child as stipulated in international declarations and conventions.

[4] Karam (1997) at 27.

women. The CEDAW Committee has been at the heart of the challenge to confront incompatible reservations. It has been particularly active with regards to its authority to determine the validity of reservations, and has staunchly confronted other UN bodies that challenged its authority on this matter.

In order to clarify the limits of this authority, the CEDAW Committee requested in its third session (1984) a legal opinion from the Treaty Section of the UN Office of Legal Affairs. In what seemed like a blow to the Committee's authority, the latter expressed the view that the functions of the CEDAW Committee "do not appear to include a determination of the incompatibility of reservations, although reservations undoubtedly affect the application of the Convention and the Committee might have to comment thereon in its reports in this context."[5] The Committee's authority was thus restricted to commenting on reservations, without being able to make declarations regarding their compatibility with the 'object and purpose' of the Convention.

In 1986, Canada requested a "general exchange of views on the question of reservations" to be included in the agenda of the third meeting of State parties.[6] The issue was also brought up in the Third Committee of the General Assembly, culminating in a heated debate between States that had entered reservations based on the Islamic *Sharīʿa* and other State parties. As a result of these discussions, the UN Secretary General was requested to seek the views of States on the issue of reservations, and to present a report on this matter to the General Assembly. Of the 87 parties to the CEDAW at the time, only 17 replied to the Secretary's General's invitation.[7] Although State parties expressed concern at the number of reservations that seemed to be incompatible with the 'object and purpose' of the CEDAW, they nonetheless agreed that it was beyond the competence of the Committee to determine the compatibility of reservations. They were unanimous, however, in recognising the need to withdraw reservations, particularly incompatible ones.[8]

---

[5] CEDAW/C/L.1/Add.20 (contained in The Work of CEDAW, Volume I, 1982 to 1985, United Nations. See "The Practice of Human Rights Treaty Bodies With Respect to Reservations to International Human Rights Treaties", Seventeenth Meeting of Chairpersons of the Human Rights Treaty Bodies (Geneva, 23–24 June 2005), Fourth Inter Committee Meeting of the Human Rights Treaty Bodies (Geneva, 20–22 June 2005) UN Doc HRI/MC/2005/5 (13 June 2005), at para 8).

[6] State parties to the CEDAW have a general meeting every two years. They have dealt with the issue of reservations to the CEDAW in two separate meetings.

[7] Liesbeth Lijnzaad, *Reservations to UN Human Rights Treaties. Ratify and Ruin?* (1995) at 330.

[8] Ibid.

In spite of the opinions expressed by States parties in its sixth session in 1987, the CEDAW Committee adopted General Recommendation 4 in which it expressed concern at the "significant number of reservations that [appear] to be incompatible with the object and purpose of the Convention."[9] The Committee further welcomed "the decision of the State parties to consider reservations at its next meeting in New York in 1988" and suggested that they reconsider any incompatible reservations "with a view to withdrawing them."[10]

However, the significance of General Recommendation 4 should not be overstated; although the Committee had denounced reservations incompatible with the CEDAW, it left the matter to be examined by the States parties themselves. Ultimately, there was little impact on the reserving States.[11] In fact, throughout the 1980's the CEDAW Committee's authority to deem reservations invalid remained very limited. However, this trend, which was initially espoused by both States as well as the UN Secretariat, seems to have lost much of its influence in the 1990's and particularly "after the emergence of the [CCPR]-led jurisprudence on reservations."[12] In order to understand the development of this novel regime and new-found activism of the CEDAW Committee in the area of incompatible reservations, it is essential to discuss the development of the regime governing reservations to multilateral treaties, particularly treaties of a so-called 'humanitarian' character including human rights treaties, which has evolved significantly over the last half century.

The Traditional Approach to Reservations to Multilateral Treaties

Traditionally, reservations to multi-lateral treaties "required the unanimous acceptance of all other treaty parties, unless the treaty otherwise provided."[13] The unanimity rule was based on the desire to protect the integrity of multilateral treaties; any objection to a reservation by any of the parties would automatically exclude the reserving State from becom-

---

[9] *General Recommendation no. 4*, Reservations, CEDAW, 6th Sess. (1987).

[10] Ibid.

[11] Tyagi (2001) at 230.

[12] Ibid.

[13] Catherine Redgwell, 'Universality or Integrity? Some Reflections on Reservations to General Multilateral Treaties', 64 *Brit. Y.B. Int'l L.* 246 (1993).

ing a party to the treaty.[14] However, this trend began to shift with the advent of decolonisation due to the sharp increase in the number of States, which created an interest in promoting widespread participation in multilateral treaties, albeit at the expense of their integrity.

The first region to depart considerably from the unanimity rule was the Pan-American region, which adopted a system that allowed a reserving state to become a party to a multilateral treaty, notwithstanding objections by other parties to its ratification.[15] The Pan-American approach evolved into a local custom for that region, affirming the State's inherent right to enter reservations to multilateral treaties. As such, objections could no longer prevent a reserving State from becoming a party. Under this system, the treaty would be in force between the reserving State and the parties that accepted the reservation; it would not enter into force for the reserving State in its relationship with any party that objected to the reservation.[16]

Eventually, a similar approach was adopted by the international community at large, based on the landmark advisory opinion of the International Court of Justice on the *Reservations to the Convention on the Prevention and Punishment of the Crime of Genocide* (1951). This approach was later codified in the 1969 Vienna Convention on the Law of Treaties.

The Development of the Current Reservations Regime

The current regime governing reservations to multilateral treaties departs from the premise that reservations are both necessary and, to a certain extent, desirable. This is so because they facilitate the ratification by States of multilateral treaties setting universal standards, in spite of widely divergent political and economic systems.[17] In other words, the current regime is based on a careful balancing act between the two competing objectives of universality and integrity of multilateral treaties.

---

[14] Jennifer Riddle, 'Making CEDAW Universal: A Critique of CEDAW's Reservation Regime Under Article 28 and the Effectiveness of the Reporting Process' 34 *Geo. Wash. Int'l L. Rev.* (2002) 605, 608.

[15] Ibid.

[16] Ibid.

[17] Redgwell (1993) at 247.

The Genocide Convention Advisory Opinion

In its breakthrough decision in the *Advisory Opinion on Reservations to the Convention on the Prevention and Punishment of the Crime of Genocide*, the ICJ administered a blow to the customary unanimity rule that previously governed reservations to multilateral treaties in two respects. Primarily, the Court held that the unanimous acceptance of a reservation by all State parties was no longer required. It stated that "the conception of the absolute integrity of a convention" did not appear to have been "transformed into a rule of international law."[18] Secondly, the ICJ established the 'object and purpose' test; it held that a reserving State may be considered a party to the Convention, notwithstanding objections, as long as the reservation was compatible with the 'object and purpose' of the treaty in question. The Court emphasised the centrality of the 'object and purpose' test to the compatibility of reservations.[19]

In effect, the Court established "a two-tier test" for addressing reservations.[20] A State could object to a reservation without deeming it incompatible with the 'object and purpose' of the treaty, thus permitting the entry into force of that treaty between the two States, as modified by the reservation. Alternatively, the objecting State could deem the reservation incompatible with the 'object and purpose' of the treaty while simultaneously objecting to the entry into force of the treaty between itself and the reserving State. The effect would thus be to preclude the enforcement of the treaty between those two States.[21] The operation of the 'object and purpose' test depended largely on the good faith of the parties, since the determination of compatibility was left to their discretion.

The 'object and purpose' test was intended to resolve the contentious issue of reservations to treaties of a humanitarian nature. According to the Court, such treaties could be treated distinctly because

---

[18] Reservations to the Convention on the Prevention and Punishment of the Crime of Genocide, Advisory Opinion 1951 I.C.J. Reports 15.

[19] Ibid. The Court also stated that "it follows that it is the compatibility of a reservation with the object and purpose of the Convention that must furnish the criterion for the attitude of a State in making the reservation on accession as well as for the appraisal by a state in objecting to the reservation."

[20] Riddle (2002) at 609–610.

[21] Ibid.

> contracting States do not have any interests of their own; they merely have, one and all, a common interest, namely, the accomplishment of those high purposes which are the *raison d'etre* of the convention. Consequentially, in a convention of this type one cannot speak of individual advantages or disadvantages to States, or of the maintenance of a perfect contractual balance between rights and duties. The high ideals which inspired the Convention provide, by virtue of the common will of the parties, the foundation and measure of all of its provisions.[22]

This widely contested departure from the unanimity rule[23] was motivated by the desire to attract the largest possible number of States to ratify a treaty, even if the price was to modify some provisions through reservations. In its sixth session (1952), the UN General Assembly eventually adopted a resolution upholding the Court's decision, in the interest of developing a more practical approach to the formulation of reservations to "legislative or normative, as opposed to contractual, treaties."[24] The 'object and purpose' test, however, proved ineffective in addressing the precise reservations it was intended to remedy, namely reservations to treaties of a humanitarian character like the Genocide Convention, which do not create horizontal obligations between States, but rather vertical obligations between a State and its subjects.

The Vienna Convention's Reservations Regime

The 1969 Vienna Convention on the Law of Treaties (VCLT) embodies the present regime governing reservations to multi-lateral treaties in its articles 2(1), and 19 to 23. It further articulates the rules enunciated by the ICJ in the Genocide Convention Advisory Opinion. According to article 2 (1) of the VCLT, any reservation has the effect of modifying, in whole or in part, the legal effect of a provision of a treaty as between the reserving State and other States. Reservations are impermissible in the following cases:

---

[22] Genocide Convention Advisory Opinion, at 12.

[23] ILC Rapporteur Sir Gerald Fitzmaurice held that the decision of the Court undermined the principle of the integrity of the treaty, and "could result in fragmenting a multilateral convention into bilateral treaties of variable content." Fitzmaurice further criticized the 'object and purpose' test on the grounds that it was fundamentally subjective and would prove impractical. See Belinda Clerk, 'The Vienna Convention's Reservations Regime and the Convention on the Elimination of All Forms of Discrimination Against Women', 85 *Am.J. Int'l. L.* 281 (April 1991) at 302.

[24] These developments "led the ILC over time to abandon its support for the unanimity principle." Ibid.

(a) The reservation is prohibited by the treaty;
(b) The treaty provides that only specified reservations, which do not include the reservation in question, may be made; or
(c) In cases not falling under sub-paragraphs (a) and (b), the reservation is incompatible with the object and purpose of the treaty.

The VCLT similarly left the authority to determine the compatibility of reservations to the discretion of States parties. The 'object and purpose' test thus remained a subjective test that allowed each State to establish individually whether a reservation was incompatible with the treaty in question.[25]

According to the Vienna Convention regime, a State may also object to another's reservation, without precluding the entry into force of the treaty as between the two States.[26] In such a case, "the provisions to which the reservation relates do not apply as between the two States to the extent of the reservation."[27] A State party's silence with regards to a reservation is tantamount to implicit acceptance.[28] It is important to note that States may also object to reservations for reasons other than incompatibility with the 'object and purpose' of the treaty.[29]

A State may thus approach reservations in four different ways. It can explicitly accept the reservation, giving it full legal effect. Alternatively, it can impliedly accept the reservation through silence (acquiescence). The third option would be to object to the reservation, in which case the treaty remains in force between the two States, to the exclusion of the reserved provision.[30] Finally, the State may object to the reservation and simultaneously preclude the treaty from entering into force as between itself and the reserving State.[31] In this case, the objecting State ceases

[25] Riddle (2002) at 610.

[26] According to article 20(4)(b) "an objection by another contracting state to a reservation does not preclude the entry into force of the treaty as between the objecting and reserving states unless a contrary intention is definitely expressed by the objecting state."

[27] Article 21(3), VCLT.

[28] Article 20(5) of the VCLT stipulates that "a reservation is considered to have been accepted by a State if it shall have raised no objection to the reservation by the end of a period of twelve months." See Riddle (2002) at 611.

[29] Ibid.

[30] Ibid. at 610. In other words the reserved provision does not enter into force between these two States. See Jan Klabbers, 'Accepting the Unacceptable? A New Nordic Approach to Reservations to Multilateral Treaties', 69 *Nordic J. Int'l L.* 179 (2000) at 181.

[31] Riddle (2002) at 610.

to have any obligations with respect to the reserving State under the whole treaty, and vice versa.

In the last two cases, the reserving State remains at an advantage. In fact, the VCLT "effectively eliminated any difference between accepting and rejecting a reservation. If a State accepts the reservation, the reserved clause is modified for both parties. If a State objects to the reservation but does not challenge that State's ratification of the treaty, then the reserved provision does not apply between the States."[32] If a State decides to preclude the entry into force of the treaty as between itself and the reserving State, it cannot enforce *any* of the treaty provisions against the latter. It is for this reason that an objecting State is usually reluctant to preclude the entry into force of a human rights treaty as between itself and a reserving State; such an arrangement would benefit only the reserving State, allowing it to evade responsibility under any of the terms of the treaty.

This inadequacy in dealing with reservations to human rights treaties, particularly incompatible reservations, has prompted several of the treaty-monitoring bodies to develop new approaches to deal with reservations. Although the evolution of a 'specific custom' applicable to all human rights treaties is widely contested, it is evident that a number of treaty-monitoring bodies, including the CEDAW Committee, have developed such a custom when it comes to the assessment of the validity of incompatible reservations. It is doubtful, however, that this 'specific custom' includes the power to sever such reservations and hold States accountable in defiance of the stated reservations, although it has been suggested "that the rule of severability could stand to be revised in certain areas of international law and, in particular, in the area of human rights."[33]

Towards a New Reservations Regime?

The subjective nature of the compatibility test resulted in the persistence of "far-reaching and detrimental reservations" that were met with very few objections.[34] In response, several UN treaty-monitoring bodies took

[32] Ibid. at 624–625.

[33] See Alain Pellet, [Special Rapporteur], 'Report on the Meeting with Human Rights Bodies', *International Law Commission, Fifty-ninth session*, UN Doc ILC(LIX)/RT/CRP.1 (26 July 2007) at para 15.

[34] Lijnzaad (1995) at 324.

it upon themselves to make pronouncements on the compatibility of such reservations.[35] A significant body of recent literature supports the view that treaty-monitoring bodies may make binding determinations on the validity of reservations, or even to declare objectionable reservations null and void.[36] Others, however, have argued that the legal merit of this approach is questionable. In general, the practice of the treaty monitoring bodies seems to suggest that there is no over-arching rule that can be applied to the issue of reservations. Each mechanism has developed a different approach to reservations over time, with some taking a more proactive role than others.

It was the activism of the Inter-American Court on Human Rights[37] and the European Court of Human Rights (ECtHR)[38] on the issue of incompatible reservations that set the stage for the development of the practice of the UN treaty bodies in this regard. Although these Courts made authoritative pronouncements on the compatibility of reservations, the significance of their jurisprudence should not be overstated. As entities endowed with the authority to give authentic and binding interpretations of the treaties they were established to monitor, State practice in the regional judicial bodies cannot be used to make generalisations

[35] The term 'treaty-monitoring body' is used to describe the mechanisms established under human rights treaties to monitor compliance with the provision of the relevant treaty. To date, nine treaty-monitoring bodies have been established: the Committee on the Elimination of Racial Discrimination established under the Convention on the Elimination of Racial Discrimination (1965), the Committee on Economic, Social and Cultural Rights established under the ICESCR (1966), the Committee on Civil and Political Rights established under the ICCPR (1966), the Committee on the Elimination of Discrimination Against Women established under the CEDAW (1979), the Committee Against Torture established under the Convention Against Torture (1984), the Committee on the Rights of the Child established under the Convention on the Rights of the Child (1989) the Committee on Migrant Workers established under the Convention on the Protection of Migrant Workers and their Families (1990), the Committee on the Rights of Persons with Disabilities, established under the Convention on the Rights of Persons with Disabilities (2006), and the Committee on Enforced Disappearances which monitors compliance with the International Convention on the Protection of all People from Enforced Disappearances (2006).

[36] Clerk (1991) at 300.

[37] The Inter-American Court was established under the American Convention on Human Rights, O.A.S. Treaty Series no. 36 (1969), 1144 U.N.T.S. 123 entered into force July 18, 1978.

[38] The ECtHR was established under the European Convention for the Protection of Human Rights and Fundamental Freedoms 213 U.N.T.S. 222, *entered into force* Sept. 3, 1953, *as amended by* Protocols Nos. 3, 5, 8, and 11 *which entered into force* on 21 September 1970, 20 December 1971, 1 January 1990, and 1 November 1998 *respectively.*

about the *quasi*-judicial treaty-monitoring bodies, whose role has been traditionally confined to an advisory one. Nonetheless, the decisions of the regional Courts are indicative of the development of the regime governing reservations to human rights treaties, inspiring much of the activism of the UN treaty-monitoring bodies in this field.

Jurisprudence of the Regional Human Rights Mechanisms

In the landmark 1982 *Advisory Opinion on the effect of reservations on the entry into force of the American Convention on Human Rights*, the Inter-American Court on Human Rights held that:

> modern human rights treaties in general, and the American Convention in particular, are not multilateral treaties of the traditional type concluded to accomplish the reciprocal exchange of rights between and for the mutual benefit of the contracting States. Their object and purpose is the protection of the basic rights of individual human beings ....[39]

The Court considered that the application of the VCLT regime was qualified by the special nature of the Convention. The Court found that a State was free to formulate any reservation as long as it wasn't incompatible with the 'object and purpose' of the Convention. It also held that the entry into force of a treaty in relation to a reserving State was not contingent upon the express acceptance of the reservation by another State party.

Although the Court's decision did not break significantly with the established multilateral-treaty reservations regime, it recognised, for the first time, that reservations to human rights treaties warranted a different approach that took into consideration the special nature of such treaties and the humanitarian objectives they were intended to achieve. This finding set the stage for future developments that differentiated between reservations to general multilateral treaties on the one hand, and human rights treaties on the other.

It was the activism of the European Court of Human Rights that radically transformed the approach to reservations to human rights treaties. In 1988, the Court dealt for the first time with the validity of a State party's reservation to the European Convention in the *Belilos* case. In its ground-breaking decision, the Court found Switzerland's interpretative

---

[39] *The Effect of Reservations on the Entry into Force of the American Convention on Human Rights*, Inter-America Court on Human Rights, Advisory Opinion OC-2/82 of september 24, 1982 at para. 29.

declaration to article 6(1) of the European Convention tantamount to a reservation, and proceeded to sever the declaration *cum* reservation on the grounds of invalidity. The Court held that Switzerland's declaration failed to meet the specificity requirement under article 64 of the ECHR, neither was it accompanied by a statement of the law involved.[40] It proceeded to sever the reservation, while maintaining that Switzerland was bound by the treaty in its entirety, including the reserved clause.[41]

Although Switzerland objected to the ECtHR's decision on the basis that it undermined the principle of State consent, the Court's justification was that when a State expresses its consents to be bound by a treaty, it also accepts that it cannot make a reservation that is incompatible with that treaty. In other words, by signing on to a treaty, the reserving State has accepted, *a fortiori* the severance of any incompatible reservations.[42]

This decision of the ECtHR shook the main pillars of the Vienna Convention's reservations regime on two fronts. Like the Inter-American Court's Advisory opinion, it challenged the previously entrenched principle that only states had the authority to judge the compatibility and validity of reservations. Furthermore, it established for the first time that an incompatible reservation could be severed, while compelling the reserving State to abide by the reserved provision. Although the Court's judgement specifically addressed reservations that didn't meet the criteria of article 64 of the ECHR, its significance lies in that it removed the validity test from the exclusive authority of States parties.

The UN Treaty-Monitoring Bodies

The Committee established under the Convention on the Elimination of Racial Discrimination (CERD) was the first to address the issue of impermissible reservations back in 1976. Needless to say, the Committee encountered significant criticism when it declared that a particular reservation was incompatible with the 'object and purpose' of the CERD.[43] The Director of the UN Human Rights Division addressed a Memorandum to the Committee, stating that it had no authority but to "take the reservations made by States parties at the time of ratification or accession into

---

40 Belilos v. Switzerland, Eur. Ct. H.R. decision of 29 April 1988.

41 Ibid.

42 Riddle (2002) at 622.

43 Tyagi (2001).

account ... A decision—even a unanimous one—by the Committee that the reservation is unacceptable cannot have any legal effect."[44]

However, this position changed considerably over time, owing to the influence of the European and Inter-American Courts' jurisprudence. In the aftermath of the *Belilos* case, a meeting of the chairpersons of the treaty-monitoring bodies agreed in 1992 that:

> treaty bodies should systematically review reservations made when considering a report and include in the list of questions to be addressed to reporting Governments a question as to whether a given reservation was still necessary and whether a State party would consider withdrawing a reservation that might be considered by the treaty body concerned as being incompatible with the object and purpose of the treaty.[45]

By 1994, the chairpersons of the treaty-monitoring bodies had become even more assertive, recommending "that treaty bodies state clearly that certain reservations to international human rights instruments are contrary to the 'object and purpose' of those instruments and consequently incompatible with treaty law."[46] The Committee on Civil and Political Rights was the first treaty-body to play an active role in this regard. That year it issued General Comment 24, through which it assumed "the power to make binding determinations on the admissibility of reservations to UN human rights treaties."[47] It affirmed its own competence to determine the validity of reservations based on their compatibility with the 'object and purpose' of the ICCPR, as well as customary international law and norms of *jus cogens*.

In order to set the foundations for this activism, the Committee opined on the special nature of human rights treaties, stating that

> the VCLT provisions on the role of State objections in relation to reservations are inappropriate to address the problem of reservations to human rights treaties. Such treaties, and the Covenant specifically, are not a web of inter-State exchanges of mutual obligations. They concern the endowment of individuals with rights. The principle of inter-State reciprocity has no place ....[48]

[44] *Report of the Committee on the Elimination of Racial Discrimination*, GAOR, 33rd Sess. at 85, Supplement no. 18, UN Doc. A/3/18 (1978). See also ibid. at 220.

[45] *Effective Implementation of International Instruments on Human Rights, including Reporting Obligations Under International Instruments on Human Rights*, Report by the UN Secretary General, UN GAOR 47th session, quoted in Schabas at 94.

[46] Ibid.

[47] Klabbers (2000) at 91.

[48] *General Comment 24*: Issues relating to reservations made upon ratification or accession to the Covenant or the Optional Protocols thereto, or in relation to declarations

It also held that the compatibility test had to be performed objectively, "with reference to legal principles," and that the Committee was "well-placed to perform this task".[49] It further justified such a role on the grounds that States have no "legal interest or need to object to reservations" because "the operation of the classic rules on reservations was so inadequate for the Covenant."[50] It was thus essential for the Committee itself to determine whether reservations were compatible with the 'object and purpose' of the ICCPR, since the "absence of protest by States [couldn't] imply that a reservation [was] either compatible or incompatible".[51]

The CCPR also arrogated to itself the authority to sever incompatible reservations because of this 'special' character of human rights treaties. It held that "the normal consequence of an unacceptable reservation is not that the Covenant will not be in effect at all for a reserving party. Rather, such a reservation will generally be severable, in the sense that the Covenant will be operative for the reserving party without benefit of the reservation."[52] In other words, the reservation would be without any legal effect.

However, the CCPR's activism did not pass unchallenged. Within six months of issuing General Comment 24, the Committee considered the first periodic report of the United States. In a highly unwelcome finding, the Committee declared that the USA's reservations to articles 6(5) and 7 of the ICCPR were incompatible with the "object and purpose" of the Covenant. The United States, which staunchly opposed the CCPR's conclusion, argued that it was "completely at odds" with established legal principles as well as the practice and express terms of adherence of many States.[53] It added that its reservations to the ICCPR formed "integral parts of its consent to be bound by the Covenant and are not severable" and hence that "[i]f it were to be determined that any one or more of them were ineffective, the ratification as a whole could thereby be nullified."[54] The USA further held that "[a] State which expressly withholds its consent from a provision cannot be presumed, on the basis

under article 41 of the Covenant, CCPR, 04/11/94, CCPR/C/21/Rev.1/Add.6, 52nd Sess. (1994) at para. 17.

49 Ibid. at para. 18.

50 Ibid.

51 Ibid.

52 Ibid.

53 Schabas (1997) at 110.

54 Ibid. at 110–111.

of some legal fiction, to be bound by it."[55] The decision also faced a great deal of criticism from the United Kingdom and France, which both objected to the Committee's opinion.

The contentious debate on the effect of invalid reservations prompted the International Law Commission in 1995 to appoint a Special Rapporteur to write a report on 'Reservations to Multilateral Treaties'. In his report, the Special Rapporteur found that "the general reservations regime is largely based on the idea of reciprocity, a concept difficult to transpose to the field of human rights or indeed to other fields."[56] However, he also held that the Vienna Convention's reservations regime was satisfactory in dealing with reservations to all multilateral treaties since it allowed States the flexibility to develop distinct reservations regimes for each separate treaty. In the case that States found particular reservations impermissible, they could explicitly prohibit them in the text of the treaty itself.[57] The view within the UN Secretariat was, similarly, to resist any notion of a separate regime for human rights treaties that granted treaty-monitoring bodies the competence to determine the validity of reservations.[58]

With time, however, States gradually accepted the CCPR's authority in monitoring incompatible reservations with a view to inducing State compliance with the reserved provisions. In fact, General Comment 24 has been widely considered as a "bold step" in the direction of establishing a separate reservations regime to govern human rights treaties.[59] It set the stage for the considerable development of State practice in the treaty-monitoring bodies, indicating a growing acceptance of the authority of such bodies to make pronouncements on the validity of reservations. It is now generally recognised that, in its capacity to interpret the treaty and monitor compliance with its provisions, a treaty-monitoring body may take an active role *vis-à-vis* incompatible reservations.

Although it is difficult to ascertain that a general customary rule has developed allowing treaty-monitoring bodies to sever reservations without affecting a State's consent to be bound by a treaty, it may be argued that there exists a specific custom in a number treaty-monitoring

55 Ibid. at 111.

56 Quoted in Schabas (1997) at 93.

57 Ibid.

58 Clerk (1991) at 300.

59 Shaheen Sardar Ali, *Gender and Human Rights in Islam and International Law* (2000), 244.

bodies that grants them a wide scope of authority when it comes to determining the incompatibility of reservations. In other words, the competence of a treaty-monitoring body to sever reservations should be examined on a case-by-case basis, rather than attempting to find a general norm that governs human rights treaties in general.

The Specific Custom within the CEDAW Committee

In spite of initial resistance throughout the 1980's, the above-mentioned developments led to the evolution of the CEDAW Committee's role with regards to incompatible reservations. The first breakthrough in this area came in the Committee's eleventh session, in 1992. In its General Recommendation 20, the CEDAW Committee called on States parties to take a number of measures *vis-à-vis* reservations to the Convention, in preparation for the Vienna World Conference on Human Rights (1993). It specifically recommended that States:

(a) Raise the question of the validity and the legal effect of reservations to the Convention in the context of reservations to other human rights treaties;
(b) Reconsider such reservations with a view to strengthening the implementation of all human rights treaties;
(c) Consider introducing a procedure on reservations to the Convention comparable with that of other human rights treaties.[60]

Although the Committee didn't explicitly state what kind of procedure it was alluding to in paragraph (c), the available options seem to be limited. One possibility would have been to introduce a procedure similar to the one applied under the CERD, which states in article 20 that a reservation is to be deemed incompatible with the 'object and purpose' of the Convention if two-thirds of the parties object to it. However, this option would not overcome the problem of subjectivity of the compatibility test, since it still relied on States' willingness to object to reservations. Alternatively, the Committee could have been alluding to the practice of the regional human rights mechanisms. In any case, no practical steps were taken to modify the reservations regime under CEDAW.

Ultimately, the issue of incompatible reservations was addressed by States in the Vienna Declaration and Programme of Action, which "encouraged" States to "consider limiting the extent of ... reservations"

[60] *General Recommendation no. 20*, Reservations, CEDAW, 11th Sess. (1992).

and to formulate them "as precisely and narrowly as possible."[61] It also encouraged them to ensure that reservations are not incompatible with the object and purpose of the treaty and "regularly review any reservations with a view to withdrawing them."[62] A far more significant stipulation ensued, specifically addressing reservations to the CEDAW, in the following terms:

> Ways and means of addressing the particularly large number of reservations to the Convention should be encouraged. *Inter alia*, the Committee on the Elimination of Discrimination against Women should continue its review of reservations to the Convention. States are urged to withdraw reservations that are contrary to the object and purpose of the Convention or which are otherwise incompatible with international treaty law.[63]

Five years after the Vienna Declaration, the CEDAW Committee adopted, in its nineteenth session, a statement on reservations in commemoration of the fiftieth anniversary of the UDHR. The statement noted that

> A number of States enter reservations to particular articles on the ground that national law, tradition, religion or culture is not congruent with Convention principles, and purport to justify the reservation on that basis. Some States enter a reservation to article 2, although their national constitutions or laws prohibit discrimination. There is therefore an inherent conflict between the provisions of the State's constitution and its reservation to the Convention. Some reservations are drawn so widely that their effect cannot be limited to specific provisions in the Convention.[64]

Apart from criticising broadly-stated reservations, the statement further identified the 'object and purpose' of the CEDAW as ending discrimination against women and achieving *de jure* and *de facto* equality between men and women. In this light, articles 2 and 16 were considered "core provisions of the Convention" and hence reservations to these articles were found to violate, in essence, the 'object and purpose' of the CEDAW.[65] The Committee identified broad reservations, including reservations to article 2 based on a perceived conflict with *Sharīʿa* law, as impermissible reservations, which "pose an acute problem for the

[61] Vienna Declaration and Programme of Action, Section II, para 5.
[62] Ibid.
[63] Ibid. Section II, para 39.
[64] *Report of the Committee on the Elimination of Discrimination against Women* 18th and 19th Sess. GAOR, Fifty-third session, Supplement No. 38, UN Doc A/53/38/Rev.1 at 47.
[65] Ibid. at 48.

implementation of the Convention and for the Committee's ability to monitor compliance with it."[66]

This position was further reinforced in the Committee's guidelines to States parties on reporting, which repeatedly asked States to withdraw reservations deemed incompatible with the 'object and purpose' of the CEDAW. In its reporting guidelines for States' initial reports, the Committee described general reservations to articles 2 and 3 of the CEDAW as incompatible reservations.[67] Moreover, in its 2003 reporting guidelines, the CEDAW Committee stated the following:

> Any reservation to or declaration as to any article of the Convention by the State party should be explained and its continued maintenance justified. ... the precise effect of any reservation or declaration in terms of national law and policy should be explained. States parties that have entered general reservations which do not refer to a specific article, or which are directed at articles 2 and/or 3 should report on the effect and the interpretation of those reservations. States parties should provide information on any reservations or declarations they may have lodged with regard to similar obligations in other human rights treaties.[68]

As such, the CEDAW Committee assumed the authority not only to scrutinise reservations and declarations to the CEDAW, but to also examine reservations to provisions addressing the rights of women in other human rights treaties. States were required to report on the "precise effects" of reservations; broadly-stated reservations were thus no longer tolerated.[69] Over time, the Committee has asserted its right to examine the compatibility of reservations, placing the burden of justifying the effect of such reservations and their continued existence on the shoulders of States. Through the summary records of its meetings, its concluding observations, and general recommendations, the Committee has expressed its concern about particular reservations that violate the 'object and purpose' of the CEDAW, appealing to States to withdraw, reconsider or limit such reservations. It has consistently commended States that ratify the CEDAW without reservations.[70] In fact, the process of

---

[66] Ibid.

[67] *Guidelines for preparation of reports by States Parties*, CEDAW Committee, 16th Sess. (13–31 Jan 1997) UN Doc CEDAW/C/7/Rev.3 26/07/96.

[68] *Compilation of Guidelines on the Form and Content of Reports to be Submitted by States Parties to the International Human Rights Treaties* UN Doc HRI/GEN/2/Rev.1/Add.2, (May 2003).

[69] Tyagi (2001) at 231.

[70] Ibid. at 232.

'constructive dialogue' with States indicates a wide toleration of the Committee's activism in this field.

The practice of the CEDAW Committee clearly surpasses the law and practice of other UN treaty monitoring bodies, such as the CERD and the CAT in this area. It may be argued that the increasing assertiveness of the CEDAW Committee, which has gone largely unchallenged in recent years, has become part of the *lex specialis* of the Committee, whereas it is still *lex ferenda* for other treaty-monitoring bodies (with the exception of the CCPR, whose "law and practice" are even more developed than that of the CEDAW Committee).[71] This *lex specialis* encompasses the competence to determine the compatibility of a reservation with the object and purpose of the treaty and the ability to call upon the reserving State to withdraw or modify its reservation. In addition, the CEDAW has consistently followed-up on the implementation of its recommendations regarding the reservations in question.[72] It is questionable, however, whether this *lex specialis* includes the authority to sever a reservation, and consider it without any legal effect. Nonetheless, the Committee has managed to assert its authority to scrutinise reservations and to engage with States to encourage them to withdraw incompatible reservations.

Egypt's Reservations to the CEDAW

Much controversy arises when examining Egypt's extensive reservations to the CEDAW. The right of a State to formulate reservations when ratifying an international treaty has traditionally been regarded as a sovereign prerogative, with direct bearings on the consensual nature of international law. As such, the issue of reservations has often been construed as "one of the most controversial subjects of contemporary international law."[73] Attempts to limit a State's ability to enter reservations have been regarded with scepticism, and are portrayed as an encroachment on the sovereign rights of States. Although the CEDAW doesn't prohibit specific reservations, article 28 (2) prohibits reservations that are incompatible with the treaty's 'object and purpose'.

---

[71] Ibid. at 239.
[72] Ibid. at 240.
[73] J.M. Ruda, 'Reservations to Treaties' 146 *Recueil de Cours III* 95–218 (1975) at 10, quoted in Ali (2000) at 240.

Upon ratifying the CEDAW, Egypt entered reservations to articles 2, 9(2),[74] 16 and 29, invoking the "Islamic *Sharīʿa*" as a basis for its reservations to articles 2 and 16.[75] These two reservations have drawn a number of objections by States parties, as well as a great deal of criticism from the CEDAW Committee.

The Incompatibility of Egypt's Reservations with the 'Object and Purpose' of CEDAW

Although the CEDAW does not expressly prohibit reservations to articles 2 and 16, reservations to these two provisions may be considered impermissible if they contradict the 'object and purpose' of CEDAW. The assessment of the compatibility or otherwise of these reservations is an objective exercise, independent of the fact that they constitute so-called 'Islamic reservations' that invoke the *Sharīʿa*.

The criteria for compatibility are two-fold. In the first place, reservations are required to be sufficiently specific. Although the VCLT doesn't state such a requirement explicitly, "*ex post facto* demonstrations of incompatibility mean that imprecise reservations 'cheat' the requirements of the Vienna Convention since the Article 19(c) test cannot be applied."[76] The result of unspecific reservations is to undermine the implementation of the treaty in question.

Egypt's reservation to article 2, which was stated in very general terms, stipulates that "the Arab Republic of Egypt is willing to comply with

[74] Egypt's reservation to article 9 (2), dealing with equal rights with respect to the nationality of children, did not invoke the *Shariʿa*, but made a general argument that seemed to rely on an implicit application of the 'child's best interest' principle, as well as the mother's consent. Egypt rationalised its reservation in the following terms: "This is in order to prevent a child's acquisition of two nationalities where his parents are of different nationalities, since this may be prejudicial to his future. It is clear that the child's acquisition of his father's nationality is the procedure most suitable for the child and that this does not infringe upon the principle of equality between men and women, since it is customary for a woman to agree, upon marrying an alien, that her children shall be of the father's nationality." In 2004, after a ten-year campaign led by women's groups in Egypt, the nationality law was amended, and the reservation to article 9 (2) was withdrawn. See Lijnzaad (1995) at 343.

[75] Egypt made a similar broad reservation, based on the *Shariʿa*, to article 18 of the African (Banjul) Charter on Human and People's Rights, to which it acceded in 1984. Whereas article 18 identifies the family as the "custodian of morals and traditional values," paragraph (3) is unequivocal in requiring State parties to eliminate "*every* discrimination against women and also ensure the protection of the rights of the woman and the child as stipulated in international declarations and conventions."

[76] Clerk (1991) at 310–311.

the content of this article, provided that such compliance does not run counter to the Islamic *Sharīʿa*." The reservation fails to point out how the provisions of the Convention, particularly the measures enumerated in article 2 may be inconsistent with the Islamic *Sharīʿa*. There is also "considerable scope for different judgments about the nature and extent of conflict between the *Sharīʿa* and the Convention" as interpretations and applications of the *Sharīʿa* may differ considerably between different States.[77] It is therefore difficult to assess the scope and effect of the reservation even with a sound knowledge of the *Sharīʿa*; "only the reserving State knows what its reservation means".[78] The articulation of a reservation in such general terms also arguably contravenes the principle of good faith, one of the cornerstones of the international legal order.

The CEDAW Committee has repeatedly asserted that article 2 is central to the CEDAW's 'object and purpose.' Reservations to article 2 signify a general reluctance to implementing the substantive provisions of CEDAW. A previous Chairperson of the CEDAW Committee has asserted that "when you enter a reservation to article 2, you are violating and nullifying the whole concept and sense of the Convention."[79] In fact, "article 2 arguably forms the crux of CEDAW by essentially requiring the ratifying States to 'incorporate the convention into domestic policy.' "[80]

Egypt's reservation to article 16 of the CEDAW has also received a large amount of criticism. The reservation, which makes similar reference to the Islamic *Sharīʿa*, is articulated in the following terms:

> Reservation to the text of article 16 concerning the equality of men and women in all matters relating to marriage and family relations during the marriage and upon its dissolution, without prejudice to the Islamic *Sharia's* provisions whereby women are accorded rights equivalent to those of their spouses so as to ensure a just balance between them. This is out of respect for the sacrosanct nature of the firm religious beliefs which govern marital relations in Egypt and which may not be called in question and in view of the fact that one of the most important bases of these relations is an equivalency of rights and duties so as to ensure complementarity which guarantees true equality between the spouses. The provisions of the *Sharīʿa* lay down that the husband shall pay bridal money to the wife and maintain her fully and shall also make a payment to her upon divorce, whereas the wife retains full rights over her property and is not obliged to spend anything on her keep. The *Sharīʿa* therefore restricts the wife's

77 Ibid.
78 Ibid.
79 Riddle (2002) at 629.
80 Ibid.

> rights to divorce by making it contingent on a judge's ruling, whereas no such restriction is laid down in the case of the husband.[81]

The wording of this reservation avoids mentioning *Sharīʿa*-derived *law*, which is essentially man-made, invoking instead the divinely ordained and 'sacrosanct' *Sharīʿa*, which affords "true equality between the spouses". This language attempts to capitalise on the exception espoused in article 23 (a), which stipulates that "nothing in the present Convention shall affect any provisions that are more conducive to the achievement of equality between men and women which may be contained in the legislation of a State Party." However, Egypt does not apply the *Sharīʿa* as such, but rather an adaptation of the *Sharīʿa* in a body of codified, man-made family laws, which, though based indeed on the *Sharīʿa*, do not incorporate all the of its egalitarian principles. Egypt's personal status laws could not be said to uphold "true equality" in all respects, particularly at the time this reservation was articulated. The clearest evidence of this is the subsequent adoption of a number of significant legal reforms that were firmly anchored in the *Sharīʿa*.

The above-mentioned reservation referred specifically to the issue of divorce. At the time the CEDAW was ratified, the relevant laws allowed the husband no-fault divorce while requiring a court decision for the wife to obtain divorce for harm. In 2002, however, Egypt's personal status law was reformed to grant the wife the right to no-fault divorce, a reform clearly grounded in the sources of the *Sharīʿa*. Although the divorce is still contingent upon a judge's decision, it is intended to be almost automatic if reconciliation attempts fail, and if the wife forfeits her financial rights. These reforms clearly contradict Egypt's contention that the laws governing family relations 'may not be called into question.'

There were other incidents in which Egypt invoked the *Sharīʿa* in a manner that subsequently changed during to reinterpretation. During the drafting of the CEDAW in the Commission on the Status of Women, the Egyptian delegate expressed his disapproval of article 15(1), which guarantees the right to freedom of movement and domicile, on the grounds that "according to the *Quran*, the husband must choose the site of the matrimonial home and the wife has the same domicile as her husband."[82] Eventually, however, Egypt accepted the terms of article 15 as its domestic law changed and became consistent with the provision. This

---

[81] *Declarations and Reservations* 1423 United Nations Treaty Series.
[82] Ali (2001) at 258–259.

attests to the fact that the sacrosanct nature of the *Sharīʿa* is often used as a convenient pretext to shield States from changing their domestic laws, even when these laws are based on an interpretation of the *Sharīʿa* that may be readily modified to meet the needs of contemporary society.

By their very nature, Egypt's reservations to the CEDAW, particularly the reservation to article 2, seem to suggest that they are "designed to avoid any obligation to bring domestic laws in conformity with the obligation to eliminate discrimination against women."[83] The effect of such reservations is to allow States to ostensibly commit themselves to the broad goal of women's equality in all fields, while acknowledging that they have no real intention of granting women these equal rights.[84] Although Egypt's substantive reservations to articles 2 and 16 of the CEDAW persist, in violation of the 'object and purpose' of the Convention, very few States have articulated objections to them. For this reason, the CEDAW Committee has taken a more active role with regards to these reservations.

The Subjectivity of the 'Object and Purpose' Test[85]

Clerk's detailed study of the application of the 'object and purpose' test by State parties to CEDAW indicates that State practice in this area is 'erratic'.[86] The subjectivity of the 'object and purpose' test, and its inconsistent application are complicating factors that leave incompatible reservations largely unaddressed. As the final arbiters of the compatibility of reservations with the 'object and purpose' of a treaty, the VCLT left it up to States parties to object to incompatible reservations. However, objections by States to reservations incompatible with the CEDAW's 'object and purpose', including those of Egypt, have been both haphazard and subjective. It is thus evident that the application of objections to human rights treaties has "a more political than a legal significance."[87]

Only four States, Germany, Mexico, the Netherlands, and Sweden, have articulated objections to Egypt's reservations. All of them have explicitly stated that their objections should not preclude the entry into force of the CEDAW in relation to Egypt. Although they haven't stated so explicitly, it can be inferred that these States hold Egypt bound by

83 Hossain (1994) at 473.
84 See, in general, Riddle (2002).
85 See Clerk (1991) at 298–302.
86 Ibid.
87 Schabas (1997) at 81.

all provisions of the Convention, including the reserved articles. In its reservation, Germany stipulated the following:

> The Federal Republic of Germany considers that the reservations made by Egypt regarding article 2, article 9, paragraph 2, and article 16 … are incompatible with the object and purpose of the Convention (article 28, paragraph 2) and therefore objects to them. In relation to the Federal Republic of Germany, they may not be invoked in support of a legal practice which does not pay due regard to the legal status afforded to women and children in the Federal Republic of Germany in conformity with the above-mentioned articles of the Convention. This objection shall not preclude the entry into force of the Convention as between Egypt … and the Federal Republic of Germany.[88]

The Netherlands made a similar objection, as did Mexico which, however, singled out Egypt's reservations to articles 9 and 16 of the CEDAW, leaving out article 2. It added that "these reservations, if implemented, would inevitably result in discrimination against women on the basis of sex, which is contrary to all the articles of the Convention."[89] Sweden further added that:

> the reason why reservations incompatible with the object and purpose of a treaty are not acceptable is precisely that otherwise they would render a basic international obligation of a contractual nature meaningless. Incompatible reservations, made in respect of the Convention on the elimination of all forms of discrimination against women, do not only cast doubts on the commitments of the reserving states to the object and purpose of this Convention, but moreover, contribute to undermine the basis of international contractual law. It is in the common interest of states that treaties to which they have chosen to become parties also are respected, as to object and purpose, by other parties.[90]

These four States have expressed similar objections vis-à-vis other reservations deemed incompatible, including those formulated by Algeria, Bangladesh, Jamaica, the Republic of Korea, Thailand, and Tunisia, among others. This is testament to the fact that the question is not one of so-called 'Islamic' reservations but of reservations that are incompatible with the CEDAW's 'object and purpose', in general.

Nonetheless, in deciding whether or not to object to reservations, States are undoubtedly motivated by political considerations, which is why very few States have been willing to formulate objections to reserva-

---

[88] *Declarations and Reservations* 1423 United Nations Treaty Series.

[89] Ibid.

[90] Ibid.

tions deemed incompatible. That is not to mention the inconsistency with which some States have articulated their objections. Norway, for instance, has objected to the reservations entered by Algeria, Saudi Arabia, Libya and the Maldives, while turning a blind eye to reservations formulated by Egypt on similar grounds. On the other hand, Mexico has objected to Egypt's reservations while failing to object to similar reservations made by Tunisia and Algeria.

Quite notable is the fact that not a single State has objected to Israel's reservation to article 16 of the CEDAW, which also subordinates the provision to "the laws on personal status which are binding on the various religious communities in Israel."[91] This reservation is very similar in scope and effect to the reservations formulated by Egypt to the text of article 16.

Although all objections refer to the 'object and purpose' test, they differ in that the objecting States did not identify the same reservations as incompatible with the 'object and purpose' of CEDAW. This attests to the lack of uniformity in the practice of objecting States, in general, as well as the internal inconsistency in the practice of each single State.[92] This uneven practice suggests that the willingness of States to object to incompatible reservations is contingent upon intervening political and other extra-legal concerns.

Are Egypt's Reservations Severable? The CEDAW Committee's Activism and the Progressive Development of International Law

Given the inconsistency of objections to Egypt's reservations, the CEDAW Committee has taken it upon itself to assume an active role in this regard. Ever since its examination of Egypt's initial report in 1983, the CEDAW Committee has repeatedly expressed its concern with regards to Egypt's sweeping reservations, particularly the reservations to articles 2 and 16, which it considers core provisions of the Convention. Egypt's reservations were, in fact, the first to be considered by the Committee.[93] In its examination of Egypt's initial report, the Committee requested clarifications on the meaning of 'complementarity,' of obligations under

[91] Ibid.

[92] Clerk (1991) at 300. Clerk adds that: "Reservations or sets of reservations entered by twelve states have been formally objected to by three other states parties. Three were objected to by all three of the objecting states, seven by two of the three states, and the other two by only one state."

[93] Lijnzaad (1995) at 342.

Islamic Law, the compatibility of polygamy and repudiation with the CEDAW, and whether women had legal recourse against discrimination in Egypt.[94] In fact, the Committee's approach has often been to disregard the existence of these reservations altogether, and to direct questions to Egypt regarding provisions to which it has entered reservations. For instance, the pre-sessional working group of the fifty-fourth session of CEDAW, which considered Egypt's combined sixth and seventh periodic reports, asked Egypt to "provide further information on steps taken to ensure equality between women and men in matters of personal status regarding marriage, divorce, consequences of divorce, and inheritance", and to "indicate whether [it was] considering abolishing the practice of polygamy, in accordance with article 16 of the Convention and the Committee's general recommendation 21 (1994) on equality in marriage and family relations."[95]

The Committee's appeals to the Egyptian Government to withdraw its reservations to the CEDAW have not passed unheeded. In fact, Egypt's representatives have consistently asserted that it is actively working on withdrawing these reservations. In its twenty-fourth session the CEDAW Committee examined Egypt's third periodic report as well as its combined fourth and fifth periodic reports. In response to a question raised in the pre-sessional working group, Egypt's representative contended that the reservation to article 2 of the CEDAW had been articulated "not because Islam was against the equality of women, but as a precautionary measure."[96] Egypt had initiated an internal process to demonstrate that the reservation, "without prejudice to the principles of *Sharīʿa*", was not intended to protect discriminatory laws. She added that "she was hopeful that the Government would drop the reservation and that the issue would gain support in Parliament."[97]

The responses of Egypt's representatives suggest both a toleration of the CEDAW Committee's authority to scrutinise reservations, as well as

---

[94] *Concluding Observations*, Egypt, CEDAW A/39/45 (1984) 34th and 39th meetings, held on 30 March and 3 April 1984 (CEDAW/C/SR.34 and 39) at para. 191.

[95] *List of Issues and Questions with regard to the Consideration of Periodic Reports*, CEDAW Pre-session Working Group 45th Session C/EFY/Q/7, Jan–Feb 2010, at para. 27–28.

[96] *Press Release of the Committee on the Elimination of Discrimination against Women* WOM/1250, 492nd Meeting, (19/01/2001) available at http://www.un.org/News/Press/docs/2001/wom1250.doc.htm; see also Third Periodic Reports of States Parties, Egypt, CEDAW CEDAW/C/EGY/3 (25 July 1996).

[97] Ibid.

a conviction that the reservations needed to be withdrawn to bring Egypt closer to fulfilling its international obligations. There was no protest or objection by Egypt's representatives to the Committee's assumption of such an activist role. Arguably, such practice is tantamount to acquiescence to the Committee's scrutiny of Egypt's reservations, and its pronouncements regarding the extent of their validity. Egypt's statement to the Committee reflects a changing attitude towards reservations, particularly its assertion that:

> the national laws had to be changed for the country to remove its reservations, and the new Law of 2000 was a step in that direction. A Committee, with the participation of specialists on *Sharīʿa*, had been formed to study the reservations, and had recently recommended withdrawal of the reservation to Article 2 of the Convention. Article 16 was still under study. The Committee had decided that if reservations needed to be made, they should be well justified. However, unless the attitudes of people were changed, the legal amendments alone would not alter the situation.[98]

In its latest report to the CEDAW Committee, Egypt similarly reported that an internal consultation mechanism had been set up to look into withdrawing its general reservation to article 2 (but not to article 16).[99] The persistence of this process for what seems to be close to ten years, however, seems to suggest it is rather fruitless.[100] The Committee has thus continued to express concern that the reservations have not yet been withdrawn, urging Egypt to "expedite the steps necessary" for their withdrawal, while reminding it "that articles 2 and 16 are central to the object and purpose of the Convention and that, in accordance with article 28, paragraph 2, they should be withdrawn."[101]

---

[98] Ibid.

[99] *Consideration of reports submitted by States parties* under article 18 of the Convention on the Elimination of All Forms of Discrimination against Women, Combined sixth and seventh periodic reports of States parties, Egypt, UN Doc CEDAW/C/EGY/7 (5 Sept 2008) at 8, 15 and 74.

[100] According to Aboul Komsan, a Committee of *Azhar* Scholars was set up in 2004 to review Egypt's reservations to the CEDAW, with a view to submitting to the legislature a proposal to withdraw them. The Committee, however, expressed the view that the reservations could not be withdrawn; in fact, they held that the CEDAW, as a whole, contravened the *Shariʿa* and that Egypt should therefore withdraw its consent to be bound by the treaty. *Interview* with Nihad Aboul Komsan, [Director Egyptian Center for Women's Rights], (November 11, 2004).

[101] *Concluding Observations*, Egypt, 492nd and 493rd meetings, (19 January 2001) UN doc CEDAW/C/SR.492 and 493, at para. 327.

It is evident that this process of constructive dialogue has precipitated some change in Egypt's attitude to its reservations, and a desire to reform legislation, including that derived from the *Sharīʿa*, so as to ensure compatibility with CEDAW. The Committee has positively engaged with Egypt's representatives on reserved provisions, holding Egypt accountable in spite of the existence of these reservations. Although Egypt has responded to such scrutiny with promises that the reservations were being reconsidered, there is some degree of inconsistency in Egypt's position, particularly with regards to its readiness to withdraw its reservation to article 16. Nonetheless, it is evident that the Committee's general position is that Egypt is bound by the principle of non-discrimination against women in all fields, including family relations, regardless of the existence of reservations. The Committee, though, has not on any occasion explicitly stated that it considers Egypt's reservations to articles 2 and 16 severed. Practically speaking, the Committee cannot force Egypt to implement these provisions; progress in this area is contingent upon the acceptance and cooperation of the State concerned.

Due to the complex and controversial nature of the topic of reservations to multilateral treaties, the International Law Commission has embarked on a process to draft a Guide to Practice on Reservations to Treaties to fill the gaps of the Vienna Convention's reservations regime. The provisional draft of the Guide to practice departs from the premise that the Vienna Convention is silent with regards to the issue of invalid reservations. In other words, the VCLT's provisions regarding the acceptance and objection to reservations are limited in their application to reservations that are valid. In part 4.5, the draft Guide to Practice states that "a reservation that does not meet the conditions of formal validity and permissibility … is null and void, and therefore devoid of legal effect."[102] In such cases, the State would be considered a party to the treaty "without the benefit of the reservation, unless a contrary intention of the said State … can be identified."[103] The intention of the State is revealed by examining the text of the reservation itself, but also its subsequent practice and the 'object and purpose' of the treaty in question.[104] This proposal of the ILC is far-reaching and goes a long way in holding States

[102] Text of the set of draft guidelines constituting the *Guide to Practice on Reservations to Treaties*, Provisionally adopted by the International Law Commission, UN Doc A/65/10, provisional draft guideline 4.5.1 at 66.

[103] Ibid., Provisional Draft Guideline 4.5.2, at 67.

[104] Ibid. at 68.

accountable under human rights treaties notwithstanding any incompatible reservations they may have entered. It grants the depositary of the treaty a role in determining the permissibility of a reservation, and in the case of human rights treaties, formally confers this right upon treaty-monitoring bodies thus removing the determination of incompatibility from the exclusive purview of States.[105] It therefore understates the role of objections by other State parties in the process of invalidating a reservation.

Whereas the Special Rapporteur on Reservations to Treaties has asserted that the Guide is grounded in State practice,[106] it is still unclear whether the proposed draft constitutes a codification of existing customary international law, or rather a progressive development of the rules related to reservations to human rights treaties. It also remains to be seen how States will react to its important formulations, and whether they will consent to this significant erosion of what was once considered a sovereign prerogative.

Other International Obligations

A reservation to a treaty provision that embodies a rule of customary international law may not modify that State's obligations under the customary rule, which therefore continues to apply. This principle was reaffirmed by the ICJ in the *Case Concerning Military and Para-Military Activities in and Against Nicaragua*, which stipulated that:

> the multilateral treaty reservation may [not] be interpreted as meaning that, once applicable to a given dispute, it would exclude the application of any rule of customary international law the content of which was the same as, or analogous to, that of the treaty-law rule which had caused the reservation to become effective.[107]

Egypt therefore cannot resort to a general reservation to shield itself from the application of the customary norm of non-discrimination on the basis of gender. When it comes to family relations, however, evidence of the existence of a customary norm of equality is less evident, making it difficult to argue that article 16 of the CEDAW is binding by virtue of customary international law.

---

105 Ibid., Draft Guideline 2.1.7 *bis* at 43 and Draft Guideline 3.2.1 at 60.

106 *Report* prepared by Mr. Alain Pellet, Special Rapporteur on the Meeting with Human Rights Bodies at para 12.

107 Military and Para-Military Activities at 84.

On the other hand, Egypt is also bound to respect the principle of non-discrimination in family relations by virtue of its obligations under general human rights treaties. The ICCPR and the ICESCR both prohibit discrimination on the basis of gender with regards to both civil and political rights as well as economic, social and cultural rights. Article 16 of the UDHR specifically prohibits discrimination in the area of family relations, as does article 23 of the ICCPR which stipulates that "all adults have the right to marry and found a family. Women and men have equal rights to marry, within marriage, and at its dissolution." However, discerning the scope of Egypt's obligations under the ICCPR and ICESCR is complicated by the existence of a general interpretative declaration that was articulated at the ratification of both Covenants. The declaration stated that Egypt accepted, supported and ratified the Covenants "taking into consideration the provisions of the Islamic *Sharī'a* and the fact that they do not conflict with the text annexed to the instrument."

As is the case with invalid reservations, the VCLT is equally silent on the issue of interpretative declarations, which have therefore also been addressed in the ILC's draft Guide to Practice. As a general rule, States, which are the primary subjects vested with the authority to interpret their own treaty obligations, have the right to "indicate [their] own understanding of the treaties to which [they are] a party."[108] There are situations, however, as the *Belilos* case has shown, in which an interpretative declaration may be deemed to constitute a reservation. This is so if the effect of the declaration is to "undermine the legal effect of one of the provisions of a treaty or the treaty as a whole",[109] allowing States to circumvent the legal rules governing reservations. In such a case the "unilateral statement which purports to be an interpretative declaration"[110] may be reclassified as a reservation, and the relevant provisions of the VCLT would then apply. In other words, whether the unilateral statement constitutes a reservation or an interpretative declaration "is determined by the legal effect it purports to produce".[111]

Similarly, conditional interpretative declarations, which subject the State's "consent to be bound by the treaty to a specific interpretation of

---

[108] *Fourteenth Report on Reservations to Treaties*, Addendum by Special Rapporteur Allain Pellet, International Law Commission, 61st Session A/CN.4/614/Add.1 (2009) at para 143.

[109] Ibid. at para 134.

[110] Ibid. Draft Guideline 3.5.1.

[111] Ibid. Draft Guideline 1.3.

the treaty ..." may in some cases be considered reservations.[112] By conditioning the State's consent to be bound by the treaty, such declarations produce the same legal effect as conditional reservations. The State is only willing to be bound by the treaty insofar as it can be given a meaning within the scope of its interpretative declaration. In such a case, it can still be considered a simple interpretative declaration if it is a genuine interpretation that is "in accordance with the authentic interpretation of the treaty."[113]

Because of the theoretical complexity of the topic, it seems very difficult to place Egypt's carefully and ambiguously worded declaration in either category. A close analysis leaves us with two possible outcomes. The first, arrived at through a literal reading of the declaration, suggests that there is no conflict between the 'Islamic *Sharīʿa*' and the text of the Covenants. In other words, the declaration doesn't seek to modify any of the Covenants' provisions, in which case it has no legal effect at all. This interpretation, while providing a simple solution to the problem, renders Egypt's articulation of the declaration superfluous and is hence unconvincing.

The second option would be to consider the declaration a conditional declaration that makes Egypt's consent to be bound by the Covenants conditional upon their conformity with the *Sharīʿa*. If this were the case, the rules on reservations would apply, with the possible effect of rendering the declaration invalid. In either case, the legal effect of the declaration cannot be to shield Egypt's laws from compliance with the Covenants.

It follows from the above that Egypt is still bound to give effect to the principle of equality in family relations, if not by virtue of its ratification of the CEDAW, or under customary international law, then by virtue of its obligations under the ICESCR and ICCPR. Although the wording of articles 16 of the UDHR and 23 of the ICCPR differ markedly from the extensive wording of article 16 of CEDAW, there is reason to presume that all these provisions cover the same range of rights. By reading the text of article 23 of the ICCPR into article 16 of CEDAW, it is evident that Egypt is bound by sub-paragraphs (1) (a) on equal rights to enter into marriage, (b) on the right to free and full consent, (c) on equal rights during marriage and at its dissolution, as well as (d) and (e) on equal

112 *Fourteenth Report on Reservations to Treaties*, at para 166.
113 Ibid. at para 172.

responsibilities relative to children and freedom of choice in the number and spacing of children.

Although the remaining provisions of CEDAW's article 16, namely sub-paragraphs (f) on equal rights with regards to guardianship and wardship of children, (g) regarding the right to choose a family name and profession, (h) on the ownership, acquisition and management of property, and paragraph (2) on minimum marriage age and registration of marriages, do not appear in article 23 of the ICCPR, a close examination of the CCPR's General Comments reveals that these provisions constitute an integral part of the right to free and full consent and of equal rights and obligations for both spouses. According to General Comment 28,

> Many factors may prevent women from being able to make the decision to marry freely. One factor relates to the minimum age for marriage. That age should be set by the state on the basis of equal criteria for men and women. These criteria should ensure women's capacity to make an informed and uncoerced decision. A second factor in some states may be that either by statutory or customary law a guardian, who is generally male, consents to the marriage instead of the woman herself, thereby preventing women from exercising a free choice .... [The state must] ensure that the matrimonial regime contains equal rights and obligations for both spouses, with regard to the custody and care of children, the children's religious and moral education, the capacity to transmit to children the parent's nationality, and the ownership or administration of property, whether common property or property in the sole ownership of either spouse.[114]

In terms of legal obligations, it is evident that having ratified the ICCPR, Egypt is bound by all the substantive provisions covered by article 16 of CEDAW. As such, Egypt could theoretically be held accountable under international law if it violated the principle of non-discrimination in the area of family relations.

In terms of policy considerations, there is a growing trend at the international level to reject incompatible and otherwise invalid reservations. The persistence of such reservations comes at a hefty price in political and diplomatic terms, given that effective membership in the community of nations, in this day and age, requires active demonstration of a commitment to universal human rights standards. Disregard for human rights is a justification for the international community to designate a State as a pariah, an outlaw that is not entitled to full sovereign rights. New the-

---

[114] *General Comment 28*: Equality of Rights Between Men and Women (Article 3), (29 March 2000) UN Doc CCPR/C/21/Rev.1/Add.10, at para 23 and 25.

ories on sovereignty, defining it as a responsibility towards the governed rather than right of the State, serve to remind States that universal human rights can no longer be violated with impunity. Benefits in trade and commerce, international aid and regional economic integration are increasingly becoming conditioned on adequate human rights protection that rises to international standards. In the context of these new realities, no State can afford to persist in a policy that attracts a large degree of international criticism, particularly if the policy concerned is not central to the interests of the State, or truly necessary to protect its value system. Incompatible reservations have not safeguarded States from the need to reform their legislation. In fact, they have served to attract further attention to the laws they are specifically designed to shield, drawing increased international criticism and pressure for reform. Such a misinformed policy is clearly counterproductive, and while it may delay the need to undertake necessary reforms for a limited amount of time, it will neither fend off international criticism, nor absolve the State from the duty to face up to its responsibilities towards its citizens, in the long run.

CHAPTER FIVE

SHARĪʿA LAW AND THE DEVELOPMENT OF EGYPT'S PERSONAL STATUS LEGISLATION

Having addressed in previous chapters the international legal framework for the protection of the rights of women, and the nature of obligations to which Egypt must adhere in the area of family relations, this chapter will lay out the basic institutions, structures and processes that underlie Egypt's family law. The Egyptian legal framework for family law is based on the idea of the personality of law,[1] or law as applied by virtue of religious affiliation. The family law for *Sunni* Muslims, which has a "broad conception of personal status that encompasses questions of marriage, divorce, paternity and successions,"[2] is derived from the Islamic *Sharīʿa*, as interpreted and codified by Egyptian jurists and legislators since the late nineteenth century.

The history of family law reform dates back to Egypt's emergence as a modern State at the dawn of the 19th century under the leadership of *Muhammad ʿAli Pasha*. The modernisation process entailed increased urbanization, technological advancement, secularization, and integration into the European-dominated world economy. Among other reforms, the *Pasha* sought to limit the power of the religious institution, to control religious learning at *Al-Azhar*, and to break the institution's economic independence. The drive towards secularization prompted the State to assert its control over the religious institution by appointing the Grand *Mufti*, the religious official who issued *fatwas* (decrees), early in the nineteenth century.[3] Although this process led to a radical

---

[1] Mark S, W. Hoyle, *Mixed Courts of Egypt* (1991).

[2] Nathalie Bernard-Maugiron and Baudouin Dupret, 'From Jihan to Susanne. Twenty Years of Personal Status Law in Egypt', 19 *Recht van de Islam* (2002) at 1.

[3] Margot Badran, *Feminists, Islam, and Nation. Gender and the Making of Modern Egypt* (1996) at 10. This practice had begun earlier, under Ottoman rule, but was only introduced to the new Egyptian state in the 19th century. The *Mufti's* pronouncements, whether liberal or conservative, influenced attitudes and behaviour, and he was expected to "lend religious legitimacy to matters of special interest to the state." It later became a feature of the reform effort of the late twentieth century to garner support for personal status law reforms through legitimation by the Grand *Mufti* of Egypt and the *Sheikh* of *Al-Azhar*.

transformation in gender relations in Egypt, the State surrendered to the religious authorities the task of regulating family or 'private' life, while taking control of more aspects of 'public' life.

The origins of Egypt's legal system can be traced back to the Ottoman reforms of the nineteenth century, which culminated in the Ottoman *majalla* issued between 1869 and 1877. Although the *majalla* was intended to be "Islamic in content" it was based on the French *Code Napoléon*.[4] As the reforms progressed, the Capitulation Agreements also expanded, granting European citizens extraterritorial status, and leading to a system of consular courts for Europeans.[5] Egypt, which enjoyed a substantial degree of autonomy from the Ottoman Empire, generally followed through with similar reforms, albeit at a different pace. In 1875 a parallel court system, the Mixed Court system was set up to adjudicate claims amongst foreigners and between foreigners and Egyptians. The Mixed Courts operated according to their own code, which was drawn heavily from the *Code Napoléon*, and remained in existence until 1949 when foreigners came under the jurisdiction of Egyptian courts.

Throughout the 1860's and 1870's 'modernisation' efforts were accelerated under *Khedive Isma'il*; increasing travel opportunities led to unprecedented interaction with European societies, architectural transformation eroded the previous seclusion of women, and expanding opportunities for women's formal education led to a heightened "gender consciousness" that was essential for the transformation of the view of women in Egyptian society.[6] In 1883, a National Court system was established applying the *Code Napoléon*, although some effort was made to incorporate Islamic elements. The new court system applied the *Code Napoléon* to all areas of law with the exception of personal status issues and endowments (*waqf*), which were adjudicated by the *Sharīʿa* Courts.[7] As such, all commercial, civil, and criminal codes were secularised, leaving only *aḥwal shakhsiya*, or personal status laws under the jurisdiction of the religious authorities.

[4] Nathan Brown, *The Rule of Law in the Arab World. Courts in Egypt and the Gulf* (1997) at 2.

[5] Ibid. at 3.

[6] Badran (1996) at 6–9.

[7] Lama Abu-Odeh, 'Modernising Muslim Family Law: The Case of Egypt', 37 *Vand. J. Transnat'l L.* 1043 (October 2004) at 1081–1083. The capitulations system was an offshoot of the widespread European influence in Egypt, and the ensuing legal privileges and concessionary benefits granted to European immigrants. Foreign nationals demanded that they be exempt from Islamic law, which was considered primitive and incapable of regulating complex economic and financial transactions.

The jurisprudence of the *Sharīʿa* Courts is an important source for understanding how Islamic law was applied in the evolving social setting of the nineteenth and twentieth centuries, and how judges were influenced by such reforms. In 1956, a procedural reform was introduced whereby the *Sharīʿa* Courts and the *Milli* Courts (which served Egypt's religious minorities) were abolished, and their work was absorbed into the National Court structure.[8] Personal status cases thus came to be adjudicated in specialised chambers of ordinary courts, and under the purview of ordinary judges educated in modern law, rather than the religiously-educated *qādīs*. This undoubtedly had an impact on the application of the principles of the *Sharīʿa* in the realm of personal status, which envisions a fluid and flexible inspiration from a multitude of sources, opinions and interpretations, rather than a commitment to a codified, and hence essentially rigid body of law.

Since the first codification of the personal status law, Egyptian feminists have struggled with attempts to develop, modify and reform such legislation, an endeavour that was often hampered by those who posited the *Sharīʿa* as unitary and immutable. The reformulation of the feminist struggle in nationalist terms, a consequence of women's activist involvement in the struggle for independence, provided a catalyst for the reform process, as women became politically active and simultaneously better organised.[9] The promulgation of the Ottoman Family Law in 1917 further inspired codification in Egypt, although Egyptian family law was far more radical.[10] Contemporary personal status legislation is still based on the legislative enactments adopted in 1920 and 1929, which deal with issues of marriage, divorce and child custody, whereas succession is covered by Law no. 77 of 1943 and Law no. 71 of 1946. Since the 1920's, changes in the law have been sluggish, and several reform attempts were aborted particularly in the 1950's and 1960's.

The rise of militant Islam in the 1970's and 1980's and the subsequent exploitation of religion to reinforce the patriarchal family structure has further hampered recent legal reforms and undermined their

---

[8] Ibid.

[9] Ron Shaham, *Family and the Courts in Modern Egypt* (1997) at 10. Towards the end of the nineteenth century the Egyptian feminist movement gained momentum, particularly when the French-educated lawyer Qassem Amin published his book "Women's Liberation" (*tahrir al-mar'a*) in which he called for the education and unveiling of women.

[10] J.N.D. Anderson, *Islamic Law in the Modern World* (1959).

application and enforcement by a conservative society and judiciary intent on circumventing the law. Eventually, "it fell to feminists and other progressives concerned with issues of gender to untangle what religion actually prescribed from what was alleged to be required by Islam."[11] The flexibility of *Sharīʿa* law, and its suitability to modern exigencies has once more been confirmed, however, through the introduction of a significant substantive reform to the personal status law in 2000. Significant procedural reforms have also been introduced in an attempt to prevent prevarication by litigants and judges of the substantive law.

A proper comprehension of this complex legislative reform process requires a consideration of the methods by which the law was allowed to evolve. Whereas the religious sources from which the positive law was derived did not change, it is the innovative selection from and reinterpretation of these sources that has allowed for a significant degree of doctrinal development.[12] This development process is evident in both the jurisprudence of the *Sharīʿa* courts before the codification of the personal status law, as well as the in legislative reforms that characterised the twentieth and twenty-first centuries.

Introduction to *Sharīʿa* Law: The Sources of Islamic Jurisprudence and the Rise of *Taqlīd* Law

The four *Sunni* jurisprudential schools, widely considered as the authoritative interpretations of the sources of Islamic law, date back to the eighth and ninth centuries AD. The schools were established through the allegiance of groups of jurists to any one of the founders, namely *Abu Hanifa* (the *Ḥanafi* School), *Mālik bin Anas* (the *Māliki* School), *Al-Imām el Shafʿi*, (the *Shafʿi* School) and *Aḥmed bin Ḥanbal* (the *Ḥanbali* School).[13] By the ninth century AD, all the schools of Islamic *fiqh* had come together and coalesced into the four surviving *Sunni* jurisprudential schools.[14]

Many authoritative scholars on Islamic law concur that in the late ninth century AD the gates of *ijtihād* (reasoning) were effectively closed, marking "an end of the development of Islamic legal doctrine."[15] Recent

[11] Ibid. at 10.

[12] Elizabeth Tucker, *In the House of the Law, Gender and Islamic Law in Ottoman Syria and Palestine* (1998) at 12.

[13] Coulson (1968) at 40–51.

[14] Behrouz (2003) at 1147.

[15] Tucker (1998) at 11.

writings, however, have undermined the presumption that the gates of *ijtihād* were ever really closed, particularly through examining the practice of the *muftis* (juristconsults) and *qādīs* (judges).[16] Nonetheless, the use of *ijtihād*, particularly in recent history, has been controversial.

In general, it is presumed that since the late ninth century, Muslim jurists have been mostly engaged in explaining and applying the law from settled doctrine rather than interpreting the sacred texts through applying their mental faculties.[17] Though the four medieval jurisprudential schools became consolidated as the authentic interpretations of "Islamic law" for *Sunni* Muslims,[18] other jurisprudential schools, including some of those associated with *Shiʿite* doctrine, remained marginally influential, most notably the *Zaydiyya*, the *Imāmiyya*, the *Ibādhiya*, and the *Gaʿafariya*.[19]

The oldest of the four *Sunni* schools, the *Ḥanafi* and *Māliki* schools, both came into existence in the early period of Islamic jurisprudence, which was characterized by the emergence of two different approaches to jurisprudence. The first espoused the use of reasoning *(ra'y)* and analogy (*qiyas*), whereas the second gave heavier weight to the Prophet's tradition (*Sunnah* or *hadīth*).[20] The *Ḥanafi* school was characterised by the "uninhibited use of personal reasoning (*ra'y*) to regulate issues not specifically addressed by *Quranic* injunctions or Prophetic traditions (*Sunnah*)."[21] On the other hand, the *Māliki* School gave greater authority to the Prophetic traditions. As such, followers of the *Ḥanafi* school was described as *ahl al-ra'y*, or the people of opinion, while adherents of the *Māliki* school were labelled *ahl al-ḥadīth*, or the people of tradition. The *Māliki* and *Ḥanafi* doctrines diverge on a number of important issues, reflecting the different social traditions of the localities where they emerged.[22]

In contrast to the localised character of the *Ḥanafi* and *Māliki* schools, the *Shafʿi* and *Ḥanbali* schools were the product of the jurisprudential controversy that surfaced during the 9th century AD, regarding the

---

[16] Ibid. at 12.

[17] Ibid. at 11.

[18] Venkatraman (1995) at 1970.

[19] Ahmed Ibrahim Bek and Wassel Ibrahim, *Aḥkām al-ʿaḥwāl al-shakhsiyya fil shariʿa al-islāmiyya walqānūn* (2003) at 29.

[20] Ibn Khaldun, *The Muqaddimah*, quoted in Herbert Liebesny, *The Law of the Near and Middle East. Readings, Cases and Materials* (1975) at 19.

[21] See Coulson (1968) at 40–51.

[22] Ibid. The *Maliki* School emerged in the Iraqi centre of *Kufa* in 767 AD, whereas the *Hanafi* School emerged in the Arabian centre of Medina in 796 AD.

sources of religious law.[23] The *Shafi* school combined aspects of both the *Ḥanafi* and *Māliki* schools; however, it opposed the teachings of the "people of tradition" on many points.[24] In the mid-9th century, the *Ḥanbali* school of jurisprudence emerged under the leadership of *Aḥmad bin Ḥanbal*. This school maintained the principle of the paramount authority of the Prophet's *Sunnah*, which it contended was being undermined by the forms of juristic reasoning recognised in the other schools.[25]

Although the different jurisprudential schools are based on similar fundamentals, they diverge on many details. By the end of the 9th century AD, the four schools were recognised as the leading authorities in Islam, and have remained as such to this day. Adherence was largely restricted to these four schools, with the caveat that Muslims could select interpretations from either of them without any formalities. The interpretations of each of the schools on any given point are considered equally valid. The technique of selection allowed Muslims to make use of the divergent opinions of the schools, a tool that has been aptly used by countries that apply *Sharīʿa*-derived personal status laws so as to allow for greater flexibility in implementing reforms.[26]

It was the *Shafi* school that formulated the systematic theory of jurisprudence known as *Usul al Fiqh*, in the 9th century AD, by classifying the sources of Islamic jurisprudence as follows: the *Quran* as the primary source, the *Sunnah* as a secondary source, followed by consensus (*ijmaʿ*) and reasoning by analogy (*qiyās*). The *Quran* is regarded as the utterance of God, and is hence indisputable. The *Quran* is not, in fact, a code of law; out of more than 6,000 verses only 600 deal strictly with legislation.[27] The *Sunnah* is the collection of Prophetic traditions and customs, or "anything that could be proven to have been the practice of the Prophet and his oldest disciples."[28] The traditions were recorded in six collections in the 9th century, now considered equally authentic sources of the *Sunnah*.[29]

---

[23] Coulson (1968) at 40–51.

[24] Liebesny (1975) at 21.

[25] Coulson (1968) at 53–61.

[26] Ibn Khaldun, quoted in Liebesny (1975) at 30–32.

[27] David Santillana, *Istituzioni di Dirrito Musulmano Malichita*, vol. 1, 32–33, quoted in Liebesny (1975) at 12.

[28] Ignaz Goldziher, *Mohammedanische Studien* Vol. 2, p. 13. Quoted in Liebesny (1975) at 13.

[29] S.G. Vesey-Fitzgerald, 'Nature and Sources of the Shari'a', in *Law in the Middle East*, Vol. 1, Khadduri and Liebesny eds. (1978) at 94.

The *Quran* and the *Sunnah* are often referred to as the "roots of the bases (*usul-al-usul*), a phrase which implies that the other foundations of the law are merely subordinate to and dependent on them."[30] *Ijma'* (consensus of the Muslim community) is the third source of law, and was deduced from both *Quranic* injunctions and Prophetic *ḥadīths* (sayings), which held that God "would not permit His people universally to be in error."[31] It refers to consensus of the scholars as well as the Islamic community as a whole. Finally, *qiyās*, or reasoning by analogy, depends on the "fallible judgement of man."[32] As such, one is to resort to *qiyās* only where the three other sources leave a matter ambiguous. It is important to note that *qiyās* does not imply purely personal judgement, on the other hand, it indicates an "inductive process governed by the rules of logic."[33] It was *Imām Shaf'i*, often labelled as vindicator of tradition (*nāsser el-ḥadīth*) who advanced the view that independent human judgement should mainly be employed to draw logical analogies from existing precedents.

Other minor sources of Islamic jurisprudence also exist, although by and large, they have been relegated to the sidelines since *Imam Shaf'i*'s elaboration of the *usul-al-fiqh*. The principle of *istiḥsān* (preference) which literally means "choosing the better" was most extensively used by the *Ḥanafi* school, particularly where the application of *qiyās* would lead to an unreasonably harsh result.[34] Another source is *istislāḥ* or *maslaḥa* (general interest), which considers the spirit of the law, or "what was aimed at for mankind in the law, that is five things, namely maintenance of religion, of life, of reason, of descendents, of property."[35] This principle was widely criticised for being too 'elastic' and allowing a great deal of human intervention with the divinely-revealed law.[36] A less flexible principle, *istisḥāb* (finding a link) was advanced by *Imām Shaf'i*, mainly as a principle of evidence rather than of general law.[37] Finally, the principle of *darura* (necessity) was applied sparingly by both the *Ḥanafi* and the *Māliki* schools.[38]

---

30 Ibid. at 95.
31 Ibid.
32 See Liebesny (1975) at 12.
33 Ibid.
34 Vesey-Fitzgerald (1978) at 101.
35 Ibid.
36 Ibid.
37 Ibid. at 102.
38 Ibid.

Since the end of the nineteenth century the practice of *usul al fiqh* was based, by and large, on "mummified knowledge that had little or nothing to do with the social experiences of Muslims over the ensuing centuries."[39] This was largely a reaction to the often chaotic and potentially contradictory decisions of the largely independent *qāḍīs*. Independent reasoning became rare among Muslim jurists; they engaged in *taqlīd* a method of reasoning or 'imitation' based on the precedents set by the four *Sunni* jurisprudential schools. The rise of *taqlīd* ushered in an era of rigidity, whereby laws were based on precedents elaborated by jurists in the Middle Ages, and left unchallenged, but for a few marginal attempts, for centuries. This method of jurisprudence effectively limited "the influence of independent value judgments on the content of the revealed law."[40] Although codified law was largely based on *taqlīd*, or an innovative variation of it, recent studies have shown that actual legal practice in the *Sharīʿa* courts before and during the early years of codification, remained susceptible to other influences.

The codification of Egypt's personal status law has evolved since the turn of the twentieth century from strict adherence to *taqlīd* law, to the development of other innovative methods. Departing from a personal status code based on the *Ḥanafi* doctrine, the reform movement initially employed the techniques of *takhayyur* (selection of the most favourable interpretation from the preponderant opinions of the four Jurisprudential schools) and *talfīq* (combining opinions from the different schools so as to arrive at a rule that exists in neither of the schools) to introduce aspects of *Māliki* law that were more favourable to the position of women in the family. The most recent reforms, however, have taken a further stride, employing the technique of *ijtihād* based on the novel interpretation of the primary sources of Islamic law, thus departing from the *fiqh* (jurisprudence) of the medieval schools that had been adhered to for centuries.

The Development of Egypt's Personal Status Law: Legislating the *Sharīʿa*

As States in the region moved towards centralisation and modernisation, *Sharīʿa*-derived rules were codified into positive law; each State selecting

[39] Tucker (1998) at 11.
[40] Behrouz (2003) at 1147.

a particular school to adhere to. The legal rules on which Egypt's personal status laws are based were mainly adopted from the *taqlīd* era and are based on the interpretations of the *Ḥanafi* school, often regarded as the most restrictive when it comes to personal status issues. The Arab Mashreq (Iraq, Jordan, Lebanon, Palestine and Syria) also adopted, for the most part, the *Ḥanafi* doctrine. The Arab Maghreb (Algeria, Morocco, Tunisia and Libya), known for its more liberal approach to personal status issues, adopted the *Māliki* doctrine, whereas Saudi Arabia and several other Arab Gulf States embraced the *Ḥanbali* doctrine. The *Shafʿi* doctrine was endorsed in Yemen and by significant minorities in several other Arab Muslim States.[41]

The first attempt to codify personal status law in Egypt was the endeavour by *Mohamed Qadri Pasha*, in 1875, to compile the provisions of the *Ḥanafi* jurisprudential school into a comprehensive code on personal status. Although the code was never officially promulgated, in 1897 *Ḥanafi* personal status law was officially endorsed by the State and *Qādis* (judges) were instructed to apply it when adjudicating on all questions of personal status.[42] According to Abu Odeh, the *Ḥanafi* doctrine:

> advocates a particularly patriarchal structure of the family. This is so because ... the *Ḥanafi*'s give women *fewer* financial rights *in* marriage as well as less means of exit *from* marriage. At the same time, they reward the husband *more* for his financial obligations by *adding* to his powers in marriage.[43]

Subsequently, since the early twentieth century, Egyptian legislators have attempted to mitigate the harsh effects of the restrictive *Ḥanafi* school by adopting interpretations of other jurisprudential schools, most notably the *Māliki* school.[44] However, *Ḥanafi* law remains a fundamental source of law in Egypt's personal status legislation, constituting the "background body of rules that the modern Egyptian statutes are seen as departing from and intervening in."[45] Until 2004, recourse had to be made to the predominant opinion in the *Ḥanafi* school, in the case of absence of a textual provision in the codified personal status laws. In this case judges usually referred to the unofficial codification of *Qadri Pasha* as

---

[41] *Islamic Family Law Project* http://www.law.emory.edu/IFL/index2.html.

[42] Oussama Arabi, 'The Dawning of the Third Millennium on Shariʿa: Egypt's Law No. 1 of 2000, or Women May Divorce at Will', *Arab Law Quarterly* 6 (2001) at 2.

[43] Abu-Odeh (2004) at 1102.

[44] Arabi (2001) at 8.

[45] Abu-Odeh (2004) at 1102.

the only concise and accessible compilation of the doctrine.[46] The law was amended in 2004 such that judges now have the option to refer to any of the jurisprudential schools.

The development of Egypt's personal status law must be viewed both in light of the country's emergence into a modern nation-State, and the subsequent embracement of "a new culture of modernity" by the Egyptian ruling elite.[47] Women's struggle to advance their status and rights within the family manifested itself in two parallel processes; the adjudication of personal status cases first in the *Sharīʿa* then the ordinary courts, and the codification of personal status laws that broke the strict gender hierarchy within the family. These two processes were permeated with the employment of innovative methods; the courts were inclined to go beyond the teachings of the *Ḥanafi* school as were legislators, who resorted to other jurisprudential schools to find more egalitarian solutions for women. However, until very recently, there was no formidable challenge to the practice of *taqlīd* law until Egypt's Supreme Constitutional Court officially enunciated a new doctrine based on *ijtihād* in 1985, which formed the basis for important legal reforms based on that doctrine in 2000.

The Role and Jurisprudence of the Sharīʿa *Courts*

Formal codification of law is alien to the *Sharīʿa*; traditionally *qādīs* had a wide discretion in applying the law, which they derived from "the voluminous legal literature of their respective schools of law".[48] During the period of Ottoman rule, the *Sharīʿa* Courts in Egypt had a wide jurisdiction, including "personal status, religious endowment (*waqf*), as well as civil, criminal and administrative affairs."[49] In the early nineteenth century, the State's quest to diminish the power of the religious establishment, led to the promulgation of a series of laws that diminished the *Sharīʿa* courts' jurisdiction, developing civil laws and codes and alternative 'secular' courts.[50] The elaborate witness system was eventually abolished with important implications for the courts'

[46] Decree-Law no. 78 of 1931, the Bill of Organization of *Shari'a* Courts, art. 280 (later abrogated by article 4 and replaced by article 3 of Law no. 1 of 2000).

[47] Badran (1996) at 3.

[48] Shaham (1997) at 14.

[49] Ibid. at 11.

[50] Judith Tucker, *Women in Nineteenth-Century Egypt* (1985) at 12.

jurisprudence which had traditionally not relied on written evidence. The 1897 Law concerning evidence and procedure further restricted the Sharīʿa courts' jurisdiction to matters of personal status and *waqf*, and established a hierarchy of degrees of litigation.[51]

Several important studies in social and legal history have examined the *Sharīʿa* courts' records to elucidate the role of *qādīs* in disputes relating to personal status and *waqf*, and to the status of women in general.[52] Focusing on the nineteenth and first half of the twentieth century, these studies have shown that the role of Egypt's *Sharīʿa* courts, which applied *Ḥanafi* doctrine since 1805, developed considerably over time.[53] Throughout the nineteenth century the *Sharīʿa* courts were gradually 'Egyptianised', with the majority of *qādīs* recruited from the ranks of the Egyptian *ʿulema*. The jurisprudence of the courts reveals that these *qādīs* applied the yet uncodified *Sharīʿa*, "tempered by a recognition of social reality".[54] This often led to outcomes favourable to women, including the frequent enforcement by the courts of *khulʿ* divorce,[55] or no-fault divorce initiated by the wife, which had disappeared in Egypt since the codification of family law in the beginning of the twentieth century, until it was reinstituted through a highly contested law in 2000. On the other hand, the application of *Ḥanafi* law often disadvantaged women, particularly in areas such as child custody and guardianship.[56]

Throughout the first half of the twentieth century, the *qādīs*, striving for the public interest and taking into account modern realities, departed at various times from the strict opinions of established jurisprudential schools. Although, in general, *qādīs* "represented a conservative outlook that was not prone to change easily in the face of new social conditions,"[57] adhering most of the time to *Ḥanafi* doctrine, they used their discretion in many instances to favour interpretations that "manifested human considerations."[58] Adhering to *Ḥanafi* doctrine was also beneficial to women when it led to a rejection of local custom that discriminated against them. In various cases, *qādīs* used their power of discretion to respond to social change. For instance, in determining when a marriage has been

51 Shaham (1997) at 11–12.
52 See Tucker, (1985), and Shaham (1997).
53 Tucker (1985) at 10.
54 Ibid. at 14.
55 Ibid. at 53.
56 Ibid. at 60.
57 Shaham (1997) at 230.
58 Ibid. at 232.

consummated for the purposes of establishing the women's right to the dower, *qādīs* took into consideration modern customary practices—not envisioned by predominant interpretations of the *Sharīʿa*—that allowed premarital meetings between couples after the signing of the marriage contract, even though the strict *Sharīʿa* rules on 'legal privacy' had not been met.[59] They also invented an innovative punishment for husbands who mistreated their wives, by exempting the wives from the duty of obedience in such cases.

The response of *qādīs* to the legal reforms of the 1920's is also a subject of much interest; particularly in areas where the law gave the *qādīs* a degree of discretion. The complex and diverse approach of the *qādīs* to the 1923 legislation on minimum marriage age and registration of marriages is a case in point. Although *Ḥanafi* doctrine sanctions marriage from the beginning of sexual maturity and creates no obligation to register marriages, the vast majority of *qādīs* demonstrated support for the reforms and hence adopted expansive interpretations that made them applicable to a larger range of cases. A minority of *qādīs*, though, intent on adhering to the strict teachings of the *Ḥanafi* school, sought to limit the scope of the legal reform by interpreting it narrowly.[60] In cases related to judicial divorce initiated by the wife, some *qādīs* employed their personal discretion in establishing 'harm' to the benefit of the wife, by resorting directly to *Māliki* texts. In general, therefore, "the deviation of the reforms from *Ḥanafi* doctrine does not appear to have been a fundamental problem for the *qādīs*."[61]

While drawing generalisations from the jurisprudence of the *Sharīʿa* courts is a futile exercise in light of the different prevailing social and political milieu that informed the decisions and power of these courts at different points in time, not to mention the constant development of the institutional setting in which they operated, there is enough evidence to suggest that the *qādīs* exercised some degree of independence and flexibility of judgement in applying the law. The conception of statutory legislation "encouraged the *qādīs* to adopt a more innovative legal approach."[62]

Although the *qādīs* remained generally committed to *taqlīd* law, and did not generally seek to challenge that *status quo*, their independence

---

[59] Tucker (1985) at 42.
[60] Ibid. at 67.
[61] Shaham (1997) at 233.
[62] Ibid. at 234.

allowed them to choose innovatively from among juristic interpretations, and in very limited cases apply the principles of *ijtihād* and *istilāḥ* to serve justice, taking into consideration the particulars of every case. This process was, however, rather *ad hoc* in nature, and represented no official policy of the State or the religious establishment, but was rather subject to the discretion of each individual *qādī*. Nonetheless, it undoubtedly informed the process of codification at the time, which equally sought to depart from the strict traditions of *Ḥanafi* doctrine. Legal modernisers took the process one step further in their attempt to institutionalise the practice of *ijtihād* in law-making.

The process of codification of *Sharīʿa*-derived family law has transformed the way in which that that law operates, as statutory legislation is incapable of being fluid and flexible. Although codifying family law generally serves the interests of predictability, objectivity, and rationality, because it simultaneously prevents the flexibility central to the application of *Sharīʿa* law,[63] the legislator must seek to introduce this flexibility in the law itself, to remain true to the spirit of the *Sharīʿa*. In other words, the imperative for incorporating Islamic notions of justice and equality through the process of codification presents itself as a priority, as well as the constant development of the law to take into account changing social realities.

Codification and the Rise of Legal Modernism

Legal developments over the past few decades in countries that apply *Sharīʿa*-derived laws, equally indicate that the *Sharīʿa* is not a rigid body of law that is insensitive to the needs of society.[64] Although the classical theory of Islamic jurisprudence, as consecrated since the tenth century AD, left little room for the modification of established juristic opinions by any legislative authority, the rise of Islamic legal modernism, born in the nineteenth century, attempted to break with the tradition of *taqlīd* and institutionalise the reinterpretation of the religious scriptures in light of modern realities. The tools proposed by the modernisers included: (a) the codification of the ethical provisions of religious law into positive law; (b) the utilisation of the doctrines of *takhayyur* and *talfīq*; (c) the reopening of the gates of *ijtihād*.[65]

---

[63] See Tucker (1998) at 184.

[64] Coulson (1968) at 4.

[65] Layish, 'The Contribution of the Modernists to the Secularization of Islamic Law', 14 *Middle East Studies* 263 (1978) at 263–264.

The process of personal status law reform can be traced back to developments in the Ottoman Empire, including the imperial edicts of the Ottoman Sultan in 1915, in which he declared for the first time that women had the right to sue for divorce under certain circumstances.[66] In 1917, an Ottoman Family Code, based on the four schools of Islamic jurisprudence, was adopted, inspiring the promulgation of a number of statutes in Egypt, including Decree-Law no. 25 of 1920 and Decree-Law no. 25 of 1929. The reforms were inspired by tools developed and advocated by the early Islamic reform movement led by figures such as *Jamal al-Din al-'Afghani* (1838–1897), *Rifa'ah Badawi Rafi' al-Tahtawi* (1801–1873), the Grand Mufti of Egypt *Muhammad 'Abduh*, (1849–1905) and his disciple *Rashīd Reda* (1865–1935), as well as "western-trained lawyers in family reform."[67]

In the early nineteenth century, *al-Tahtawi* advocated the use of *takhayyur*—the principle by which a Muslim could select a position from any of the major *Sunni* schools—excluding the other three—to adapt the *Sharī'a* to changing circumstances.[68] *Takhayyur* allowed jurists to embrace the prevailing interpretations of the other Sunni schools in certain circumstances.[69] In fact, *takhayyur* "played a decisive role in facilitating interpretations favouring women" in the early twentieth century.[70] This technique was used in the adoption of the 1920 and 1929 personal status Decree-Laws, among others, where the provisions of the *Māliki* school were selected in order to increase the grounds on which women could obtain judicial divorce. Eventually, the technique of *takhayyur* evolved, as legislators began to seek the opinions of individual scholars within a particular school, even if these opinions were in conflict with the predominant doctrines of the principal schools.[71] This was a clear departure from the traditional understanding of *takhayyur*, which originally mandated the adoption of only a dominant opinion within one of the four *Sunni* schools.

The reformers availed themselves of yet another technique—*talfīq*—or the mixing between the positions of the schools "so as to produce a

[66] Esposito (1982) at 3–10.
[67] Shaham (1997) at 8. Shaham argues that the secular lawyers had a larger impact on the reform process than the official *'ulema*.
[68] Venkatraman (1995) at 1985.
[69] Arabi (2001) at 19.
[70] Venkatraman (1995) at 1985.
[71] Coulson (1968) at 40–51.

hybrid ruling which does not belong to any of them."[72] Such combination and fusion often led to the articulation of rules that existed in none of the orthodox schools, and thus arguably departed considerably from *taqlīd* law. In fact, any claim that this process constituted *taqlīd* was "nothing more than a thin veil of pretence, a purely formal and superficial adherence to the established principles of jurisprudence."[73] As such, it has been termed by many scholars as neo-*ijtihād*. Notwithstanding this reality, reformers chose to stick to that pretence; acknowledging that they had departed from the doctrine of the four schools would have potentially aborted the whole reform process. The method of *talfīq* was used most extensively in the area of inheritance and testamentary bequests (*waqf*).

The twin processes of *takhayyur* and *talfīq* were used repeatedly from the 1920's till the 1980's to legitimate reforms that placed limits on the husband's right to divorce, while simultaneously granting the wife more leeway in ending the marriage.

By far the most widely employed reform tools, they emanated from the doctrine of supra-*madhhab*, or the notion that "the state should not be confined to the rules of one *madhhab* but should be free when appropriate to seek the rules for its purposes in the doctrine of any school of law."[74]

The third tool, *ijtihād*, advocated by *Sheikh Muhammad ʿAbduh*, the Grand Mufti of Egypt, was reinterpreted so as to include a 'humanistic-liberal' element, namely the principles of *istislāḥ* and *maslaḥa* (public welfare and public interest).[75] If any particular social need was not covered by the canonical sources of Islamic law, then "a jurist should select an interpretation that best accorded with the public interest."[76] The principle of *maslaḥa* became the cornerstone of *ʿAbduh's* reforms allowing for alternative ways of legislating based on *Sharīʿa* law, in essence through modifying the hierarchy of the sources of law advocated by the theory of *Usul-al-fiqh*.[77] However, the use of *ijtihād* remained very limited.

The tools of the reform movement were successfully used to break down the strict power structure entrenched in *Ḥanafi* law. Through "selecting elements from the legal doctrines of the four *Sunnı* law schools,

[72] Esposito (1982) at 3–10.
[73] Coulson (1968) at 201.
[74] Abu-Odeh (2004) at 1091.
[75] See Layish (1978) at 264 and Abu-Odeh (2004) at 1091.
[76] Abu-Odeh (2004) at 1091–1092.
[77] Ibid.

the framers of these laws sought to adapt elements of Islamic family law to the needs of modern times and to improve the legal status of women vis-à-vis their husbands and paternal relatives."[78] Whereas early reforms were confined within the limits of *taqlīd* law (the strict adherence to the four orthodox schools), recent reforms have arguably departed from the strict doctrine of the four schools. The recent adoption of article 20 of Law no. 1 of 2000 arguably re-opened the gates of *ijtihād*, theoretically completing the elements of *ʿAbduh's* utilitarian reform project.

Personal Status Law Reform in the 20th and 21st Centuries

The process of reforming Egypt's *Ḥanafi*-based personal status law is still very much an ongoing process. The earliest reforms were achieved through a legal strategy that introduced procedural restrictions on the jurisdiction of the *Sharīʿa* courts in order to enforce the registration of marriages and prevent the marriage of minors. In 1911, the courts were banned from hearing a dispute in the absence of written evidence of the marriage contract. Similarly, after the failure in 1914 of an initiative to legally ban marriage for girls under 16 years of age, a law was adopted in 1923 to prevent the courts from hearing personal status disputes if the wife and husband were less than sixteen years and eighteen years of age, respectively, *at the time of marriage*[79] (the same principle was reaffirmed by the 1931 *Sharīʿa* Court Regulations).

The most significant reforms in Egypt's family law have been associated with divorce legislation, which has changed considerably since the turn of the twentieth century, granting women near-equality rights in the area of divorce. According to the *Ḥanafi* doctrine, the wife could obtain a judicial divorce on very limited grounds, namely the "incapacity of the husband to consummate the marriage, his apostasy from Islam" or in the case of "a fraudulent marriage contracted prior to puberty."[80] Feminists maintained that the husband's undeterred right to divorce the wife at any time coupled with the wife's inability to terminate the marriage was a major indication of asymmetry in the marital relationship. As such, limiting the husband's right to divorce and simultaneously increasing the

---

[78] *Dawoud El Alami*, quoted in Bernard-Maugiron and Dupret (2002) at 2.

[79] Shaham (1997) at 54–55. This provision was amended by article 17 (1) of Law No. 1 of 2000 which stipulated that the couple must have attained the minimum marriage age *ate the time of hearing*.

[80] See Qadri Pasha'a Egyptian Hanafi Code of Personal Status (1875), articles 298 and 303.

grounds on which a woman could obtain a judicial divorce were among the major feminist demands throughout the 1920's.

Decree Laws no. 25 of 1920 and no. 25 of 1929 represented a watershed by increasing the grounds on which a wife could obtain judicial divorce. The laws, which departed substantially from traditional *Ḥanafi* teachings and relied on various provisions of the *Māliki* school, were "cloaked under the veil of the 'acceptable' reform mechanism of *takhayyur*."[81] Basing themselves on the wide interpretation of 'harm' (*darar*) of the *Māliki* school, Laws no. 25 of 1920 and 25 of 1929 provided for irrevocable divorce initiated by the wife, through judicial decree. Articles 4 and 5 of Law no. 25 of 1920 stipulated that the husband's failure to provide maintenance (*nafaqa*) may be considered grounds for judicial divorce. Article 6 of Law no. 25 of 1929 further stipulated that "if the wife claims that the husband has caused her harm (*darar*) rendering the resumption of conjugal relations impossible, she may sue for a separation, in which case the divorce is irrevocable, if the existence of 'harm' is proven, and reconciliation fails."

Articles 12 and 13, which deal with divorce for the prolonged absence of the husband, aptly illustrate the employment of the technique of *talfīq* to come up with a single legal rule. In conformity with the *Māliki* legal doctrine, articles 12 stipulated that prolonged absence of the husband (for more than a year) constituted grounds for divorce. However, the provisions also adopted aspects of *Ḥanbali* law; divorce is only granted if the husband is absent for no 'justifiable' reason. Absence for any reason that does not violate the *Sharīʿa*, including work, education, and trade is considered 'justifiable'. This is in stark contrast to *Māliki* doctrine, which does not make judicial divorce for 'prolonged absence' of the husband conditional on the cause for such absence. Reverting to *Māliki* legal doctrine once more, article 13 establishes that judicial divorce for the prolonged absence of the husband is an irrevocable divorce.[82]

Combining the opinions of *Imam Mālik* and *Ibn Taymiya*, article 14 of Law no. 25 of 1929 stipulated that the imprisonment of the husband for three or more years also constituted grounds for divorce. The wife could sue for divorce only after a year of the prison term had lapsed.

---

[81] Venkatraman (1995) at 1988.

[82] Ahmed Nasr el-Guindy, *al-ta'liq 'ala nussuss qanun tanzim ba'dh awda' wa igra'at al-taqadhi fi masa'il al-ahwal al-shakhsiyya* [Commentary on the text of the Law to Organise Certain Conditions and Procedures of Matters of Personal Status] (2000), 419.

In addition, Articles 9, 10 and 11 of Law no. 25 of 1920 made a similar pronouncement with regards to 'harm' caused by the husband's incurable 'disease or defect' (*marad aw 'ayb*). The wife loses the right to sue for divorce if she was aware of the 'disease or defect' before marriage, or if she learnt about it after the marriage and acquiesced. Going beyond the teachings of the four *Sunni* schools, as well as the *Shi'i* and *Zaydi* schools, the law widened the definition of 'disease or defect' to encompass any incurable disease, rather than restricting the definition to a disease that obstructed normal conjugal relations. Basing themselves on the opinion of *Ibn al-Qayyim*, the legislators of Law no. 25 of 1920 granted the judge discretion in deciding whether the 'disease or defect' in question justified judicial divorce.[83] In suing for a divorce on the basis of 'harm', the burden of proof was placed on the wife; she could be granted the divorce only if she succeeded in proving to the judge that she had, in fact, suffered from some kind of 'harm' for any of the above-mentioned reasons.

Simultaneously, feminists demanded that the husband's unconditional right to divorce be restricted in order to challenge the gender hierarchy within the family. Traditionally, under the teachings of the *Ḥanafi* school, the husband has the right to unilateral and unconditional divorce (*talāq*) also known as repudiation. The divorce is effective even if the husband is intoxicated or under duress, and may be conditional (meaning the husband may make the divorce effective on condition of any particular behaviour on the part of the wife. If the wife engages in such behaviour, she is automatically divorced.) The divorce is not effective if the husband states the repudiation formula when in a state of anger, such that he was acting irrationally. According to the *Ḥanafi* school, the wife could also stipulate in the marriage contract that she has the right to divorce herself at will.[84]

In the 1920's, feminists demanded that the provisions of *Ḥanafi* law be modified so as to restrict the husband's unfettered right to divorce the wife. They suggested limiting the husband's right to unilateral divorce to 'serious' cases only, and after an attempted reconciliation by a *qādī* (judge).[85] Although these demands were based on direct interpretations of *Quranic* provisions, they were not backed by the opinions of the four

[83] Ibid. at 322.

[84] Mostafa Al-Siba'ie, *Al-Mar'a bayn al-fiqh wal qanun* [Women between Jurisprudence and Law] (2002), 94.

[85] Badran (1996) at 131.

schools and hence were not well-received by the legislature.[86] Nonetheless, Decree-Law no. 25 of 1929 placed several restrictions on the husband's right to unilateral divorce, derived from several different juristic opinions. Among the reforms, the law selected interpretations from the *Shafi'i*, *Māliki*, and *Hanbali* schools in order to prohibit a divorce declared by a man who was intoxicated or under duress.[87] In contravention of the teachings of the *Ḥanafi* school, it also stipulated that repudiation could not be conditional; neither could its wording be ambiguous.[88] The husband must explicitly state the repudiation formula (*anti taliq*) in order for the separation to be effective. This provision was based on the minority opinions of the Meccan scholar, *'Ata* and the Iraqi scholar, *Shurayh*.[89]

Similarly, article 3 of Law no. 25 of 1929 adopted the minority opinions of *Ibn Taymiya* and *Ibn el Qayim* to stipulate that a divorce would only be considered irrevocable after three separate pronouncements of the repudiation formula.[90] This was a clear departure from the teachings of the *Ḥanafi* School, which held that in cases where the husband makes three repudiations in one statement, the divorce becomes irrevocable.[91]

The two personal status decree laws of 1920 and 1929 led to the official endorsement of the doctrines of *takhayyur* and *talfīq* as a legislative policy. The two decree-laws did not, however, displace all of the provisions of the *Ḥanafi* doctrine. For instance, divorce stated in a moment of anger would remain invalid, a provision that did not conform to *Māliki* teachings. Moreover, the law retained the wife's right to divorce herself, upon the husband's explicit delegation in the marriage contract, a *Ḥanafi* school interpretation that remains relevant today (although it is used sparingly).[92] Together, the two decree-laws had the effect of turning Egypt's personal status law into a hybrid law that brought together provisions from each of the four schools, including minority opinions.

The process of selecting and combining from the different jurisprudential schools to achieve reforms in the area of personal status law wasn't limited to the early reform period. In 1979, President *Sadat* issued Decree Law no. 44 (commonly known as *Jihan*'s Law) by presidential decree

[86] Similar provisions, however, were later adopted in Tunisia and Syria. They were based on *ijtihād* from the text of the *Quran* and *Sunnah*.

[87] Decree Law no. 25 of 1929, art. 1.

[88] Ibid. Art. 2 and art. 4.

[89] Coulson (1968) at 194–195.

[90] Al-Siba'ie (2002) at 92.

[91] Ibid.

[92] Badran (1996) at 131.

during parliamentary recess. The procedural caveat was employed in order to prevent the People's Assembly from blocking the controversial law.[93] Inspired by *Māliki* jurisprudence, Law no. 44 of 1979 covered many of the most important feminist demands of the previous half a century. It extended the grounds on which the wife could obtain a judicial divorce, established her right to the conjugal home if she had custody of the children, as well as her right to compensation (*mut'a*) if she was divorced against her will or for no fault of her own. The most controversial aspect of the new law was its approach to polygyny, which it sought to effectively limit by granting the wife the right to an automatic judicial divorce if she produced evidence that her husband had taken another wife without her knowledge, without needing to establish that the subsequent marriage caused her 'harm'.

Law no. 44 of 1979 thus assumed that any polygamous union between a married man and a second wife constituted, in essence, a type of 'harm' to the first wife, if it happened without her knowledge and consent, as stipulated in the *Māliki* and *Ḥanbali* doctrines. Once again, by adopting the technique of *takhayyur* and invoking the *Māliki* and *Ḥanbali* doctrines, important reforms were achieved within the framework of Islamic legitimacy.[94]

In 1985, however, as a result of widespread opposition, the law came before Egypt's Supreme Constitutional Court for review, and was repealed. Although the Court's decision was based on the procedural grounds that there was no constitutional basis for adopting it during parliamentary recess through Presidential Decree, the Court's judgement was, nonetheless, considered "a success for Islamicists and a blow to reformers."[95] It has often been cited as evidence that patriarchal social attitudes may block reforms that are in complete accord with the *Sharī'a*.

Two months after the law was rescinded, a massive effort by feminists led to the promulgation of Law no. 100 of 1985, a watered-down version of the 1979 law.[96] The new law (the first personal status law ever adopted by the People's Assembly) modified the provision on the wife's 'automatic' divorce in the case of the husband's subsequent marriage, by making such divorce subject to the court's discretion. Article 11*bis*(1) of the 1985 law requires the wife to prove that the polygamous marriage caused her

[93] Venkatraman (1995) at 1988–1989.
[94] Ibid. at 1989.
[95] Bernard-Maugiron and Dupret (2002) at 5.
[96] Dahl (1997) at 195.

moral or material 'harm' that obstructs normal cohabitation as husband and wife. The article further stipulated that the first wife may only seek judicial divorce if she had no knowledge of and did not consent to the second marriage. The wife was required to file the lawsuit for divorce within one year of learning of her husband's second marriage. If she didn't meet that deadline, she would have forfeited that right. The second wife was also allowed to seek judicial divorce on the basis of 'harm' if she was ignorant to the fact that the husband had other wives at the time of marriage.

Although, Law no. 100 of 1985 did not grant the wife the right to an automatic divorce, it treated polygyny as a special type of harm, based on which the wife could sue for divorce. It also included a procedural restriction on polygyny by requiring that the first wife be notified of the husband's subsequent marriage. Nonetheless, the law was widely criticised for adopting a very loose definition of 'harm' which was often used to the disadvantage of women, as well as for limiting the time period during which the first wife could sue for divorce. The removal of the provision granting the wife the conjugal home during the period of custody was also widely criticised. Instead, the text of the new law ordered the husband to pay housing costs. The removal of these two provisions was regarded by many critics as a compromise in favour of conservatives.

The new law also introduced a new type of divorce; under article 11*bis*(2) divorce could be granted in the case of discord or *khilāf mustaḥkam*.[97] Derived from the principle of 'obedience'[98] as interpreted by the *Ḥanafi* legal doctrine, this type of divorce is detached from divorce on the basis of 'harm'. According to article 11*bis*(2), failure to obey the husband results in the forfeiture of the right to maintenance. A wife is considered disobedient if she leaves the matrimonial home and refuses to return, in spite of the husband's 'invitation' (*daʿwa*) to do so, at the hands of an officer.

The wife may object to this procedure before the Court, on the basis that she has legitimate reasons (*awgoh sharʿiya*) to leave the matrimonial home. Although the law does not specify what reasons may be considered legitimate, according to *el-Giundy*, the Courts have interpreted the phrase to include: the husband's failure to provide a matrimonial home consistent with the requirements of the *Sharīʿa*, his systematic

[97] Law no. 25 of 1929 as amended by Law no. 100 of 1985, art. 11 in *Qawanin al Aḥwal al-Shakhsiyya* (2004), 32.

[98] El-Guindy (2000) at 399.

maltreatment of the wife, or if he cannot be trusted with her wealth and property.[99] In either of these cases, the wife may request a judicial divorce based on discord, in which case the court must first attempt reconciliation before granting the divorce.[100] The divorce is accompanied by a financial settlement, which is proportionate to the allocation of blame as determined by the arbitrators.[101]

Although Law no. 100 of 1985 was a result of an impressive mobilization of civil society, many commentators "deplored the fact that Egypt, in this way, had taken three steps forward in 1979, only to take two steps back again in 1985."[102] Coupled with these major flaws in the substantive law, the largest obstacle confronting women remained the cumbersome litigation procedures. Compounded by the gaps in the legal system, and its inherent bias against women, the procedural law had the effect of rendering personal status cases into protracted legal battles.[103]

In March 2000, an important attempt was made to address these challenges when Law no. 1 of 2000 came into force. The law, which was largely procedural in nature, began a process to introduce a "new legal framework" for family disputes, which "came into effect in three tranches of legislation" that were completed in 2004.[104] It modified the procedures for personal-status cases, addressing the legal inefficiencies of the previous laws. It also introduced two important provisions, namely no-fault divorce (*khulʿ*), initiated at the wife's prerogative and the right to divorce in the context of an unregistered (*ʿurfi*) marriage.[105]

Until 2000, most personal status law reforms were based on the employment of *takhayyur* and *talfīq*, including reference to minority opinions within the four *Sunni* jurisprudential schools, and in some rare cases other schools of *fiqh*. The adoption of Law No. 1 of 2000 arguably ushered in a new era, by codifying into law an interpretation of the religious

99 Ibid. at 409.

100 Ibid. at 414.

101 Law no. 25 of 1929 as amended by Law no. 100 of 1985, art. 10(b).

102 Ibid.

103 Mulki Al-Sharmani, 'Egypt's Family Courts: Route to Empowerment?' (Published 7 Sept. 2007) http://www.opendemocracy.net/article/democracy_power/5050/egypt_family_law. See also, by the same author, 'Egyptian Family Courts: Pathway to Women's Empowerment?', *Hawwa: Journal of Women of the Middle East and the Islamic World* 7 (2009) at 89–119; and 'Legal Reform, Women's Empowerment, and Social Change: The Case of Egypt', *IDS Bulletin* 41, No. 2 (2010) at 10–17.

104 Ibid.

105 Law no. 1 of 2000, Regarding the Promulgation of a Law to Organize Certain Conditions and Procedures in Matters of Personal Status, Official Gazette, Arab Republic of Egypt, no. 4; 29 (January 2000).

texts that did not conform, in its entirety, to the teachings of any of the classical jurisprudential schools.

Although the procedure of *khulʿ* exists in all four *Sunni* schools, they all require consent of the husband in order to effect the divorce. The law as adopted by the Egyptian legislature, however, does not require the husband's consent, a clear departure from the predominant views of the *Shafʿi*, *Ḥanbali*, *Māliki* and *Ḥanafi* schools. In justifying its novel formulation of the *khulʿ* formula, proponents made direct references to the text of the *Quran* and *Sunnah*. In so doing, the Egyptian legislature shifted from its traditional use of the tools of *takhayyur* and *talfīq*, adopting the liberal tool of *Ijtihād* based on the primary sources of the *Sharīʿa*.

In March 2004, the People's Assembly promulgated Law no. 10 of 2004, which came into force the following October. The law, which dealt with matters of procedure, established a court system to adjudicate all personal status law cases, known as the family courts. The consolidation of personal status cases in one court, and before one judge was hailed as a positive development that would save both time and resources.[106] In the same year, Law no. 11 of 2004 was promulgated, establishing the Family Insurance Fund to enable female litigants to collect court-ordered alimony and child support through Nasser Bank.[107]

According to article 2 of Law no. 10 of 2004, the Family Court is composed of three judges and two specialists trained in social work and psychology. At least one of them must be a woman. Each court also operates a "Family Dispute Settlement Office" which enforces Law no. 1 of 2000's provisions on compulsory mediation.[108] Although the family court model aims to establish "an efficient and non-adversarial legal system that is based on mediation"[109] it has been widely criticised for subjecting only judicial divorce (mostly initiated by the wife) to compulsory mediation, while granting men the freedom to divorce their wives at will.[110] Nonetheless, compulsory mediation has resulted in actual

---

[106] 'Divorced from Justice Women's Unequal Access to Divorce in Egypt', *Human Rights Watch* Vol. 16, no. 8(E) (December 2004) at 52.

[107] Al-Sharmani, 'Egypt's Family Courts: Route to Empowerment?'

[108] Law no. 10 of 2004, art. 5.

[109] Al-Sharmani, 'Egypt's Family Courts: Route to Empowerment?'

[110] According to article 21 of Law no. 1 of 2000, upon registering a divorce:

The registrar must warn the couple of the harms associated with divorce, and must *invite* them to appoint a mediator from each of their families to attempt conciliation. However, if the couple insist on the divorce, or if they agree that divorce has already taken

reconciliation in about half of the cases brought before it since the entry into force of the new system,[111] saving both time and unnecessary costs.

It is noteworthy that those who operate the system (judges, social workers, psychologists, etc.) assert that the intent and purpose of the family courts model is to protect and uphold the rights of the family, and not those of the wife. Therefore, some have contended that it is erroneous to characterise these procedural reforms as advances in the rights of women.[112] Others are inimical to the concept of formal mediation itself, arguing that it is "an alien concept borrowed from western legal models".[113] Such opinions show the extent to which the legal empowerment of women, in spite of conscious and organised reform efforts, can be held hostage to conservative attitudes and patriarchal considerations.

In spite of the use of these innovative tools to reform Egypt's family law, some of the major demands articulated by feminists since the 1920's have not yet been met. These demands include making repudiation by the husband contingent upon a court's decision, restricting polygyny through requiring a court order for its validation, increasing women's maintenance rights, and the abolition of the institution of *ṭāʿah* (obedience).[114] Although the introduction of judicial *khulʿ* was an important success for the feminist movement, critics lament the fact that Law no. 1 of 2000 was largely procedural and failed to address the majority of substantive demands by feminists. By focusing on procedural issues and making very few substantive reforms, the law is arguably cosmetic and may have actually presented a setback for women's rights. According to this view, procedural hurdles are difficult to remedy through piecemeal reforms, and require an overhaul and restructuring of the whole judicial system in a manner that makes it more egalitarian. By selling Law no. 1 of 2000 as a significant reform, both domestically and internationally, the government was able to put off genuine substantive reforms while effectively pre-empting feminists from making further demands.

Although these concerns are indeed legitimate, they underestimate the magnitude of recent reforms, and what they represent in terms of introducing a new legislative policy that departs from established interpreta-

---

place, or if the husband decides that he has already divorced the wife, the registrar must register the divorce [without a conciliation attempt].

[111] Adham Faheem, [Deputy Chief Justice of the Southern Cairo Court *Mahkamet Ganoub al-Qahira*], *Interview*, (Nov. 15, 2004).

[112] Ibid.

[113] Al-Sharmani, 'Egypt's Family Courts: Route to Empowerment?'

[114] *Divorced from Justice* at 10.

tions of the religious texts. This new policy has been endorsed and upheld by Egypt's Supreme Constitutional Court in its interpretation of Egypt's ambiguous and apparently contradictory constitutional provisions on non-discrimination on the basis of gender, and is constantly defended by the Court when adjudicating the constitutionality of *Sharīʿa*-derived reforms. Although there is still much to be desired in terms of possible areas of legal reform, this pragmatic policy presents exciting prospects for the gradual, yet effective, reform of Egypt's family laws without breaking with the legitimacy of Islamic reform methods. A decade after Law no. 1 of 2000 was successfully promulgated, it can only be hoped that Egypt's legislature will capitalise on this momentum, and the legitimating cover provided by a progressive Supreme Constitutional Court, to embark on a process of transformation of the basic foundations of Egypt's family law to conform with the underlying egalitarian and just principles of the *Sharīʿa*.

CHAPTER SIX

GENDER (IN)EQUALITY AND THE *SHARĪʿA* IN EGYPT'S CONSTITUTION: THE ROLE OF THE SUPREME CONSTITUTIONAL COURT

Constitutional provisions affect gender equality at multiple levels. At the most basic level, constitutional provisions that make direct reference to equality between men and women inform and affect all other legislative enactments, as the basic law of the land. But over and above that, contradictory constitutional language, as well as the recognition of religious law, on the one hand, and international law, on the other, within the legal hierarchy, all impact women's enjoyment of their equality rights. Ultimately, the balancing of the various rights and the impact of different sources of law is left to the processes of constitutional interpretation. Gender non-discrimination is consecrated in almost every contemporary constitution, Egypt's being no exception. Egypt's constitutional provisions on gender equality, however, are not absolute; they include qualifications related to the role of women in the family, and especially as mothers. The question of how to resolve a potential conflict between the individual rights of a woman, on the one hand, and the rights of the family as a unit, on the other is basically left unanswered, and it is a question that seems to constantly concern the State when adopting new laws and policies. The success of such reforms hinges upon the ability of the State to justify them in terms of conservative family values that appeal to patriarchal mentalities.

The Egyptian constitution's treatment of the relationship between domestic law and international law, whether in the form of international treaties, custom, or general principles of law is also rather unclear. Although the Egyptian legal system is based on the monist tradition, many of the rights in question are non self-executing by nature, and hence require the modification of national laws. The implications of this are, unfortunately, that there is an inevitable gap between Egypt's obligations at the international level and its domestic legislation.

Another complex issue, one that arises in many legal jurisdictions, is the position of religious law in the State's legal system. Egypt's constitution stipulates in article 2 that the Islamic *Sharīʿa* is the principle source of legislation. This has often been lamented by advocates of women's rights, particularly those espousing a secular approach, as potentially eroding the equality rights of women. However, the actual enjoyment by women of their equality rights is really a factor of how such constitutional provisions are interpreted. As the sole body entrusted with the authority to interpret constitutional provisions, Egypt's Supreme Constitutional Court (SCC) has played an extremely important role in defining the framework within which women's family rights can be advanced. Although historically the SCC had a mixed record in dealing with legislation favourable to the human rights of women (it repealed a law granting the wife an automatic divorce for in the case of polygyny, as well as a law instituting quota for women in parliament) its interpretation of article 2 of the constitution has contributed to an environment of progressive reform. Through such interpretations, the SCC has advanced a moderate social reform agenda that favours the gradual consolidation of women's family rights without departing from the principles of the *Sharīʿa*.

Gender Equality in Egypt's Constitution

Egypt's current Constitution, adopted in 1971 and subsequently amended on May 22nd 1980, and more recently in 2005 and 2007, is a manifestation of the apparent conflict between women's equality rights, on the one hand, and traditional conceptions of family and gender roles, on the other. Egypt's official position is that the Constitution clearly guarantees gender equality by virtue of articles 8, which guarantees "equality of opportunity to all citizens" and 40, which stipulates that "all citizens are equal before the law. They have equal public rights and duties without discrimination between them due to sex,[1] race, ethnic origin, language, religion or creed". The Constitution equally, though, includes a number of provisions, namely articles 9, 10 and 11, which arguably institutional-

[1] Egypt. Const. art. 40. The exact wording of the Constitutional provision has been subject to some debate. The Arabic text prohibits discrimination on the basis of a number of criteria, including "*jins*", which can be translated to mean either "sex" or "race". Regardless of such competing interpretations, however, the Supreme Constitutional Court held that the list contained in Article 40 was not exhaustive, and that it prohibited discrimination on all grounds, not just the ones mentioned in the text (Case no. 6, 13th Judicial year, SCC, (16 May 1992).)

ize the view of women as mothers and emphasize their primary role as members of family units. Article 9 stipulates that:

> the family is the basis of the society founded on religion, morality and patriotism. The State is keen to preserve the genuine character of the Egyptian family—with all values and traditions represented by it—while affirming and promoting this character in the interplay of relations within Egyptian society.

Article 10 further states that "the State shall guarantee the protection of motherhood and childhood …", whereas article 11 stipulates that "the State shall guarantee coordination between a woman's duties towards her family and her work in the society, considering her equal to man in the political, social, cultural and economic spheres without detriment to the rules of Islamic jurisprudence."

Critics have maintained that the wording of constitutional provisions allows for the separation of the 'private' or family rights of women, which are governed by religious-based laws, from their other 'public' rights, which are based on the principle of equality.[2] By qualifying the principle of gender equality with reference to 'Islamic jurisprudence', the Constitution arguably presupposes that the *Shariʿa* doesn't allow for gender equality. The constant development of Islamic jurisprudence, however, which at times demonstrates greater commitment to women's equality than at others, is not fairly represented by the deterministic wording of the aforementioned provisions.

The inclusion of constitutional language that guarantees the protection of the family as a unit is not unique to Egypt's Constitution. In fact, such language exists in article 23 of the ICCPR, as well as many constitutions (such as the German Basic Law and Spanish constitution) which deem the family worthy of special protection by society and the State.[3] Articles 9, 10 and 11, of Egypt's Constitution do not give precedence to a woman's family duties over other roles and responsibilities, neither do they make women solely responsible for the family.[4] According to Egypt's reports to the CEDAW Committee, these provisions are actually intended to permit the differential and preferential treatment of women, such as

[2] Eschel Rhoodie, *Discrimination Against Women. A Global Survey* (1989), 364.

[3] See discussion *supra* at p. 15, and note 18.

[4] *Combined sixth and seventh periodic reports* CEDAW/C/EGY/7 (2010) at section 2.4.

under the labour law, in response to major feminist demands at the time the Constitution was promulgated.[5]

However, the striking thing about these provisions is the ambiguity with which they accord the State a role in 'coordinating the balance' between a woman's family duties and work in society. This advances the stereotype that women who work are less capable of taking care of their families, and that women's primary responsibility is towards the home.[6] Taken together, a literal reading of these provisions seems to tip the balance in favour of the rights of the family, as a unit, and against the rights of the wife and mother, as an individual. This view was reaffirmed by the CEDAW Committee in its consideration of Egypt's third periodic report and its combined fourth and fifth periodic reports, during which it expressed concern that:

> Article 11 of the Egyptian Constitution, which states that the State shall enable a woman to reconcile her duties towards her family with her work in society and guarantee her equality with men in the sphere of political, social, cultural and economic life, appears to entrench the woman's primary role as mother and homemaker.[7]

Over-emphasising the rights of the family, as a unit, moreover, may limit the State's ability to intervene in family affairs to regulate harmful and discriminatory conduct, such as domestic violence and marital rape. By simultaneously espousing in article 40 an unequivocal guarantee of gender equality under the law, only to advance the view, in articles 9, 10 and 11, that a woman's primary role is as a wife and a mother, the Constitution is inherently ambiguous or even contradictory in its approach to gender equality. In an attempt to reconcile these seemingly conflicting constitutional provisions, the SCC's jurisprudence has reaffirmed the complementarity of articles 11 and 40, affirming that neither should take precedence over the other, but rather that advancing the values underlying the Constitution necessitates a concurrent reading of all its provisions.[8] Ironically, in 1985 article 40 was successfully applied to challenge legislation that distinguished between men and women, only this legislation actually established a quota for women in parliament. Law no. 22

---

[5] Ibid.

[6] See also *Constitution Review Group Report, The Family*. Online http://www.constitution.ie/reports/ConstitutionReviewGroupReport.pdf (last accessed Feb. 25th, 2010).

[7] *Concluding Observations of the Committee on Elimination of Discrimination Against Women*: Egypt, Twenty-fifth Session (15 Jan–2 Feb 2001) UN Doc CEDAW/C/2001/I/Add.2 at para. 332.

[8] Case no. 144, 18th Judicial year, SCC, (1 Sept 1997).

of 1979 was thus repealed on the grounds of discriminating on the basis of gender.[9] In other words, article 40 has been used to block affirmative action favourable to women (although such action is foreseen by article 4 of CEDAW) rather than to advance women's human rights and protect them against discriminatory legislation.

Although Egypt's Constitution was significantly reformed in 2005 and again in 2007, there was no attempt to review any of the above-mentioned provisions relevant to the family rights of women. In the area of political rights, however, the benefit of hindsight prompted the amendment of article 62 of the Constitution to allow for a minimum quota for women's representation in parliament.[10] This was followed by the adoption of relevant legislation which resulted in 64 seats being allocated to women. The process was thus carefully planned in order to avoid any potential challenges to the constitutionality of the new law.

Having discussed the substantive content of Egypt's constitutional provisions and their apparently contradictory treatment of women's equality, the question that subsequently arises is how to address possible conflicts between Egypt's Constitution, on the one hand, and its international human rights law obligations, on the other. Although article 27 of the VCLT provides a straightforward answer to this question, in practice, Egypt's legal system does not accord precedence to the rules of international law over domestic legislation. Practice also shows that Egypt's international legal obligations are of limited immediate value, in the absence of relevant domestic legislation to give effect to such obligations, as well as inadequate enforcement by domestic courts.

Positioning International Law within the Hierarchy of Legal Sources

Egypt's legal system is based on a variation of the monist tradition. According to article 151 of the Constitution, international treaties are directly enforceable once ratified. In other words, no promulgating legislation is required in order to enforce their provisions in Egyptian courts. All international treaties and agreements come into force upon the President's ratification, except for a number of exceptions (namely treaties

[9] *Combined sixth and seventh periodic reports of States parties, Egypt*, UN Doc CEDAW/C/EGY/7 at 7, note 4.

[10] Ibid. at 7; 18; 21.

establishing alliances, peace agreements, international agreements relating to navigation and trade, as well as any treaty that affects the State's sovereign rights or its budget) which require the consent of the People's Assembly. Human rights treaties, which arguably affect the States' sovereignty, require ratification by the President, with the consent of the People's Assembly.[11] Once ratified, the provisions of human rights treaties supposedly have the force of law, and are hence directly enforceable in domestic courts without the need for promulgating legislation.

Egypt has repeatedly asserted this position when questioned by the CEDAW Committee about the status of CEDAW as an international human rights treaty *vis-à-vis* domestic legislation. During the presentation of its periodic reports, Egypt has affirmed that upon ratification, the CEDAW became "an integral part of the national law."[12] As such, it could theoretically be "be directly invoked before courts of law."[13] In order to assess the effectiveness of this process, the Committee requested Egypt's Delegation, during its examination of the combined sixth and seventh periodic reports, to give examples of specific cases in which the CEDAW was directly invoked in domestic courts.[14] Although such questions have been repeatedly raised by various treaty-monitoring bodies within the UN human rights framework, in general they are inadequately addressed in Egypt's responses.

Although the CEDAW and other human rights treaties have been referred to sparingly by the Supreme Constitutional Court, this does not seem to be the case in the lower courts. This indicates that although human rights treaties can be invoked in theory, they seldom are in practice, reflecting a general lack of awareness in the judiciary and amongst lawyers and litigants, not only of the CEDAW, but of the binding nature of international human rights law and its creation of legal rights. Moreover, the very nature of many family rights does not seem to allow for direct enforceability. For example, prosecuting a husband for marital rape cannot rely on vague provisions regarding equality between

[11] Ibrahim Badawy El-Sheikh, *Nafath Iltizamat Masr al-dawliyya fi Majal Huquq al-Insan fi alNizam al-Qanuni al-Masry* [The Enforcement of Egypt's International Human Rights Obligations in the Egyptian Legal System] (2003) at 239.

[12] *Concluding observations of the Committee on the Elimination of Discrimination against Women, Egypt*, Ninth session, (22 Jan–2 Feb 1990), UN Doc CEDAW A/45/38 (1990) at para. 405.

[13] Ibid.

[14] *Concluding observations of the Committee on the Elimination of Discrimination against Women, Egypt*, Forty-fifth session, (18 Jan–5 Feb 2010), UN Doc CEDAW/C/EGY/CO/7at para 17.

spouses or a general prohibition of all forms of violence, but requires the incorporation in domestic criminal law of a particular crime, with a prescribed punishment. Without such a modification of the law, the principle of *nullem crimen sine lege* would apply, making any prosecution impossible. Practically speaking, therefore, direct incorporation of international human rights treaties into the Egyptian legal system cannot replace the promulgation of specific legislation when the rights in question are non self-executing by nature.[15]

In the case of conflict between domestic and international law, it is still unclear which of the two takes precedence according to Egypt's legal system. Egypt's Constitution does not grant international law a status superior to either domestic constitutional or legislative provisions, as required by article 27 of the VCLT.[16] Rather, it accords international treaties an ambiguous position; failing to clearly indicate where they are placed in the hierarchy of laws.[17] Domestic courts consistently treat international treaties as having an equal status to legislation, applying the general principles of *lex specialis derogat lege generali*, and *lex posterior derogat lege priori* to determine which provisions take precedence in the case of conflict.[18]

On the other hand, the Supreme Constitutional Court has accorded treaty provisions a special status by insisting that "the human rights clauses of Egypt's Constitution be interpreted in accordance with those human rights standards generally recognised and applied by democratic States, as reflected in international human rights instruments."[19] It has accordingly relied, in a few rare cases, on international human rights standards in its interpretation of Egypt's constitutional provisions and domestic legislation. For instance, in its judgement in Case no. 23 (1996) concerning the right to marriage, the Court asserted that the right to marriage was protected by the Islamic *Shariʿa*, and added that:

---

[15] See also Badawy El-Sheikh (2003) at 206.

[16] Art. 27 of the Vienna Convention on the Law of Treaties stipulates that: "A party may not invoke the provisions of its internal law as justification for its failure to perform a treaty."

[17] Adel Omar Sherif, 'Unshakable Tendency in the Protection of Human Rights: Adherence to International Instruments on Human Rights by the Supreme Constitutional Court of Egypt', in Eugene Cotran and Adel Omar Sherif (eds.), *The Role of the Judiciary in the Protection of Human Rights* (1997), 36.

[18] See Badawy El-Sheikh (2003) at 239–250.

[19] Ibid.

> The right to marry for whomever reaches the age of majority is also endorsed by international instruments, including the Convention on Consent to Marriage, Minimum Age for Marriage, and Registration of Marriages (1962); the Convention on the Elimination of All forms of Racial Discrimination (1965); the International Covenant on Civil and Political Rights (1966); the Declaration on the Elimination of Discrimination Against Women (1967); the Convention on the Elimination of All Forms of Discrimination Against Women (1979); and the European Convention for the Protection of Human Rights and Fundamental Freedoms. This last instrument, in Articles 8 and 12, states that everyone has the right to respect for his private and family life, his home and correspondence, and that men and women of marriageable age have the right to marry and to found a family.[20]

The Court's allusion to these international instruments is, seemingly, for their persuasive value rather than out of a sense of legal obligation. This is evident in the Court's reference to specific provisions of the ECHR, to which Egypt is not a party. In general, the SCC has not pursued a consistent policy of referring to international instruments in its jurisprudence. Its readiness to invoke international law has been sporadic at best, depending on the inclinations of the Court's Chief Justice at any given time.[21]

Theoretically, if a legislative statute or executive decree contravenes international human rights obligations that are reflected in the constitution, it can be challenged before the SCC and repealed. However, in practice, neither article 40 of the Constitution not the CEDAW or any other international human rights treaty have been invoked to challenge provisions of Egypt domestic legislation that violate the rights of women.[22] It also remains to be seen how the SCC would address a case in which there was a perceived conflict between Constitutional provisions, including article 2 which entrenches the *Sharīʿa* as the principal source of legislation, and international human rights standards.

As for rules derived from customary international law, and general principles of law, the Egyptian Constitution makes no mention of their status in the legal hierarchy. Judicial decisions have, however, granted

---

[20] Case no. 23 of the 16th Judicial Year, SCC, decided on March 18th, 1995, published in the Official Gazette no. 14, on April 6, 1995.

[21] The vast majority of cases that refer to international obligations are confined to the period in which Supreme Court Judge Awad El Morr was Chief Justice of the SCC.

[22] Constitutional claims against provisions of the personal status law have always been based on alleged incompatibility with article 2 of the Constitution rather than the contrary claim of incompatibility with the equality provision of article 40.

them the force of law, as long as they do not conflict with existing legislative provisions.[23] This reverse logic seems to suggest that Courts in Egypt have given domestic legislation precedence over both customary international law and general principles of law, in direct contravention of article 27 of the VCLT.

The Supreme Constitutional Court's Jurisprudence

As the sole authority entrusted with adjudicating the constitutionality of domestic legislation and interpreting legislative and constitutional provisions, the SCC has played a multi-faceted role in enforcing women's equality rights in the area of family relations. The SCC's power of judicial review (its authority to repeal legislation that violates the constitution or uphold legislation that conforms to it) has important consequences for the guarantee of women's equality rights. Although the SCC's exercise of its adjudicative function has had mixed results, it's rich jurisprudence indicates an employment of its powers of interpretation to distinguish between immutable aspects of the *Sharīʿa*, and other aspects which were left clearly ambiguous in the religious texts, and were therefore susceptible to constant development to meet the needs of society.

The SCC's Adjudicative Role and the Endorsement of Ijtihād

Interest in the SCC's jurisprudence in the area of women's rights centres mainly on its progressive approach to constitutional provisions related to the application of *Sharīʿa* law. Article 2 of the Constitution, amended in 1980 to appease the growing Islamic revivalist trend that characterised Egypt's political scene at the time, stipulates that the "*Sharīʿa* is *the* principal source of legislation", as opposed to the previous formulation of the *Sharīʿa* as *a* principal source of legislation. Opposed by sceptics on the grounds that it would severely undermine women's exercise of their equality rights and obstruct legal reforms,[24] article 2 actually proved to be a useful tool in the hands of a progressive SCC, intent on interpreting the text in a manner that allowed for novel formulations of Islamic jurisprudence.

[23] Badawy El-Sheikh (2003) at 239.
[24] See in general Rhoodie (1989) at 364.

The SCC's jurisprudence has evolved significantly in terms of its receptivity to challenges against the constitutionality of personal status laws that are favourable to women. Initially, it avoided determining the compatibility of legislation with the *Sharīʿa* by employing two tactics: (1) declaring the non-retroactivity of the article 2 amendment, thus avoiding the substantive ramifications for all laws promulgated prior to 1980 (a strategy employed on twelve different occasions); and, (2) revoking legislation challenged under article 2, when the need arose, on procedural rather than substantive grounds.[25] This approach was used to repeal Decree Law no. 44 of 1979, widely criticised by conservatives for restricting polygyny by extending the grounds on which a wife could obtain judicial divorce. The law, popularly known as *Jihan*'s law[26] also awarded the wife the conjugal home in the case of divorce, during the period of custody. Although the SCC ultimately found the law unconstitutional in 1985, it did not base its ruling on any substantive argument. Departing from what was in essence a procedural point, the SCC held that "there was no sufficient constitutional basis for modifying family Law no. 25 of 1929 by means of a Presidential Decree."[27]

A series of landmark cases in the 1990's, however, ushered in a new era of activism for the SCC, based on the doctrine enunciated in its judgement of May 4th, 1985 that:

> According to the report of the Commission [charged with preparing the Constitutional reform], the aim of the new formulation of Article 2 of the Constitution is to "force the legislator to have recourse to the commands of the *Sharīʿa*, to the exclusion of any other source, in order to discover what he is searching for; then, if he does not find there an explicit ruling, he is to employ the *Sharīʿa* resources of interpretive effort (*al-ijtihādiyya*) in order to arrive at the proper rules to follow and which do not transgress the foundations and general principles of *Sharīʿa*."[28]

The SCC's jurisprudence over the past quarter of a century demonstrates a strong commitment to this doctrine. In 1993, the SCC clearly distinguished between the "explicit rulings (or principles) of the *Sharīʿa*", which are not subject to interpretation, and other rules which can change to

---

[25] Abu-Odeh (2004) at 1139.

[26] In reference to Egypt's First Lady at the time, Jihan Sadat, who played a major part in the adoption of the law.

[27] Bernard-Maugiron and Dupret (2002) at 7. See discussion *supra* at p. 138–139.

[28] Supreme Constitutional Court, Judgment of May 4th, 1985, translation in Oussama Arabi, 'The Dawning of the Third Millennium on Shari'a: Egypt's Law no. 1 of 2000, or Women May Divorce at Will', *Arab Law Quarterly* 1 (2001) at 6.

adapt to the changing needs of society. Explicit rulings, i.e. those directly derived from the religious scriptures (the *Quranic* text and the Prophet's *ḥadīth*) or *an-nass*, take precedence over other rules that are not absolute in their origin and meaning. In other words, it espoused the view that "beyond the revealed text, there is no appeal (*la ijtihād maʿa an-nass*)."[29] In its judgement of May 13th, 1993, the Court stated that:

> This signifies that no legislative text may contradict those formal rules of *Sharīʿa* whose origin and meaning are definitive (*qātiʿat al-thubut wa'l dalāla*): these rules and their delimitation cannot be the object of interpretive effort (*ijtihād*) .... It is inconceivable, therefore, that the content thereof be modified according to changes in time and place. The authority of the Supreme Constitutional Court in this regard is limited to safeguarding their implementation and their overruling any other legal rule that contradicts them.[30]

The SCC further elaborated on the principle of *ijtihād*, employing this principle as well as *istiḥsān* (preference) and *istislāḥ* (general interest) in a number of other landmark decisions, consecrated as "judicial principles". It held that the *Sharīʿa* envisioned "the employment of reasoning in cases where a text is absent, by way of developing practical guidelines—in content more benevolent to human beings, more sensitive to their affairs and more answerable to their true interests than the legal rules are originally legislated to achieve."[31] The SCC also explicitly stated that it was possible to depart from the reasoning of the established Sunni jurisprudential schools. It held that the *Sharīʿa* "does not vest sacredness on the arguments of any Muslim scholar on any affair i.e. sacredness that precludes revision and reconsideration, even substitution ... it is correct to say that the independent reasoning by any one Muslim scholar is not necessarily worthy of being followed than that by any other."[32]

In order to grant legitimacy to the government's practice of relying on minority opinions in order to introduce reforms in the area of family law, the SCC further stated that "it could be that the least supported opinions be the most conducive to changing situations, even if they are contradictory to opinions that have prevailed for some time. Such are the

---

[29] Arabi (2001) at 7.

[30] Judgement of the Supreme Constitutional Court, May 15th 1993; trans B. Dupret, 'A propos de la constitutionalité de la Shari'a: Présentation et traduction de l'arrêt du 26 Mars 1994 de Haut Cour Constitutionnelle égyptienne', *Islamic Law and Society* 4, 1, 96 (1997).

[31] Case no. 8, 17th Judicial year, Supreme Constitutional Court, 18 May 1996.

[32] Ibid.

roots and origins of the *Sharīʿa*, which is by necessity evolving, eschewing rigidity, allowing for independent reasoning."[33]

The SCC's jurisprudence has also explicitly conferred legitimacy upon the government's departure from the reasoning of the established juristic schools, by reference to the *Sharīʿa*'s endorsement of the ruler's authority and discretion in matters that affect the people's affairs. It also endorsed the principle that the *Sharīʿa* seeks to apply the legal rule that is less burdensome to the people. In Case no. 82 (1997), the Court held that,

> independent reasoning in indecisive legal rules ... is a right given to Muslim scholars, but the ruler is more entitled thereto so that he can consider each issue individually ... with the help of those Muslim scholars, but without being necessarily restricted by the opinions of others. He may give different legal rules after referring to [the *Quran*] and [the *Sunnah*] to regulate people's affairs in a certain environment with its special circumstances, considering that the interests to be regarded are those which agree with the objectives of the *Sharīʿa*, defined in light of their development, since they are unlimited. Thus the ruler, when choosing between two opinions, should consider the easier, unless it is a sin, and not give a legal rule that is hard upon the people, or else he will be contradicting the Quranic verse "Allah would not place a burden on you."[34]

The SCC relied on the doctrine of *ijtihād*, and elaborated on it further in a number of seminal cases dealing specifically with women's rights. In 1994, it was confronted with the issue of the constitutionality of article 11 of Law no. 100 of 1985, which expanded the grounds on which a wife could obtain judicial divorce to include harm caused by her husband's polygamous union.[35] In its judgment, the SCC rejected the plaintiff's argument that by granting the wife such a right, article 11 violated the explicit dictates of the *Quran*, which allowed the husband to marry up to four wives. Although in its reasoning, the SCC agreed with the plaintiff that the *Quran* granted the husband the right to practice polygyny, and to marry up to four wives, it held that allowing the wife to request judicial divorce on the basis of harm could not be considered tantamount to preventing the husband from practicing polygyny. This was so because the law required the wife to prove that her husband's polygamous marriage had caused her harm that was "real not illusory, actual not imagined, demonstrable not assumed, independent of the

[33] Ibid.

[34] Case no. 82, 17th Judicial year, Supreme Constitutional Court (5 July 1997).

[35] Case no. 35, 9th Judicial year, Supreme Constitutional Court, (14 August 1994). See Abu-Odeh (2004) at 1145.

incident of the later marriage . . . " and occasioned by the husband's failure to abide by the strict limits imposed on the practice of polygyny by the *Sharīʿa*.[36] Granting the judge discretion in determining the existence of harm ensured that the harm claimed by the wife was "objective and not whimsical."[37]

In the same case, the SCC upheld the wife's right to place a condition in the marriage contract prohibiting her husband from taking on a second wife, and consequently to opt for a termination of the contract if it is breached by the husband. Although the SCC didn't go as far as challenging the husband's right to marry more than one wife, it held that article 11 of the law in question was in conformity with article 2 of the Constitution.

Two years later, the SCC issued a judgement concerning Islamic attire in secondary schools.[38] In this case, the Court was confronted with a claim against the constitutionality of an executive order issued by the Minister of Education, prohibiting schoolgirls from wearing the face-veil (*niqāb*) and headscarf (*hijāb*) in all schools.[39] The edict resulted in such public outrage that the government was forced to amend it, such that girls would be allowed to wear the headscarf if they were un-coerced and had obtained explicit permission from their parents. *Niqāb* or covering of the face was not to be permitted under any circumstance.[40]

This amendment, however, didn't bring an end to the fierce campaign launched by Islamists against the edict, which eventually came before the SCC for review. In its judgment, the Court examined the *Quranic* verses relevant to the issue and concluded that the *Quran* recommended that women cover various parts of their body. However, it found no evidence in the *Quran* of any necessary obligation for women to cover their hair or face. The Court added that the *Sunnah* was equally ambiguous on the matter, as were the opinions of the Sunni jurisprudential schools, which disagreed with regards to the specific parts of the woman's body that should be covered.[41] The Court proceeded to stipulate that the rationale

[36] Ibid.

[37] Abu-Odeh (2004) at 1145.

[38] Case no. 8, 18th Judicial Year, decided on May 18th, 1996.

[39] Edict no. 113, 1994.

[40] Edict no. 208 of 1994.

[41] Case no. 8, 18th Judicial Year, decided on May 18th, 1996, Supreme Constitutional Court. Translation in Awad Mohamed El-Morr, 'Judicial Sources for Supporting the

behind regulations on women's dress was the principle of modesty, whose underlying purpose was to prevent illicit sexual activity. It further found that an edict banning the veil wouldn't necessarily encourage men and women to engage in illicit sexual activity, and accordingly such a measure could not be found to violate the principle of modesty. Concluding that the edict was in conformity with article 2 of the Constitution, the SCC reemphasised that:

> unlike Islamic 'principles' which lie beyond controversial points of view as to their mandatory application, all other Islamic 'rules' are susceptible to different interpretations, and due to this are changeable, in order to ensure that they adapt to new realities with continued vivacity and elasticity.[42]

The SCC further asserted that Islam was a "framework by which its adherents should manage themselves in a manner compatible with their recognizable interests."[43] The Court thus recognised that the *Sharī'a* is sufficiently flexible and adaptable to accommodate modern realities.

In 1997, the SCC was once more confronted with a controversial question regarding the constitutionality of article 11 of Law no. 25 of 1929. The article in question allowed the wife to seek judicial divorce based on the notion of discord, or the judge's determination that reconciliation with the spouse was impossible.[44] In its reasoning, the Court agreed with the plaintiff that the *Quran* granted the husband the absolute right of unilateral divorce. On the other hand, it held that there was another stipulation in the *Quran* that was relevant to the case. This rule mandated the appointment of an arbitrator from the families of each of the spouses to mediate between them in the case of discord. Although the arbitrators are entrusted with the task of reconciling the spouses, the *Quran* is silent on what the arbitrators should do if the reconciliation attempt fails. Taken in this light, the Court held that article 11 should be seen as granting the arbitrators the right to recommend divorce to the judge. This provision was thus "within the realm of human-made legislation (or *ijtihād* as the Court sometimes called it) since it touched on the question of what extra

---

Protection of Human Rights', in Eugene Cotran and Adel Omar Sherif (eds.), *The Role of the Judiciary in the Protection of Human Rights* (1997) at 8.

42 Ibid.

43 Ibid. at 16.

44 Case no. 82, 17th Judicial Year, SCC, (1997).

powers arbitrators should be given—itself a subject of dispute among the various medieval schools of jurisprudence."[45]

Another clearly discriminatory legal provision came before the SCC for review in 2000. Until then, an edict issued by the Minister of the interior required a wife to obtain her husband's permission in order to travel. Although attempts to pass legislation to cancel the edict failed, in its November 4th decision, the SCC repealed the aforementioned decree.[46] The SCC's decisions have gradually paved the way for the adoption of one of the most ambitious reforms in the evolutionary history of Egypt's personal status law: the introduction of *khulʿ* divorce initiated at the wife's prerogative.[47] In the Explanatory Memorandum of the new law, reference was made to the SCC's jurisprudence on the use of *ijtihād* to justify the law's departure from the opinions of the four Sunni jurisprudential schools.

The Court was forced to defend the *khulʿ* provision when it was challenged before it in 2002, on the grounds of failing to require the husband's consent in order to effect the divorce.[48] After recounting the evidence for *khulʿ* divorce in the *Quran* and the *Sunnah*, the SCC, held that this type of divorce constituted one of the formal rules of *Sharīʿa* whose origin and meaning are definitive (*qātiʿat al-thubut wa'l dalāla*), and hence could not be contested. In defence of the woman's right to seek *khulʿ* divorce without the consent of her husband, the SCC held that the religious scriptures had been deliberately silent on the matter, allowing for legislative discretion in choosing the outcome that serves the interests of both parties in the relationship being regulated. Effecting the divorce in spite of the husband's opposition thus emanated from the dictates of reason and necessity. Forcing the wife to remain in a marriage she no longer wanted was clearly not in her interest, causing her harm in contradiction with the rules of the *Sharīʿa*, and undermining the essential principles underpinning marriage, namely quietude (*sakan*), compassion (*mawada*), and mercy (*raḥma* or *taraḥom*).

The SCC's jurisprudence has also reaffirmed the wife's right to initiate *khulʿ* divorce for the simple reason that she 'detests' life with her husband, without the need for any further justification or proof of harm. Emphasizing the wife's "psychological state" at the moment of requesting *khulʿ*

[45] Abu-Odeh (2004) at 1141.
[46] Case no. 243, 21st Judicial year, SCC (4 Nov 2000).
[47] See statement of the Speaker of the People's Assembly.
[48] Case no. 201, 23rd Judicial year, SCC, (15 Dec. 2002).

divorce, and her inability to continue sharing a life with her husband, the Court also upheld the nature of *khulʿ* as an irrevocable divorce that cannot be subject to appeal.[49]

Appraising the Role of the SCC

The SCC's jurisprudence may seem insufficiently progressive particularly on issues such as polygyny and obedience. The SCC's jurisprudence has reaffirmed the principle of a wife's obedience in return for maintenance[50] as well as the husband's right to marry more than one wife. However, it has also annulled the decree requiring the husband's consent for travel, upheld procedural restrictions on polygyny, veiling in schools, the *khulʿ* provision, as well as legislation favouring the mother, and female members of her family in child custody disputes, and extending the period of the mother's custody over her children.[51] Enthusiasts of judicial activism may advocate a more radical role for the SCC in its capacity as the institution most capable of defining the limits not only of other branches of government, but also of an increasingly conservative society that is often hostile to women's equality rights. In practical terms, however, it is evident that the Court's assumption of this moderate and intermediate position between the 'conservative' and the 'feminist' has allowed it to successfully promote a moderate, pragmatic and relatively uncontroversial social agenda that has allowed for important, albeit gradual, progress.

In almost all of the challenges brought before it, the SCC has adopted a balancing approach, in which the result was a middle ground between the two competing interests of conservatives on the one hand, and feminists on the other. For instance, while religious conservatives argued for unrestricted polygyny and unilateral divorce for the husband, and feminists sought a prohibition of polygyny and equal divorce rights for the wife, the SCC upheld a law that restricted the practice of polygyny and granted the first wife a way out, as well as a law that permitted judicial intervention to allow the wife to escape a bad marriage.[52] Similarly, "while some religious groups think that women should be veiled, and feminists believe that the law should not regulate women's dress, the SCC affirmed the principle

[49] Ibid.

[50] Case no. 164, 19th Judicial year, SCC, (3 July 1999).

[51] See Case no. 7, 8th Judicial year, SCC (15 May 1993) and Case no. 74, 17th Judicial year, SCC (1 March 1997).

[52] Abu-Odeh (2004) at 1145.

of modesty as the limit of the legislature's reach and as a compromise between the two positions."[53]

Through these decisions, the SCC has mandated the employment of *ijtihād* to adapt the relative 'rules' of the *Sharīʿa* to the changing needs of society, specifically when a rule is not governed by absolute 'principles.' In the area of law where explicit rulings exist, Egypt's legislators could go beyond the doctrines of the four schools by applying the sacred texts directly. There was also an explicit endorsement of the choice of juristic opinions that were 'easiest' on the people, that conformed to their true interests and to the spirit of the *Sharīʿa*. After more than a century since *Sheikh Muhammad ʿAbduh* enunciated his legal reform doctrine, the SCC thus formally endorsed the process of "going back to the revealed sources of *Sharīʿa* for inspiration in all modern legislation," departing from the commitment to the established doctrine of the four schools (*madhāhib*) and culturally sedimented customary rules (*ʿurf*).[54]

The SCC's approach clearly departs from any purported moratorium imposed on reasoning or *ijtihād*, and from the practice of *taqlīd* law that has arguably predominated law-making based on the *Sharīʿa* for over ten centuries. Not only has this new doctrine consolidated legal reforms challenged on the basis of non-conformity with the *Sharīʿa*, and paved the way for the adoption of even more sweeping reforms, but it is formulated in a way that legitimises constant development and evolution of interpretations in order to serve the changing interests of society. By advocating a less literal approach, doing away with rigidity and propagating a more active scrutiny of the spirit and object of the religious texts, particularly in areas that are indeterminate and thus susceptible to the employment of *ijtihād*, the SCC's jurisprudence opens the door to the adoption of a legislative policy informed by the egalitarian principles of the religious scriptures, with huge promises for the empowerment of Egyptian women.

[53] Ibid.
[54] Arabi (2001).

CHAPTER SEVEN

MARRIAGE, DIVORCE AND INHERITANCE: UNEQUAL POWER STRUCTURES AND WOMEN'S EQUALITY RIGHTS

The extent to which the body of laws that currently governs family relations in Egypt conforms to international standards on women's human rights is a complex and multifaceted question that admits no easy answer. Egypt's current personal status law is a fragmented body of legislative acts, based on the legal reforms of the 1920's, yet with a legacy of constant evolution. Comparing these laws with international standards that are based on inherently different fundamentals necessitates an inevitable element of reductionism. For while international law is seemingly gender-neutral, promoting formal equality between the sexes in all fields, laws derived from the Islamic *Sharīʿa* are highly gendered, since "many, though not all, legal rights and obligations are informed by the sexual identity of the individual."[1] Nonetheless, the hierarchical relationship established by the VCLT between international and municipal law, necessitates such an analysis, for practical reasons, in order to assess the degree of compliance of Egypt's domestic law with its international obligations.

The international standard for equality in family relations is potentially at odds with *Sharīʿa*-derived family law in five main areas: the right to enter into marriage (including full consent in marriage, minimum marriage age and marriage registration), rights during marriage, rights with regards to children, the dissolution of marriage, and the ownership and acquisition of property. This analysis therefore does not cover paragraphs (e) and (g) of article 16 of CEDAW as they do not raise much controversy; a Muslim woman is entitled to retain her maiden name, and decisions regarding occupation as well as number and spacing of children are dictated by the personal choices of the couple rather than by law. Paragraph (d) on equal rights and responsibilities as parents in matters

[1] Tucker (1998) at 185.

relating to children raises the same questions of custody, guardianship and wardship that are addressed within the context of paragraph (f) of article 16.

In most of the areas covered by this analysis, Egypt's family law does not treat women as equal in rights to men; in some cases their rights are clearly subordinate, while in others they are evidently superior. In general, Egypt's personal status law is built on a structure that restricts some of women's substantive rights in return for offering them a greater degree of financial rights. For instance, whereas the husband may divorce the wife with almost no restrictions, the wife may only obtain judicial divorce under limited circumstances. In turn, she is entitled to financial compensation from the husband in the case that he initiates divorce, whereas the opposite is not true. Recent attempts to grant women greater equality rights in the area of divorce through introducing *khulʿ* separation have come at the expense of some of the woman's post-divorce financial rights. In the areas of guardianship over children and inheritance, it can similarly be seen that men's greater maintenance obligations have been translated into more extensive substantive rights.

Whereas placing the burden of financial care squarely on the shoulders of the husband may be viewed as a mechanism to perpetuate the financial dependence of women, and hence entrench gender hierarchies, conversely, it may be regarded as a system of interdependence based on the value of reciprocity between the husband and wife. The large gap between what is envisioned by the principles of the *Sharīʿa*, in theory, and what the law, the courts, and social realities mandate, in practice, often means that what are intended as obligations to be assumed by the husband are translated into relationships of authority and domination. In spite of what the intention of the religious scriptures may be, statutory law is often at odds with egalitarian principles, and hence with international standards. Although several of the most discriminatory provisions of Egypt's family law have been addressed over the years, bringing it closer to international standards of equality, various aspects of the law remain in urgent need of reassessment.

The Same Right to Enter into Marriage; The Same Right Freely to Choose a Spouse and to Enter into Marriage with Their Free and Full Consent[2]

Free choice and consent in marriage are the main pillars of a healthy and equitable marital relationship, and are considered basic and inalienable human rights for both men and women. Although men may also be affected by a denial of their freedom to choose a spouse, it is women who suffer disproportionately from violations of this right. According to Egypt's family law, a marriage may not be contracted without the prospective wife's consent. If consent is lacking, the marriage is considered void and may be dissolved by a court.[3]

However, a number of Egypt's legal provisions and practices raise questions regarding the full enjoyment of the right to enter freely into marriage. The legal provisions most relevant to this question are those concerned with the regulation of minimum marriage age, registration of marriages and guardianship of women by a male relative for the purposes of concluding a marriage contract. Another important issue, one that is often overlooked in analyses of the right to consent in marriage, arises in the context of a forced resumption of a marriage that has ended through divorce or the return of a once missing husband, even in cases where his previous wife has remarried.

Minimum Marriage Age

The establishment of a minimum age for marriage is a basic right, which aims to protect the girl child from forced marriage, as well uphold her right to education and the highest attainable standard of health. Establishing a minimum age for marriage was amongst the first demands of the Egyptian feminist movement, and was finally achieved in 1923 after years of lobbying.[4] Law no. 56 of 1923 on Marriage Age, which remained in force until 2008, stipulated that the legal age for marriage was 16 years for girls and 18 years for boys. According to article 99/5 of the 1931

---

[2] Art. 16(1)(a), (b) and 16(2) of CEDAW; art. 23(3) of ICCPR.

[3] Combined 6th and 7th periodic reports of states parties, Egypt, Consideration of reports submitted by States parties under article 18 of the Convention on the Elimination of All Forms of Discrimination against Women, UN Doc CEDAW/C/EGY/7 (5 Sept 2008), at 75.

[4] Badran (1996) at 128. Twice in 1937, proposals submitted to the Chamber of Deputies failed to abolish the law.

Sharīʿa Court Regulations, no marital claim could be adjudicated in court unless both parties had attained the minimum marriage age *at the time of marriage*.[5]

These legislative provisions fell short of the international standards established by the CEDAW Committee, relying on the CRC's definition of a child, on a number of counts: the minimum age for women was below 18 years, and there was a clear distinction between the minimum ages required for women and for men. Moreover, the law did not prohibit child marriages; instead it relied on a procedural tool in the form of a restriction on the jurisdiction of courts to hear disputes arising from marriage contracts that were contracted prior to the parties reaching the legal age. As such, it sought to discourage child marriages by ensuring that the parties' rights would not be protected and enforced by the courts in case of denial of such rights. The law, however, was often circumvented through the forgery of birth certificates or bribing marriage notaries to overlook the young age of one or both of the parties. The procedural hurdles imposed by the State thus did not prove effective. Moreover, by denying recourse to the judiciary for parties of such marriage contracts, the law only served to further disadvantage girls that had been coerced into an early marriage.

In its consideration of Egypt's third periodic report and combined fourth and fifth periodic reports in 2001, the CEDAW Committee recommended that Egypt "amend the law on the legal age of marriage to prevent early marriage, in line with its obligations as a State Party to the Convention."[6] Embarking on a process to bring the relevant provisions in line with its international obligations, article 17 of Law no. 1 of 2000 stipulated that claims will not be adjudicated unless the spouses have attained the minimum marriage age *at the time of the claim*. This amendment aimed to address abuse faced by women whose marriages were contracted prior to attaining the legal age, and who suffered disproportionately as a result of the exclusion of their marriage contracts from the purview of the courts. In 2008, a new article, 31*bis*, was added

[5] *Shari'a* Court Regulations (1931). Replaced by article 17 (1) of Law no. 1 of 2000 which amended the jurisdictional bar to cases where the couple had not attained the minimum marriage age *at the time of hearing*.

[6] Report of the Committee on the Elimination of Discrimination against Women Twenty-fourth session (15 Jan–2 Feb 2001) and Twenty-fifth session (2–20 July 2001), UN Doc A/56/38, at para 353.

to the Civil Status Act No. 143 of 1994, stipulating that no marriage contract would be authenticated if the parties had not reached the legal age of 18 years, while prescribing administrative punishment in the case of violation.[7]

It has been argued that this law, which faced widespread criticism, will hardly deter guardians who are intent on marrying off their children at a younger age than the legal minimum, and who often go to great lengths to falsify birth certificates to that end.[8] Until recently, the fact that legal guardians faced no criminal penalty for such conduct[9] meant that girls were often married at ages far below the legal age for marriage. A field study conducted by Egypt's Ministry of Health in Upper Egypt in the late 1980s indicated that 44% of rural women married in the previous five years were under the legal age of 16 at the time of marriage.[10] However, the State stepped up its enforcement mechanisms in 2009, when it successfully brought charges against a number of officials involved in illegal child marriages, who received penalties ranging from fines to one-year prison sentences.[11] Legal guardians who have contracted their daughters' marriages prior to the legal age have also been punished as accomplices.

Marriage Registration

Article 16 (2) of CEDAW as well as the Convention on Consent to Marriage, Minimum Age for Marriage and Registration of Marriage (1964), to which Egypt is not a party, require States to make the registration of marriages compulsory. Obligatory registration of marriages places some checks on the ability of guardians to marry off minors,[12] and ensures women access to the judicial system to protect the rights arising from the marriage contract.

---

[7] Law No. 126 of 2008 amending the provisions of the Child Act (No. 12/1996); the Penal Code (No. 58/1937); and the Code on Civil Affairs (No. 143/1994), *Al-Jarida Al-Rasmiya* 15-06-2008, No. 24*Bis*, at 2–27. See Consideration of Egypt's combined 4th and 5th report, Committee on the Rights of the Child at para 92.

[8] Guenena and Wassef (1999) at 23.

[9] Ibid.

[10] 'Early Marriage: Child Spouses', *Innocenti Digest* no. 7 (United Nations Children Fund Innocenti Research Centre, March 2001) at 5.

[11] *Consideration of reports* submitted by States parties under article 12 (1) of the Optional Protocol to the Convention on the Rights of the Child on the sale of children, child prostitution and child pornography, Egypt, Committee on the Rights of the Child (7 March 2010) UN Doc CRC/C/OPSC/EGY/1 at para 57.

[12] 'Early Marriage', at 5.

When registering the marriage, the registrar (*ma'dhun*) must ensure that both spouses have consented to the marriage. Registration of marriages also guarantees that women can demand their rights, including maintenance (alimony) in the case of divorce. Women may also add provisions to the marriage contract claiming more extensive rights within the marriage; however, for all intents and purposes, this privilege is seldom utilized due to the social stigma attached to it.[13]

Registration of marriages has been obligatory in Egypt ever since the promulgation of Law no. 56 of 1923. The 1923 law also stipulates clearly that both parties must consent to the marriage. The issue of marriage registration arises with respect to customary or un-registered (*'urfi*) marriages. According to Decree-Law no. 78 of 1931, judges could not adjudicate cases in which the marriage was not registered, thus excluding *'urfi* marriages from the purview of the courts. This provision, originally intended to discourage unregistered marriages, was often abused by husbands who could easily deny that the marriage had taken place, thus depriving their wives of their legal rights.

The recently promulgated Law no. 1 of 2000 attempted to remedy this situation. Article 17 stipulates that customary marriages (*zawāj 'urfi*) previously unrecognised by the State, will be recognised in divorce cases as long as there is some form of documentation to prove the marriage.[14] Documentation typically takes the form of a contract signed informally by the parties, often in the presence of witnesses. In such cases, the wife may obtain a judicial divorce by recourse to the family court. Although this departs from the international obligation not to recognise unregistered marriages, it provides important protection for women who seek judicial divorces or sue for denial of parentage in the context of customary marriages. It thus constitutes an imperative demanded by feminist groups and dictated by social realities not foreseen by CEDAW.

Guardianship in Contracting a Marriage

The principle of guardianship is often erroneously understood as a license to force women into marriage without their consent. Guardianship in marriage is unregulated by statute in Egypt. As such, it is subject to the opinion of the *Ḥanafi* school according to which the principle of

[13] Rhoodie (1989) at 365.
[14] Law no. 1 of 2000, *Al-Jarida Al-Rasmiya*, (29 Jan 2000), Issue No. 4Bis, at 2–30.

guardianship is not based on compulsion, but rather on the principle of delegation. The guardian (*waly-al-amr*) may not, under any circumstance compel his ward to marry; he merely acts as the minor's agent or representative.[15] According to *Ḥanafi* doctrine, consent of the guardian is obligatory to contract a marriage by minors in general, be they men or women.[16] Consent of the guardian is unnecessary if the ward has attained majority age[17] (Egypt's Civil Code places that age at 21 years for both men and women).

The legal provisions on guardianship do not, therefore, discriminate between men and women, at face value. Consent of the parent or guardian in the case of the marriage of minors is a general principle that exists in the majority of the world's legal systems, and aims to uphold the voluntary nature of marriage and to ensure that the person contracting the marriage is capable of making a mature, fully informed decision.[18] In other words, the modern State "depends on age as a surrogate for maturity,"[19] which is the same approach adopted in Egypt's legal system.

The *Ḥanafi* school differs markedly from the *Māliki*, *Hanbali* and *Shafi'i* schools, on the determinant of 'maturity'. Whereas the latter three schools consider a woman 'mature' if she has been married previously (i.e. is no longer a virgin), according to *Ḥanafi* doctrine, maturity is a consequence of age. According to the three other schools, the woman may not contract her first marriage without her guardian's consent, even if she has reached majority age.[20] Any woman marrying for the first time is considered lacking in the maturity required to make an informed decision regarding her marriage, irrespective of her age.

Although the guardian may not, under any circumstances compel his ward to marry, according to the *Ḥanafi* school, he may invalidate a marriage contracted without his consent by virtue of the *kafā'a* (compatibility) doctrine. The principle of *kafā'a* is exclusively used to judge a man's compatibility or competence as a husband. Men, on other hand, are not required to prove the competence of the women they seek to marry, and a marriage may not be invalidated if the incompetence arises on the part

[15] Bek and Ibrahim (2003) at 120–121.

[16] Article 34 of Qadri Pasha's Collection of Shari'a Rules on Personal Status According to the Ḥanafi Doctrine. Full compilation in Bek and Ibrahim (2003).

[17] Article 51 of Qadri Pasha's collection.

[18] 'Developments—The Family', 93 *Harv. L. Rev* 1979–1980 at 1258–1259.

[19] Ibid. at 1258.

[20] Al-Hibri (1997).

of the wife.[21] The rules on *kafā'a* are derived from a number of prophetic traditions encouraging legal guardians to marry their ward to compatible men. The text of these *aḥādith* seems to suggest that the principle of *kafā'a* is intended to obligate guardians to act in the best interest of their ward, rather than as a license to annul a marriage contracted without the guardians' consent. The principle seems to apply equally, in theory, to men as well as to women.

Although there is no precise definition of *kafā'a*, *Qadri Pasha*'s collection considers family origin, occupation, and the amount of dower, factors in determining compatibility.[22] Other interpretations, however, which are also based on *Ḥanafi* doctrine, hold that social status and the amount of dower cannot be considered grounds for the invalidation of the marriage on the basis of incompatibility.[23] Such opinions define compatibility as strictly pertaining to the husband's piety in religious matters. Because the *Māliki*, *Ḥanbali* and *Shafi'i* schools do not allow for the woman to contract her own marriage without the guardian's consent, they do not recognise the right of the guardian to invalidate the marriage based on *kafā'a*.[24]

Although Egypt's family law allows for women who have reached majority age to contract their own marriage, this seldom occurs in practice. Social norms require women to be accompanied by a male guardian while contracting their marriage. Courts have also annulled marriages by reference to the *kafā'a* doctrine, although there are no studies to indicate the prevalence of this practice in recent jurisprudence.

It is often argued that the notion of guardianship, when practiced by women that have reached majority age, perpetuates the stereotype of women as dependent and immature, and hence demanding of a male family-member's protection. In practice, guardians may abuse their roles and, in some circumstances, invalidate their wards' marriages against the latter's will. The practice of guardianship may also exclude women from negotiating their marriage contracts, and hence prevent them from upholding many of their rights at the outset of marriage.[25] On the other hand, in cases where the guardian is well-informed and aware of the

---

[21] Article 62 of Qadri Pasha's collection.
[22] Articles 63–69. Ibid.
[23] *Egypt, Islamic Family Law Project*, available at http://www.law.emory.edu/ifl/legal/egypt.htm.
[24] Al-Hibri (1997).
[25] *Divorced from Justice* at 17.

ward's rights, guardianship has the potential to support and help the ward demand her rights in cases where the potential spouse is recalcitrant.

Fully enforcing the principle of consent requires positive steps to review the rules on guardianship in marriage, particularly the possible termination of a marriage contract by a guardian, as well as to prevent abuses of guardianship. Registrars should be required, by law, to seek the consent of the woman in person, and to explain to her directly the rights she has in marriage and the conditions she may stipulate in the marriage contract. Violations of this obligation should be deterred through serious penalties. According to some juristic opinions, guardianship may also be exercised by female relatives,[26] which is an option that should be examined and institutionalised.

Return of a Husband Who Is Missing or Assumed Dead

The issue of consent doesn't only arise at the outset of marriage. The personal status law provisions dealing with a 'lost' or 'missing' husband also raise important questions regarding the consent of the wife. According to the relevant legal provisions, the husband is considered deceased if he has been missing for a period of 4 years.[27] A decree may be given to that effect, after the specified time-period has elapsed, according to which the wife is allowed to remarry after observing the waiting period.

Having said that, controversy arises in cases where it is subsequently discovered that the 'missing' husband is, in fact, alive whether he actually returns to claim the wife or not. The law here differentiates between two separate cases. According to article 8 of Law no. 25 of 1920 as amended by Law no. 100 of 1985, if the wife has not remarried, and the 'missing' husband returns, or appears to be alive, then the wife 'is his' (i.e. she is still held to be his wife). In other words, she is automatically 'returned' to the once-missing husband, without requiring a new expression of consent. The second case, which is even more controversial, arises when the wife re-marries and her second husband 'consummates the marriage'. In such a case, the law distinguishes between a second husband that has acted in good faith, meaning that he is unaware that the previous

---

[26] Bek and Ibrahim (2003).

[27] Article 21 of Law no. 25 of 1929. This period is shorter if the husband was on board a sunken ship or in a plane crash or was a member of the armed forces and was engaged in hostilities.

husband is alive, and one acting in bad faith. In the case of good faith, the second husband is entitled to keep the wife, as long as the marriage was not contracted during the waiting period. The law is silent as to how to deal with a marriage contracted in bad faith, i.e with the second husband knowingly and deliberately concealing the fact that the first husband is alive. By implication, it seems that the second marriage would be annulled and the wife 'returned' to the first husband if he claimed her.

The continuation of the second marriage is, in essence, predicated on the second husband's intentions. The wife is literally treated as an object to be handed over between the two husbands, without any say in the decision. These provisions, which have no grounds in the *Sharīʿa*, deal with the wife like an object devoid of any desires, needs, feelings, or rights[28] in direct contravention of the principle of consent.

The Same Rights and Responsibilities during Marriage[29]

Egypt's personal status law distinguishes between the roles—and hence rights and obligations—of the husband and wife within the marital relationship. The husband is responsible for maintaining the wife and family, whereas the wife has no concomitant obligation. Although, in theory, this arrangement should result in greater financial security for women, and the support of a relationship based on partnership, in practice it leads to hierarchy in the marital relationship. Tradition imposes on women a duty to 'obey' their husbands, with several detrimental consequences, primary among which is the husband's perceived right to discipline the wife. The law further grants the husband additional privileges that lead to asymmetry in the marital relationship, including the right to marry polymagously.

The Husband's Maintenance of the Wife

Egypt's family law places the obligation to maintain the wife and family squarely on the husband's shoulders. The wife is not required to contribute to household expenditures, and is entitled to "full financial support during marriage and during the waiting period (*ʿiddah*) in case of

[28] See Nihad Aboul Komsan, 'Women Between Islamic Shari'a and Personal Status Laws', *The Egyptian Centre for Women's Rights* http://www.ecwregypt.org/English/researches/index.htm

[29] Art. 16(1)(c) of CEDAW and art. 23(4) of the ICCPR.

divorce."[30] The rationale is to guarantee women financial support in all stages of their lives either as daughters, wives, mothers or sisters, the financial burden of their sustenance falling onto male relatives. According to article 1 of Law no. 100 of 1985, maintenance is the obligation of the husband from the point at which the marriage contract comes into effect. The maintenance obligation includes the provision of food, housing, and clothing,[31] including cases where the wife has her own personal resources or is of another religion. Law no. 100 of 1985 departed from *Ḥanafi* doctrine by including medical expenses as part of the husband's maintenance obligation.[32]

According to Law no. 62 of 1976, maintenance claims are to be decided in a timely fashion and the Nasser Social Bank is to pay overdue maintenance debts. It specifies the exact portions of the husband's income that can be appropriated for maintenance dues as follows: 25 % for the wife and 35 % for one or two children (to be divided between the children by court). If he has both a wife *and* one or two children, they receive 40 % of his income to be shared between them.[33] The same rules apply in the case of alimony payments for a divorced wife and child support. In cases where the husband refuses to provide maintenance (or alimony), a court order may be executed on his property.[34] The value of the overdue maintenance is assessed in accordance with the husband's wealth when it was due (i.e. from the moment the husband stopped providing it) rather than at the time of the court's ruling. If the husband has no property, the wife is granted an immediate divorce.[35]

In order to overcome the problem of the non-payment of maintenance, Law no. 1 of 2000 revitalised the role of the Nasser Social Bank in enforcing overdue maintenance payments. According to the law, the Bank may automatically deduct maintenance dues from the husband's salary or pension if he is a public-sector employee. For non-public sector employees, the law requires that the maintenance dues be deposited in the Bank at the beginning of every month.[36] This system became operational in October 2004 with the promulgation of Law no. 10 of

[30] Jamal Badawy, 'Gender Equity in Islam', *World Assembly of Muslim Youth—Studies on Islam* at http://www.iad.org/books/GEI.html (last accessed 12/5/2005).

[31] Law no. 25 of 1920 as amended by Law no. 100 of 1985, art. 1.

[32] See Abu-Odeh (2004) at 1129.

[33] Law No. 62 of 1976 Modifying Some Rulings on Maintenance.

[34] Law no. 25 of 1920 as amended by Law no. of 100 of 1985, art. 4.

[35] Ibid.

[36] Law no. 1 of 2000, art. 72–75.

2004. If the husband still fails to pay his dues, he may face imprisonment for up to 30 days.[37]

Obedience of the Wife to Her Husband

Although maintenance of the wife theoretically provides some degree of financial security, it is contingent on the wife's 'obedience' to her husband. The wife may thus lose her right to maintenance if she proves to be 'disobedient' (*nāshiz*). According to article 212 of *Qadri Pasha*'s compilation, the wife must obey her husband in all matters that are considered his conjugal rights, and that are 'legitimate' under the *Sharīʿa*. Obedience entails that the wife must not leave the matrimonial home without her husband's permission, must share his bed when he asks her unless she has a legitimate excuse, 'preserve' herself and her honour, look after his wealth and property, and refrain from disposing of his property without his permission.[38]

The concept of 'obedience' (or *ṭāʿah*) as codified in Egypt's personal status law is described by al-Hibri as a "patriarchal, hierarchical construct" that forces the wife to 'submit' to her husband in fulfilment of the marriage contract. According to article 1 of Law no. 25 of 1920, as amended by Law no. 100 of 1985, the wife loses her right to maintenance in three cases: (1) if she commits apostasy; (2) if she refuses to 'surrender' herself to her husband (i.e. if she denies her husband conjugal rights, without a legitimate justification or for reasons out of the husband's control); (3) if the wife leaves the matrimonial home without the husband's permission, except in cases sanctioned by law, 'custom' or 'necessity'. Until 2000, the wife also needed her husband's formal consent in order to travel.[39] Article 1 also stipulates that a wife is considered disobedient, and thus subject to losing her maintenance, if she insists on working in spite of her husband's explicit disapproval. However, feminists succeeded in including a provision that the wife's work in such a case must involve 'abuse of right' or must be contrary to the interests of the family, which is a clear departure from *Ḥanafi* doctrine.[40]

---

[37] Law no. 1 of 2000 as amended by Law no. 91 of 2000, art. 76bis, *Al-Jareeda Al-Rasmiya*, Issue 21(a) (18 May 2000).

[38] See also Helal Youssef Ibrahim, *Mawsoo'at al ahwal al Shakhseya* [Encyclopaedia of Personal Status Law] (2002), 170.

[39] See discussion *supra* at p. 159.

[40] This article was upheld by the Supreme Constitutional Court, Decision no. 18, 14th Judicial year, *Official Gazette*, Issue 20, (15 May 1997).

According to article 11*bis*2 of Law no. 25 of 1929, as amended by Law no. 100 of 1985, the wife is not entitled to the husband's maintenance if she is disobedient. Such is the case if the wife refuses to return to the matrimonial home or *bayt al-ṭāʿah* (house of obedience) within a period of thirty days after the husband recalls her through a court order. According to article 6*bis*(2) of Law no. 100 of 1985, the wife may object to the court order recalling her to the 'house of obedience' within the thirty day limit, indicating her reasons for 'disobedience'. The court must attempt a conciliation upon whose failure the wife may initiate a procedure for divorce. If the wife fails to object within the specified time-limit, she loses her right to maintenance.

The wife's obedience is contingent upon the husband's good treatment and his protection of the wife's property rights. According to el-Guindy, the 'house of obedience' must fulfil a number of criteria. Primarily, the wife must feel secure in the home as well as have access to all the necessary facilities and sanitation services, an issue which is relative to the couple's social standing. The house must allow for the couple's privacy, but should be situated between 'good' neighbours who are near enough to be able to hear the wife's call for help and therefore be witnesses to what takes place between the couple.[41] This last requirement attests to the perversity of the relationship between the spouses in the 'house of obedience'; it is assumed that the husband may act violently against the wife, such that she needs the neighbours to stand witness in court.

The principle of obedience has been criticised fiercely for placing women in a subordinate position within the family. According to al-Hibri, the practice of *bayt al- ṭāʿah*, which originates from "the belief that a wife must remain in the conjugal home and obey her husband in exchange for his financial support," has no basis in either the *Quran* or the *Sunnah*.[42] Based on this proposition, the principle has been repeatedly contested by feminists who have succeeded in slightly eroding the husband's right to obedience. In 1967, after a large campaign led by Egyptian feminists, a Ministerial Order prohibited the use of the police to bring the wife back to the matrimonial home by force, which was previously possible under the *bayt al- ṭaʿah* provision. However, the principle of *ṭāʿah* still persists in Egypt's personal status law as a legal duty owed by wives

[41] El-Guindy (2000) at 406–407.
[42] Guenena and Wassef (1999) at 23.

to their husbands. Although it can no longer be used to force the wife to return to the conjugal home, it is often "used by men as a loophole to avoid alimony payments" to their wives.[43]

The principle of obedience as codified in Egypt's personal status law goes against the very core of the principle of gender equality espoused by the CEDAW. It proposes a stereotyped role for the husband as the dominant head of the household, and subsequently a role for the wife as necessarily submissive. This hierarchy between the genders is supposedly predicated on the principle of *qiwama*, by virtue of which it has been claimed that men have authority over their wives.[44] Such patriarchal interpretations of the principle of *qiwama*, on which present-day personal status law is based, clearly go against the spirit and the letter of articles 2(f) and 5 of the CEDAW, which place an obligation on State parties to change patriarchal views of the family that proscribe stereotyped and hierarchical roles for men and women. Although reforms have succeeded in increasing the wife's maintenance rights, and eroding the husband's obedience rights, they are still far from international standards of equality.

Violence against Women and the Husband's Right to Discipline the Wife

The principle of *ṭāʿah* or the wife's requisite obedience to her husband has entrenched the view that the husband has the right to discipline the wife in cases where she is disobedient. This view is supported by reference to verse 4:34 of the *Quran*, although various interpretations have been proposed for the word '*iḍribūhun*' that appears in the above-mentioned verse, including to 'abandon', 'admonish', and 'avoid' as opposed to the traditional interpretation that reads 'beat' or 'strike'.[45] Feminists have

[43] Ibid.

[44] Muslim feminists have longed discussed the principle of *qiwama* and its effects on gender relations in Islamic societies. For an analysis of the principle of *qiwama* see Al Hibri (1997), who argues that the word *qawwam* (the noun from *qiwama*) may simultaneously be interpreted to mean "head", "boss", "protector", "manager", "guide" or "advisor." Over the centuries, jurists have chosen the more authoritarian and patriarchal interpretations of the word to lend credence to the view that men have a superior status to women. See discussion *infra* at pp. 277–278.

[45] A detailed discussion of the rich linguistic debate over the actual meaning and intention of this verse, although extremely important, unfortunately lies outside the scope of this study. It should be noted, however, that there have been proposals to prohibit wife disciplining by reference to the prophetic tradition (in a process that uses arguments similar to those used to abolish slavery).

also referred to the Prophet's *Sunnah* to assert 'striking' was considered metaphorical, and not intended to hurt and humiliate.

A recent study by UNICEF indicated that 35% of women in Egypt "reported being beaten by their husband at some point in their marriage."[46] The husband's right to discipline the wife is not regulated by statute in Egypt. As such, the predominant opinion of the *Ḥanafi* school governs, allowing the husband to physically punish the wife in the case of disobedience "so long as no permanent damage is inflicted."[47] This provision grants judges a large degree of discretion in determining what extent of physical abuse is acceptable.

Although wife battering resulting in permanent damage is punishable under Egypt's criminal law, marital rape is not considered a criminal offence. In its third periodic report to the CEDAW Committee, Egypt claimed that its penal code (Law no. 58 of 1937) criminalised all forms of violence against women and regarded the degree of consanguinity as an aggravating factor.[48] The fourth and fifth periodic reports referred to Law no. 6 of 1998, which criminalises intimidation and the threat or use of force or violence against wives, children and parents. However, the shadow report of the World Organization Against Torture asserted that the abovementioned law was inadequate in protecting women, since wife battering was only considered a crime if it exceeded "the accepted limits of disciplining or if it result[ed] in certain injuries."[49] Furthermore, section 60 of the Criminal Code stipulates that "the provisions of the penal code shall not apply to any deed committed in good faith, pursuant to a right determined by virtue of the *Sharīʿa*."[50] This provision may potentially have the effect of shielding abusive husbands from legal penalty. The issue is thus one of inadequate penal provisions and poor interpretation and enforcement of the law, with the result that husbands may evade penal sanctions for perpetrating acts of violence acts against their wives.

---

46 Amnesty International, *Making Violence against Women Count Facts and Figures—a Summary*, Media Briefing, (March 5th, 2004) available at http://www.amnesty.org/fr/library/asset/ACT77/034/2004/fr/301b0c48-fabb-11dd-b6c4-73b1aa157d32/act770342004en.pdf.

47 Guenena and Wassef (1999) at 38.

48 See *Egypt's 3rd Periodic Report*, submitted to the CEDAW Committee, Part I, Chapter II.

49 Benninger-Budel, Carrin, *Violence against Women in Egypt*, Report prepared for the CEDAW Committee, 24th Sess., World Organization Against Torture (2001) available at http://www.omct.org/files/2001/01/2175/egypteng2001.pdf.

50 Law no. 58 of 1937, Egyptian Penal Code.

Such impunity is exacerbated by the widespread social acceptance of domestic violence as a legitimate means to discipline the wife. According to the 1995 National Population Centre Survey, almost 86 percent of women thought men were justified in beating their wives under certain circumstances. About 70 percent of the women aged fifteen to forty-nine thought that violence was justified if the wife refused sex. About 70 percent of women aged twenty to twenty-nine believed that a husband could beat his wife if she 'talked back' to him.[51] The prevalence of domestic violence in Egyptian society is indicative of the entrenched structural inequality between men and women.

Feminists in Egypt have tried to limit the incidence of violence against wives by giving battered women 'a way out' through making violence a ground for divorce based on harm. Law no. 25 of 1920 restricted the husband's ability to abuse the wife, since the concept of 'harm' was taken to include systematic maltreatment, in accordance with *Māliki* jurisprudence. However, judicial divorce for harm is up to the discretion of the judge, and the burden of proof, in such cases, lies on the plaintiff (the wife). It is often very difficult to prove that the wife has been subjected to violence, and that this violence has caused her 'harm' justifying a judicial divorce.

The problem is compounded by the predominantly male and largely conservative judiciary. Judicial conservatism is consecrated through adherence by courts to a number of so-called judicial 'principles' or legal precedents widely considered as having authoritative value. Among these is Principle 59 which stipulates that "a wife's return back to the home after having been harmed means that life could continue between them [the spouses], which does not constitute grounds for divorce later."[52] The courts also make exceptions based on the social standing of the wife. Mistreatment constituting 'harm' often has a higher threshold when dealing with women from poorer backgrounds. For instance, the Court of Cassation previously defined harm as the infliction of verbal or physical abuse on the wife in a way that does not befit her social standing.[53] Similarly, the Court of Appeals held that "what a woman of a particular social class

[51] *Divorced from Justice* at 14.

[52] Hajjar (2005) at 25. When the Court of Cassation enunciates a rule in three separate decisions of the Court, it becomes a legal principle that binds it in future cases. Although such precedents do not theoretically bind the lower courts, in practice, they usually strictly abide by them.

[53] Court of Cassation, Case no. 28, 29 (18/4/1962) See Abu-Odeh (2004) at 1137.

finds tolerable, another of a different social class, may not."[54] Such exercise of judicial discretion finds its foundations in the text of the law itself, which stipulates in article 6 that harm exists when the situation is intolerable "for her likes".[55]

Taken together, the practice of courts in Egypt suggests a gap between the legal protections afforded to women against domestic violence, on the one hand, and international standards, on the other. The 1996 Report of the UN Special Rapporteur on Domestic Violence indicates that the international definition of violence against women has a very low threshold. It is not limited to harm causing serious injury, but includes psychological and moral harm, intimidation, verbal abuse, and marital rape. In its consideration of Egypt's reports in 2000, the CEDAW Committee expressed its concern that "although efforts have been made, there is no holistic approach to the prevention and elimination of violence against women, including domestic violence, [and] marital rape."[56] Egyptian legislation should therefore be adapted to prohibit all forms of domestic violence, including intimidation, psychological violence, physical violence and marital rape. It should also put in place effective legal remedies for women that are victims of violence, including mechanisms to end impunity for perpetrators.

On the other hand, it should be noted that the government has exerted a notable effort to end the practice of female genital mutilation (FGM) also considered a form of violence that occurs within the family. Apart from the large-scale media and public education campaign instituted to end the practice, Law No. 126 of 2008 criminalized FGM by imposing a penalty on perpetrators that amounts to imprisonment for a period between three months and two years, or a fine.[57]

Polygyny: The Husband's Right to Marry Polygamously

Polygyny is permissible under Egyptian family law; a man may legally marry up to four wives, albeit with some restrictions. The battle to legally abolish or restrict polygyny has raged ever since the birth of the Egyptian

[54] Court of Appeals, Case no. 89, 82 (11/12/1965).

[55] Law no. 25 of 1929.

[56] *Report of the CEDAW Committee* 24th and 25th sessions at para 344.

[57] *The Shadow Report on the Status of Egyptian women* in matters of personal status and forms of violence against women according to CEDAW convention, Centre for Egyptian Women's Legal Assistance, available at http://www2.ohchr.org/english/bodies/cedaw/docs/ngos/CEWLAEgypt_45.pdf.

feminist movement. In the 1920's, feminists in Egypt campaigned against polygyny as an "attack on the dignity of the wife and the mother."[58] They called for the prohibition of polygyny, except in cases where the first wife could not bear children or suffered from an incurable disease.[59] Their demands were not based on attempted secularisation, but on a direct interpretation of the relevant *Quranic* verses, which stipulate that

> "If ye fear that ye shall not Be able to deal justly With the orphans, Marry women of your choice, Two, or three, or four; But if ye fear that ye shall not Be able to deal justly (with them) Then only one ... That will be more suitable, To prevent you From doing injustice."[60]

The feminist perspective is supported by a literal reading of the text. According to this interpretation, a man could marry up to four wives provided he treated them with perfect equality. Such equality was required with regards to both material as well as immaterial things, including affection.[61] Verse 4:3 stipulates that "Ye are never able to be fair and just as between women, Even if it is Your ardent desire ..."[62] According to the feminist interpretation, fulfilling the conditions for polygyny was practically impossible, and the recommendation was thus logically towards monogamy. Since the *Quran* had been revealed in a society that widely practiced polygamy, it was difficult to address through an absolute and immediate prohibition. The aim of these verses was to restrict the practice to four wives only, and adopt gradualism to eventually discredit it. Feminists thus assert that the persistence of polygyny goes against the spirit of the *Quran*. Similar interpretations were used to prohibit polygyny in Tunisia's personal status code.[63]

Among the first attempts to discourage polygyny was *Sheikh Muhammed 'Abdu's* proposal that the matter be placed under the authority of the courts. He suggested that a man be prohibited from taking on

---

[58] Feminist leader Hoda Sha'rawi, quoted in Badran (1996) at 128.

[59] Ibid.

[60] Verse 4:3, Translation by A. Youssef Ali.

[61] Commentary to Verse 4:3 by A. Youssef Ali. Available at http://www.quran4u.com/Tafsiraya/Index.htm.

[62] Verse 4:129. Translation by A. Youssef Ali. Pikthal's translation reads "Ye will not be able to deal equally between (your) wives, however much ye wish (to do so)."

[63] Amira Mashour, 'Islamic Law and Gender Equality. Could There Be A Common Ground?', 27 *Human Rights Quarterly* 2 (May 2005) at 568.

additional wives unless able to prove his financial capacity before a court, as well as pledging to "accord his wives equal attention."[64] Ten years later, in 1926, the *Mufti*'s suggestion was incorporated in the proposal for a revised personal status law.[65] The proposal was approved by the Cabinet, only to be vetoed by the King.[66] Later attempts to prohibit or restrict polygyny were also aborted.

In 1972 and 1974, *Aisha Rateb* (a feminist figure and former Minister of Social Affairs) made a similar proposal, eliciting strong opposition from conservatives. The proposal precipitated a protest march by *al-Azhar* scholars before the People's Assembly, forcing President *Sadat* to announce publicly that the Assembly would not contemplate any action on it.[67] In a less ambitious, yet important step in 1979, Decree-Law no. 44 was promulgated, restricting polygyny by granting the first wife the right to an automatic divorce in the case that her husband took on a second wife, without the need to establish the existence of 'harm.' While falling short of earlier feminist demands to prohibit the practice, this provision granted women a way out of a polygamous union.

However, with the annulment of the law, the wife's ability to get a judicial divorce became once more subject to proving that the polygamous marriage caused her 'harm', placing the matter within the court's discretion. Although polygyny is a 'dying custom' in Egypt, the reason for that is neither the existence of legal prohibitions nor procedural hurdles, but rather socio-economic factors which make it difficult for a man to support more than one household.[68] The campaign against polygyny is, however, "more than a fight against a declining social practice; it [is] an attack against patriarchal supremacy expressed in legalized asymmetrical sexual relations with psychological, social and economic implications for women."[69] According to this view, any legal culture that tolerates polygyny contributes to the prevalence of patriarchy, and perpetuates the subordination of women in all fields.

---

64 Badran (1996) at 129.
65 Articles 1 and 2 of the Draft Law Personal Status Law of 1926, in Bek and Ibrahim (2003) at 1055–1059.
66 Badran (1996) at 130.
67 Guenena and Wassef (1999) at 21.
68 Badran (1996) at 130.
69 Ibid.

The persistence of polygyny clearly contradicts Egypt's obligations under CEDAW and other international instruments. According to General Recommendation 21 of the CEDAW Committee,

> Polygamous marriage contravenes a woman's right to equality with men, and can have such serious emotional and financial consequences for her and her dependents that such marriages ought to be discouraged and prohibited. The Committee notes with concern that some States parties, whose constitutions guarantee equal rights, permit polygamous marriage in accordance with personal or customary law. This violates the constitutional rights of women, and breaches the provisions of article 5 (a) of the Convention.

In its consideration of Egypt's third periodic report and combined fourth and fifth periodic reports, the CEDAW Committee expressed concern at the "continued legal authorization of polygamy" and urged Egypt to "take measures to prevent the practice of polygamy in accordance with the provisions of the Convention and the Committee's General Recommendation 21."[70]

In 2009, the National Democratic Party announced that it would propose an amended personal status law that would restrict polygyny by requiring the express authorisation of a court. The law would also place more weight on ending the practice through stipulations in the marriage contract by both the wife and the husband. On one hand, the wife's inclusion of a condition in the marriage contract preventing her husband's subsequent marriage would have to be enforced by the court. On the other hand, the wife would be entitled to an immediate and automatic divorce if her husband took on a second wife without having reserved such a right clearly in the first marriage contract.[71] The draft law, which was due to be presented to parliament in 2010, has been postponed.

In support of the government's efforts, various scholars from *al-Azhar* have put forward the argument that Islam only allows for polygyny in very limited circumstances. They assert that a literal reading of the *Quranic* verses on polygyny, in their proper context, reveals that this practice is permitted only if the second wife is a widow that cannot

[70] *Report of the CEDAW Committee* 24th and 25th sessions at para 355.

[71] *Ishtirāt huṣūl arragol ʿala mowafaqat al-maḥkama itijāh litaqyīd taʿadud azawjāt bimisr, wal-azhar yarfoḍ al-talāq al-shīʿi* [Requiring the Court's Approval with a view to Restricting Polygyny in Egypt, and al-Azhar Rejects Shiʾite Divorce] Available at www.alarabiya.net (16 Feb 2009).

maintain her orphaned children. In other words, polygyny was tolerated in the early days of Islam as a form of social solidarity when men were lost in battle leaving behind widows and orphans with no source of income.[72] Although it doesn't prohibit polygyny altogether, the proposed draft has been staunchly opposed by many scholars[73] and is expected to draw a great deal of hostility when presented to parliament. If promulgated, it would undoubtedly represent an important achievement for Egyptian women, bridging the gap between Egypt's domestic law and international standards of protection.

The Same Rights As Parents; The Same Rights and Responsibilities with Regard to Guardianship and Wardship[74]

Egypt's personal status law also differentiates between the rights and responsibilities of spouses, vis-à-vis their children, based on the traditional division of labour between the genders that renders the father as guardian and provider, and the mother as caregiver. This view has many implications for guardianship and maintenance of children, as well as custody rights for divorced couples. Although women are disadvantaged in relation to legal guardianship rights, the law clearly favours them in the area of child custody.

Guardianship of Children and Maintenance (Child Support)

In accordance with *Ḥanafi* doctrine, Egypt's personal status law differentiates between custody (*ḥaḍānah*) over children, on the one hand, and legal guardianship (*wilāyah*) and maintenance (including child support in the case of divorce), on the other. The latter are primarily the obligation of the father, even in cases where the children are in the mother's exclusive custody. As such, the father is always the legal guardian over his children, and in his absence guardianship passes on to the paternal grandfather. Although the law does envisage the possibility of granting the mother guardianship, this does not seem to be the case except in exceptional circumstances. The father has a concomitant obligation to provide financially for his children.

---

72 Ibid.

73 Ibid.

74 Art. 16(1)(d) and (f) of *CEDAW* and art. 23(4) of the *ICCPR*.

The father's maintenance obligation towards the child differs markedly from that towards the wife; it extends beyond food, clothing and lodging to include education and preparation for adulthood.[75] The child's disobedience does not relieve the father of providing maintenance. Article 18*bis*2 of Law no. 25 of 1929 as amended by Law no. 100 of 1985 stipulates that the father is under an obligation to provide his minor children with maintenance, if they don't have their own personal resources, until the son reaches the age of fifteen and the girl marries or is able to earn her own income. Where the son suffers a handicap or is unable to earn a living for any other reason, including the desire to pursue studies, the father is obliged to provide maintenance even if the son is over fifteen years of age.[76] Maintenance is provided according to both the child's needs and the father's means (*biqadr yassrihi*), and is due retroactively from the point at which the father stopped providing for the child.[77] These provisions are enforced through the Family Insurance System Fund of the Nasser Social Bank, under whose terms the father may face imprisonment for failure to comply.[78] The same rules apply in the case that the man and woman are divorced, in which case the father pays his maintenance dues as child support, even when the children are in the mother's custody. The father is also required to provide a suitable dwelling for the divorced wife and their children as long as they are in her custody.

The maintenance liability placed on the father entails that he has the right to 'generally supervise' his child's upbringing. More specifically, the father is considered the child's legal guardian, and as such has the right to manage and dispose of his/her property. Guardianship rights also comprise the responsibility to act as the marriage guardian. According to article 1 of the Egyptian Law on Rules of Guardianship over Money,[79] the father has guardianship rights over his children, whether sons or daughters, until they attain the age of twenty-one. The law severely restricts the guardian's ability to dispose of the child's property, requiring the Courts' permission for transactions of significant value. In 2008, the Child Law was amended to allow the parent exercising custody to

[75] Keith Hodkinson, *Muslim Family Law: A Sourcebook* (1984) at 310.
[76] Law no. 25 of 1929 as amended by Law no. 100 of 1985, art. 18*bis*2.
[77] Ibid.
[78] Law no. 10 of 2004.
[79] Law no. 119 of 1952.

exercise guardianship with regards to the child's education.[80] The effect of this provision is to almost exclusively establish the divorced mother's guardianship rights over her children's education, since the law grants her custody for almost the whole duration of their schooling.

If the father is incapable of exercising guardianship rights (if he has, for instance, been convicted of any number of specific crimes, including rape)[81] guardianship is passed on to the paternal grandfather unless the father has specifically appointed another legal guardian. In certain cases, the Court may appoint a guardian.[82] Unlike common perception, the mother may also be awarded guardianship over her children, according to article 12 of Law no. 118 of 1952,[83] although this is rarely practiced.

Placing the maintenance obligation squarely on the father's shoulders, while granting him priority with regards to guardianship seems to be at odds with the text of article 16(f) of the CEDAW, which calls for "equal rights and responsibilities as parents," including guardianship and wardship. In its General Recommendation 21, the Committee held that "most States recognize the shared responsibility of parents for the care, protection and maintenance of children" and that,

> The shared rights and responsibilities enunciated in the Convention should be enforced as law and as appropriate through legal concepts of guardianship, wardship, trusteeship and adoption. States parties should ensure that by their laws both parents, regardless of their marital status and whether they live with their children or not, share equal rights and responsibilities for their children.[84]

This interpretation seems to equate between 'shared' and 'equal' rights and responsibilities. Its strict application would require the wife to contribute to maintenance expenses, while allowing the divorced husband greater custody rights. The father's obligation to provide for the family, however, is a principal tenet of *Sharīʿa*-derived personal status law. Its aim is to relieve the wife of the burden of maintenance, particularly since she traditionally bears the brunt of child-rearing and hence may not have

[80] *Second Shadow Report for the CEDAW Coalition*, Egyptian Association for Community Participation Enhancement (EACPE), (2009), at 60 available at http://www2.ohchr.org/english/bodies/cedaw/docs/EACPE_E.pdf.

[81] Article 2 of Law no. 118 of 1952.

[82] Articles 29–31 of Law no. 118 of 1952.

[83] But see *Shadow Report of the Egyptian NGOs coalition on the CEDAW* (December 2000) at 36.

[84] General Recommendation no. 21, CEDAW, 13th Session, (1994).

the opportunity to earn a living to support herself as well as her children. Although the father (husband) is obliged to maintain the mother (wife) and the children, she has no such commitment, regardless of her wealth. This distinction and the concomitant financial obligations of the man, is one that is consistently demanded by women in court, yet is not envisioned by CEDAW.

Although the Egyptian legal framework for guardianship, custody and child support is not one of 'equal' responsibility, it can be said to conform to a standard of 'shared' responsibility that seems to be alien to the strict equality provisions of the CEDAW. Many Egyptian women resort to the judiciary to demand maintenance rights for themselves and their children. Feminists have also long demanded the broadening of such rights in return for the wife's burden of child-bearing, nursing and child-rearing, a relationship widely accepted "as part of a system of interdependence and reciprocity".[85]

This different conception of rights, and the specific socio-economic environment in which it operates, must be taken into consideration when evaluating the compatibility of Egypt's laws with international human rights standards. If a standard of complete equality is to be applied, it would necessarily entail that the maintenance (and child support) obligation also be shared equally between the father and mother, an obligation that not all women would be ready to accept. It should be noted however, that recalcitrant husbands and fathers have found ways to circumvent court procedures regarding maintenance. Certain reforms should therefore be introduced to deal with cases where the mother is the *de facto* provider, due to the absence of the father or a male agnate legally required to provide maintenance. In cases where the father defaults on child support, certain measures should be considered including possibly transferring legal guardianship to the mother.

Child Custody

Egypt's personal status law has very specific provisions relating to custody over children in the case of the dissolution of marriage. The child's custody is shared consecutively between both parents. Traditionally, mothers in Egypt retained custody over their children until the sons turned seven years of age and the daughters nine. Custody would then

---

[85] Behrouz (2003) at 1151.

pass on to the father, in accordance with the teachings of the *Ḥanafi*, *Ḥanbali* and *Shafiʿi* jurisprudential schools. The rationale was that the younger child was in need of maternal love and affection, while the maturing child was more in need of the father's discipline and guidance.[86]

The *Maliki* school held similar views with regards to custody over the son; however, the mother was to be granted custody over the daughter until the latter's marriage. In 1985, feminists achieved an important victory by incorporating the provisions of the *Maliki* school into Law no. 100 of 1985, extending maternal custody until the son turned ten years old and the daughter twelve, during which time the mother received a custody fee from the father. According to article 18 of the same law, throughout the duration of the mother's custody, the father was obliged to provide an independent residence for the children and their mother. The judge could prolong the mother's custody until the son turned fifteen and the daughter married if this was considered to constitute 'the child's best interest.' However, in the latter case, the wife would not not earn the custody fee for the duration prolonged by the judge, neither would she be entitled to a residence.

According to article 20 of Law no. 25 of 1929 as amended by Law no. 100 of 1985, both parents have the right to visit their children (as do the grandparents in the case that the parents are deceased) upon their mutual agreement. If the parents fail to reach an agreement on the frequency of such meetings and the venue, the judge may decide on their behalf. This provision is in full agreement with article 9 of the Convention on the Rights of the Child, which stipulates that in cases where the child is separated from a parent through a court decision, the State must ensure the child's right to "maintain personal relations and direct contact with both parents on a regular basis, except if it is contrary to the child's best interests."[87]

Custody over children is not limited to the child's parents, but extends to the whole extended family. According to article 20, in cases where the mother is deceased, or loses custody over the child, the maternal grandmother is awarded custody, followed in line by the paternal grandmother, then full sisters, then half-sisters, and so on. Priority is always granted to

---

86 Badran (1996) at 132. Arguably, such reasoning perpetuates the stereotype of women as necessarily emotional and men as more rational and hence more mentally capable.

87 Article 9 of the *Convention on the Rights of the Child*.

women in the family as long as the child is in the early childhood years. Once the child has passed the legal age, or there are no women in the family, custody passes on to the father, and male agnates from the father's family, then males from the mother's family. If the mother remarries, she may lose custody to another family member, in the following order: the maternal grandmother, maternal aunt, paternal grandmother and paternal aunt.

The provisions on child custody in the 1985 law were criticised on a number of grounds, particularly for discriminating between the girl child and the boy-child, whose custody originally reverted automatically to the father at age ten. In March 2005, however, article 20 was amended so as to treat both children equally and to give the mother more extensive custody rights.[88] According to this amendment, both children would remain in their mother's custody until they reached fifteen years of age. At that point, instead of automatically transferring custody of the son to the father, the judge would have to consider the son's preference. The same provision holds true for the daughter. According to article 70 of Law no. 1 of 2000, were a dispute to arise regarding custody, the Public Prosecutor may carry out an investigation to discern where the 'best interest of the child' lies, and to grant custody on that basis, until a court ruling is issued resolving the matter.

These amendments are particularly significant for a number of reasons. First and foremost, they take into consideration the issue of the best interest of the child. As it stands, the law does not seek to grant either the mother or the father a distinctive advantage because of their gender. The arrangement stems from a genuine belief that the interest of the child is best served if they spend their early childhood years with a female family member. At age 15, the child is arguably old enough to make an informed decision regarding his/her own custody arrangements, and may thus choose to be with either parent.

It cannot be argued that sharing custody between the parents in such a way constitutes discrimination against women. Article 16(f) of the CEDAW clearly establishes the equality of the spouses with regards to guardianship, wardship and trusteeship, which includes custody rights. Although the CEDAW Committee did not clarify the precise meaning of

---

[88] See Reem Leila, 'More Maternal Rights', *Al-Ahram Weekly* 10–16 March 2005, available at http://weekly.ahram.org.eg/2005/733/eg9.htm.

equality in custody rights, it affirmed the principle that "the best interests of the child shall be the paramount consideration."[89] Equality in custody rights is therefore not an absolute right; it is qualified by the principle of the 'best interests of the child.'

Although the 'best interest' standard enjoys international consensus as a general principle governing custody arrangements, its exact meaning is highly contested. As such, the 'best interest' principle is decidedly subjective, and may fall under different interpretations depending on the cultural context.[90] In practice, the standard of the 'best interest of the child' is left to the discretion of domestic judges and is therefore a principle whose application differs from one setting to another and from one culture to another.[91]

Until the recent amendments were introduced, the 'best interest of the child' was upheld through granting custody to the mother in early childhood years and then transferring it to the father at the age of 'maturity'. It was argued that the judge may always use his discretion to prolong the mother's custody in cases where the application of the law would lead to a situation that was not in the child's 'best interest.' However, the legislators' understanding of the 'best interest' principle has evolved since then. It is now seen as entailing that the child spend more time with the mother (until they reach fifteen years of age) and then take part in the decision affecting later custody arrangements.

The new draft personal status law due to be presented to parliament includes important amendments in the area of parent's visitation rights. As long as the child is in the mother's custody, they must be accompanied by the mother or grandfather when visiting the father. The recently proposed amendments thus greatly increase the mother's rights in the area of child custody, giving her the upper hand in raising her children and influencing them throughout the period of upbringing. The expansion of such rights is clearly not based on a principle of absolute 'equality' of the spouses, which if applied, would greatly erode the mother's rights, and arguably disadvantage the child.

---

89 *General Recommendation no. 21*, CEDAW.

90 Abdullahi An Naim, 'Cultural Transformation and Normative Consensus on the Best Interest of the Child', 8 *Int'l J. of L. & Family* (1994) at 62.

91 Ibid.

The Same Rights and Responsibilities upon the Dissolution of Marriage[92]

According to the CEDAW, the husband and wife should have equal rights in ending the marriage, just as they had equal rights to begin within, and throughout the duration of the marriage. In Egypt, divorce legislation is the area of personal status law that has been most extensively reformed, particularly with the adoption of Law no. 1 of 2000 which granted women important rights in the area of divorce.

Under Egypt's personal status law, divorce results in three different outcomes: (1) revocable divorce (*talāq raji'i*), whereby the husband can retrieve the wife without the need for a new marriage contract; (2) irrevocable divorce (*talāq bā'in baiynouna soghra*), whereby the couple must write a new marriage contract if they wish to resume the marriage; (3) irrevocable separation (*talāq bā'in baiynouna kobra*), in which case the couple may not remarry unless the wife marries another man and divorces (or is widowed). This final type of divorce occurs in the case that the husband has divorced the wife three times, or if the wife resorts to *khul'* divorce.

In each of the three scenarios the wife must observe a *'iddah* or waiting period during which she has the right to receive maintenance, but may not re-marry. The waiting period lasts for three menstrual cycles, or a period of three months if the woman is no longer menstruating. For a pregnant woman, the waiting period lasts until she gives birth (or miscarries). In any case, it may not exceed one year from the date of divorce.[93]

Whereas there has been much criticism of the *'iddah* in recent scholarship on Muslim women's rights, one must examine the issue in its proper context in order to arrive at a fair judgment. The objective of observing the *'iddah* is two-fold; first of all, it grants the couple a 'cooling off' period in the case of revocable divorce, during which time they can reconsider and resume the marriage without the need for a new contract. At another level, it ensures that any children conceived to the separated couple are attributed to their rightful father. Although it may be argued that modern technology has rendered the second justification of *'iddah* obsolete, in all

---

92 Art. 16(1)(c) of *CEDAW*, and art. 23(4) of the *ICCPR*.

93 Law no. 25 of 1929, art. 18.

practicality, it would be nearly impossible to employ modern technology (such as DNA testing) to the thousands of divorce cases that occur every year, in order ascertain the child's true father.

*Unilateral Divorce (*Talāq*) by the Husband*

Under Egypt's family law, the husband has the right to unilateral and unconditional divorce (*talāq*) also known as repudiation. This type of divorce is revocable, up to the third time. However, after three divorces, it becomes an irrevocable separation. As described earlier, the Decree-Laws of 1920 and 1929 placed a number of limits on the husband's right to unilateral divorce. This type of divorce also gave rise to various financial rights guaranteed to the divorced wife. In addition to the deferred dowry (*mahr*) and maintenance during the waiting period, the divorced wife is entitled to compensation (*mut'a*) assessed at two years' maintenance, at least. Further marginal restrictions on unilateral repudiation were incorporated into Law no. 100 of 1985, which placed procedural prerequisites for repudiation, with the aim of ensuring that the husband would not resort to unilateral divorce recklessly. For instance, article 5*bis* of Law no. 25 of 1929 as amended by Law no. 100 of 1985 requires the husband to register the divorce within 30 days of its occurrence. If the wife is absent from the registration proceedings, the registrar is under an obligation to inform her of the divorce. According to article 23*bis* of Law no. 25 of 1929 as amended by Law no. 100 of 1985, the husband's failure to abide by this provision may lead to a six month prison sentence. The registrar's failure to comply with his duties is also penalised; he may face a fine and a one-month prison term.

Feminist efforts throughout the decades to make unilateral divorce subject to a court decision have been unsuccessful to date. The draft personal status law introduced in 2009 supposedly included a provision that would require the presence of two witnesses in order for the divorce to take legal effect. However, this proposal was rejected by the Islamic Research Academy (*magma' al behooth al-Islāmiyya*)[94] on the grounds that it was based on Shi'ite jurisprudence and obstructed the husband's right to divorce.[95] Such reasoning is problematic, since various provisions

[94] According to Law no. 103 of 1961, the Islamic Research Academy is the highest institution for theological research, and therefore has the mandate to research and approve issues related to the *Shari'a*.

[95] *Ishtirāt huṣūl arragol ...*

in Egypt's family law have been inspired by Shiʿite doctrine, particularly in the area of inheritance. Unfortunately, the husband's right to divorce his wife at will thus remains largely unrestricted, with very slim prospects for reform in the near future.

*Unilateral Divorce through Delegation (*ʿIsma*)*

Egypt's personal status law grants the wife equal rights in the area of divorce by granting her the option of unilateral repudiation through delegation, known as *ʿisma*. This is in accordance with *Ḥanafi* doctrine, which allows the husband to delegate to his wife the right to divorce herself, before or after the marriage takes place. Although this option has always been legally available to Egyptian women, it is seldom practiced for the negative social stigma it carries.[96] It has been argued that *ʿisma* doesn't grant women an equal right to divorce, since it is contingent upon the husband's concurrence at the signing of the marriage contract. However, it is a legal right granted to women by law and they may insist on resorting to it if they so desire at the outset of marriage. The fact that divorce through delegation is rarely practiced indicates poor awareness and determination by women to exercise their rights.

In the 1980's, a new marriage contract was proposed, which granted both spouses the right to divorce. Although it allowed for "the inclusion of conditions agreed upon by the partners" by failing to include a checklist of such conditions, the new marriage contract intimidated and discouraged women from using this tool.[97] The new standard-format marriage contract was not adopted until the year 2000.[98] It created for the first time a checklist of conditions which the wife could demand in order to place herself on an equal footing with her husband. None of these clauses were compulsory; however, they allowed the prospective wife to be fully aware of her rights before the marriage took place.[99]

Although the right to divorce by delegation of the husband exists in theory, and is included in the marriage contract checklist, sharing the right to divorce is a rare phenomenon in Egypt. Its use has been widely curtailed due to social pressures that discourage women, as well as the widely prevalent stereotype that women, by virtue of their emotional

[96] Rhoodie (1989).
[97] Ibid.
[98] Bernard-Maugiron and Dupret (2002) at 15.
[99] Guenena and Wassef (1999) at 44.

nature, would abuse any right to automatic divorce, leading to instability in the family.[100] Divorce by delegation does not affect women's full enjoyment of their post-divorce financial rights.

*Judicial Divorce (*Tatlīq*)*

Women gained the right to sue for a judicial divorce based on 'harm' or 'injury' (*ḍarar*) under Law no. 25 of 1929, which was amended by Law no. 100 of 1985. According to article 6 of the amended law, a wife may obtain an irrevocable judicial divorce if she proves harm caused by: (1) non-maintenance of the husband (2) serious or incurable defect of the husband, (3) harm caused by discord (4) moral or material harm due to the husband's polygamous marriage, (5) the husband's disappearance or imprisonment. According to decision no. 432 of the Court of Appeals of 1964, the definition of 'harm' includes the husband's systematic maltreatment of the wife, in either a verbal or physical manner, that is not suitable to women of her standing (*la yalīq bimithliha*).[101] Judicial divorce is considered a single irrevocable divorce that is subject to appeal.

Law no. 100 of 1985 proved detrimental when enforced by the courts. Women seeking judicial divorce often spent several years in the process (according to estimates, the average life of a judicial divorce case was about seven years).[102] Even if the wife obtained a ruling for divorce, it could not be executed unless it passed through all three degrees of litigation.[103] This was to avoid a situation where a woman would obtain a judicial divorce and subsequently re-marry, only to have the court's decision reversed by a higher court. In such cases the woman would find herself in a situation of bigamy; her new marriage could be forcibly annulled, and she would have to return to her first husband.

In spite of its shortcomings, judicial divorce for harm was initially considered a substantial advancement for women, who previously could not hope to initiate divorce proceedings except in very limited circumstances. When put to practice, however, thousands of women suffered significant hardship for their inability to prove the existence of 'harm' justifying divorce. Divorce procedures were also often protracted, with

100 Ibid.

101 Ibrahim (2002) at 397.

102 Brown (1997).

103 *Shadow Report of the Egyptian NGOs Coalition on the CEDAW* at 35.

no guarantee of success at the end of the process. The situation was compounded by a conservative judiciary, completely dominated by male judges, who unnecessarily restricted application of the relevant legislative provisions. Many women thus remained stranded in unhappy marriages with little possibility of separation. Media reports estimate that there are three-quarters of a million unsettled divorce cases in Egypt's family courts.[104]

Law no. 1 of 2000 addressed the administrative hurdles delaying divorce procedures by streamlining the judicial process and decreasing all fees related to the litigation process. It also stipulated that the Court of Cassation must issue decisions on divorce cases within six months of filing the case, during which time the wife could not remarry. This was meant to ensure that women would only remarry after all stages of the litigation process had been overcome and the judgment was final. As such, there would be no more room for a court's judgement to be overturned after the wife had remarried, forcing her to return to her first husband in violation of the principle of consent. In cases of judicial divorce, as in the case of unilateral divorce by the husband, the wife is entitled to her full financial rights.

Khulʿ *Divorce*

On January 26th, 2000, the Speaker of Egypt's People's Assembly announced the adoption of Law no. 1 of 2000. After ten years of negotiation, the law introduced a third type of divorce, known as *khulʿ*, by virtue of which the wife may obtain an irrevocable judicial separation, if she so desires, for no fault of the husband's. Article 20 of the new law granted women the right to obtain an irrevocable judicial divorce (*khulʿ*), on condition of the restitution of the dower to the husband and the relinquishment of the right to alimony.[105] According to article 20,

> The two spouses may agree between themselves upon *khulʿ*, but if they do not agree mutually and the wife files a claim requesting *khulʿ*, and ransoms herself and releases herself from her husband by *khulʿ* (*khālaʿat zawjiha*) by forfeiting all of her lawful financial rights, and restores to him the dower he gave to her, then the court is to divorce her from him.[106]

---

[104] Arabi (2001) at note 8.
[105] Ibid. at 3.
[106] Law no. 1 of 2000, art. 20.

In its current formulation, the provision accords full weight to the wife's desire to separate from her husband. His consent is not necessary; the wife may literally divorce herself if she so wishes, on condition of the forfeiture of all her financial rights.[107] The wife must, however, submit to a reconciliation attempt, carried out by two mediators appointed by the court. The reconciliation attempt may not exceed 3 months.[108]

In the case that the couple have children, there may be a second reconciliation attempt of three months, which is separated from the first attempt by a period of thirty to sixty days. If the spouses are not reconciled, the judge "is required to pronounce the divorce, even against the husband's will."[109] The wife is not required to prove 'harm' or to ground her petition in any reason other than that she can no longer bear life with her husband. According to section 2 of article 20,

> The court shall not grant a divorce by *khulʿ* until there has been an attempt at reconciling the two spouses, and after it has appointed two arbitrators to undertake the endeavour to reconcile them within a period not exceeding three months … and after the wife declares explicitly that she detests life with her husband and that continuation of married life between them is impossible and that she fears that she will not maintain God's limits due to this detestation.

All four *Sunni* schools agree that the wife's right to custody over her children is not affected by the *khulʿ* procedure, neither are the children's maintenance rights. This is reflected in section 3 of article 20. They are also in agreement as to the necessity of a reconciliation attempt before the court grants the divorce.[110] According to sections 4 and 5 of article 20:

> The separation effected by *khulʿ* is, under all circumstances, an irrevocable divorce (*talāq bāʾin*); and the court's decision is, under all circumstances, not subject to appeal (*taʿn*), in any of the forms of appeal.

As such, the law stipulates that divorce by *khulʿ*, unlike judicial divorce on the grounds of 'harm' is a single irrevocable divorce, and is not subject to appeal. This provision is also in accordance with the opinions of all four jurisprudential schools. In sum, there are four main elements of the *khulʿ* procedure as envisioned by article 20, namely: (1) it is initiated by the wife; (2) the wife must forfeit her financial rights, including the

[107] Bernard-Maugiron and Dupret (2002).
[108] Ibid.
[109] Ibid. at 14.
[110] El-Guindy (2000) at 349.

dowry and alimony, but not her rights with regards to child custody and support; (3) the consent of the husband is not required; (4) the divorce is irrevocable and may not be appealed. Although the *khulʿ* law does not grant women the right to divorce on an equal footing with men, it undoubtedly represents a huge advancement for women intent on leaving an unhappy marriage. It demonstrates that Egypt's legislature has endorsed the practice of *ijtihād* to legislate new laws that grant women more extensive rights, without prejudice to the principles of the *Sharīʿa*.

In its consideration of Egypt's third, and its combined fourth and fifth periodic reports, the CEDAW Committee 'took note' of the adoption of the new law, but expressed concern that it discriminated against poorer women, who wouldn't be able to afford repaying the dowry and relinquishing the right to alimony (maintenance).[111] The Committee recommended that Egypt reconsider the law so as to allow women the right to unilateral divorce without having to forego their financial rights.

However, a correct understanding of the practice of dowry and alimony payment reveals that this argument is inaccurate. Dowry and alimony are, as a general custom, proportionate to the woman's financial and social standing; the richer the wife the more she receives in terms of both dowry and alimony, and thus the more she will be giving up if she opts for *khulʿ* divorce. Although the prospect of giving up the dowry and alimony could arguably act as a disincentive for all women, in a general sense, it is short-sighted to claim that the law discriminates between rich and poor women. Unlike divorce initiated by the husband, the law also does not require women who initiate divorce to pay additional compensation or alimony to their divorced husbands, although equal treatment would mandate such a settlement.

In practice the financial aspect of the new law doesn't seem to have deterred women from initiating *khulʿ* divorce. However, many feminist activists have called for an amendment of the procedure to require that the wife return only her dowry, and no more, in conformity with the prophetic precedent,[112] without needing to forfeit all financial rights. Although such an amendment might be conceivable,[113] the CEDAW

[111] *Report of the CEDAW Committee* 24th and 25th sessions at para 323, 328.

[112] Aboul Komsan, 'Women Between Islamic Shari'a and Personal Status Laws'.

[113] This, of course, is countered by the notion that alimony is intended to offset the harm suffered by the wife, which does not arise in no-fault divorce.

Committee's recommendation that *khul*ʿ be amended so as not to affect any of the wife's financial rights is not only short-sighted, but also manifestly inequitable towards a man who is divorced for no fault of his own.

Post-Divorce Financial Rights

The principle of equality in the dissolution of marriage theoretically includes equality in post-divorce financial rights. According to the 'Western liberal' model, the law should treat the husband and wife equally, including in the payment of divorce settlements, alimony and child support. For example, the US Supreme Court ruled in 1979 that it is unconstitutional to limit alimony payments to the divorced wife while excluding the husband.[114] Personal status legislation in Egypt clearly distinguishes between the financial obligations of the wife and the husband, the latter usually bearing the brunt of such obligations after divorce, as he does throughout the duration of marriage. By law, the wife is compensated for divorce initiated by the husband and for divorce based on harm. In these two cases, the divorced wife is entitled to certain financial rights, whereas the husband generally is not.

Article 18*bis* of Law no. 25 of 1929 as amended by Law no. 100 of 1985 provides that the divorced wife is entitled to alimony (*nafaqa*) throughout the waiting period or until the termination of pregnancy or nursing, when applicable, and to compensation (*mut*ʿ*a*) in the case that the divorce occurred without her consent and "was not due to any cause on her part."[115] The value of the compensation is established by a judge, in accordance with the husband's means, the duration of the marriage and the circumstances of the divorce, and may not be less than two years' maintenance.[116] The distribution of alimony payments and child support is enforced through the Nasser Social Bank, as is the case with maintenance dues.[117]

The unequivocal demand for 'equal rights' for men and women upon the dissolution of marriage is at odds with the extensive financial rights granted to women upon divorce, to the exclusion of men. It seems counter-intuitive for feminists to continue demanding greater substantive rights, while refusing to relinquish some of the financial rights they

[114] See *Orr v. Orr*, Supreme Court of the United States of America, 440 US 268 (1979).
[115] Bernard-Maugiron and Dupret (2002) at 10.
[116] Law no. 25 of 1929 as amended by Law no. 100 of 1985, art. 18*bis*.
[117] Law no. 10 of 2004.

have acquired over the years. In 2009, the Egyptian media reported that there was a proposal to grant divorced women, in the new draft personal status law, a share of the husband's assets that were acquired throughout the duration of the marriage. This proposal, widely attacked as a Western importation, was eventually shelved, although feminists continue to demand its endorsement.[118]

Equal Rights in Respect of the Ownership, Acquisition, Management, Administration, Enjoyment and Disposition of Property[119]

A woman's right to own and administer her own property individually is of paramount importance. Economic independence naturally translates into greater empowerment and hence more leverage within the family, as well as in society as a whole. Article 16 (1) (h) of CEDAW raises two important issues, namely freedom in owning and disposing of property, as well as inheritance rights.

Sharīʿa-derived legislation very clearly grants women full rights over their property throughout the marriage, and at its dissolution, rights women in Egypt have always enjoyed. Throughout the duration of the marriage, the wife retains a completely independent legal personality and complete ownership of her property and any property the husband gives her. The area of inheritance rights, however, has received a considerable degree of international criticism, and is widely misrepresented as discriminating against women because they are women. Upon closer scrutiny, it is evident that inheritance laws based on the Islamic scheme, do not necessarily disadvantage women, nor are they based on any inherent notion of inferiority of women.

The Wife's Full Right to Own and Dispose of Property

The *Sharīʿa* recognizes the full property rights of women before, during and at the dissolution of marriage, which include the full right to dispose of and maintain property. After marriage, the wife retains both her juridical personality and any property that she owns. Her private property, as well as any interest or profit that accrues, is independent of the husband, who also has no guardianship rights over the wife's property.

---

[118] See *The Shadow Report on the Status of Egyptian women*, CEWLA.
[119] CEDAW, art. 16(1)(h) and ICCPR, article 23 (4).

The right to property also includes full control over its disposition and maintenance. Married women aren't required to contribute to household expenses, and are entitled to full financial support at all times during marriage and throughout the waiting period (*'iddah*) in the case of divorce. The dowry, a gift made by the husband to the wife upon marriage (and not to her family) is the wife's exclusive property and may not be reclaimed by the husband, except in cases of *khulʿ* divorce. Women are not required to share any of their own property as a condition for divorce settlements. Apart from the dowry, the only property right acquired by the wife after marriage is the right to inherit from her husband in the case that he dies. The husband also has the right to inherit from his deceased wife, subject to the shares prescribed by the *Quran* and the *ḥadīth*.

Inheritance (Succession)

Inheritance law is one of the few areas of law that is largely derived from the explicit text of the *Quran*. As such, it's been subject to minimal contestation by legal reformers. Egypt's complex inheritance rules are mainly expounded in Law no. 77 of 1943. It has been erroneously portrayed that under *Sharīʿa*-derived inheritance laws, women always receive half the share that is due to men. There is thus a widespread belief among critics that Islamic inheritance schemes consistently discriminate against women *because* they are women.

The CEDAW Committee itself has a mixed record in this regard. Although the CEDAW is silent on the issue of inheritance, it implicitly endorses the right to equal inheritance in a number of articles, including article 15 which demands equality in civil capacity and ownership of property, and article 16(1)(h), which stipulates that men and women have equal rights with regards to the ownership, acquisition, management, administration, enjoyment and disposition of property. This includes equal access to, as well as equal rights in, inheritance. Any 'distinction' between men and women in these fields would thus amount to discrimination under the Convention.

Nonetheless, in some instances, the CEDAW Committee has shown a degree of tolerance for unequal inheritance shares based on *Sharīʿa* law. For instance, the Committee accepted Libya's explanation, during its consideration of Libya's report, that the 'Islamic' rationale behind unequal inheritance shares was that men inherited their shares with concomitant obligations, including the payment of dowry and maintenance, whereas women had no similar commitments.[120] However, in other cases, the Committee flatly rejected this proposition. In General Recommendation 21, it asserted that:

> Any discrimination in the division of property that rests on the premise that the man alone is responsible for the support of the women and children of his family and that he can and will honourably discharge this responsibility is clearly unrealistic. Consequently, any law or custom that grants men a right to a greater share of property at the end of a marriage or *de facto* relationship, or on the death of a relative, is discriminatory and will have a serious impact on a woman's practical ability to divorce her husband, to support herself or her family and to live in dignity as an independent person.[121]

Unequal inheritance shares were thus considered discriminatory because the premise on which they were based, namely that the husband is the primary bread-earner and supporter of the family, is 'clearly unrealistic'. There are, however, no accurate studies to demonstrate that men, as a general rule, and in different cultural settings, do not disproportionately bear the brunt of maintaining the family. The trend at the international level, whether within the CEDAW Committee, the Human Rights Council or other international fora, is still to consider Islamic inheritance schemes incompatible with the Convention.

Because inheritance is based on a number of complex formulae and dozens of different configurations, only a brief overview of the rules affecting women's inheritance will be possible here. As a starting point, it must be noted that by allowing women to inherit property, the *Sharīʿa*—which overturned pre-Islamic Arabia's prohibition on women's inheritance—was considered revolutionary at the time.[122] It descended on a society in which women were, themselves, considered part of the estates to be inherited exclusively by men.

According to the *Sharīʿa*, there are several categories of kin who constitute legal heirs, including wives, mothers, daughters and sisters. The law on inheritance distinguishes between three classes of heirs: the *Quranic* heirs (*ʿasḥāb elfurōḍ* or *sharers*), whose shares are stated

[120] See discussion *supra*, p. 81–82.

[121] General Recommendation no. 21, CEDAW.

[122] See Fatima Mernissi, *The Veil and the Male Elite* (1991) at 120–121. According to Mernissi, Islam affirmed for the first time the idea of women as sovereign individuals that would no longer be inherited but would, themselves, inherit a share of the estate.

explicitly in the text of the *Quran*, agnatic heirs (*aʿasāb* or *residuaries*)[123] who inherit the remainder of the estate after sharers, and uterine heirs (*thawu al-arḥām*).[124] Not all heirs always inherit; often a particular heir may inherit to the exclusion of others. In general, *sharers* take precedence over all other classes. Among the classes of heirs there is a cross-cutting group of primary heirs that can never be excluded from the estate, namely the spouses, parents and children of the deceased, of whichever gender. However, in some cases their shares may be decreased in order to accommodate the rights of other heirs.[125] All agnates and uterine heirs may be excluded in some circumstances, such as the presence of the son or father of the deceased (known as *ḥajb*), or the extinction of the estate after the *Quranic* heirs receive their shares. Out of a total of twelve sharers (*Quranic* heirs), eight are women.[126] By specifying their shares explicitly in the Quran, they are guaranteed a certain share of the estate when they are entitled to inherit.

In some cases, women sharers receive the majority of the estate through allotted shares. For instance, if the deceased has no son, his daughter receives half the estate whereas two daughters receive two-thirds, to be divided equally among them. The remainder of the estate goes to other relatives.[127] Certain heirs may be shifted from one class to another in the presence of other heirs.

Once the *Quranic* shares are distributed, the *residuaries*, who are agnatic heirs, inherit the remainder of the estate, according to articles 16–19 of Law no. 77 of 1943. For instance, in the case that the deceased leaves behind a son, he inherits the remainder of the estate after all sharers (the deceased's parents and spouse) and prevents all other residuaries from sharing in the estate (such as uncles and brothers). If there is also a

---

[123] Agnatic heirs are those whose relation with the deceased can be traced without the intervention of any female links. They include the son, the son's son (however low), the father, brother, paternal uncle, and in the case that they have switched classes from sharers to residuaries, the daughter, son's daughter full sister and consanguine sister.

[124] Badawy, 'Gender Equity in Islam'.

[125] Zeinab Chaudhry, 'The Myth of Misogyny: A Reanalysis of Women's Inheritance in Islamic Law', 61 *Albany L. Rev.* 511–555 (1997) at 529–530.

[126] The eight women sharers are the wife, mother, daughter, son's daughter, true grandmother (i.e. father's mother, and mother's mother), full sister, consanguine sister (half sister from the same father) and uterine sister (half sister from the same mother), whereas the four men are the husband, father, true grandfather (i.e. father's father, or grandfather), and uterine brother.

[127] Ahmed El Nagdy Zahw, *Ahkam al-mirāth fil sharīʿa al-islāmiyya* [Inheritance Law in the Islamic *Sharīʿa*] (2003) at 87.

daughter, she splits the son's share, taking what amounts to a third of his total share, and leaving him with two thirds. In other words, the daughter changes classes from a sharer to a residuary, and receives half (and not a third) of what is now due to the son. In the case that a descendent has no other relatives, the uterine heirs (blood relatives through a female link) inherit part of the estate.[128]

The shares of women, as is the case with other relatives, differ according to the specific circumstances of every case. In some cases, there is a clear inequality between males and females of the same degree of relationship to the deceased. This includes the above-mentioned case of a son and daughter of the deceased inheriting together, as well as full or consanguine brothers and sisters inheriting together. Another pertinent example is the difference in shares accorded to spouses. Whereas a wife inherits a quarter of her deceased husband's estate if they have no descendents,[129] the husband, on the other hand, inherits half the wife's estate.[130]

Although this provision indicates that the wife inherits a smaller share because of her gender, in other instances, when a wife and husband inherit together from their deceased son or daughter, they inherit equal shares. For instance, verse 4:11 of the *Quran* stipulates that "And to each of his parents a sixth of the inheritance, if he have a [child]; and if he have no [child] and his parents are his heirs, then to his mother appertaineth the third".

This means that the parents of a deceased man each inherit one sixth of the estate if the deceased has a child, who is also entitled to a share of the inheritance.[131] Between them, the parents of the deceased are thus entitled to a third of the estate, to be shared equally among them. If the deceased has left behind a son, then each parent receives a sixth of the estate, and the son the remainder of the estate. If the child is a daughter, however, she receives half the estate, and the parents a sixth each. The father may then inherit what remains of the estate, over and above his share, as a residuary. This is so "because he is the agnate relative closest to the deceased, excluding all collaterals."[132]

[128] Chaudhry (1997) at 539.

[129] Children or their descendents (i.e. grand children, great grand-children, etc.)

[130] If there are descendents, the wife inherits one eighth of the estate, whereas the husband inherits a quarter.

[131] Law no. 77 of 1943, art. 21.

[132] Chaudhry (1997) at 534–535.

If the deceased leaves behind no children, but two parents, then controversy arises. The *Quran* stipulates that the mother is entitled to a third of the estate, while it is silent with regards to the share of the father. If the inheritance is limited between the mother and father (i.e. there are no agnatic relatives of the deceased entitled to a share of the inheritance) the mother receives a third of the estate, and the father is granted the remainder as the only residuary. The mother's share is guaranteed through a clear *Quranic* stipulation, whereas the father inherits as a residuary based on the prophetic traditions.

In some cases, the deceased may leave behind his parents and no children, but also other relatives who are entitled to share in the estate. In such cases, Egypt's law differentiates between the mother and father, although that is not evident in the text of the relevant *Quranic* stipulations. Let us consider two possible scenarios by way of illustration. The first scenario is that the deceased is a woman, leaving behind a husband and two parents. In this scenario, strictly applying the *Quranic* shares means the deceased's husband would receive half the estate first as his *Quranic* share, and the mother a third of the estate while the father would be left with only a sixth of the estate, as a residuary. In other words, the mother would receive double the share of the father. According to the minority opinion of *Ibn Abbas*, this is the proper distribution envisioned by the *Quran*.[133]

Egypt's law, however, does not apply this interpretation. Instead, it adheres to the opinion of the *Caliph* Omar, who was confronted with this question historically. After consulting with the companions, he held that in this case, the mother should receive a third of the remainder of the estate (rather than her *Quranic* share which is a third of the estate in its totality). This yields the same results as applying the principle by which the male receives the share of two females, such that the father would receive a third of the estate and the mother a sixth.

Let us now consider a second scenario, in which the deceased is a man leaving behind a wife and his two parents. In this case, if one is to follow a strict textual reading of the Quran, the wife would receive a quarter of the estate as a *Quranic* sharer, while the mother would receive a third, and the

---

[133] Al Qaradawy (1997). According to this scholar, the view that the mother inherits an equal or even larger share than the father has been supported by the Prophet's nephew, Caliph *Ali ibn Abi Talib*, and Caliph *Usman* and *Zaid ibn Thabit*. This view was also supported by Imam's *Mālik*, *Abu Hanifa*, and *Al-Shafi'i* and therefore is not a minority opinion.

father would be left with what remains of the estate, which is little under half (five twelfths), if there are no other relatives. However, the law here stipulates that the mother receives not a third of the estate, but a third of the *remainder* of the estate. The father thus receives two-thirds of the remainder (which amounts to half the estate), while the mother receives only one third (amounting to a quarter of the estate), thereby decreasing the share allotted to her by the *Quran*. If there are other relatives, the mother and father would receive even smaller shares.

In order to justify this departure from the relevant *Quranic* text, jurists have restricted the application of the second part of verse 4:11, to cases where the parents are the *only* heirs. In this case, the mother would receive a third of the estate as a sharer, and the father two thirds of the estate as a residuary, and hence the result conformed to the principle that the male inherits the share of two females. In cases where the deceased was survived by a spouse or other relatives, the wife would not receive a third of the estate, but a third of the remainder of the estate.

Although strict adherence to *Quranic* stipulations was supported by the opinion of *Ibn Abbas*, who held that residuaries had to accept that they always received what remained of the estate regardless of the size of that share, it was disregarded by Egypt's legislature. Instead, Law no. 77 of 1943 adopted the opinion that granted the mother a third of the remainder of the estate so that her share would not be greater than or almost equal to that of her husband (the father). This is curious in light of the fact that verse 4:11 establishes, at its beginning, the principle that the parents may inherit equal shares by granting them each a sixth in the case that they are inheriting along with the child of the deceased. Surely, this specific rule would overrule any general principle that applies to the relationship between other classes of heirs. It is notable that in other countries that apply *Sharīʿa*-based laws, the mother and father are always granted equal shares.[134]

Notwithstanding the above-mentioned cases, in which some women may receive shares that are half those of their male counterparts, there are numerous other cases, in which the law grants women equal, if not bigger shares than male heirs. This is so whether or not they are of the same degree and relationship to the deceased. For instance, in the case that the deceased has uterine brothers and sisters, they inherit a third of the

[134] According to Chaudry, these provisions "emphasize the equality of a husband and wife, both living, inheriting equally from their children as father and mother", see Chaudry (1997) at 535.

estate, to be shared equally between them, regardless of their gender.[135] In the case that a woman dies leaving only her husband and a full sister as heirs, the husband (who is a *sharer*) will inherit half the estate and the sister, another *sharer* will inherit the remaining half. If the deceased has also left behind a half-brother from her father, he receives nothing as a residuary, whereas if she left behind a half-sister, she would receive a sixth.[136]

To take a more complex case, one may consider the case in which a woman dies, leaving behind a husband, daughter and full brother. The husband will receive a quarter of the estate, the daughter, as an only child will receive half, and the brother will inherit the remaining quarter. Another interesting example is if the deceased leaves behind two daughters and any number of brothers. In this case, the daughters inherit two-thirds of the estate and all the brothers, regardless of how numerous they are, share the remaining third equally between them. All these configurations allow females to inherit equal, if not greater shares than their male relatives.[137]

There are other cases worth mentioning. One of them is the case that the deceased leaves behind a daughter and full sister, as well as other agnatic relatives (not including a son or full brother). In this case, the daughter inherits half of the estate, and the sister changes classes to become a residuary, inheriting the remainder of the estate, while eliminating all other male agnates such as uncles and paternal half - brothers, through the principle of *ḥajb*.

It is thus evident that only in a minority of cases do women receive half the share of men in the same category, namely the deceased's off-spring, which include sons and daughters, and agnatic grandsons and granddaughters, as well as full or consanguine brothers and sisters, when these men and women are inheriting together. In some cases, the mother and father inheriting together may inherit unequal shares, although this is not reflected in the relevant *Quranic* stipulations. As a general rule, the share due to each heir, including women, will depend on the existence of other heirs to the estate. In the majority of cases, women will end up receiving equal, if not bigger shares than their male relatives, particularly since they are guaranteed majority shares rather than inheriting what is left over as residuaries.

---

135 Zahw at 98.
136 Al Qaradawy (1997).
137 Chaudry (1997) at 535–536.

In order to increase the wife's share in cases where she suffers a disadvantage, Law no. 71 of 1946 (the Law of Bequest) legalised testamentary bequests (*wassiya*) to heirs, within a limit of up to a third of the estate. As such, a husband may choose to grant his wife a third of his estate over and above her legal share. The law also extended the doctrine of *raḍ* to apply to spouses, such that they may inherit more than their share if part of the estate remains after all heirs have inherited.[138] These amendments created new tools to increase a woman's share of the inheritance, particularly if the deceased is her husband, by allowing widows to share in the residue of the deceased husband's estate. As such, the widow would inherit first as a *sharer* then receive part of what is left over as a *residuary*.

Although the rationale behind unequal inheritance shares has, on certain occasions, been dismissed by the CEDAW Committee, the actual intent of these rules is not to discriminate against women but to offset the financial obligations placed on male family members, by virtue of the Islamic vision of a family as a network of reciprocal and complementary relations. These obligations include the payment of dowry, provision of maintenance, and the provision of a matrimonial home. Although such a scheme could conceivably disadvantage a woman that doesn't benefit from such financial rights, several solutions have been proposed to mitigate these possibly harsh effects. Many of these solutions are based, themselves on Islamic principles, and include the aforementioned practices of *raḍ* and of *wassiya*, which may amount to up to a third of the estate, and must be paid before the estate is distributed among the heirs. The law also allows the granting of *hiba* (gifts) and *waqf* (endowments). These tools allow for the equal or fair distribution of the estate in cases where women may be disadvantaged by inheritance rules, or are not, in actuality, benefiting from the males' maintenance obligation, as required by the *Sharīʿa*.[139]

---

[138] *Egypt, Islamic Family Law Project.*

[139] For a comprehensive analysis of such alternative schemes, see Chaudhry (1997), who also proposes a more controversial proposition based on the notions of *maqasid* (intent) and *taʿlil* (ratiocination). According to this view, the rationale or cause (*ʿillah*) for unequal shares is that the male relative is obliged to maintain the female relative. In the absence of the *ʿillah* (i.e. if the man does not maintain the female), the rules can be modified, in light of the intent of the *Sharīʿa*. In other words, in a society where men do not maintain the women, the laws on inheritance may be changed for absence of the *ʿillah*. This view can be contested by Islamic scholars, though, on the basis that reasoning or *ijtihād* is limited to questions which are not addressed by clear *Quranic* provisions, which is clearly not the case with inheritance. Aboul Komsan also proposes the application of the *Shiʿite* Imami doctrine, according to which men and women are entitled to equal shares of inheritance.

Based on the above, it is inaccurate and short-sighted to maintain that inheritance laws derived from the *Sharīʿa* necessarily discriminate against women, and disadvantage them by consistently granting them half the share of male relatives. Not only is there protection for women who inherit as sharers, but many cases exist where women inherit shares greater than men of different relationships to the deceased, or even exclude them altogether from the estate. Legal reforms have been introduced to increase the potential shares of disadvantaged women; benefiting from such exceptions, however, requires a considerable degree of awareness and is contingent on the cooperation and fairness of the deceased prior to his/her death.

The existence of such a complex scheme limits the potential for abuse, and deliberate exclusion of certain heirs, which is always possible in a system that allows for absolute discretion through writing a will that disposes of the estate in an unfair and unjust manner. Inheritance is a matter that poses great difficulties in all legal systems; not only does the distribution of property occur during times of bereavement, but the process has to be managed by those closely affected by the death. The problem can be exacerbated by uncertainty and anxiety about the future of money or belongings, which is where the importance of a predictable and comprehensive scheme becomes evident. Moreover, under the complex *Sharīʿa*-based scheme, it is impossible to disinherit children, unlike many Western schemes of intestate succession, which pass the whole of the estate, or its vast majority to the surviving spouse, thus disinheriting children from a previous relationship, and possibly children from the current relationship in the case of the spouse's subsequent marriage.[140] Conversely, the *Sharīʿa*-based scheme attempts to provide shares for a larger number of surviving relatives. Although this scheme is not based on absolute equality, not every 'distinction' between men and women amounts to discrimination, particularly in cases where women are accorded larger shares than male relatives.

Nonetheless, there is potential room for reform of Egypt's laws on inheritance, particularly in cases where women have been allotted smaller shares than ordained by *Quranic* stipulations. Equally important is the legal empowerment of women in a way that allows them to know their

[140] For a general overview of the system of intestate succession in the United Kingdom, from which these arguments are derived, see *Intestacy and Family Provision Claims on Death*, Law Commission, Consultation Paper No. 191 (Overview), 29 Oct 2009 available at http://www.lawcom.gov.uk/docs/cp191_overview.pdf.

rights and protect them from possible encroachments by male relatives, who may seek to strip them of their inheritance. The National Council for Women is, in fact, in the process of drafting new legislation to address the issue of depriving women of their legal inheritance rights, under which disinheriting women in contravention of the law would be met with severe penalties.

The Way Forward in the Area of Legislative Reform

It is evident that several provisions of Egypt's personal status law are at odds with international standards of equality, as well as the notions of justice and righteousness envisioned by Islam, particularly the provisions on disappearance of the husband, obedience and polygyny, and the inadequate treatment of domestic violence. According to some juristic opinions, these provisions may be amended through alternative interpretations that do not depart from the principles of the *Sharīʿa*. In other areas such as guardianship over children and inheritance, there may be room for some minor reforms, which must simultaneously be met with a more flexible interpretation of international standards in a way that accommodates the values of reciprocity (based on different roles and responsibilities) that underpin *Shariʿa*-derived law. Where the principle of reciprocity is not being met by a recalcitrant husband or male family member, ways should be sought to deprive him of privileges afforded to him by law, or to further enhance the woman's position. In areas such as registration of customary marriages and child custody, the law benefits and protects women in a way not envisioned by CEDAW, and not in line with an 'absolute equality' standard, but which is more suitable to the specific cultural setting the law is intended to regulate.

In areas such as divorce by delegation (*ʿisma*), divorce by *khulʿ*, and the new marriage contract, Egypt has met international standards of equality through employing its own indigenous reform tools. Much still needs to be done in terms of educating women and raising awareness amongst them, as well as in the judiciary and legal profession, in order for them to fully enjoy their rights, and benefit from adequate enforcement. The reform process should also be stepped up, as amendments to the law have often occurred at a pace that is less than satisfactory.

Under Egypt's personal status law, there doesn't seem to be room for absolute or formal equality in all areas of life, unless there is a complete break with the principles of the *Sharīʿa*, a development which is unlikely to be accepted by society. The majority of Egyptian feminists have therefore relied on a different conception of non-discrimination than the one envisioned by CEDAW. Their model is reminiscent of the cultural feminist approach to women's rights, which acknowledges the inherent differences between men and women, and is willing to grant women different rights and responsibilities. For instance, Egyptian feminists have campaigned to increase women's maintenance rights, a right that is not based on a model of absolute equality with men. The *sine qua non* for these increased financial rights has been the acceptance of a lesser share of inheritance in some cases, and a compromise on various substantive rights such as in the area of guardianship over children. Since the aim of these distinctions is not to oppress women but to attain justice according to a different social standard, in a culture that accepts distinct but reciprocal roles for men and women, they do not always amount to discrimination, with the negative connotation that the word carries.

However, there is a very thin line between what does and what does not constitute discrimination and disadvantage. The principle of obedience, for instance, has been used to justify oppressive practices that subjugate women, including toleration of domestic violence. The same can be said of polygyny, a practice with severe repercussions for the rights and dignity of women. Whereas piecemeal legislative reforms have succeeded in overcoming the most oppressive practices against women, they have failed to bring about the large-scale transformation in their rights and social status envisioned by the CEDAW. It is thus imperative for personal status law reform to persist, using the same indigenously derived tools, while underlining the egalitarian nature of the Islamic scriptures from which such legislation is derived. The aim should be to arrive at a new comprehensive personal status law that would completely replace the geriatric decree-laws of the 1920's that still govern personal status matters. The new law must be based on a fundamentally different premise that women are equal to men in dignity, enjoying equal mental faculties and judgement, in spite of having different responsibilities within the family. Such an approach will preserve the accomplishments achieved by the Egyptian feminist movement in areas such as maintenance and child custody, while paving the way for more reforms, such as expansion of guardianship rights over children, restriction of polygny and unilateral divorce by the husband, and the punishment of all forms of domestic violence, including marital rape. The comprehensive law should address cases in which the reciprocal model is not being adequately applied, granting women more extensive rights in such cases.

It should also guarantee the adequate enforcement by the judiciary of the legal rights of women, and the application of deterrent penalties in cases of circumvention of legal rules, particularly in the area of inheritance.

Article 2 of CEDAW recognises that it is impractical to seek to immediately eliminate discrimination against women. Egypt can be seen as slowly progressing towards the fulfilment of the right of non-discrimination in family relations through employing innovative tools to interpret the religious texts, namely *takhayyur*, *talfīq*, and *ijtihād*. This process often seems slow and protracted, but it presents the only practical and legitimate way to adapt the Muslim family institution to modern-day perceptions. Although it may be perceived, at face value, as an attempt to defy the universal human rights movement, what this approach represents, to the contrary, is an attempt to join that movement in a way that makes sense to Muslim women, by combining human rights and dignity with the pillars of their own faith.

CHAPTER EIGHT

THE POSITIVE PROSPECTS FOR PERSONAL STATUS LAW REFORM: TWO STEPS FORWARD

The preservation of the *Sharīʿa* in the area of personal status law has often been presented as the 'sacrificial lamb' of modernisers who had been intent on imposing secular codes in the areas of civil, criminal and commercial matters at the turn of the twentieth century. The piecemeal and fragmentary reform of family law that ensued meant that gains by women remained at the margins, and hence could not achieve true equality. It has thus been argued that serving justice to women and meeting the requirements of modernity, requires a secularisation of the family law altogether, and the application of a standard of absolute equality.[1] This approach, however, ignores the fact that any law must be compatible with the social setting in which it operates. The public has to readily accept the laws they are required to conform with and give effect to. Disrupting the careful balance between social and legal norms "creates tensions, and usually does not stand the test of daily life."[2]

Since the turn of the twenty-first century Egypt's personal status law has undergone a gradual reform process that demonstrates the possibility of further developing these laws, without the need to secularise them altogether. Although reforms have often been slow to come, they have gradually granted women greater equality rights. Every national, religious and cultural group have the right to practice and manifest their own religious and cultural beliefs; depriving them of such a right would, in itself, constitute a violation of international human rights standards. *Sharīʿa*-derived personal status legislation is engrained in the identities of many Muslim women as well as men. Depriving them of the right to adhere to the principles that form the pillars of their belief system cannot possibly be considered as a legitimate aim. Although the CEDAW is unequivocal in its demand for equality between the genders in family

[1] Abu-Odeh (2004) at 1047.
[2] Shaham (1997) at 228.

relations, the intent of the CEDAW cannot possibly be to force different groups of women into lifestyles which they themselves do not approve of. It is inconceivable for the international human rights movement to remain impervious to the reality that cultural particularities and diverse worldviews exist, and that they have the potential to achieve standards of equality through internal validation processes. According to Behrouz,

> imposed foreign values are not easily internalized. As a matter of both ethics and policy, then, restrictions on the rights of Muslim women can best be challenged by showing that such restrictions are not in fact required by Islam in the context of present-day Islamic societies. This is not an unrealistic task.[3]

It is narrow-minded to construe the relationship between international human rights standards and religious beliefs as inherently antagonistic. Rather than engaging in such polemics, what is required is a heightened respect for pluralism in the human rights debate in order to adequately address the needs of diverse groups of women. Such an exercise is not an apology for discriminatory practices and laws; it requires the highest degree of scrutiny of prevailing rules and a radical break with those that disadvantage women and deviate from the principles of human dignity. In other words, if a core group of women's human rights can be recognised as constituting universal standards that are to apply without regard to religion and culture, there are other rights that would have to be culturally qualified, without jeopardising women's dignity. Achieving equality for women is a two-way road that requires a compromise solution, with the aim of genuinely improving their status, rather than serving the ideological purposes of an international and academic elite, detached from the realities and preferences of the women on whose behalf they purport to speak.

The elimination of gender discrimination requires that Egypt, as a party to the CEDAW "assume a role in the reform process to ensure that its international duty is fulfilled."[4] However, this raises the question of whether this obligation is met if legal reforms are introduced by the State, but rejected by the people and those who represent them. In such a case, would the State have absolved itself of any responsibility for the persistence of discriminatory laws and practices?

In spite of its mixed record, Egypt has demonstrated a commitment to reforming its family law over the past ten years. This process began with

---

[3] Behrouz (2003) at 1139–1140.

[4] Ibid. at 1157.

the adoption of Law no. 1 of 2000. While the new law may not represent a major transformation in Egypt's personal status legislation, it undoubtedly marks a novel approach by the government, and a newfound commitment to legal modernism in spite of ideological and social resistance. In 2004, Law no. 10 was promulgated to institute procedural reforms with the intention of facilitating litigation in personal status matters. Then, in March 2005, a new law was passed reforming the provisions on child custody. A wide debate on further reforming the personal status law was initiated in 2009, when the Women's Committee of the previously ruling National Democratic Party sought to present a new draft law to the People's Assembly. The draft, which was widely debated in the media, was eventually postponed in light of widespread opposition. In the wake of the 25th January 2011 revolution, however, the fate of the draft remains unknown.

It is apparent, that the State is further obliged to embark on a process of transformation of social values in order to eradicate the root causes of discrimination against women. While legal reforms in and of themselves are not sufficient to achieve such a transformation, they "reflect social change, grant sanction to the social behaviour that legislators are interested to encourage, and serve as a medium for teaching the social values inherent in the reforms."[5] Recent legal reforms have encouraged important internal deliberations on the status of women within the family, which act as a precursor to internalising new changes to family structure. Applying innovative reform techniques will undoubtedly allow for more extensive reforms that deviate from patriarchal interpretations of the sources of the *Sharīʿa* handed down over the centuries, to the detriment of Egyptian women.

Changing Interpretations in a Changing Society

The CEDAW Committee has, on several occasions, called upon States that apply *Sharīʿa*-derived personal status law to seek innovative methods, within the context of the *Sharīʿa*, to reform legislation, particularly laws that discriminate against women. Although this is a welcome proposition, it contradicts other views of the Committee which reject, outright, the very foundation on which *Sharīʿa*-derived law is based, namely the

[5] Shaham (1997) at 235.

complementarity of rights and obligations within the family, as opposed to a strict equality standard. Even when significant reforms have been achieved, such as the adoption of no-fault (*khulʿ*) divorce for the wife, they haven't been met with sufficient approval by the Committee, which has only 'taken note' but not welcomed this development.

It was the plight of women who waited years for a divorce ruling and, worse still, those whose cases were eventually dismissed, that prompted the adoption by Parliament of the new Law Regarding Certain Conditions and Procedures of Litigation in Matters of Personal Status, Law no. 1 of 2000. Applying innovative tools of interpretation, the People's Assembly succeeded in granting women unprecedented rights in initiating divorce. The law, which consists of 81 articles, was widely criticized in the popular press for its endorsement of no-fault divorce initiated at the wife's prerogative, on condition of restitution of the dower and forfeiture of alimony. The deep schism in religious opinions with regards to this provision, exhibited by both legislators in the People's Assembly as well as some religious scholars at the state-sponsored Islamic Research Academy resulted in a nine-year-long negotiating and drafting process. In spite of the objection of many religious scholars, the Grand *Sheikh* of *Al-Azhar* and the Islamic Research Academy declared that the new law, including the provision on judicial *khulʿ*, was in conformity with the Islamic *Sharīʿa*.

Hailed as a victory for feminists and women's rights activists, the law was eventually adopted in January 2000. The most striking aspect of Law no. 1 of 2000 is its substantial departure from the interpretations of the four Sunni jurisprudential schools in its codification of the article 20 provision on judicial *khulʿ*. This is revealed through a close examination of the Minutes of the Parliamentary Sessions in which the law was discussed, and the attached Annexes. Whereas the four *Sunni* jurisprudential schools, including the *Ḥanafi* school require the consent of the husband in order to effect separation by *khulʿ*, Law no. 1 of 2000 makes no such requirement. The provision was widely contested between conservatives who held that it didn't conform to the interpretations of the four schools, and was therefore inconsistent with the *Sharīʿa*, and liberals who argued that the *khulʿ* provision was consistent with the absolute and unambiguous text of the *Quran* and the Prophet's tradition (*Sunnah*).

Perhaps most illuminating was the statement made by the Chairman of the People's Assembly, immediately following the law's promulgation. He emphasized that in drafting Law no. 1 of 2000, the People's Assembly had been intent on:

> Complying with Article 2 of the Egyptian Constitution, which stipulates that the *Sharīʿa* is the primary source of legislation. In spite of the controversy surrounding the opinions of the jurists, the Assembly has conformed to the Supreme Constitutional Court's interpretation of the phrase "principles of Islamic *Sharīʿa*" as the clear-cut decrees of the *Quran* and the *Sunnah*. *Ijtihād* is limited to issues that are ambiguous and therefore the Assembly has referred to the decrees of the *Quran* and the *Sunnah*, disregarding specific juristic opinions and *ijtihādat*. The Assembly has selected the interpretations that reinforce the clear-cut decrees [of the *Quran* and *Sunnah*] since the issue at hand does not involve ambiguous provisions. The principles of the *Sharīʿa* are limited to what was decreed by the *Quran* and the *Sunnah*, and the Assembly has respected these sources.[6]

This statement, and several others, indicates that the promulgation of Law no. 1 of 2000 marks a newfound willingness to go back to the sacred texts and legislate afresh, leading to the adoption of laws that are not necessarily based on the predominant interpretations of any of the jurisprudential schools. In effect, the statement asserts that the People's Assembly relied on absolute 'principles' in the sacred texts (whose meaning is definitive and unambiguous as defined by the SCC[7]) and suggests that in the face of such provisions, the historical doctrines of the major schools lost their once-privileged authority as interpretations of what the *Sharīʿa* said about *khulʿ* divorce. Although the process was not framed as one of *ijtihād*, the very fact that the legislature went back to the religious text to reinterpret the provisions on *khulʿ* divorce involved an element of reasoning and value judgement that was independent of existing interpretations.

This clear departure from the traditional practice of *taqlīd* law, by virtue of which Egyptian legislators selected the most favourable interpretation from the preponderant opinions of the four schools (*takhayyur*) or patched up opinions from the different schools (*talfīq*), is very rare in the history of personal status legislation in Egypt. Whereas reforms since the 1920's have been largely based on *taqlīd*, the 2000 reforms indicate a move away from these practices in favour of *ijtihād*, or reasoning based directly on the text of the primary sources (the *Quran* and the *Sunnah*). In justifying its novel formulation of the *khulʿ* formula,

---

[6] Fathi Sorour, (Chairman of the People's Assembly) Statement before the People's Assembly (Jan 26th, 2000) Minutes of the 29th Parliamentary Session *Official Gazette* 79 (March 9, 2000).

[7] *See* discussion *supra* at p. 153–160.

the government referred to the text of the religious scriptures without making reference to any juristic interpretations, even minority views. According to Arabi, the State thus formally endorsed, a century later, "*Muhammad ʿAbduh*'s program of going back to the revealed sources of *Sharīʿa* for inspiration in all modern legislation, and [abandoning] any prior commitment to either the historically established school doctrines of Islamic law (*madhāhib*) or to culturally sedimented rules of behaviour (*ʿurf*)."[8] The following sections will address precisely how the *khulʿ* provision departed from the teachings of the four schools, and the parliamentary debates surrounding the adoption of the new provision.

Evidence for Judicial Khulʿ in the *Quran* and *Sunnah*

Article 20 of Law no. 1 of 2000 is based on a *ḥadīth* of the Prophet Mohammed, involving *Thabit bin Qays* and his wife *Habība* (or *Jamīla* in some recounts of the tradition), who was granted a divorce by the Prophet, although her husband was free of any "fault of his own." According to *Al-Bukhari's* Compendium (*al-Jamiʿ al-Sahih*), the following *ḥadīth* was narrated by *bin ʿAbbas* (the Prophet's cousin and widely recognised authority):

> The wife of *Thabit bin Qays* came to the Prophet and said, "O Allah's Apostle! I do not blame *Thabit* for defects in his character or his religion, but I, being a Muslim, dislike to behave in un-Islamic manner (if I remain with him)." On that Allah's Apostle said (to her), "Will you give back the garden which your husband has given you [as dowry: *mahr*]?" She said, "Yes." Then the Prophet said to Thabit, "O Thabit! Accept (*iqbal*) your garden, and divorce her once (*talliqha*)."[9]

According to the above *ḥadīth*, the divorce is contingent on the wife's restoration of the dower she received at the time of marriage. A literal reading of the *ḥadīth* indicates that the Prophet addressed *Thabit* in the imperative, ordering him to accept it (*iqbal* or *khudh*), which he did. This formulation leaves no room for the assumption that the husband's

---

[8] Arabi (2001) at 6.

[9] *Sahih al-Bukhari*, Volume 7, Book 63, *Ḥadith* number 197, available at *University of South California Centre for Muslim-Jewish Engagement* http://www.usc.edu/schools/college/crcc/engagement/resources/texts/muslim/hadith/bukhari/063.sbt.html (last accessed 10/11/2010).

consent was necessary for the divorce to take place. The same account of the tradition was recorded in *al-Nissai*'s compendium; it was these two compendia that the People's Assembly referred to in drafting the new law.

Although the Prophetic tradition involving *khul*ʿ was compulsory for the husband, the classical schools have invoked certain verses of the *Quran* to propose the view that *khul*ʿ divorce is a negotiated settlement that requires the consent of the husband. However, these verses seem to envision a distinct kind of separation, which should not be confused with *khul*ʿ. There is a certain incongruity in meaning between judicial *khul*ʿ as practiced by the Prophet, and the *Quran*'s endorsement of the wife's right to 'ransom' or release (*taftadi*) herself through a negotiated settlement. Verse 1:229 of the *Quran* stipulates that:

> And it is not lawful for you that ye take from women aught of that which ye have given them; except (in the case) when both fear that they may not be able to keep within the limits (imposed by) Allah. And if ye fear that they may not be able to keep the limits of Allah, in that case it is no sin for either of them if the woman ransom herself.

The *Quranic* verse has been interpreted by the four Islamic jurisprudential schools to allow a woman to 'buy' her divorce through relinquishing her financial rights, even in the case that the husband is guilty of no fault of his own. They share the common understanding that the *khul*ʿ procedure involves the notions of "ransoming and mutual exchange," necessitating the husband's consent as a *sine qua non* to effect the separation.[10] This is different from the Prophet's tradition, which clearly indicates that the husband had no choice, but to accept the dowry and divorce the wife. The medieval jurists came to terms with this seeming inconsistency between the stipulations of the *Quran* and the *Sunnah* by "allowing the *Quranic* implication of a consensual transaction to overrule the Prophetic ruling in *Ḥabiba*'s *khul*ʿ separation case."[11]

Khulʿ *in the Four* Sunni *Jurisprudential Schools*

Each of the four *Sunni* schools expressly recognises the *khul*ʿ procedure, albeit with some notable differences. All four schools seem to approach the issue of *khul*ʿ as a right of the husband, rather than the wife; they are predominantly concerned with the question of the husband's right to reclaim the dowry and gifts he gave to the wife upon marriage. The

[10] Arabi (2001) at 15–16.
[11] Ibid. at 18.

Shafiʿi, *Ḥanafi* and *Ḥanbali* schools all treat *khulʿ* as a sale transaction, which requires the explicit consent of the husband. In his Compendium *al-Umm*, *al-Shafiʿi* explicitly describes the *khulʿ* procedure as a sale transaction, underlining both the consensual and negotiated character of the divorce. He states that:

> Were a man to separate from his wife by *khulʿ* (*khalaʿ al-rajul imraʾatah*) then the separation is a single irrevocable divorce because it is a sale like other sales. It is not permissible for him to take possession of her money while continuing to possess her.[12]

It is noteworthy that *al-Shafiʿi* refers to the divorce by *khulʿ* as an action carried out at the husband's prerogative (it is the husband that separates from his wife, and not vice-versa). As such, it is clear that the decision to effect the divorce lies ultimately with the husband, who may choose to either 'possess' the wife or, alternately, the money and gifts he gave her. Although *al-Shafiʿi* made clear reference to the Prophet's order to *Thabit* to divorce his wife, without asking for his consent, he proceeds to elaborate on the *Quran's* doctrine on *khulʿ* as a negotiated ransom, which necessitates the husband's agreement. According to *Imam al-Shafiʿi*, *khulʿ* as described in the *Quran* is a type of sale, which allows "the amount that the vendor and buyer mutually agree to without any (prior) specification."[13] Similarly, the *Ḥanbali* and *Ḥanafi* schools described the *khulʿ* procedure as a 'transactional bargaining' process.[14] *Ḥanbali* scholar *Muwaffaq al-Din bin Qudāma* describes it as a "transaction, similar to a sale or a marriage contract; it does not require a judge ... and is a dissolution of a contract by mutual consent."[15] He further stresses that this is the position each of *Aḥmed bin Ḥanbal*, *Imam Mālik*, *Imam al-Shafiʿi* and *ahl-al-raʾy* (or the people of opinion, in reference to the *Ḥanafi* School).[16]

This opinion is further reinforced in *Qadri Pasha*'s compilation of *Ḥanafi* law, which describes *khulʿ* as a procedure initiated by the husband, and subject to his will,[17] and is the position reflected in the Model Arab Unified Personal Status Law, which describes *khulʿ* in article 100 as a process that occurs with the agreement of both spouses.

---

[12] Ibid.
[13] Ibid. at 15.
[14] Ibid.
[15] Ibid. at 14.
[16] Ibid.
[17] Articles 276, 279 and 280 of *Qadri Pasha*'s Compilation.

Although the *Maliki* interpretation of *khulʿ* departs significantly from the approach of the other three schools; however, no *Maliki* scholar expressly states that the *khulʿ* separation may take effect in spite of the husband's objection. Conversely, *Imam Mālik* explicitly introduces the husband's consent as a necessary factor by citing a different account of the Prophetic precedent involving *Habiba* and *Thabit*. According to this account, reported on the authority of *Said bin Mussayib*, a seventh century jurist from *Medina*,

> The Prophet invited *Thabit bin Qays* to be present, and he told him about *Habiba* and about her positive response to the Prophet's asking her whether she would be willing to give him back his garden. *Thabit* said: "This is to my liking; yes." The Prophet (p.b.u.h) said: "Then she gives it back" ... and he told Thabit: "It is just one statement (*hiya wāḥida*)."[18]

The above-mentioned account is the only one that makes explicit reference to the consent of the husband, and was quoted in *Imam Mālik's* Compendium in order to arrive at the opinion that divorce by *khulʿ* is irrevocable. Jurists have referred to another passage in the Compendium to suggest that *Imam Mālik* envisaged a type of *khulʿ* that would not require the consent of the husband, and that would take place at the hands of a judicial authority. However, a close reading of the passage, which appears in the section on divorce for harm (*darar*) suggests otherwise:

> Were the dispute between the couple to aggravate and were they to refer to the governor [judge], he is to appoint two arbitrators, one from his family and the other from hers .... If the arbitrators establish that the harm (*darar*) originates from the husband, they are to separate them (*farraqa baynahuma*) without the wife being liable ...; if the harm originates from both, they are to separate them, with the wife paying back a portion of the dower, either its half or more or less, depending whether the mutual harm is equal on both sides, or more from her, or more from him.[19]

Although the statement "they are to separate them" does indeed suggest that the judgement of the arbitrators is decisive, regardless of the opinion of the husband, it is important to note that the above applies to situations where there is 'mutual harm.' It is therefore applicable to divorce on the basis of discord, and does not envision a case where the wife demands a no fault divorce, without a claim of harm, and without the husband's

[18] Arabi (2001) at 14.
[19] Ibid. at 13.

consent. In the case of divorce for discord, addressed in the above passage, the husband may also receive compensation from the wife, if the harm is exclusively the wife's fault.

The argument that the *Māliki* school does not recognise judicial *khulʿ* without consent of the husband is further confirmed by the debates that took place in the 9th Session of the Council of the Islamic Research Academy, which discussed the conformity of draft Law no. 1 of 2000 with the Islamic *Sharīʿa*. Regarding the husband's consent, *Sheikh Ibrahim El-Dessouky* asserted that allowing for a judicial settlement of the dispute doesn't necessarily mean that the husband's consent is automatically waived. In fact, according to *el-Dessouky* all four *Imams* agreed that:

> both spouses must be present in the *Majlis* [now court] where the decision regarding the divorce is delivered. If either of them leaves or objects to the procedure at any point, even with a lowered voice, the divorce is not accepted.[20]

Only one of the thirteen members of the Academy objected to *el-Dessouky's* statement, without providing detailed evidence to the contrary (the objection was of a procedural nature, based on the grounds that the debate on the topic had been closed in the previous session.) *El-Dessouky* was urged to record his opinion in the Explanatory Memorandum (*muthakira iḍaḥiyya*) of the new law.[21] However, no indication of his views is to be found in either the law, or its Explanatory Memorandum. A brief exposé of the positions of the four schools was incorporated into the Annex to the Minutes of the 22nd Parliamentary Session. It is evident that the document was hastily prepared; citing the reference *Al-fiqh ʿala el-madhahib el-ʾarbaʿ*, the document asserts that consent of the husband is requisite in all four jurisprudential schools. In sum, neither the *Māliki* school, nor any of the other three classical schools make *khulʿ* separation compulsory once the wife persists in demanding it, which is the case with article 20 of the new law.

Khulʿ *As Envisioned in Article 20*

Article 20 of Law no. 1 of 2000 grants the wife the right to separate from her husband without his consent. Curiously enough, however, the Explanatory Memorandum of the law asserts that the *khulʿ* provision is

[20] Annex to the Minutes of the Meeting of the 22nd Parliamentary Session (Jan. 16, 2000) (On file with author) at 307.

[21] Ibid. at 295–297.

in complete conformity with the *Sharīʿa* basic principle (*al-ʾasl al-sharʿi)* that *khulʿ* occurs through *mutual* consent. If such consent is not possible, the dispute is referred to adjudication, in the case that the wife maintains that she can no longer live with her husband, and fears transgression of God's limits.

Based on the above, it seems that article 20 differentiated between two types of *khulʿ*. The first type occurs through mutual consent, and is dealt with in the first section of article 20 of the new law. It is based on the verses of the *Quran* that describe *khulʿ* as a ransoming procedure. The second is a different type of *khulʿ* that does not require the husband's consent, and which is detailed in the second section of article 20. It is based on the *Ḥabiba* (or *Jamila)* incident as recorded in the Compendia of *al-Bukhari* and *al-Nissaʾi*. In other words, the *Ḥabiba* precedent is allowed to "stand distinctly on its own, separate from the *Quranic* settlement separation, as an autonomous divorce structure, in which the judge, at the determined request of a woman, compels her husband to separate from her."[22]

This radical break with the *fiqh* of the schools caused a great deal of criticism and opposition to article 20, some of which resurfaced in the debates of the People's Assembly, although the provision had passed through nine years of prior debate and negotiation. As such, the debates in the People's Assembly capture only the tip of the iceberg, particularly since the vast majority of seats in the Assembly were, at the time, monopolised by the National Democratic Party (NDP), which introduced Law no. 1 of 2000.

Debating *Khulʿ* in the People's Assembly

The debates that took place in the People's Assembly aptly reflect the effect of patriarchal social attitudes on personal status law reform. Throughout the five parliamentary sessions in which Law no. 1 of 2000 was debated,[23] several MP's expressed arguments against the new law, particularly the article 20 provision on judicial *khulʿ*. Out of a total of about 100 MPs

---

[22] Arabi (2001) at 18. This is based on the general principle expounded by *Imam al-Shafʿi* that there exists a category of rulings that God explicated in the tradition of the Prophet, without a *Quranic* text.

[23] The 22nd Parliamentary Session (16 Jan. 2000), 23rd Parliamentary Session (16 Jan. 2000), 27th Parliamentary Session (25th Jan., 2000), 28th Parliamentary Session (26th Jan. 2000), and 29th Parliamentary Session (26th Jan. 2000), 5th Ordinary Session, 7th, legislative year.

that commented on the new law, less than 15 openly spoke up against the *khulʿ* provision. This evident lack of opposition, however, is less an indication of societal consensus than one of the paucity of parliamentary seats occupied by members of the opposition and independents at the time (about 40 out of 454 seats, or less than 10%), not to mention the prevailing restrictions that prevented members of the opposition Muslim Brotherhood from joining the People's Assembly.

The fact that Law no. 1 passed through nine years of deliberation confirms that the *khulʿ* provision, the only substantive provision of the law, was considered highly controversial. In the People's Assembly, several amendments to the text of article 20 were proposed, on the grounds that the provision ignored the opinions of the four *Sunni* schools, and therefore violated the Islamic *Sharīʿa*. It was proposed that article 20 of the draft law be amended so as to require the husband's consent.[24] This motion failed, as did a separate motion raised by five Members of the People's Assembly (MP's) to remove article 20 from the draft law altogether. Several other proposed amendments to the article didn't gain the support of the majority, including a proposal to render the *khulʿ* suit automatically into a case of divorce for harm in the event of the husband's opposition to the separation. Another amendment introduced by eight MP's sought to make the court's decision in *khulʿ* separation subject to legal contestation (appeal).[25]

In fact, the only amendment that achieved majority approval was the one introduced by the government, with a view to appeasing opposition, and which made judicial separation by *khulʿ* contingent upon compulsory mediation. The purpose of mediation would be to try to 'save' the family through reconciliation before giving effect to the divorce.[26] This provision, introduced as a concession to conservatives, was criticised by some for denying women the full right to *khulʿ* divorce as described in the *Quran* and *Sunnah*.[27] In order to pass the provision on judicial *khulʿ*, a compromise was made to remove another proposed provision, which

[24] *Ragab Helal Hemeida* (a Member of Parliament from the *Al-Ahrar* party, which has Islamist inclinations). Minutes of the 28th Parliamentary Session, Published in the Official Gazette, Fifth Legislative Year (March 9, 2000) at 61.

[25] Ibid. at 59.

[26] See Mariz Tadros, 'The Third Option', *Al-Ahram Weekly* 31 October–5 November 2002.

[27] Aboul Komsan, 'Women Between Islamic Shariʾa and Personal Status Laws'.

would have allowed a wife to obtain the Court's authorization to travel without her husband's consent. This latter provision had also aroused a huge amount of controversy, leading to its eventual abandonment, as a *quid pro quo* for the adoption of judicial *khul*ʿ.[28]

Critics of the proposed article 20 based their views on a number of rhetorical arguments, summarised below, which weren't limited to religiously-based considerations, but included social concerns as well as procedural objectives, the latter having been used repeatedly in the past to forestall reforms in personal status law. However, Government officials succeeded in appeasing conservatives by appealing to patriarchal mentalities, and introducing the above-mentioned limitations to the *khul*ʿ procedure, without affecting the essence of the new amendment and its endorsement of no-fault divorce initiated by the wife.

Arguments against the Current Formulation of Article 20

Opponents of article 20 based themselves on five main arguments, mapped out in the following sub-sections. Most of those arguments did not rely on religious claims. Some of the critical comments came from within the ranks of the NDP, although the vast majority supported the new reform. All statements in opposition to the new law reflect the pervasiveness of patriarchal attitudes, as well as the existence of negative stereotypes regarding the role of women.

Rhetorical Argument 1: Instability of the Family

Perhaps the most widely stated argument against the new law was the allegation that it would create an unprecedented degree of instability in family relations, causing the dissolution of many families. According to this view, *khul*ʿ should be opposed because it would inevitably lead to societal chaos.[29] One MP made the broad assertion that social conditions had changed considerably since the *khul*ʿ of *Habiba* (also known as the first *khul*ʿ in Islam) and that *khul*ʿ was thus not suitable in light of modern realities. He argued that granting the wife the right to seek judicial *khul*ʿ would lead to the disintegration of social values, and ultimately to an

[28] The Supreme Constitutional Court eventually annulled the edict requiring the wife to seek her husband's approval in order to travel. See discussion *supra* at p. 159.

[29] This argument was widely propagated by the media, which predicted that between 1.5 and 2 million women would apply for *khul*ʿ; however, only a few thousand cases were filed in the first two years after the law was passed. See Mariz Tadros, 'The Third Option'.

increase in the crime rate.[30] According to another MP, the tradition involving *Thabit bin Qays* should not be generalised into a general legal rule, since the wife in that specific incident had no children.[31] It is unclear what this proposition suggests, but perhaps it could mean that the *Ḥabiba* case was governed by specific circumstances which are not applicable in most other cases of *khulʿ* separation, or that where there are no children, the family is not really in need of protection and hence *khulʿ* separation becomes more tolerable. Alternatively, this argument could imply that *Habiba*'s separation was a type of divorce for harm because her husband was incapable of bearing children. In any case, the text of the *ḥadith* shows no indication that the question of whether or not the couple had children had any bearing on the decision to allow for *khulʿ* divorce.

Surprisingly, the view that no-fault divorce would lead to a disruption of family relations was also expressed by *Yassin Serag Eddin*, Head of the Parliamentary Committee of the *Wafd* Party, a party traditionally seen as liberal, and supportive of women's rights.[32] His statement advanced a stereotypical view of women as emotionally unstable, and hence more prone to destroy the family on an irrational impulse.

Rhetorical Argument 2: The Khulʿ *Procedure is Limited in Application to Rich Women*

A small number of MP's criticised article 20 of Law no. 1 of 2000 on the basis that it was limited in its application to rich women, who could afford to 'ransom' themselves from their husbands. They maintained that the provision did not adequately meet the needs of poor Egyptian women, who constituted more than 60% of the female population.[33] Relying on this notion, MP *Abdel Moneim el-Oleimy* argued that the provision contravened the stipulation in article 40 of the Constitution that all citizens are equal before the law, for discriminating against poor women.[34] Although this argument didn't constitute a major basis for opposition

---

[30] Allam Mohamed Abdel Halim, 22nd Parliamentary Session at 29–30.

[31] Badr Mahrous Mohamed Soliman Sha'arawy (National Democratic Party). Ibid.

[32] Serageddin was one of law's fiercest opponents and walked out in the midst of the parliamentary discussions on the new law, on the pretext that the sessions were being conducted in an undemocratic manner. He was of the view that the People's Assembly was dealing with the law in a hasty manner, and that the *khulʿ* provision was in clear violation of the *Shari'a*. See Mariz Tadros, 'Rooster's Wrath', *Al-Ahram Weekly* 20–26 January 2000.

[33] Allam Mohamed Abdel Halim, 22nd Parliamentary Session at 29–30.

[34] Abdel Moneim El-Olaimy (Independent), 22nd Parliamentary Session at 31.

to the new law in the People's Assembly, it was widely propagated by the popular media.[35] It has also been advanced by non-governmental organisations, and even by the CEDAW Committee in its examination of Egypt's periodic reports.

Rhetorical Argument 3: As a Procedural Law, Law No. 1 of 2000 Should Exclude Matters of Substance

Challenging reforms to personal status legislation on the grounds of procedure is a well-known strategy in Egypt, and was utilised against Decree Law no. 44 of 1979, which was repealed by the SCC on procedural grounds. In a similar vein, a number of MP's attempted to challenge article 20 of Law no. 1 of 2000 on the grounds that the new law was exclusively procedural, and hence ought not to deal with substantive issues.[36] This argument, however, had few supporters, particularly since personal status laws in Egypt are generally comprised of a combination of procedural and substantive matters. In fact, it has been suggested, that introducing the *khulʿ* provision through a procedural law was a deliberate strategy by the government, to minimise opposition to the new law.

Rhetorical Argument 4: Khulʿ *Violates the Husband's Right to Guardianship (*Qiwama*)*

One basic argument against granting the wife the right to initiate *khulʿ* divorce was that such a right would violate the principle of *qiwama* or guardianship of the husband, which is arguably enshrined in the *Sharīʿa*. One MP went far enough to argue that a strict adherence to the letter and spirit of the *Quran* necessitated that women remain confined to the home.[37] Although these opinions were relatively limited, they clearly indicate the persistence of strictly conservative views that propagate a very restrictive approach to women's rights and status under the *Sharīʿa*. Such voices are hence openly hostile to any reform of the personal status law that breaks the power hierarchy within the family, or tips the balance slightly to the advantage of women. It is such misinformed and bigoted views that threaten to erode the achievements made by Egyptian women over the past decades.

---

[35] See, for instance, Amina El-Bendary 'Conditional Surrenders', *Al-Ahram Weekly* 13–19 January 2000, Mariz Tadros, 'What Price Freedom?', *Al-Ahram Weekly* 7–13 March 2002.

[36] Abdel Moneim El-Olaimy (Independent), 22nd Parliamentary Session at 32.

[37] This argument invoked the *Quranic* verse commanding the wives of the Prophet to remain within their matrimonial home (*waqarn fee biyutikinna*).

Rhetorical Argument 5: Khulʿ Requires Consent of the Husband
According to this view, judicial *khulʿ*, as properly applied, requires the husband's consent in order for the separation to take effect. Proponents of this view based their argument on a different account (*riwaya*) of the prophetic tradition involving *Habiba* and her husband *Thabit*. According to this account, the Prophet when approached by *Habiba* regarding the separation, asked her to go back to her husband and seek his consent.[38] They also site the previously mentioned *Quranic* verses, which require the husband's consent in order for the wife to 'ransom' herself and the divorce to take place, as well as the interpretations of the four classical schools, which maintain that *khulʿ* is a consensual transaction that may only be executed by the prior agreement of the two parties.[39]

According to this view, since the decision on judicial *khulʿ* is taken by both spouses concomitantly, there is no room for judicial action, let alone such action without the husband's consent. Even if judicial intervention were to be permitted, it cannot be done in the manner provided for in article 20, which leaves absolutely no room for judicial discretion in effecting the divorce, granting the wife, in effect, an automatic divorce if she so insists. This was, perhaps, the most challenging argument articulated against the new law and the most difficult to counter. Only by introducing *ijtihād* as a reform tool, and disregarding the prevailing opinions of the four classical schools, could this argument be challenged and defeated.

Arguments in Favour of the Current Formulation of Article 20

Equally, there were many arguments expressed in support of article 20, primarily by members of the previously ruling NDP, as well as other government representatives. Given the composition of the People's Assembly at the time, these arguments naturally outnumbered those expressed against the law. An obvious trend in most of the statements of support was the tendency to rely on patriarchal argumentation to appeal to conservatives and avoid unnecessary hostility. Very few arguments were articu-

---

[38] They include Yassin Serag Eddin (*Wafd* Perty), Ragab Helal Hemeida (*Al-Ahrar* party) *Minutes of the Twenty-Second Parliamentary Session* at 37; Abdel Aziz Mohamed Ahmed Shahin *Minutes of the Twenty-Eighth Parliamentary Session* at 13.

[39] See, for instance, the Statements of Ragab Helal Hemeida (*al-Ahrar party*); Mohamed Abdel Fattah Elmissry; Mohamed Ahmed Marzouk; Abdel Moniem el-Olaimy (Independent); Abdel Aziz Mohamed Shahin recorded in: Minutes of the 28th Parliamentary Session.

lated in terms of the rights of women or standards of equality, or conformity with international obligations. Conversely, most proponents of the new law vehemently argued against its characterisation as an achievement for women.

Rhetorical Argument 1: Khul' *Can Be Beneficial to the Husband and Family*

Faced with the critique that the new law would inevitably lead to a breakdown in family structure, proponents of article 20, held that the new provision on *khul'* would actually contribute to the stability of family relations. This line of argumentation, which attempted to promote the potential advantages to the family and the husband to be reaped through the *khul'* procedure, sought to avoid any reference to the rights of women. Precisely, the argument was framed in the terms that no healthy family could be based on hatred and oppression, and that the husband stood to benefit from the *khul'* separation, through restoration of the dowry and maintaining his dignity (since no dignified man could accept to hold a wife that loathed him). In expressing this argument, the Minister of Justice claimed that the new law "does not take from the man to give to the woman, neither does it take from the woman to give to the man."[40]

In fact, in order to sell article 20, the Minister of Justice asserted that the intention of the law was not to grant women the right to no-fault divorce according to their whims. Conversely, it was envisaged to govern only situations of extreme injustice and oppression. This portrayal of *khul'* as a type of divorce for harm was clearly intended to appeal to conservative mentalities, whose patriarchal approach to family relations would not allow for a law that placed women on an equal footing with their husbands.[41] The reform was thus sold as upholding the rights of the man and the family. Any reference to equality rights for women would have arguably aborted the whole process.

Rhetorical Argument 2: The Law Does Not Discriminate against Poor Women

In response to allegations that the *khul'* procedure was only restricted to rich women who could afford to ransom themselves from inconvenient marriages, Dr. *Abdel Rahman el-'Adawy*[42] provided a counter-argument,

[40] Minister of Justice, *Minutes of the 22nd Parliamentary Session* at 7.

[41] This argumentation was also adopted in the *Explanatory Memorandum* of the new law.

[42] The Government's representative in the Islamic Research Academy.

based on purely logical considerations. He explained that the *khulʿ* procedure only required the wife to return the dowry she was given by her husband. If the woman was rich, that would likely amount to a large sum of money; however, if she were poor, it would in all likelihood be much less. As such, poor women and rich women were treated equally under the new law, as paying back a small dowry would not prevent or deter poor women from seeking divorce through *khulʿ*.

Rhetorical Argument 3: The Draft-Law Has Been Aptly Examined and Approved

Many proponents of article 20 suggested that since the law had been examined by several high-level committees, and had passed through a nine-year review process, the Assembly should accept the validity of the draft provision, without need for further debate or commentary. It was repeatedly iterated that the law had been examined by a Committee of representatives from the Ministry of Justice, as well as the Islamic Research Academy of *al-Azhar*, chaired by the Grand *Sheikh of al-Azhar*, which had approved the provision by a majority of 35 out of 40 members. The draft provision had also received the approval of the Legislative Committee of the State Council (*majlis al-dawla*) which meant that it must have been adequately scrutinised for conformity with the *Sharīʿa*.

The argument that the draft law should not even be debated because it had already been vetted by the above-mentioned authorities was advanced by the representatives of the Parliamentary Committee of the National Democratic Party.[43] This attests to the important role played by the religious institutions in legitimating reform of *Sharīʿa*-derived legislation, and the close relationship these institutions had with the government. A similar argument was upheld by the Parliamentary Committee of the left-leaning *Tagamuʿ* party. This position, though serving to expedite the adoption of legislative reforms, also raises questions regarding the role of the People's Assembly and its legislative mandate, and what may be characterised as submission to government-introduced initiatives.

Rhetorical Argument 4: Khulʿ *Exists in Other Arab and Islamic Countries*

The argument that the *khulʿ* procedure exists in the laws of other Arab and Islamic countries, specifically Libya, Morocco, Jordan, Syria, Yemen and Kuwait lent credence to the claim that *khulʿ* was not a novel *ijtihād* of

[43] Ahmed el-Alfy (National Democratic Party); Khaled Mohy Eddin.

the Egyptian jurists.[44] Reference was also made to the draft Arab Model Unified Law on Personal Status, which includes a provision on *khul'*. To support the claim that *khul'* does not necessarily require the husband's consent, reference was made to article 14 of the Libyan Personal Status Law, which states that if the spouses do not consent to the separation, a judge may decide to effect the *khul'* divorce in exchange for a reasonable sum of money.[45] No mention was made as to whether other Arab countries waived the requirement of obtaining the husband's consent. This argument was later incorporated in the Explanatory Memorandum of Law no. 1 of 2000.

Rhetorical Argument 5: The Khul' *Procedure Upholds Justice*
Another important argument was that the new law was necessary to meet the evolving needs of society and to avoid oppression. Several MP's suggested that the *khul'* procedure established justice by giving the wife a means to evade 'repression', 'slavery' and 'imprisonment'. The *Sheikh* of *al-Azhar's*, intervention was the only statement that advanced a Muslim-feminist perspective, namely that the *khul'* procedure was necessary to put an end to the wife's suffering at the hands of an oppressive husband, and that it could find support in the *Sharīʿa*'s conception of justice, and of marital relations based on compassion and mercy (*mawadda wa raḥma.*) He further asserted that the *Sharīʿa* view of social justice upholds the equality of the genders in particular areas, including equality in dignity and equality of religious obligations, and does not tolerate oppression.[46]

Although this view attempted to create a perception of *khul'* as a type of divorce for harm, to be applied in extreme cases where the wife was 'oppressed' by the husband, it also emphasised the egalitarian principles of the *Quran* that could be used to justify reforms in family law. The significance of this argument, articulated by the highest religious authority in Egypt, is its reference to the issue of equality between men and women, albeit beneath the cloak of the more general rhetoric on social justice. It demonstrates the important role of the religious institution in advancing a moderate interpretation of the religious scriptures, and a cautious reform agenda, in spite of widespread opposition by conservatives.

---

[44] Supporters of this argument include Mohamed Mohamed Aboul Einein (National Democratic Party) *Minutes of the 28th Parliamentary Session* at 30.

[45] Ibid.

[46] Sheikh Tantawy, Grand Sheikh of Al-Azhar, *Minutes of the 22nd Parliamentary Session*.

Rhetorical Argument 6: Khulʿ *Will End the Suffering of the Wife*

This essentially feminist view, proposed by only one MP, held that the *khulʿ* law was necessary in order to ensure women's equal rights, and to end their suffering through the procedure of divorce for harm, which often took as long as eight or nine years to be completed. This strand of argument was based on the *Quranic* stipulation that women have rights equal to their obligations (*lahunna mithl alathy ʿalayhinna*),[47] thus finding legitimacy by reference to religious scriptures. It is quite surprising that such arguments, which are at the very heart of the proposed reform that essentially targeted women's divorce rights, were extremely limited.

Rhetorical Argument 7: There Is Strong Evidence for Khulʿ *in the* Quran *and* Sunnah

A common thread that ran through the arguments of the Minister of Justice, Grand *Sheikh* of *Al-Azhar*, and representatives of the government was that the *khulʿ* procedure was well-grounded in the verses of the *Quran* and the Prophet's tradition. In expounding this opinion, they asserted that the *khulʿ* procedure existed in the *Quran* and the *Sunnah*, as well as the four *Sunni* jurisprudential schools and the *ijmaʿ* of the religious scholars. However, they avoided commenting on whether the procedure envisaged by the four schools was the same as the one codified in article 20 of the new law.

Although there was hardly any reference to the precise opinions of the four schools, to confirm that *khulʿ* did not require the husband's consent, there was plenty of reference to the specific accounts of the ḥadith recorded by *al-Bukhari* and *al-Nissa'i*. These accounts of the prophetic tradition involving *Ḥabiba* and *Thabit* clearly indicate that the prophet did not seek *Thabit*'s consent, but granted *Ḥabiba* the separation automatically when she expressed her willingness to return the dowry. In light of the obvious lack of support of the four schools, reference to their opinions was both sparse and superficial.

The Minster of Justice, however, held that the *Māliki* school acknowledged the right of the couple to refer the dispute to a judge, in the case that they failed to reach an agreement. It followed that, based on pure logic, this school envisaged a situation where the wife could be granted the divorce, even without the husband's consent.[48] This argument was

---

[47] Farran, *Minutes of the 28th Parliamentary Session.*

[48] Sheikh of al-Azhar, *Minutes of the 22nd Parliamentary Session* at 13.

further expounded by *el-ʿAdawy* who maintained that the *Māliki* school allowed for judicial intervention at the hands of two arbitrators in the case that the spouses failed to reach agreement on separation. The decision of the arbitrators in such cases was binding. If the arbitrators disagreed amongst themselves, the decision would be up to the judge's discretion. *El-ʿAdawy* used this reasoning to argue that the *Māliki* school did not require the husband's consent in order for the divorce to take place. The text of article 20 is thus reconcilable with the interpretation of that school.

However, a close reading of article 20, in its current formulation, reveals that there is no room for the judge to exercise any discretion; he has no choice but to submit to the wife's will. If the wife maintains that she "fears transgression of God's limits," she is automatically granted the divorce. Moreover, as mentioned previously, the repeated references to the interpretations of the *Māliki* school seem to confuse divorce for mutual harm (or discord) described in the relevant passage of *Imam Mālik's* Compendium and *khulʿ*. It is thus quite evident that article 20 departed from the established opinion of the *Māliki* school, although there was a reluctance to admit that during the drafting process.

In fact, the chairman of the Committee of Religious, Social Affairs and *Waqf* asserted that the Assembly was actually going back to apply the true *Sharīʿa* once more, proving that it is flexible, and adaptable to modern realities. He maintained that article 20 was in complete conformity with the direct and unambiguous stipulations (*qāti'at al thubūt wal dalāla*) of the canonical sources of the *Sharīʿa*, and that the Assembly could therefore sidestep juristic opinions that opposed these sources.[49]

On the other hand, without referring to direct passages from the Compendia of the four *Sunni* schools, the *Sheikh* of *al-Azhar* asserted that "we are not basing this law on our own *ijtihādāt*".[50] This statement reveals two things; first, that any official acknowledgement of *ijtihād* could potentially alienate many supporters and provoke many opponents of the law. And second, although any mental exercise that leads to a different interpretation of the religious scriptures is, in essence, *ijtihād*, the official position was that in this specific case there was no need for either new *ijtihād* or the *ijtihād* of the classical schools because the

[49] Ahmed Omar Hashem (Chairman of the Committee of Religious and Social Affairs and Waqf) *Minutes of 22nd Parliamentary Session* at 27–28.

[50] Ibid.

religious scriptures were absolute and unambiguous in their meaning. The majority of proponents of article 20 thus emphasised the evidence for *khulʿ* as a non-consensual procedure in the Prophetic traditions, repeatedly making reference to the account recorded by *al-Bukhari* and *al-Nissa'i*, while eschewing the jurisprudence of the classical jurists.

Taken together, the government's policy, supported by the religious establishment, and backed by the jurisprudence of the Supreme Constitutional Court, whether deliberately or inadvertently, endorsed *ijtihād* as a reform tool, while maintaining an appearance of continuity with the past. This cautious approach has served the articulation of a pragmatic and gradual reform agenda that succeeded in alienating extremist positions and promoting a moderate legislative reform policy.

Explanatory Memorandum to Law No. 1 of 2000

The Explanatory Memorandum to the law further indicates that article 20 was sold to conservatives by reference to family rights rather than the rights of women. The Memorandum, which designates a whole section to article 20, rationalises *khulʿ* by construing it as a means to uphold the man's financial rights, and maintain the woman's modesty. The Memorandum begins by explicitly stating that the basis for *khulʿ* is to be found in the relevant *Quranic* verses and the account of the Prophet's tradition involving *Thabit bin Qays* as recorded in the Compendia of *al-Bukhari* and *al-Nissa'i*. The Memorandum proceeds to explain that the *khulʿ* procedure is not unknown to Egyptian legislation; it existed in principle under Law no. 78 of 1931 on the Organisation of the *Sharīʿa* Courts. As such, Law no. 1 of 2000 didn't introduce a new concept, but simply codified the exact procedures that would allow for *khulʿ* separation, while maintaining the rights of both spouses. It emphasises that:

> the law upholds the rights of the husband by reinstating the material gifts he gave to his wife, and absolves him of any of the financial burdens of divorce. As such, insisting on 'holding on' to the wife would cause her harm, which contravenes the principle of the *Sharīʿa* that one is to avoid harm to oneself and to others (*la ḍarar walā ḍirār*). It also relieves the wife of the need to sue for divorce on the basis of harm, which could force her to reveal the secrets of her conjugal relations, a matter of great difficulty for modest women, who may feel that revealing such secrets would harm their children.[51]

[51] *Explanatory Memorandum*, Law no. 1 of 2000 (author's translation).

The Explanatory Memorandum asserts that the Court will exert its utmost to reconcile the spouses, and if that fails, the divorce will be granted on condition that the wife return the dower and forfeit her right to alimony. It concludes by stating that the *khulʿ* procedure has the effect of relieving the 'disturbed' family, and the 'confused' wife. However, in reality, the law does much more than that. It grants women, on a basis of equality with men, the right to no-fault divorce, previously unforeseen by Egypt's family law. It thus strikes at the very heart of the belief that a man may hold his wife against her will, and force her into 'obedience' if she no longer desires to share a life with him, extending to the wife the traditionally male prerogative to leave the marriage at will.

In order to advance the *khulʿ* provision it was imperative that the law-maker address and appeal to patriarchal mentalities in order to neutralise conservatives. It is through such "patriarchal pronouncements on the outer limits that the 'reformer' gains legitimacy for his or her reforms in the eyes of watchful religious contenders."[52] *Khulʿ* arguably could never succeed if it had been promoted as an equality right for women, although, in essence, that is what the law ultimately achieved.

Procedural Reforms and the Establishment of the Family Court

The introduction of *khulʿ* divorce was supplemented by the institution of several significant reforms in litigation procedures. The intention of the reforms was to streamline judicial procedures by consolidating all personal status disputes into a single case brought before one court. In October 2004, the People's Assembly promulgated Law no. 10 of 2004, which created a Family Court with the capacity to facilitate personal status lawsuits and provide prompt legal redress to women. By virtue of the new system, all stages of the case are presented to the same court, composed of a panel of three judges, which theoretically facilitates court proceedings.

The procedural reforms introduced by Law no. 1 of 2000 also seek to relieve the parties of unnecessary administrative expenses. Article 3 of the law stipulates that fees are eliminated at all stages of litigation in cases

---

52 Abu-Odeh (2004) at 1048.

dealing with maintenance and alimony, whereas articles 61–63 seek to reduce overall delays in personal status cases. Articles 10 and 15 stipulate that when a divorce is granted, all matters relating to that case (such as child custody and alimony) will be resolved by the same court.

The law makes an attempted reconciliation, through the newly-established Family Dispute Settlement Offices (*makātib taswiyāt munāzaʿāt al-usra*) mandatory before any judgement on the case is to be delivered. Such mediation is only required when the wife initiates the divorce[53] although there are current proposals to establish mandatory dispute settlement procedures in the case of divorce initiated by the husband.

Although commentators are divided on the merits of compulsory mediation in personal status cases, in general,[54] this analysis will be confined to assessing the new system as it now stands. Under the new law, a report on the family dispute is prepared by a psychologist and a social worker, one of whom has to be a woman. They will also offer mediation and counselling to couples free of charge, which may potentially avoid extensive legal procedures.[55] The public prosecutor may intervene in the dispute by submitting a memorandum of opinion to the court.[56]

While the new law is obviously an important development, and was welcomed by many women's right groups, it has also been the subject of significant criticism. It has been argued that the changes brought about by these procedural reforms are purely cosmetic; the Family Courts exist on the same premises as the regular court system, but with different entrance and exit points. They are equally overcrowded, apply the same substantive laws, and are staffed by the same male judges,[57] who have often shown bias against women and conservatism in the enforcement of reforms. Moreover, it has been argued that the psychologists and social workers that are entrusted with mediation are not sufficiently trained, and are inclined to compromise the rights of the wife for the supposed benefit of preserving the family. That is not to mention the unnecessary delays

---

[53] Law no. 10 of 2004. See *Divorced from Justice* at 54.

[54] For a comprehensive analysis of this subject, and the shortcomings of the new Family Court system, see Mulki Al-Sharmani, 'Recent Reforms in Personal Status Laws and Women's Empowerment. Family Courts in Egypt', *American University in Cairo Social Research Centre* (2007) at 58.

[55] *Divorced from Justice* at 54.

[56] Al-Sharmani, 'Recent Reforms in Personal Status Laws', at 58.

[57] Zeinab Mohamed, [Lawyer specialized in personal status cases], *Interview* (November 5th, 2004).

that result from the application of the new system, as a judgement is only rendered if all reconciliation attempts fail.[58]

It has also been argued that this new alternative dispute resolution mechanism "lack[s] authoritative legal structure, adequate training and resources, enforcement mechanisms, and a supportive legal and societal environment."[59] The public prosecutor's role has been slated as insufficient, failing to contribute in any significant way to the adjudication process, and therefore unnecessarily prolonging it. Finally, the fact that the judges in the new courts are not specialised Family Court judges "hinders the development of adequate judicial expertise and accordingly impacts the quality of the adjudication process."[60]

On the other hand, to be fair in judging the new system, the fact that the Court is composed of a panel of three judges, unlike the regular Courts of First Instance, may contribute towards a due and fair process.[61] Moreover, in purely statistical terms, the new law seems to have achieved some of its stated objectives since it came into force in October 2004. In its first year of operation, purportedly 50% of all personal status cases brought to the Court were settled through conciliation.[62] Although this is a positive indication of sorts, possibly signifying women's success in having their grievances addressed through the conciliation mechanism, it could equally imply that women are pressured to compromise on their rights through the conciliation process, in light of the social stigma attached to adjudication.

Another major development has been the establishment of the Family Insurance Fund through Law no. 11 of 2004, which seeks to ensure the enforcement of alimony and child support payments. Under the previous system, the Nasser Social Bank, a government entity, provided alimony and child support to women in the case that their husbands evaded payment. The Bank later collected the payments from the ex-husbands by direct deduction. However, the Bank was eventually forced to halt its operations due to its inability to collect the necessary funds, particularly from men who worked in the private or informal sectors.[63]

58 Aboul Komsan, *Interview.*

59 Al-Sharmani, 'Recent Reforms in Personal Status Laws', at 58.

60 Ibid.

61 Ibid. at 58.

62 Interview with Adham Faheem, Counsellor *Mahkamet Ganoub Al Qahira* [South Cairo Court] (October 20th, 2004).

63 *Divorced from Justice* at 52.

The newly-established Fund, which is attached to Nasser's Social Bank, generates its resources through the administrative fees levied for the registration of births, marriages, and divorces, as well as governmental contributions.[64] The system does, however, have a major shortcoming; the Fund's maximum payment is only 500 Egyptian pounds per month. Although such support is expected to assist a large number of Egyptian women, "the payments will not be sufficient for many middle class women and will do nothing to help women in debt because of years of accumulated unpaid support."[65] Moreover, the system suffers from another major lacuna, namely its failure to address the situation of divorced women who have no children from their ex-husbands. Such women still suffer from the problems associated with poor enforcement of court decisions with regards to alimony.[66] Finally, the Bank recently decided not to enforce maintenance agreements issued by mediation offices.[67] Overcoming these obstacles would undoubtedly provide women with an important mechanism with which to enforce their legal rights.

In balance, it is too early to judge whether these reforms will really overcome the procedural burdens that hamper women's ability to enjoy the protections afforded to them by law. In spite of the persistence of a number of legal gaps and shortcomings, the new procedural law undoubtedly represents an important step for women seeking a more effective and speedy settlement of family disputes.

To date, legal reforms in the area of family law seem to have been imposed from above, through a top-down model that is more difficult to defend before a conservative public, and less amenable to rapid internalisation. However, the sheer numbers of women resorting to the Family Courts to settle their family disputes attests to the existence of some degree of trust and acceptance of the system. With the passage of time, new values reflected by the legal reforms will start to take root, and gradually transform the strict power hierarchy within the family. More important than the specific outcome of each legal reform, therefore, is the socialising effect of these legal developments, and the concomitant debates regarding the legal status of women under the *Sharīʿa*. It is

---

[64] Law no. 11 of 2004, art. 2.

[65] *Divorced from Justice* at 52.

[66] Saeed Halwa, 'Thaghrat Shar'iyya fi qanun al-ahwal ashakhsiyya' [Legal Lacuna in the Personal Status Law] *Al-Ahram* 8 (18 February 2005).

[67] Al-Sharmani, 'Recent Reforms in Personal Status Laws', at 58.

through such debates that the process of validation and absorption of the new social norms, inherent in important legal reforms, begins. This process however, is a complex and gradual one that is bound to run up against numerous economic, political and cultural challenges. Although some of these challenges have, and will continue to be addressed by the government, there are others that require the participation of other stakeholders, such as civil society, in a broad and comprehensive strategy to advance the family rights of women. Of these challenges, the most daunting is, perhaps, opposition by traditionalists and radical Islamists, intent on sabotaging the modernisation effort in a bid to achieve their own political ends.

CHAPTER NINE

DOMESTIC ENFORCEMENT OF WOMEN'S HUMAN RIGHTS

The actual implementation and enforcement of human rights, including women's rights, takes place, by and large, in the domestic sphere. International standards are useful only to the extent that they are incorporated into a State's domestic law, allowing direct access through the judicial system. In other words, an abundance of legal standards and instruments at the international level will hardly trickle down to affect the lives of women on the ground unless there are adequate domestic tools to enforce such standards. Legally binding international treaties are not effective without a commitment on the part of a government to actually enforce them, through implementing national laws that prohibit gender discrimination.[1] The CEDAW thus places the burden of enforcement of women's equality rights on the domestic legal institutions of the State.[2] Hossain asserts that the international principle of non-discrimination on the basis of gender,

> constitutes "invaluable ammunition" for expanding, establishing, and enforcing standards in domestic law. Applying the international equality norm to inform the content of constitutional and legislative provisions in domestic courts remains the most effective mechanism for protecting women's rights in the family as elsewhere.[3]

According to article 24 of the CEDAW "State parties undertake to adopt all necessary measures at the national level aimed at achieving the full realisation of the rights recognised in the present Convention." Although the wording of article 24 suggests that States have discretion in adopting "methods that suit the political traditions, constitutional conventions and idiosyncrasies of their legal and political orders" to enforce the CEDAW,[4] such discretion is most certainly not unfettered. In exercising

---

1 Plattner (1995/1996) at 1254.
2 Suneja (2002) at 38.
3 Hossain (1994) at 485.
4 Cook, *State Accountability under the Women's Convention*, at 247.

this 'margin of appreciation', States must display good faith in interpreting their treaty obligations, and due diligence in achieving non-discrimination.

Enforcing international human rights standards domestically is a challenge that confronts women in many societies. According to the Beijing Declaration and Programme of Action:

> The gap between the existence of rights and their effective enjoyment derives from a lack of commitment by Governments to promoting and protecting those rights and the failure of Governments to inform women and men alike about them. The lack of appropriate recourse mechanisms at the national and international levels, and inadequate resources at both levels, compound the problem.[5]

In turn, while reforming the law may address the worst forms of discrimination faced by women, it cannot immediately have the effect of modifying social values that discriminate against them. This gap between *de jure* and *de facto* discrimination is even more difficult to bridge in conservative societies, where struggles over the human rights of women often transpire into "contestations over legal jurisdictions and authority, namely whether international legal standards will prevail to guide State policy, or whether other bodies of law (constitutional, religious, customary) are accorded precedence when there is a contradiction."[6] Principles of gender equality can, and have, been construed as secular in nature, or even 'anti-Islamic' and hence incompatible with the rules of the *Sharīʿa*. Although legislative reforms are a step in the right direction, they are challenged by a conservative judiciary, coupled with the persistence of patriarchal attitudes and cultural practices that fuel the ideological resistance to women's equality rights. Since the success of legal reforms is contingent on a positive attitude from the public and accurate interpretation by judges, such reforms can be completely defeated if the public finds ways to circumvent, them or if judges depart in their application from the 'intention' of the legislator.[7]

The change in the status of women is thus a historical process that depends on a number of factors, including economic, social and cultural factors. The hierarchical family structure has been affected through women's access to education, their entry into the workforce, as well as social and political action by the State and by non-governmental

[5] *Beijing Declaration and Programme of Action* at para. 217.
[6] Southard (1996) at 10.
[7] Shaham (1997) at 17.

organisations.[8] Although the rise of militant Islam, the weakness of grass-roots feminist organisations, women's inadequate awareness of their own rights, as well their under-representation within the judicial system have all hampered the pace of women's empowerment, family reform still persists at a steady pace.

In order to understand the obstacles to the process of reform in Egypt, it is imperative to "understand the nature and dynamics of the behaviour of governments as political entities acting within the context of specific political, economic and social conditions" as well as the nature and dynamics of prevailing power relations.[9] This is essential as "no government can afford to disregard the politically articulated positions of powerful groups or segments of its population who might want to maintain religious and customary laws."[10] The result has been that throughout the years, the State has often adopted a rather ambiguous and self-contradictory stance towards women's equality rights.

Discrimination against women in Egypt must therefore be understood within the context of several interrelated 'root causes' such as the gap between law and society, and the gap between the ruler and the ruled. Although Egypt's ousted regime was officially committed to advancing the rights of women, in the same manner as the *Nasser* and *Sadat* regimes were before it, many of its policies did not find resonance among Egypt's public. The result has been that many government-led initiatives, often perceived as policies imposed by an elite that is detached from the problems and realities of the people, have not achieved the requisite "broadly-based political support", particularly when such reforms affect entrenched cultural attitudes.[11]

According to Hajjar, lessons can be drawn from the Tunisian experience to inspire law reform strategies elsewhere in the Arab-Muslim world. Whereas reforms in Tunisia were a product of wide-spread support for the nationalist Bourguiba regime in the 1950's, their ultimate success was conditional upon the legitimacy of the regime and the "parallel mobilisation of socialist forces at the grassroots level."[12] The socialist party, which advocated and led the reform effort,

[8] Ibid. at 235.

[9] An-Naim, 'State Responsibility Under Human Rights Law to Change Religious and Customary Laws', at 169.

[10] Ibid.

[11] See Ibid. at 178.

[12] Hajjar (2005) at 1981.

> undertook to educate the general population about the need for change, created the National Union for Tunisian Women, and included women on its electoral slates. Thus women were enfranchised socially, economically, and politically due in significant part to the efforts of extra-governmental actors.[13]

Notwithstanding these realities, Egyptian women have made some substantial gains through articulating a domestic discourse on women's human rights, inspired by the principles of the *Shari'a*. The convergence of the efforts of NGOs, the government and other stakeholders led to significant reforms of the personal status law in recent years, both substantively and procedurally. Such piecemeal reforms, however, are insufficient, in and of themselves, to transform the status of women in Egyptian society and break the strict power hierarchy within the family.

The Challenges Confronting Domestic Enforcement

The obstacles to the domestic enforcement of women's equality rights in the area of family relations are numerous and complex. They can be divided into five main categories: (1) a conservative judiciary that is unwilling to adequately enforce the law; (2) the mixed impact of grassroots feminist organisations; (3) the rise of political Islam and the government's appeasement policy; (4) the prevalence of patriarchal attitudes and the negative social stigmas attached to women's enjoyment of their equality rights, particularly in the area of family relations; (5) women's lack of awareness of their rights, and hence their complicity in the violation of their own human rights. These factors will each be considered in the sections below, with particular emphasis on the State's obligation to address these obstacles in compliance with its international obligations.

Judicial Conservatism

The judiciary is universally recognised as the "safety valve which balances human rights on the one hand, and public order or the stability of society on the other."[14] Egypt's obligations as a State-party to the

[13] Ibid.

[14] Abdel Rahman Nosseir, 'The Supreme Constitutional Court of Egypt and the Protection of Human Rights', in Eugene Cotran and Adel Omar Sherif (eds.), *The Role of the Judiciary in the Protection of Human Rights* (1997) at 50.

CEDAW include ensuring adequate judicial application of the principles incorporated in the Convention. Judicial enforcement of international human rights standards depends on the independence of the judiciary, and the extent to which judges are willing to resort to international human rights norms as a source of interpretation of domestic legislation.[15]

In Egypt, women frequently resort to the judiciary to claim their rights in cases involving divorce, maintenance, child custody, alimony and other personal status matters. This litigation process previously took place through the regular court system, (summary courts, courts of first instance, appeals courts, and the Court of Cassation). However, in October 2004, with the introduction of Law no. 10 of 2004, a consolidated system of specialised Family Courts was established.

In spite of these changes, the fact remains that the system is overwhelmingly presided by the same male judges that spearheaded the previous adjudication process. Journalistic accounts suggest that these judges are more inclined towards conservative argumentation in personal status issues.[16] This is particularly evident in cases where women file for judicial divorce based on 'harm', in which case they are required to meet very high thresholds of harm in order to satisfy the judge.

Judicial conservatism is evident in how members of the judiciary have approached the recent reforms in personal status law. One senior judicial authority stated that the philosophy behind these reforms was not to protect the rights of women, but to protect the family unit, stressing that they should not be construed otherwise.[17] The insistence on giving priority to the protection of the family over the rights of the woman suggests a resistance among some officials in the judiciary to granting women more extensive equality rights.

The problem of judicial conservatism has been exacerbated by the exclusion of women from the judiciary. Although this exclusion is neither codified in Egypt's laws nor its Constitution, it is a matter of

---

[15] Ibrahim Badawy El Sheikh, *Nafāth Iltizamāt Masr al-dawliyya fi Majāl Huqūq al-Insan fi alNizām al-Qanūni al-Masry* [The Enforcement of Egypt's International Human Rights Obligations in the Egyptian Legal System] (2003) at 203–204.

[16] See Fatma Khafagy, 'Traps of Empowerment', *Al-Ahram Weekly* 10–16 March 2005, available at http://weekly.ahram.org.eg/2005/733/fe1.htm; see also Tadros, 'The Third Option'

[17] Judge Adham Faheem, [Deputy President of the *Ganoub Al Quhira* Court] Interview.

"standard practice based on stereotypical and biased views about women."[18] Recently, however, a woman was appointed by presidential decree to the Supreme Constitutional Court, and thirty women were appointed in judicial positions throughout the country. These developments, however, are unlikely to lead to a widespread change in approach to the appointment of women judges in the near future, particularly in light of the recent conundrum related to the attempted barring of women judges from the Administrative Court system.

Egypt's Courts have traditionally adhered to so-called 'judicial principles' established by the Court of Cassation, which—although theoretically non-binding—have been used by judges as persuasive precedents. These principles have further reinforced the negative effects of a restrictive divorce structure, including cases of spousal violence.[19] Among these principles is the one that stipulates that "a husband's inappropriate conduct is not considered [by itself] grounds for divorce." Another principle stipulates that "a wife's return back to the home after having been harmed means that life could continue between [the spouses], which does not constitute grounds for divorce later."[20] That is not to mention that where reforms in legislation have been achieved, judges have proved reluctant to implement laws adequately. A telling example is the repeated attempts by judges to unnecessarily delay the implementation of divorce procedures under Law no. 1 of 2000, which the law was intended to facilitate.[21] Recent studies regarding the enforcement of Law no. 1 of 2000 have been described as 'disquieting' since they demonstrate the prevalent sexism and bias of judges against women. It has been observed that in a number of courts, specifically in rural areas, "judges have put pressure on women to withdraw their *khulʿ* cases by suggesting that they will have to give their husbands the deferred dower, return their *shabka* [gifts of jewellery], and generally increasing their financial losses beyond the intention of the law."[22]

---

[18] *Divorced from Justice* at 14.

[19] Hajjar (2005).

[20] Ibid.

[21] Reem Leila, 'A Family Affair', *Al-Ahram Weekly* 16–22 January 2003, available at http://weekly.ahram.org.eg/2003/621/fe1.htm; and Tadros, 'What Price Freedom?'.

[22] Diane Singerman, 'Rewriting divorce in Egypt: Reclaiming Islam, Legal activism and Coalition Politics', in Robert Hefner (ed.), *Civic Pluralist Islam: Prospects and Policies for a Changing Muslim World* (forthcoming), 36. Available at http://www.ucis.unc.edu/programs/Middle_East/Diane%20Singerman.pdf.

In a recent survey, it was revealed that "many judges, government officials, and others in the legal system share the prevailing societal view of women as inherently irrational and child-like."[23] This negative stereotype, as well as the patriarchal attitude of many judges, has placed Egyptian women in an uncertain legal position, adversely affecting their ability to demand already precarious legal rights before the Family Courts.

Whereas Egypt's Supreme Constitutional Court has recognised the importance of advancing the human rights of women in recent years, it is evident that such awareness is not reflected in courts at lower levels of the judicial system. Judicial ignorance and conservatism, often developing into outright obstructionism, thus represent sizeable challenges, depriving many reforms of their legal value. Countering this trend necessitates an active effort to properly disseminate the CEDAW and provide adequate training for judges, psychologists, social workers and lawyers, who form the backbone of the new Family Court structure.

The Mixed Impact of Non-Governmental Feminist Organisations

The role of feminist organizations is indispensable in changing attitudes towards women. Effective protection of women's rights is contingent upon a twin process of legal reform and societal change; women's groups are most aptly situated to contribute to both processes. The importance of women's non-governmental organisations cannot be overstated, as they represent the voice of those most adversely affected by discriminatory laws and practices. Without their wide participation in reassessing cultural practices, with broad-based support from interested women, "customs will continue to seem natural, continue to be unquestioned, and continue to be actively practiced and excused on the grounds of culture."[24] The lack of resolve by other actors to modify attitudes towards women can only be altered through persistent efforts by domestic pressure groups.[25]

There is no doubt that grassroots efforts are central in effecting feminist transformations.[26] The importance of such movements stems from their ability to 'indigenise' international standards, and to raise awareness

---

[23] *Divorced from Justice* at 28.

[24] Southard (1996) at 61–62.

[25] Suneja (2002) at 42.

[26] Sherifa Zuhur, 'The Mixed Impact of Feminist Struggles in Egypt During the 1990's', 5 *Middle East Review of International Affairs* (March 2001) available at http://meria.idc.ac.il/journal/2001/issue1/jv5n1a6.html.

among local constituencies about their existence. They play an important role in lobbying for legislative reforms, as well as in disseminating knowledge of international women's rights standards. That is not to mention their privileged position among all sectors of society, which enables them to integrate international standards in the social fabric through providing alternative, indigenous, feminist discourses. For these reasons, the CEDAW Committee in its General Recommendation 10, requested State parties to encourage "national women's organizations and non-governmental organizations at the national, regional and international levels to publicize the Convention and its implementation."[27] The Vienna Declaration and Programme of Action has also recognised "the important role of non-governmental organizations in the promotion of all human rights … at national, regional and international levels."[28] It further urged "governments, institutions, intergovernmental and non-governmental organizations to intensify their efforts for the protection and promotion of human rights of women and the girl-child."[29] Similarly, the Final Declaration of the International Population Conference, convened in Cairo in 1994, emphasised the centrality of the role of non-governmental organisations, and underscored the State's role in this regard. It stipulated that "every effort should be made to encourage the expansion and strengthening of grassroots, community-based and activist groups for women."[30] It encouraged the elaboration of national campaigns to "foster women's awareness of the full range of their legal rights, including their rights within the family, and to help women organize to achieve those rights."[31]

A State cannot possibly succeed in bringing about the wide-scale change in popular beliefs and attitudes foreseen by the CEDAW on its own. Strengthening the role of civil society is an important prerequisite to modifying cultural attitudes that discriminate against women, as required by articles 2 (f) and 5 of CEDAW. Changing laws based on religious or customary norms requires action by "a strongly motivated and

---

[27] *General Recommendation 10*, (1989) tenth anniversary of the adoption of CEDAW, CEDAW 8th Sess. (1989).

[28] *Vienna Declaration and Program of Action*, World Conference on Human Rights, A/CONF.157/23 (12 July 1993) para. 38.

[29] Ibid, para 18.

[30] *Report of the International Conference on Population and Development*, Resolution 1, Programme of Action, para 4.12 A/CONF.171/13 (18 October 1994) [Hereinafter ICPD Final Declaration].

[31] Ibid.

well-informed local constituency, willing and able to engage in organised action."[32] In the absence of such a local constituency, there will be no pressure on the State to effectuate its commitments or "implement change in accordance with human rights law."[33] In other words, no sea-change in attitudes towards the role of women will occur in the absence of a strong grassroots movement that will work at a local level to indigenise international standards, while simultaneously lobbying for further reform of discriminatory laws.

The history of the 'feminist movement' in Egypt dates back to the mid-nineteenth century. Towards the end of that century the 'woman question' (*qadiyat al-mar'ah*) which encompassed all aspects of women's role in society had become an issue of frequent public debate.[34] There have been many important studies of Egypt's 'feminist movement', with its internal divisions, and its impact on family law reform. These studies indicate that this movement was not simply a single 'movement', but rather "a collection of diverse groups—including women activists, local NGOs, government agencies and officials, prominent lawyers and judges".[35] These diverse groups had different ideas and agendas, which led to different views about what kinds of family law reforms were needed. Some efforts, for example, targeted the existing, substantive law to amend articles that discriminated against women and/or introduce provisions that would enhance women's rights. Others focused on reforming the procedures for litigation, while some championed initiatives intended to preserve the cohesion and stability of Egyptian families.[36]

Throughout its long history, the women's rights movement in Egypt has therefore achieved mixed results, passing through a number of peaks and low-points. The first high-point coincided with the so-called 'renaissance' of the late nineteenth century[37] and remained at a peak throughout the nationalist movement of the 1920's. Conversely, the period of the 1980's, was one of decline, due to the rise of political Islam. This period, which persisted until the end of the 1990's, witnessed an erosion of previous reforms, as the government struggled with policies to contain radical

[32] An-Naim, 'State Responsibility Under Human Rights Law to Change Religious and Customary Laws', at 178.
[33] Ibid. at 179.
[34] Guenena and Wassef (1999) at 12.
[35] Al-Sharmani, 'Egypt's Family Courts: Route to Empowerment?'.
[36] Ibid.
[37] Ibid.

Islamist groups. Since the turn of the twenty-first century, however, the reform project has once more gained important momentum, although it has recently been characterised by a more elitist constituency that is arguably removed from the grassroots.

In general, the feminist movement in Egypt has not succeeded in creating a widespread internal discourse on women's equality rights that is not viewed as an external, Western imposition, but as an authentically domestic (and hence by necessity 'Islamic') approach. Although each generation of Egyptian feminists has had the reform of personal status legislation at the top of its agenda, they "have been most successful in the public sphere and most thwarted in the private sphere."[38]

The past decade has witnessed a notable increase in the number of Non-Governmental Organisations in Egypt, including those specifically dealing with women's issues; however, this trend hasn't led to a concomitant advancement in the rights and status of Egyptian women.[39] Out of about 16,000 NGOs registered in Egypt, only 3 % deal specifically with women's issues. According to a purely functional classification, women's rights organizations can be divided into three broad categories.[40] The first and largest, comprised of charity organisations, mainly focuses on providing financial assistance in the form of donations to women and female-headed households. Such organisations play no role in legislative and social change and show little interest in modifying legislation that affects women's human rights. The second category comprises development NGOs, which develop sources of income for women most notably through providing micro-credit. They constitute about a quarter of the total number of women's NGOs and also play no direct part in lobbying for legislative reform.[41] Finally, advocacy NGOs, which lobby for changes in government policy and legislation, constitute less than 5 % of the total, or a mere ten NGOs.[42]

---

[38] Badran (1993) 129.

[39] Zuhur (2001).

[40] Aboul Komsan, *Interview*.

[41] However, their role is indispensable to advocacy NGO's since their grassroots work allows them to provide somewhat reliable statistics on issues related to women.

[42] Women's advocacy NGOs include: The Egyptian Center for Women's Rights, the Women and Society Association, the Alliance of Arab Women, the New Woman Research Center, the Center for Egyptian Women Legal Aid, the Forum for Women in Development as well as several general human rights organizations that also advocate for women's rights, including the Center for Legal Studies and Information for Human Rights, and the Cairo Institute for Human Rights Studies.

Throughout the 1980's, the Egyptian government was openly hostile to the few existing women's rights activist organisations, particularly in cases where they were affiliated to the political opposition. A widely cited case is that of the Arab Women's Solidarity Association (AWSA) established by Egyptian feminist *Nawal El-Sa'dawi* in 1985. The AWSA adopted a clearly confrontational attitude towards conservative positions on gender, particularly those labelled 'Islamic'.[43] In 1991, the government shut down AWSA, prompting women's groups to come together informally in order to avoid dissolution throughout the 1980's and 1990's.[44]

In the 1990's, however, it became more difficult for the government to take an actively inimical stance to women's organisations, particularly after the 1994 UN Population and Development Conference. The conference awakened not only the international community, but also domestic constituencies to the existence of institutionalised discrimination against women in Egypt. All of a sudden, and for the first time, discriminatory provisions of Egypt's criminal code, nationality law and personal status law came under international scrutiny. The conference thus came as a great boost for the ten-year campaign to amend these laws. In their campaign, Egyptian feminists made reference both to Egypt's international obligations, particularly under the CEDAW, as well as article 40 of the Constitution.[45] After ten years of campaigning, the coalition finally succeeded in amending the nationality law so as to allow Egyptian women to equally pass on the nationality to children from a foreign husband (albeit with some restrictions).

The women's rights movement has been further hampered by legal restrictions on the formation of NGO's. Although the amended Association Law, Law no. 84 of 2002 marked a significant change in the government's sceptical attitude towards NGO's, restrictions on the formation of civil society organisations still persisted. The law requires all associations to register with the Ministry of Social Affairs, subsequently granting the government the power to approve some NGOs and prohibit others. These measures have adversely affected several women's rights organisations, including the New Woman Research Centre established for the purpose of raising awareness on women's issues (particularly FGM and domestic violence), whose application to register under

[43] Badran (1993) at 142.
[44] Ibid.
[45] Aboul Komsan, *Interview*.

the new law was initially rejected.[46] Eventually, however, the decision was challenged before the State Council and reversed. Although the government is currently working on amending the NGO law, no official draft has been made available for public discussion. It therefore remains to be seen how the proposed amendments will facilitate the work of civil society.

It has also been argued that the establishment of so-called 'government-oriented' national mechanisms has marginalised grassroots movements and promoted an elitist reform agenda that favours cosmetic reforms instead of real substantive changes.[47] The CEDAW Committee has encouraged States to establish national mechanisms to help advance the rights and status of women. In its General Recommendation 6, the Committee stipulated that States must establish "effective national machinery ... at a high level of government" with the mandate to:

(a) Advise on the impact on women of all government policies;
(b) Monitor the situation of women comprehensively;
(c) Help formulate new policies and effectively carry out strategies and measures to eliminate discrimination.[48]

In 1978, the Egyptian government established the National Council for Women (NCW), in preparation for the International Women's Year Conference in Mexico City. It was often lamented that the NCW failed initially to bring about any significant change in the rights of women.[49] The National Council for Childhood and Motherhood (NCCM) was established in 1989. Prompted by the imminence of the Beijing Conference, Egypt renewed the national machinery's mandate, revitalising the NCW in 1993.[50] Throughout the last decade both Councils have been active in a number of fields; the NCW has drafted legislation in the areas of child custody and an impending draft personal status law, whereas the NCCM has launched an overall successful campaign to end FGM and to criminalise the sexual exploitation of children. In 2009 the head of the

---

[46] *Divorced from Justice* at 10.

[47] Aboul Komsan, *Interview*. See also Sherifa Zuhur and Amany Kandil, Address at the *Third Annual Conference of the Arab International Women's Forum* (June 8th, 2004).

[48] *General Recommendation no. 6*, National Machinery, CEDAW, 7th Session (1988).

[49] Mervat Tallawy, 'International Organizations, National Machinery, Islam and Foreign Policy', in Mahnaz Afkhami and Erika Friedl (eds.), *Muslim Women and the Politics of Participation. Implementing the Beijing Platform* (1997), 133.

[50] Singerman (forthcoming) at 28.

NCCM was selected to head Egypt's first Ministry for Family and Population, increasing the number of serving women Ministers to three for the first time in any serving Egyptian cabinet.

Although the NCW and NCCM have a progressive reform agenda and significant resources and technical expertise at their disposal that enable them to propose legal reforms and conduct wide-scale national campaigns, they have been subjected to three main criticisms. Often labelling them 'Government-Oriented' NGOs (or GONGO's), critics contend that the relationship between the NCW and activist NGOs is a "purely decorative" one.[51] Arguably, these mechanisms have the effect of curtailing the activism of advocacy NGOs, while maintaining the pretence of an active civil society. According to this view, the establishment of the two councils was prompted by the government's fear of increased civic activity, and desire to restrain NGO's, rather than a genuine commitment to advancing the rights of women. The direct effect has been the disempowerment and marginalisation of existing advocacy NGOs and the promotion of a milder, more elite form of feminism that has focused on more moderate reforms.[52]

According to some accounts, the marginalising role of the NCW was particularly evident during the final adoption of the amended nationality law and the personal status procedural law, whose drafts were shrouded in an atmosphere of secrecy before being presented to the People's Assembly.[53] The advocacy NGOs that had been part of the lobbying process for over a decade were not consulted, and only those included in the NCW's NGO Committee were involved, namely the "tamed development NGOs adopting the official government line."[54] In other words, the large and collaborative effort that gave birth to these laws was hijacked by the NCW near the end of the process.

Another grievance expressed by activists is that the NCW has a near monopoly over civil society representation at international conferences. It also purportedly attempted to take over the process of preparing the Shadow Report intended to assist the CEDAW Committee in its examination of Egypt's periodic reports. During the Committee's examination of Egypt's initial report in 2000, twenty-two NGOs came together

[51] *Shadow Report of the Egyptian Non-Governmental Organisations Coalition.*

[52] Several women's rights advocates, including Aboul Komsan and Zuhur, advance this view.

[53] Aboul Komsan, *Interview.*

[54] Ibid.

to prepare a Shadow Report, that was deeply critical of Egypt's policies with regards to women's equality rights. As a result, the government demanded that in the future one joint report, prepared by both the government and the NGO community, be submitted to the CEDAW Committee. However, none of the activist NGOs was invited to participate in the drafting process.[55]

Several NGOs have further expressed the concern that the NCW draws a considerable amount of foreign funding, diverting resources from NGO's and marginalising them further. This has facilitated the government's control of the women's rights agenda,[56] which has developed into "a moderate, elitist form of feminism which [the government] perceives to be helpful to the development process but does not necessarily [introduce] any disruptive social change regarding gender roles or women's status."[57]

On the other hand, recent reforms possibly would not have succeeded without the support of the country's political leadership and the joint and collaborative work of a coalition of activists, NGO's, lawyers, government departments, political leaders, legislators, and scholars.[58] The NCW, with its close links to the previous political leadership (it was headed by Egypt's former First Lady) played an important role in placing personal status law reform on the government's agenda. The disempowering effect of the NCW might also be an indication of the limited support base of NGO's, and their inability to impose themselves through the large-scale mobilisation of people, or make themselves sufficiently relevant through implementing coherent and sustainable programs. The recent revolution in Egypt has presented a historic opportunity for feminist NGO's to rebuild a popular support base, away from any political interference.

During the consideration of Egypt's combined sixth and seventh periodic reports to the CEDAW Committee in 2010, eight Shadow Reports were submitted by separate NGO's or NGO coalitions, of which five were Egyptian. This indicates that NGO's, including the most radical feminist NGO's have found a voice in this process, if not through consultation in the process of drafting the national report, then through the presentation of detailed Shadow Reports. While local NGO's developed their exper-

---

55 Ibid. For a list of participating NGO's, see *Shadow Report of the Egyptian Non-Governmental Organisations Coalition*.

56 *Divorced from Justice* at 10.

57 Zuhur (2001).

58 Singerman (forthcoming).

tise and capacity in order to actively participate in the reporting process, the government exhibited a greater degree of readiness to accept what sometimes amounted to rather harsh criticism. The recent move towards democratic governance in Egypt promises to usher in an era where NGO participation is no longer cosmetic, but is rather based on a mature and effective relationship with the State and political leadership.

Religious Conservatism and Resistance to Women's Equality Rights

Recent developments in Egypt indicate that the greatest contemporary threat to women's human rights arises from the "resurgence of radical fundamentalist thought and politics."[59] Since the 1970's, radical Islamist groups have accumulated both strength and supporters. While there is no single identifiable cause for this phenomenon, commentators have suggested a variety of contributing factors including economic hardship, the disillusionment with Egypt's defeat in the 1967 war with Israel, and the influx of Egyptian labour to the religiously conservative Arab Gulf (and their subsequent return in the 1980's). This process was encouraged throughout the 1970's by the "exploitation or use of religion from above by the government, for purposes of legitimization."[60] President Sadat's support for political Islam, in an attempt to overpower the remnants of the predecessor regime, was also a contributing factor. Given its strong potential for politicization, Islam became an undeniable force in Egyptian political discourse; "replac[ing] Arab nationalism as the ideology of dissent."[61] Women themselves became drawn to 'the Islamist ideology' in the hope for "economic deliverance and a badly needed sense of dignity and worth."[62]

As Islamist groups turned towards political violence, however, their relationship with the State gradually deteriorated, and the government's reaction was to crack down on them. As long as their utterances were restricted to issues of morality and social practices, however, Islamist groups were widely tolerated.

---

[59] Mahnaz Afkhami, "Gender Apartheid, Cultural Relativism, and Women's Human Rights in Muslim Societies", in Marjorie Agosín (ed.), *Women, Gender, and Human Rights: A Global Perspective* (2001).

[60] For a more detailed analysis of the rise of Islamic conservatism and the effect on the feminist movement in Egypt see Duval (1998) at 48–49.

[61] Duval (1998) at 52.

[62] Ghada Hashem Talhami, *Egyptian Feminism in the Balance. The Mobilisation of Muslim Women in Egypt* (1996) at 142.

In light of this political context, the 1980s and 1990s have been considered as the beginning of the era of Egyptian women's 'endangered rights.'[63] The widespread opposition to the 1979 reforms as well as the recent antagonism to the 2000 reforms both seem to be related to the "continuing rise of Islamist influence and an increasingly strong profile of religious authority within Egypt."[64] During this period, the feminist movement suffered several blows due to the government's 'flirtations' with political Islam.[65] The struggle between the government and extremists led to a precarious balancing act; whereas the former wasn't willing to strengthen these groups, it couldn't afford to completely overpower them either, particularly as the 'Islamic threat' became a convenient scarecrow and legitimising tool.[66]

A widely cited example of the State's attempts to incorporate the legitimating aspects of the Islamic discourse was the adoption in 1981 of the Constitutional amendment to article 2, which made the *Shari'a the* principal source of legislation (as opposed to *a* principle source of legislation). Many political parties in Egypt now agree—or at least purport to agree—that Islamic law should be the principle source of legislation.[67] Evidence can be found in the "evolving language of political discourse which now abounds with references to the *Quran* and the traditions of the Prophet as well as quotations from the writings of Muslim jurists and philosophers."[68] The result of these political dynamics was that no matter how hard the State tried to promote a progressive social agenda, its efforts were often rendered futile.

On the other hand, Islamist groups, vying for power, claimed that they were the true mantle-bearers of Islam, politicising the struggle for women's equality rights. As Shaheed observes,

> In reality, these claims and the often violent dynamics they entail, have little to do with religion. It is just that political parties and groups have found it expedient to use a religious idiom to express and mobilise support for their political agendas. Such politico-religious groups also find it convenient to cite so-called Islamic laws already being applied in different Muslim

---

[63] *Divorced from Justice* at 9.

[64] Zuhur (2001).

[65] Aboul Komsan, *Interview*.

[66] Karam (1997) at 25.

[67] Ibid.

[68] Mustapha Kamel el-Sayyed, 'The Islamic Movement in Egypt: Social and Political Implications', in Ibrahim M. Oweiss (ed.), *The Political Economy of Contemporary Egypt* (1990) at 234.

> countries in support of their own demands for more stringent, essentially undemocratic or discriminatory 'Islamic' laws, that amongst other things usually militate against the rights of women and minorities.[69]

The State and 'political Islam' were involved in a mutually reinforcing power dynamic, one that can only be broken through the promotion of alternative discourses presented by diverse local narratives.[70] In order for a solid transformation to occur in the way Egyptian society views and values women, it is therefore necessary to change the role of "fundamentalist political actors in defining the role of women in societies."[71]

It is within this political context, and in light of the historical background of interaction between the State and the religious institution in Egypt that the role of the religious establishment must be understood. In order to maintain its influence in daily life, *Al-Azhar* has adopted a dualistic response to the State while simultaneously asserting a certain degree of autonomy for itself. As such, it has been willing to accommodate and legitimate State policies, as long as the *Shari'a* "was not touched."[72] However, Egyptian feminists have argued that while compliant with the State's demands at the official level, "*al-Azhar's* contributions to educational thought and practice contradicted and even opposed the modernist premises of the State."[73] The tension between various forces in *al-Azhar* was evident during the promulgation of Law no. 1 of 2000. Although the law was backed by the Grand *Sheikh* of *al-Azhar*, the country's highest religious authority, it was opposed by 31 of the institution's scholars who sent a petition to the President demanding the law's revision.[74]

At another level, whereas *al-Azhar* publicly endorses many of the State's reforms, Mosque preachers who have an enormous following maintain a particularly conservative position with regards to women's

69 Shaheed (2001).

70 See Karam (1997) at 26, who also states that "as long as the discussion revolves around who is the better Muslim, one can expect a vicious circle wherein the more the State uses religious discourses to counter Islamist political hegemony, the more Islamists will rigidify their boundaries between good and bad or Muslim and Unbeliever."

71 Suneja (2002) at 42.

72 Guenana and Wassef (1999) at 8.

73 Ghada Talhami, *The Mobilization of Muslim Women in Egypt* (1996).

74 Mariz Tadros, 'Khul' Passes Major Test', *Al-Ahram Weekly* 19–25 December 2002. In addition, Zuhur describes public opinion towards the law as hostile, depicted by cartoons in many national magazines featuring "female harridans pursuing frantic husbands with their brooms, women rushing to the airports, or men donning women's clothes and headscarves and assuming domestic chores."

equality rights.[75] Given the huge amount of influence they wield in shaping the public's consciousness, it is absolutely necessary that the State invest in transforming preachers into a positive agent for change through adequate education, certification and monitoring. Just as the Mosques have the potential for rendering any reform effort futile, they are a potentially effective force for legitimation of reform policies. The centrality of this role must be recognised and adequately utilised in any comprehensive strategy to address the rights of women in the highly controversial area of family law.

The Prevalence of Patriarchal Social Attitudes

The public's hostility to government-introduced legislative reforms and their intense criticism in the media are all manifestations of the rise of social conservatism, and a fierce ideological resistance to women's equality rights. It is in this light that "the subject of personal status legislation [has] often given rise to criticism and public debate, bordering on public fury."[76] Whereas it cannot be denied that changes in law almost certainly have an impact on society, law reform strategies are most effective when "the social value base is in concordance with the desired new norms."[77] Legal reforms are thus more likely to succeed when society is more receptive to them, for "as long as the old regime of values is in effect, the tasks of making the new norms operative, or activating the educative function of law to change values, will be difficult and require action on many fronts."[78] The effect of the top-down process of reforming family law in Egypt will, therefore, be dampened unless there is a genuine and concerted effort to modify culturally-entrenched ideas and modes of behaviour that discriminate against women.

Patriarchal attitudes and the negative social stigmas that militate against the full enjoyment by women of their rights are shared equally by both men and women, often leading to women's complicity in the violation of their own equality rights. Several opinion polls, including one conducted by *Al-Mishkat* Research Centre in 2001, and by Freedom

---

75 Aboul Komsan, *Interview*.
76 Dahl (1997) at 192.
77 Hajjar (2005) at n. 13.
78 Ibid.

House in 2004 indicate that general societal attitudes towards personal status law reform in Egypt are quite negative. Such is the case among men and women alike.[79]

Journalistic accounts suggest similar findings; in March 2001, *Al Ahram Weekly* published a special issue on attitudes towards the Procedural Personal Status Law of 2000, commenting that in the aftermath of the adoption of the law, "massive campaigns were launched by opposition papers such as the liberal *Al-Wafd*, the Nasserite *Al-'Arabi* and Islamist *Al-Sha'b*" resisting the adoption of the new law.[80] Whereas it was predicted that up to two million women would file for divorce under the new law, only several thousand actually did so in the first five years.[81] The troubling indication is that even when reforms are executed, women are obviously reluctant to make use of their newly gained rights.

Social stigmas and patriarchal attitudes are further reinforced by Egypt's entertainment media, with an adverse effect on women's exercise of their rights. In general, the media portrays women as mothers and wives, usually in need of protection, which is provided by fathers, husbands and brothers. In exchange, women are expected to submit to male authority; rebellion against such authority is portrayed as deviance.[82] In addition, the media has contributed largely to the view that women's work outside the home results in negative social consequences, including the disruption of the family.[83] The stereotypes portrayed by the media are legitimised by reference to essentialist arguments, that women are, by their very constitution, emotional and erratic, that they are both fragile and vulnerable and hence require constant protection, and that they are incapable of independent and rational decision-making.

The situation is further expounded by the general lack of awareness among Egyptians, men and women alike, not only of the international protection afforded to women, but also of the egalitarian spirit

---

79 Fayza Hassan et al., *The Ultimate Emancipation of Women is in the Minds. Preliminary Results of an Opinion Poll* (2001) Available at http://www.almishkat.org/engdoc01/rn14/rn14.htm#2.

80 Tadros, 'The Third Option'. In addition, newspapers reported a large degree of hostility towards the law when it was being discussed in the People's Assembly.

81 Leila, 'A Family Affair'.

82 Guenena and Wassef (1999) at 33.

83 See Lila Abu Lughod, 'The Marriage of Islamism and Feminism in Egypt: Selective Repudiation as a Dynamic of Postcolonial Cultural Politics', in Lila Abu Lughod, (ed.), *Remaking Women. Feminism and Modernity in the Middle East* (1998) at 248–254.

of the *Quran* which is often underplayed in the interest of other agendas. Lawyers, legal professionals and judicial officials, let alone laymen have little knowledge and awareness of international human rights norms and standards, and of how to invoke them domestically or make use of enforcement mechanisms and complaints procedures internationally. Hardly any reference is made to international law in the course of litigation in personal status matters.[84] Interviews with two practicing lawyers (a man and a woman)[85] and one Prosecutor[86] confirmed that there was insufficient knowledge of international human rights law among lawyers, judges and law school students. Although the CEDAW has been published in Egypt's Official Gazette in Arabic, its equality provisions are seldom utilised to challenge discriminatory legislation. In spite of efforts by some NGO's to disseminate the CEDAW and provide training to lawyers on relevant international mechanisms, such efforts are, at best, sporadic and the language of human rights law remains restricted to a Western educated elite with hardly any impact on society.

Women's Lack of Awareness of Their Own Rights

Demands to educate women and inform them of their rights are often viewed with scepticism for implying the superiority of one value system over another. It is thus important that women's rights education eschew attempts at imposing a foreign value system that is alien to those expected to benefit from its precepts. Having said that, there are many egalitarian values that are in complete accord with the Islamic worldview, yet which are underrepresented or completely overlooked when societies tend towards essentialist thinking and conservatism.

Negative portrayals of women are indicative of the underlying value system that motivates the behaviour of the vast majority of Egyptians, affecting the way society views women and the way women view themselves. Studies indicate that the media's negative portrayals have increased women's receptiveness to conservative ideologies and stereotypes. A significant proportion of Egyptian women "find the traditional role models of mother and wife more appealing than the more complex reality of professional women who might also be wives and mothers."[87]

---

[84] Aboul Komsan, *Interview*.
[85] Mohamed Farouk, *Interview* and Zeinab Mohamed, *Interview*.
[86] Khaled Ghazi, *Interview*.
[87] Guenena and Wassef (1999) at 34.

The poor awareness among Egyptian women of their human rights, the high rate of illiteracy, in general, and the lack of legal literacy, in particular, has made it much easier for a patriarchal society to keep women at bay. In some instances, women are aware of their rights and accept them in theory but are either reluctant or powerless to exercise them in practice.[88] Their reluctance to exploit these gains can be associated with the negative social stigma that attaches to them. For example, women who resort to *khulʿ* are often portrayed as "lewd and immoral."[89] Similarly, the 2001 survey conducted by *Al-Mishkat* indicated that a staggering 85 % of the people interviewed opposed the use of *ʿisma*, or divorce by delegation, by the wife.[90] That is not to mention the negative attitude attached to settling family disputes through adjudication.

On the other hand, it is erroneous to assume that Egyptian women are submissive and subdued, oppressed and unable to lead a life of equality with their male counterparts. Women in Egypt have entered all areas of public life and occupy the highest positions in government and the private sector. The large numbers of women that do, in spite of negative social stigmas, resort to the Family Court to settle their disputes, or who opt for divorce in a society that once shunned this practice, hardly supports the perception of Egyptian women as weak and disempowered. Feminist groups in Egypt repeatedly cite the adoption of Law no. 1 of 2000 and the amendment of the nationality law as prime examples of the agency of Egyptian women, their determination to mobilise, and their capitalisation on *Shari'a*-derived domestic discourses to pressure for change.

Nonetheless, lack of access to information remains a huge obstacle to the advancement of women's family rights, particularly among the illiterate and the less well-educated. Vulnerable women, such as those in relationships of economic dependency are also disproportionately disadvantaged, and suffer most from hierarchical structures of male authority. Access to knowledge and economic empowerment are thus important prerequisites to the elaboration of a 'rights consciousness' among Egyptian women, and grassroots feminist organisations will need to go a long way before these goals are achieved. Collaboration with the media and educational institutions is also essential to raise awareness among

[88] Packer (2002).
[89] Tadros, 'Khulʿ Passes Major Test'.
[90] Fayza Hassan et al. (2001).

different groups of women of the elaborate rights they enjoy under the *Shari'a*, in order to reverse the negative views they often hold of their own position and roles in society. A process of indoctrination, starting with schoolchildren at a very young age would have to be implemented, giving rise to a new generation that is more open to the values of gender equality, tolerance, and justice and more receptive to the rights of women and accepting of their role as equal partners.

The Interplay between Domestic and International Mechanisms

It has often been argued that reforms in the area of human rights in Egypt generally materialise as a direct reaction to international pressure, rather than domestic reform initiatives. According to this view, human rights reforms initiated by the previous regime, such as the abolition of the hard labour prison sentence, and the State Security Courts, followed by the amendment of the Constitution to allow for directly contested presidential elections, are nothing but a 'hesitant' reaction to mounting international criticism of Egypt's human rights record.[91] Proponents of this view hold that Egypt's ratification of the CEDAW was motivated by external political considerations rather than domestic pressure, and was intended by President *Sadat* to demonstrate Egypt's progressiveness to the West.[92] The decision to institute affirmative action policies in favour of women in the 1970's, in the form of a quota in parliament for women, was taken in anticipation of the ratification of CEDAW, and Law no. 1 of 2000 was motivated by the desire to 'look good' in the Beijing review conference. Another argument is that advancements in the areas of women's and children's rights are used by the government as a ruse, in order to create the illusion of commitment to human rights, without having to act on more controversial issues.[93]

However, it is unrealistic to assume that domestic pressures have had absolutely no impact on the reform process. Domestic interest groups and human rights organisations may have capitalised on the momentum

[91] Gamal Essam El-Din, 'Only Half the Story', *Al-Ahram Weekly* 13–19 March 2003.

[92] See A. Jenefsky, 'Permissibility of Egypt's Reservations to the Convention on the Elimination of All forms of Discrimination Against Women', 15 *Maryland J. of Int'l L. and Trade* 199–234.

[93] Aboul Komsan, *Interview*.

and pressure created by international mechanisms and processes in order to advance their own agendas, but that is not the same as saying that their role is marginal or secondary. In many of the cases where the State has responded to domestic initiatives, it has done so at times where there was concomitant international pressure, and the need to demonstrate progress in the field of human rights internationally. The government's assertive response to FGM, for example, came in the aftermath of the broadcast by CNN of the genital cutting of a young girl at a barber's store. The incident, brought by satellite channels into people's living rooms all over the world, coincided with the 1994 UN Conference on Population and Development, which was taking place in Cairo, resulting in an international outcry.[94] Simultaneously, a grassroots movement sprung to life, starting a campaign against FGM that lasted for more than a decade, until the practice was finally criminalised in 2008. Although it is unclear which factor prompted the Egyptian government to act in this case, the international or the domestic, it was the interplay and mutually reinforcing dynamic between those two factors that contributed to real change on the ground.

Similarly, the Amended Personal Status Law adopted in 2000 was the product of more than a decade of domestic activism and internal debate, although the decisive factor in finally adopting the law, at that precise moment, seemed to be the desire to introduce progressive reforms before the Beijing +5 Conference, in which progress in each country would be scrutinized. Law no. 1 of 2000 "was the culmination of a fifteen-year campaign to facilitate divorce for women, orchestrated by a coalition of activists, lawyers, government officials, NGO leaders, legislators, and scholars."[95] This diverse coalition succeeded, through this strategy of legal activism, in challenging the predominant religious discourse on women, while averting accusations of being either pro-Western or aligned to any particular political ideology.[96] The 2000 reforms were a local initiative, inspired by authentically Islamic ideas, and promoted through indigenous lobbying and advocacy techniques which served as a launching pad for a "trans-national movement of new Muslim intellectuals and activists that are re-imagining the past and the Islamic canon, contesting dominant frames."[97] The international factor, in this case, served to expedite

94 Zuhur (2001).
95 Singerman (forthcoming) at 4.
96 Ibid. at 6.
97 Ibid. at 4.

a process that had already begun domestically and create a transnational support base that could reach a wider audience and provide a broader scope than any local NGO acting on its own.

Whereas international norms are of limited use unless they are adequately enforced at the domestic level, the standards they set provide a benchmark or frame of reference that can be useful in assessing how well a State treats it citizens. The international scrutiny of domestic legislation and policies, and the 'naming and shaming' process, which is the linchpin of the UN human rights system, become much more effective when local NGO's familiar with domestic policies and processes, are invited to participate. Simultaneously, local grassroots and interest groups can take advantage of international mechanisms as a platform to make their voices heard, and to pragmatically advance domestic agendas. This mutually reinforcing dynamic between domestic and international enforcement mechanisms is necessary for the success of any law reform strategy, and has driven several important reforms in Egypt's personal status law.

Although a significant degree of progress has been made in the area of family law reform, such reforms have proven insufficient in bringing about the social transformation necessary for women's full enjoyment of their rights. In order to meet the increasing demands of a globalised world, one that values the principles of human rights, including the empowerment and equality of women, and considers their effective implementation necessary prerequisites for responsible membership in the international community, Egypt must take a tougher stance against gender discrimination through a comprehensive strategy that combines legal reform with public education. The strategy should include a new, innovative legislative policy to draft an all-encompassing personal status code that would replace the current arcane and fragmented legal framework, while emphasizing the egalitarian principles of the religious scriptures. The strategy would also require the training of judges, legal professionals and law enforcement officials, in order to adequately enforce the law, and the institutionalisation of extensive public-education campaigns, revision of school curricula, and utilisation of the news and entertainment media to challenge stereotypical views and raise awareness, including among women, of gender-equality rights. The success of such a strategy will depend on the ability to empower popular forces to mobilise at the grassroots level, as well as to institute cooperation with *Al-Azhar* in order to contend with conservative forces, regulate the content of religious education, and monitor mosque sermons. The strategy should have one central aim that is arrived at through a coherent and consistent message that reinforces the egalitarian values of the Islamic religious scriptures regarding women and their role in society.

CONCLUSION

The Way Forward

Over the past ten years, a number of independent incidents have inspired extensive public debates on the human rights and status of women living in societies that apply *Shari'a*-derived laws. In September 2001, two planes were crashed into the Twin Towers in New York by terrorists who were nationals of Saudi Arabia and Egypt. Although this regrettable incident was accompanied by an unfortunate trend of discrimination against people of Arab and Muslim decent, and misinformed criticism and vilification of a religion that has at its very heart a message of peace and equality, it also renewed interest in studies related to the Arab world and its predominant religion, Islam, as people struggled to understand the political, economic, social and cultural settings that would contribute to such political violence. The situation of human rights and the rights of women in Arab and majority-Muslim countries were among the subjects of renewed academic, as well as political interest, as the United States and several international players took it upon themselves to pursue policies that were perceived as encouraging (or forcing) liberalism, political reform and emancipation of women in these countries.

Simultaneously, academics and scholars of Islamic law stepped up efforts to underscore the egalitarian message of the Islamic religious scriptures, and their potential reconcilability with international human rights standards. In one controversial incident in 2005, Amena Wadud, a Sudanese-born American professor of Islamic law, led a congregation of Muslim men and women in prayer, challenging the centuries-old conception that such a role was the monopoly of men. Some of the women participating didn't wear a headscarf throughout the duration of the prayer. The incident, which was captured by the global media, aroused a great deal of opposition, but also spurred an essential debate on the rights and status of Muslim women in the religious scriptures, and as practiced in modern societies. It also raised questions regarding the extent to which the limits placed by religion could be stretched to accommodate what some may consider 'modern' or 'liberal', and others 'Western' or 'secular', views and the kind of backlash that could ensue.

Important local developments were also unfolding, also questioning assumptions that had predominated the legal and religious discourse. After a process of internal consultation, Egypt finally declared to the CEDAW Committee that it would soon revise its reservation to article 2 of the CEDAW, which had attracted an immense amount of international criticism for attempting to shield Egypt's laws by reference to the *Sharīʿa*. It seems, however, that internal opposition to this stated government objective has been too great; almost a year has passed with no action taken to implement the government's pledge. Egypt also adopted, once again a system of quotas to ensure adequate representation of women in parliament, although a similar measure had been deemed unconstitutional in 1986. This time, the government made sure it amended the Constitution first. When the general assembly of the State Council (which settles administrative disputes) voted with an overwhelming majority in 2010 against appointing women judges in the Council, a legal battle ensued in which the Supreme Constitutional Court overturned the decision and affirmed women's right, on a basis of equality with men, to hold judicial office. All these incidents highlight the tensions between persistent patriarchal worldviews, and the official policies of the State, which often attempts unsuccessfully to advance the rights of women. This reality underscores the need for a fundamental shift in how the 'woman question' is addressed in Egypt.

Although tackling questions related to the human rights of women under laws derived from the *Sharīʿa* is a gargantuan task, bringing into play centuries of debate, convergence and divergence of views, addressing these complex questions rather than shying away from them is now imperative. Every Muslim has both the right and moral duty to question the assumptions that underlie laws and practices justified in the name of religion, particularly if these laws seem unjust and decidedly un-Islamic. *Shari'a*-derived legislation has proven over time to be both accommodating and adaptable, and it is time that Muslim societies made full use of that adaptability by engaging in an informed and enlightened debate for a more dynamic future. Islam's rich heritage is well placed to allow for such dynamism. No society can progress without some degree of consensus, some foundation for a common value-system and a vision to aspire to. The aftermath of the January 25th, 2011 revolution presents a historic opportunity to reach such a consensus for a society that has at its heart the values of equality, justice and dignity for Egyptian women and men alike. Women can no longer be left outside this process of national development, or regarded as passive and subordinate beings, to be driven by laws and policies that fail to recognise their best interest or subordinate that interest to parochial political considerations.

Piecemeal reforms of family law cannot adequately and effectively result in the large-scale transformation that is necessary to truly empower Egyptian women. What is required is a bold and courageous break with the past, a move away from the stagnancy of centuries of inherited customs and patriarchal interpretations to a new reality that has at its core the principles of justice, equality and dignity. Various aspects of Egypt's family laws discriminate against women; that is a fact that can neither be concealed nor ignored. Neither can we shy away from the fact that society places constraints on women that cannot be justified in terms of any objective and truthful reading of the religious texts, and the rich humanistic tradition of the Islamic faith. Nevertheless, it is impractical to simply demand that laws be transformed so as to conform to international standards, regardless of the will and the needs of the people concerned. Such a formalistic approach cannot possibly lead to the desired sea-change in the way women are perceived and their ability to lead a life of dignity and fulfilment. The realities on the ground are much more complex and warrant a holistic approach that emphasizes the role of indigenous agents of social change. Equally important is the realisation, at the international level, that some degree of cultural sensitivity is required in the interpretation and enforcement of international human rights norms and standards, to accommodate different belief systems and cultural settings.

Having said that, the most obvious question to be addressed is: How can we bring Egypt's personal status laws in conformity with its international obligations? To achieve this goal, a holistic legal reform strategy is necessary, one that takes into consideration the potentially useful role of international standards and enforcement mechanisms rather than viewing them as foreign and alien impositions. Domestically, there are factors that could be capitalised on, including the State's official commitment to advancing women's rights, whereas others need to be developed in a more positive manner. The role of the judiciary must be reversed to better enforce women's human rights, and grassroots activism encouraged and developed. In order to uncover the elements of this holistic strategy, which builds on the interplay between international and domestic factors, it is essential to contend with the following difficult questions:

Can Women's Human Rights Be Universal?

The human rights of women represent a front line between the universality of human rights on the one hand, and demands for pluralism, tolerance, and cultural sensitivity, on the other. Whereas universality predicates that human rights are to be afforded equally to all human beings by virtue of being human, relativity safeguards a people's collective interest in its cultural and religious diversity and autonomy. Nonetheless, universal instruments and standards undoubtedly provide an important normative legal basis on which women worldwide can base their struggle for human rights, and hold governments accountable for violations. It is indeed both possible and desirable to agree on a 'core' set of universal rights that all women would be entitled to, regardless of differences in culture, religion, faith, or nationality. However, it seems impossible to agree on every single right, covering each possible aspect of human endeavour, without encroaching on the freedoms to which women are entitled to practice their faith and uphold their distinct identities.

The major challenge to universality is, therefore that States and people have failed to agree on what exactly constitutes discrimination against women, particularly in the area of family relations, which is most likely to be regulated by religious law. The CEDAW Committee is well placed to act as arbiter when conflict arises at those fault lines where equality rights and religious identity clash. However, one of the main critiques levelled against women's international human rights law, particularly as articulated in the CEDAW is that it defines women's human rights against a male standard. To become more relevant, international human rights law must be re-characterised in a way that makes it more responsive to the realities and needs of women from diverse backgrounds.

A possible solution is to adopt a 'disadvantage' rather than a 'similarity/difference' model for non-discrimination, while maintaining very stringent restrictions (in order to avoid manipulation by States). Such an approach promises to address women's distinctive characteristics, as well as their unique needs and rights, while simultaneously avoiding the trap of lumping women worldwide into one homogenous group, regardless of differences in nationality, culture, religion, ethnicity, class or other background. The CEDAW Committee's heightened sensitivity to cultural and religious particularities is imperative, and has the potential to further engage States rather than antagonise them, while simultaneously advancing women's human rights with due regard to their own unique desires and needs.

How Can Universal Human Rights Standards Be Legitimized without Surrendering to Either 'Homogenizing Universalism' or the Stagnancy of 'Cultural Relativism'?[1]

The cultural legitimacy of women's international human rights standards is of paramount importance if such standards are to be effective in precipitating the desired changes in the status of Egyptian women. A major challenge confronting the women's human rights movement in Egypt is the existence of social and cultural values that perpetuate discrimination against women, necessitating the identification of different ways to discredit such values. This task is particularly complicated since discriminatory laws and patterns of conduct are ardently defended by conservative groups that either vehemently deny that they disadvantage women, or assert that such laws are essential to preserve the religious, social, and/or cultural character of Egyptian society.

Nonetheless, the success of various reforms indicates that it is possible to discredit particular traditional, conservative views of the rights and status of women. One particularly significant reform was the introduction, in the year 2000, of *khulʿ* divorce for women, which made use of the tool of *ijtihād* to come up with a rule that did not conform, in its entirety, to the doctrine of the four *Sunni* jurisprudential schools, in spite of the open hostility of conservatives. Nonetheless, the law was largely justified through appealing to patriarchal argumentation, maintaining that it did not represent an innovation of the Egyptian parliament since similar laws were in force elsewhere. The eventual promulgation of this law by the People's Assembly reveals that year-long delays in reform efforts are a product of political circumstances and the prevalence of rigid and uncompromising social attitudes, rather than any purported inflexibility of the *Sharīʿa*.

Consistently, reforms of Egypt's personal status law indicate three important facts: (1) that this body of law is potentially amenable to change as long as it is supported by a well-informed and sufficiently wide indigenous constituency; (2) that the State is officially committed to reform the family law, both substantively and procedurally. Although the pace of reform may not be completely satisfactory, it is inaccurate to assume that the government is simply refusing to meet its obligations under relevant human rights law; and (3) that *Sharīʿa*-derived

[1] See Rebecca J. Cook, 'Women's International Human Rights Law: The Way Forward', in Rebecca J. Cook, (ed.), *Human Rights of Women: National and International Perspectives* (1994), 3–36.

legislation may be preserved, albeit with some important future reforms, while simultaneously observing international obligations.

How Can International Human Rights Law Be Utilised to Promote Women's Equality in Egypt?

Internationally, the implementation and enforcement of women's international human rights law is largely dependent on the voluntary compliance by States and, to lesser extent, on moral pressure exerted by international enforcement mechanisms, through constructive engagement and 'naming and shaming'. The CEDAW Committee has succeeded, through the process of constructive dialogue, in positively engaging Egypt, particularly in attempting to encourage Egypt to remove its reservations to CEDAW. High-profile international conferences addressing women's human rights have also acted as a source of pressure, in conjunction with domestic efforts, to precipitate reforms. Nonetheless, international human rights law has more potential to effect change if it is adequately utilised by domestic channels.

Domestically, international human rights law has not yet been applied effectively in Egypt. Although international treaties are theoretically directly enforceable, they are not invoked in the litigation process, or referred to by judges, with the exception of a few cases where the Supreme Constitutional Court referred to international treaties as a source of interpretation, rather than a binding source of law. It is also questionable whether human rights that are non self-executing by nature, such as the prohibition of domestic violence and marital rape can be enforced without promulgating legislation that criminalises certain behaviour and proscribes specific penalties. Egypt's Constitution also fails to accord international treaties, custom and general principles of law a status superior to domestic legislation, which contravenes the relevant articles of the Vienna Convention on the Law of Treaties. The lack of awareness among both the judiciary and the general public has also meant that the impact of CEDAW and other international instruments is rather limited.

What Are Egypt's Precise Obligations under International Law?

Egypt cannot evade the obligation to eliminate discrimination in the area of family relations by virtue of its reservations to the CEDAW, particularly in light of the evolving rules on reservations to international human rights treaties, but also by virtue of its existing obligations under other treaties. It may be argued that Egypt's reservations to CEDAW are invalid, and therefore have no legal effect. This view is reflected in the draft ILC Guide to Practice on reservations. Under both the CEDAW and the ICCPR, rights are not progressive; according to CEDAW Egypt must pursue "without delay" a number of policies to give effect to its international obligations. This view has been reinforced by a number of 'soft-law' instruments, including the Beijing Platform for action. Additional measures that Egypt should implement include the following:

- *Constitutional measures*: Egypt is required to ensure that constitutional provisions unequivocally guarantee non-discrimination between the genders in all fields. It should therefore look into amending relevant constitutional provisions, particularly article 11, which authorises the State to 'guarantee coordination between a woman's duties towards her family and her work' arguably perpetuating a stereotyped view of women.
- *Legislative measures*: Egypt has already taken important steps to repeal and amend legislation that is discriminatory in nature. Reforms have allowed no-fault divorce for women, raised the minimum marriage age to eighteen years, and extended the mother's custody over her children until they reach fifteen years, at which point they may participate in the decision regarding their custody. Further reforms could target the following areas:
  - As a matter of urgent priority, reforms must address legal provisions regarding the wife's consent in the case of the return of a husband presumed missing or dead, obedience of the wife, and the toleration of almost unrestricted polygyny[2] unless it cases 'harm'.
  - Provisions on unlimited repudiation rights for the husband should also be reassessed, with a view to limited this practice through compulsory mediation. Feminists have emphasized that several countries that apply *Shari'a*-derived legislation, such as Malaysia and Tunisia,[3] compel both the husband and the wife to go to court in order to initiate divorce. They must also both submit to arbitration, which attests to the equality

[2] For an analysis of the interpretations favouring the restriction or prohibition of polygyny, see Sayeh and Morse (1995) at 328–329.

[3] See Wadud, *Qur'an and Woman* (1999) at 80.

between the spouses, and the genuine desire to protect the integrity of the family, regardless of which party initiates the divorce.[4]

- All forms of domestic violence, including both mental and physical violence, regardless of its severity, should be clearly prohibited and deterred through adequate penalties. The social standing of the wife should not be a determinant factor of whether she has been subject to spousal abuse. The prohibition should also cover marital rape.
- Reforms should also address the ability of a marriage guardian to invalidate a marriage contracted without his consent, based on the compatibility doctrine, and seek ways to prevent abuse of the rules on guardianship, particularly if it leads to coercion in marriage.
- Enforce laws on minimum marriage age, and consent of women in marriage, and promote better utilisation by women of the new standard marriage contract to guarantee their rights. Adequate enforcement of maintenance decisions should be guaranteed, and the State should address the needs of divorced women with no children by making the Family Insurance Fund system applicable to such cases.
- Some of the provisions on guardianship and inheritance could be revised, within the limits placed by the *Sharīʿa*, to expand women's rights, such as the case where two parents are inheriting the estate of their deceased child. The feminist demand to make *khulʿ* divorce contingent only on re-payment of the dowry, without the need to relinquish alimony payments should also be examined (although it is the opinion of the present author that forfeiture of financial rights in the case of no-fault divorce is a fair proposition). This demand is based on the alternative transmission (*riwaya*) of the prophetic tradition involving the wife of *Thabit bin Qays*, in which he told her to give back the garden and no more.
- Institute adequate penalties (in the form of both civil and criminal penalties), to deter and prevent circumvention of the law by public officials and private individuals.

[4] This view is supported by the Prophetic *hadīth* " Never did God allow anything more hateful to Him than divorce", in *Sunan Abu Dawud* (Book 12, *hadīth* 2173).

  - Provide legal remedies for women who are subject to discrimination, including compensation.
- *Judicial measures*: The judiciary is "the primary instrument through which State parties to the [CEDAW] discharge their responsibility" under the convention.[5] The State is in violation of its obligations under articles 2, 3, and 24 if its "judicial organs enunciate decisions that perpetuate inequality."[6] The independence of the judiciary may not be used as a pretext to evade responsibility in this field. Judicial measures require that Egypt:
  - Disseminate knowledge of the CEDAW and its provisions among personal status lawyers, family court judges, psychologists and sociologists, and promote legal literacy among women.
  - Make sure judges adequately enforce legal reforms, and refrain from using procedures to hamper the enjoyment by women of their rights.
  - Ensure the adequate representation of women in the judicial system through increasing the number of women appointed in the judiciary.
  - Guarantee the adequate and effective enforcement of court rulings in personal status cases.
- *Social measures*: Legislative and judicial reforms are, in themselves, not sufficient to ensure adequate enjoyment by women of their rights. Legal reforms must be internalised in order to resonate in society at large. Egypt should therefore adopt measures to:
  - Continue to intensify public information and education campaigns spearheaded by the Ministries of Education, Culture and Information,[7] aimed at eliminating stereotypes and promoting the norm of non-discrimination. Such campaigns should target children at an early age, and seek to discredit patriarchal interpretations that have the effect of perpetuating discrimination against women.
  - Reform the education system at all levels of primary, secondary, and university education to promote the view of wom en as equals and as partners.

[5] Wadud (1999) at 80.
[6] Hossain (1994) at 469.
[7] *Combined sixth and seventh periodic report*, section 5.a.2.

- Promote and strengthen the role of civil society and non-governmental organizations acting in this field, through the reform of the NGO law. The activism of civil society is of paramount importance in the process of indigenizing international standards of women's human rights. A useful operative framework used by such NGO's is emphasising the egalitarian message of the *Quran*, as well as the Islamic principles of public interest, justice, and equity. This moderate trend should be encouraged by the State, by providing opportunities for NGO activism, as partners to the State in the social development process.
- Utilise Mosque preachers and local leaders in promoting a more egalitarian approach towards women.

Can Egypt Be Held Accountable for Violations of Its International Obligations?

Since Egypt is not a party to CEDAW's Optional Protocol, which establishes the individual and group complaints procedure, the only available international enforcement mechanism is State reporting to the CEDAW Committee. This mechanism depends on the State's cooperation, and does not provide any tools to hold States accountable for violations.

Theoretically, Egypt may be held responsible for violations of international human rights law through the international law on State Responsibility. A State is legally accountable for violations of its international obligations, as long as they may be attributed or imputed to it. States may therefore be held accountable if their domestic law does not conform to international human rights conventions, if the result is a denial of rights.[8] They are thus required to repeal or amend discriminatory legislation and to give effect to their obligations through positive legislation. The responsibility of the State may be incurred "when its legislature proves unable to repeal offensive legislation or to enact necessary legislation."[9] According to Cook, as soon as the CEDAW Committee maintains that particular legislative provisions are discriminatory in one State, other parties are obligated to repeal similar legislation immediately, without waiting for it to be challenged in the courts.[10]

---

[8] Cook, 'State Responsibility for Violations of Women's Human Rights', at 149.
[9] Ibid. at 167.
[10] Cook, 'State Accountability under the Women's Convention', at 250.

States are also responsible for acts of omission, or their failure to meet international obligations, even when violations originate in the conduct of private persons.[11] With regards to private discrimination, States must demonstrate due diligence in eliminating or reducing discrimination.[12] The objective here is not to replace one wrong-doer (the individual) with another (the State), but rather to give effect to legal rights by constructing mechanisms for protection, prevention, investigation, punishment and compensation. The human rights obligations of the State include making the original violation that triggers the responsibility illegal, and adequately punishing the perpetrator.[13]

In a seminal judgment, the European Court of Human Rights recently found Turkey responsible for domestic violence committed by an individual.[14] The Court found that by failing to prevent the incident, which led to the death of the mother in law, Turkey had violated the right to gender non-discrimination, among other rights. It held that domestic violence was "tolerated by the authorities and that the remedies indicated by the government do not function effectively." It cited the "unreasonable delays in issuing injunctions by courts," the lack of dissuasive punishments and the "general and discriminatory judicial passivity" as reasons for incurring the responsibility of the State.

Nonetheless, the international law of State Responsibility remains largely a *terra incognita* for human rights lawyers.[15] Developing and applying its norms to violations of women's human rights is absolutely essential to hold recalcitrant States accountable for violations of the CEDAW.

---

[11] Ibid. For a Comprehensive analysis of the laws of State responsibility and how they can be applied to violations of the human rights of women see Celina Romany, 'State Responsibility Goes Private: A Feminist Critique of the Public/Private Distinction in International Human Rights Law', in Rebecca J. Cook (ed.), *Human Rights of Women. National and International Perspectives* (1994), 85–115, and Kenneth Roth, 'Domestic Violence as an International Human Rights Issue', in Rebecca J. Cook (ed.), *Human Rights of Women. National and International Perspectives* (1994), 326–339.

[12] Romany (1994) at 96.

[13] *Respect, Protect, Fulfill—Women's human rights. State Responsibility for abuses by non-state actors*, Amnesty International, IOR 50/01/00 (Sept 2000) at 11.

[14] Opuz v. Turkey, ECtHR 33401/02 (9 June 2009).

[15] See Velasquez Rodriguez v. Honduras, Inter-American court of Human Rights (1988).

How Can Egypt Bring Its Personal Status Law in Line with Its International Obligations?

Egypt must act quickly to adopt a new and comprehensive personal status code to replace the plethora of existing laws that govern women's family rights. Such a law must deal with women as subjects, with independent and capable mental faculties, rather than as passive objects and *de facto* minors. A reasonable starting point is the Model Arab Unified Personal Status Law which is structured in a way that comprehensively addresses all personal status matters, as well as explicitly spelling out the obligations of the wife and husband towards the family in a way which differentiates between such rights and duties, without departing from the principle of egalitarianism. Although certain specific provisions of the Model Law need revisiting, its structure and general thrust offer an acceptable practical guide.

Not all provisions of Egypt's current personal status law are discriminatory, and not all reforms in this critical body of legislation have been ineffective. There have been significant advances in the area of personal status law reform in the past few years, including the adoption of *khul*ʿ divorce and extended custody rights for the mother. Similarly, the law upholds women's financial rights when contracting the marriage, throughout its duration and at its dissolution. It also deals with the issue of recognition of customary marriages in a way that meets the distinct needs of Egyptian women.

However, the personal status laws, which are based on the legislative enactments of the 1920's, have at their very core, a subordinating view of women, evidenced in the principle of obedience, which often gives rise to domestic violence, and the provisions regarding the return of a husband presumed missing or dead. Such provisions are in complete contradiction with the Islamic principles of justice, equity and human dignity. What is required, therefore, is a radical break with this construction of the marital relationship. Before any specific legal reforms can take effect, it is essential to modify the way in which the law and society both perceive women and break the strict gender hierarchy that has placed women in a perpetually subordinate position.

Feminist literature is replete with accounts of how the *Quran* describes the marital relationship as one based on mercy, compassion, and mutual respect between the spouses. There is an abundance of literature on the *Quran's* positive approach to women, its use of egalitarian language (the *Quran* uses both the masculine and feminine forms, and thus equally addresses both men and women) as well as early Islamic society's elevation of the status of women in a way that was revolutionary as compared to pre-Islamic Arabia.[16] Feminist literature has also attempted to revisit and reassess two important principles that inform all *Sharīʿa*-derived family laws, the principles of *qiwama* and *daraja*,[17] which have often been used to perpetuate subordination of women.

Zeinab Radwan and *Ahmed el-ʿAssal*, both Egyptian Muslim feminist scholars, advance the view that *qiwama*, which may be translated as 'authority', 'protection' or 'guidance', is not the monopoly of men over women;[18] women may also enjoy *qiwama* in various instances, such as the example of a woman that is caring for an elderly father, or a sick husband. The principle of *qiwama* may not be used to justify oppression by any means. They also advance the view that *daraja*, often taken to mean a degree of distinction of men over women, is actually an added responsibility and not a privilege. *Al-ʿAssal* contends that the principle refers to the husband's duty to maintain the wife.[19] *Wadud*, on the other hand, maintains that it refers to the husband's expanded rights in divorce.[20] In either case, both these scholars, each living in markedly different societies and under radically different circumstances, recognise the need to emphasize the more egalitarian interpretations of these *Quranic* principles. According to *Radwan*, Egypt is in need of a new *fiqh* that rightly represents Islam, departing from the principle that *fiqh* or jurisprudence is no more than a means to deduce legal rules, and is hence amenable to change and adaptation in a way that ensures public welfare.[21]

---

16 Among the many arguments proposed by such scholars are that the *Quran* addressed both women and men in the text, the *Quran* is free of any portrayal of women as evil or cunning, and any claims that Eve was the reason behind Adam's fall from grace, the Quran granted women legal capacity and allowed them to inherit, etc. See in general al-Hibri; Sayeh and Morse (1995).

17 Translations of verse 4:34 of the *Quran* differ slightly. Whereas A. Youssef Ali's translation states that "Men are the protectors and maintainers of women, because God has given the one more (strength) than the other, and because they support them from their means ...", Pikthall's translation stipulates that "Men are in charge of women, because Allah hath made the one of them to excel the other, and because they spend of their property (for the support of women) ...."

18 Amany Maged, 'al mar'a ansafha al islam wa thalamaha al-muslimun' [Women: Vindicated by Islam yet Oppressed by Muslims] *Al-Ahram* 36 (6 May 2005).

19 Ibid.

20 See Wadud (1999).

21 Zeinab Radwan, 'Al mar'a wa mabda' al-mosawah bayn atashriʿ waltatbeeq' [Women and the principle of equality, between legislation and application] (2009) at 52.

Verse 4:34 of the *Quran* is also used to justify the principle of obedience by the wife to her husband.[22] However, feminists counter that the *Quran* also clearly stipulates (in verse 4:128) that: "If a woman feareth ill treatment from her husband, or desertion, it is no sin for them twain [the spouses] if they make terms of peace between themselves. Peace is better" and (in verse 2:231) "... retain them in kindness or release them in kindness. Retain them not to their hurt so that ye transgress (the limits). He who doeth that hath wronged his soul." According to Wadud, these verses indicate that the oppressive concept of forced obedience is clearly un-Islamic.[23] Al-Hibri further argues that the concept of obedience in Islam, whether it be to a ruler, an elder, or any other human being, is based on the notions of consultation and general consent (rather than hierarchy).[24] She also contends that whereas the principle of *qiwama* (guardianship) does indeed exist in the *Shari'a*, it does not grant men a superior status over women, nor does it allow them to proscribe rights that have been ordained by God.[25]

There are also numerous prophetic precedents that emphasize the importance of treating women in a respectful and dignified manner. In his farewell sermon, the Prophet specifically commanded his followers to "treat your women well and be kind to them for they are your partners and committed helpers". The Prophet was also known to have said "the most perfect man in his faith among the believers is the one whose behaviour is most excellent; and the best of you are those who are the best to their wives"[26] and to have commanded his followers to "give them [your wives] food what you have for yourself, and clothe them by which

---

[22] According to Pikthal's translation, the second part of verse 4:34 reads ".... good women are the obedient, guarding in secret that which Allah hath guarded. As for those from whom ye fear rebellion, admonish them and banish them to beds apart, and scourge them. Then if they obey you, seek not a way against them." Yousef Ali's translation is slightly different, stipulating that "the righteous women are devoutly obedient, and guard in (the husband's) absence what Allah would have them guard. As to those women on whose part ye fear disloyalty and ill-conduct, admonish them (first), (Next), refuse to share their beds, (And last) beat them (lightly); but if they return to obedience, seek not against them Means (of annoyance)."

[23] Wadud (1999) at 80.

[24] Al-Hibri (1997) at 20. She proposes that Muslims be encouraged to include conditions in their marriage contracts that mitigate the effects of the principle of obedience.

[25] Unfortunately, it will not be possible to delve into a detailed discussion of the principle of *qiwama* within the limits of this study. However, for a comprehensive examination of the different interpretations of this principle, see al-Hibri (1997).

[26] Narrated by *Abu Huraira*, in *Sunan At-Tirmidhi*, (*hadith* 628).

you clothe yourself, and do not beat them, and do not revile them."[27] The marital relationship envisioned by the *Sharīʿa* is thus one of partnership and mutual respect, and not one based on hierarchy or oppression. This is hardly consonant with the view advanced by extremists on both sides of the debate, whether extreme universalists who claim that the *Sharīʿa* oppresses women and hence should be replaced by secular law, or extreme cultural relativists who try to justify tyrannical patriarchal practices by reference to the Islamic faith.

Interpretations of the principles of the *Shari'a*, vary markedly between Muslim scholars, even between those in the same country or geographic location. However, it is precisely this flexibility that makes the *Shari'a* the superior and divine body of law that it is. The progress of people living in Muslim societies depends on their ability to propose interpretations that advance their societies rather than hinder them, allow for human progress, innovation and development rather than stifle change, interpretations that seek to emancipate women rather than oppress them. Muslim women and men worldwide are now busy reviewing centuries of jurisprudence and uncovering egalitarian interpretations of the Islamic religious scriptures that can equip their societies with utilities to face the new challenges and demands of the twenty-first century. It is through such efforts that we will hopefully find the seeds of a more tolerant and just personal status law that allows women to simultaneously uphold both their faith and identity as Muslims, as well as their dignity as human beings.

[27] *Sunan Abu Dawud* (Book 11, *hadīth* 2139).

SELECT BIBLIOGRAPHY

Studies, Reports, UN Documents and Resolutions

Amnesty International, *Making Violence against Women Count Facts and Figures—a Summary*, Media Briefing (March 5th, 2004), available at http://www.amnesty.org/fr/library/asset/ACT77/034/2004/fr/301b0c48-fabb-11dd-b6c4-73b1aa157d32/act770342004en.pdf

——, *Respect, Protect, Fulfil—Women's human rights. State Responsibility for abuses by non-state actors*, IOR 50/01/00 (Sept 2000).

Benninger-Budel, Carrin, *Violence against Women in Egypt*, Report prepared for the CEDAW Committee, 24th Sess., World Organization Against Torture (2001) available at http://www.omct.org/files/2001/01/2175/egypteng2001.pdf

CEDAW Committee, *Concluding Observations, Egypt*, CEDAW A/39/45 (1984) 34th and 39th meetings, held on 30 March and 3 April 1984 (CEDAW/C/SR.34 and 39).

——, *Concluding Observations, Egypt*, 492nd and 493rd meetings, held on 19 January 2001, UN Doc CEDAW/C/SR.492 and 493.

——, *Consideration of reports* submitted by States parties under article 18 of the Convention on the Elimination of All Forms of Discrimination against Women, *Combined 1st and 2nd periodic reports of states parties, Egypt (1984),*

——, *Consideration of reports, Combined 3rd, 4th and 5th periodic reports of states parties, Egypt* (1996).

——, *Consideration of reports, Combined 6th and 7th periodic reports of states parties, Egypt*, UN Doc CEDAW/C/EGY/7 (5 Sept 2008).

——, *Decision 3*, CEDAW, 6th Sess. (1987) in The Work of CEDAW. Reports of the Committee on the Elimination of Discrimination Against Women, Volume II, 1986–1987 (New York: United Nations; 1990).

——, *Decision 4*, CEDAW Committee, 6th Sess. (1987) in The Work of CEDAW. Reports of the Committee on the Elimination of Discrimination Against Women, Volume II, 1986–1987 (New York: United Nations; 1990).

——, *General Recommendation No. 3, Education and Public Information Programmes*, 6th Sess. (1987).

——, *General Recommendation No. 4, Reservations*, CEDAW, 6th Sess. (1987).

——, *General Recommendation No. 10, 10th Anniversary of the Adoption of CEDAW*, CEDAW 8th Sess. (1989)

——, *General Recommendation No. 12, Violence Against Women*, CEDAW, 8th Sess. (1989).

——, *General Recommendation No. 14, Female Circumcision*, CEDAW, 9th Sess. (1990).

——, *General Recommendation No. 19, Violence Against Women*, CEDAW, 19th Sess. (1992)

——, *General Recommendation No. 20, Reservations*, CEDAW, 11th Sess. (1992).

——, *General Recommendation No. 21, Equality in Marriage and Family Relations*, CEDAW, 13th Sess. (1994).

——, *General Recommendation No. 25, Temporary special measures*, 13th Sess. (2004).

——, *Guidelines for preparation of reports by States Parties*, CEDAW Committee, Sixteenth session (13–31 Jan 1997) UN Doc CEDAW/C/7/Rev.3 (26 July 1996).

——, *List of Issues and Questions with regard to the Consideration of Periodic Reports*, CEDAW Pre-session Working Group 45th Session C/EFY/Q/7 (Jan–Feb 2010).

——, *Press Release*, WOM/1250, 492nd Meeting (19/01/2001), available at http://www.un.org/News/Press/docs/2001/wom1250.doc.htm

——, *Report*, 18th and 19th Sess. (1998), UN General Assembly Official Records (GAOR), 53rd Sess. Supplement No. 38 (A/53/38/Rev.1).

——, *Report*, 13th Sess. (1994), UN GAOR, 49th Sess., Supp. No. 38, Annex I (A/49/38).

——, *Report*, 24th Sess. (15 Jan–2 Feb 2001) and 25th Sess. (2–20 July 2001), GAOR, 56th Sess., Supp. No. 38 (A/56/38).

——, *The Practice of Human Rights Treaty Bodies With Respect to Reservations to International Human Rights Treaties*, Seventeenth Meeting of Chairpersons of the Human Rights Treaty Bodies (Geneva, 23–24 June 2005).

Committee on Civil and Political Rights, *General Comment No. 3*, Implementation at the National Level (Article 21) (1981).

——, *General Comment No. 18*, Non-discrimination, CCPR, 37th Sess. (1989) Compilation of General Comments and General Recommendations Adopted by Human Rights Treaty Bodies, U.N. Doc. HRI\GEN\1\Rev.1 (1994)

——, *General Comment No. 24*, Issues relating to reservations made upon ratification or accession to the Covenant or the Optional Protocols thereto, or in relation to declarations under article 41 of the Covenant, HRC, 04 Nov 1994, UN Doc CCPR/C/21/Rev.1/Add.6, 52nd Sess. (1994).

——, *General Comment no. 28*, Equality of Rights between Men and Women (Article 3) (29 March 2000). UN Doc CCPR/C/21/Rev.1/Add.10, adopted by the Committee at its 1834th meeting (68th session).

Compilation of Guidelines on the Form and Content of Reports to be Submitted by States Parties to the International Human Rights Treaties, UN Doc HRI/GEN/2/Rev.1/Add.2 (May 2003).

Committee on Economic, Social and Cultural Rights, *General Comment no. 3, The Nature of States Parties Obligations (Art. 2, par. 1)* (14 Dec 1990), 5th Sess. (1990), UN Doc E/1991/23, reprinted in HRI/GEN/1/Rev.9 (Vol. I).

Committee on the Elimination of Racial Discrimination, *Report on its 17th and 18th Sess.* (1978), UN GAOR, 33rd Sess., Supp. No. 18 (A/33/18).

ILC Draft guidelines constituting the Guide to Practice on Reservations to Treaties, Provisionally adopted by the International Law Commission, UN Doc A/65/10.

——, *Fourteenth Report on Reservations to Treaties*, Addendum by Special Rapporteur Allain Pellet, International Law Commission, 61st Session A/CN.4/614/Add.1 (2009).

——, *Report of the Special Rapporteur on the Meeting with Human Rights Bodies*, International Law Commission, Fifty-ninth session, UN Doc ILC(LIX)/RT/CRP.1 (26 July 2007)

'Early Marriage: Child Spouses', *Innocenti Digest* no. 7 (United Nations Children Fund Innocenti Research Centre, March 2001).

Elimination of Discrimination against Women, Resolution of the 12th Sess. of the Human Rights Council (28 Sept. 2009), UN Doc. A/HRC/12/L.3/Rev.1.

The Elimination of Violence against Women, Resolution of the 51st Sess. of the Commission on Human Rights (8 March 1995) UN Doc CHR Res. 85 http://www.unhchr.ch/huridocda/huridoca.nsf/70ef163b25b2333fc12569910 04de370/74cd465a4110840b802566ef005e0818?OpenDocumentE/CN.4/RES/1995/85.

——, Resolution of the 52nd Sess. of the CHR (19 April 1996) CHR Res. 49, UN Doc http://www.unhchr.ch/huridocda/huridoca.nsf/70ef163b25b2333fc 1256991004de370/e2b218da137a27e1802566900035af26?OpenDocumentE/CN.4/RES/1996/49.

——, Resolution of the 53rd Sess. of the CHR (11 April 1997) CHR Res. 44, UN Doc http://www.unhchr.ch/huridocda/huridoca.nsf/70ef163b25b2333fc 1256991004de370 / 08a61b451a2b7432802566480004edc0b?OpenDocument E/CN.4/RES/1997/44.

——, Resolution of the 54th Sess. of the CHR (17 April 1998) CHR Res. 52, UN Doc http://www.unhchr.ch/huridocda/huridoca.nsf/70ef163b25b2333fc 1256991004de370 / 91c1c86c50a04a6e8025666b0031288a?OpenDocument E/CN.4/RES/1998/52.

Fayza Hassan et al. *The Ultimate Emancipation of Women is in the Minds. Preliminary Results of an Opinion Poll* (Al-Mishkat Research Center, 2001), available at http://www.almishkat.org/engdoc01/rn14/rn14.htm#2.

Human Rights Watch, *Divorced from Justice Women's Unequal Access to Divorce in Egypt*, Vol. 16, No. 8 (E). (December 2004).

Minutes of the 22nd Parliamentary Session (16 Jan. 2000), 7th Legislative term, *Majlis ash-sha'b* publications (on file with author).

Minutes of the 23rd Parliamentary Session (16 Jan. 2000), 7th Legislative term, *Majlis ash-sha'b* publications (on file with author).

Minutes of the 27th Parliamentary Session (25 Jan., 2000), 7th Legislative term, *Majlis ash-sha'b* publications (on file with author).

Minutes of the 28th Parliamentary Session (26 Jan 2000), Official Gazette (Parliamentary section), Issue 28 (9 March 2000).

Minutes of the 29th Parliamentary Session (26 Jan 2000), Official Gazette (Parliamentary section), Issue 29 (9 March 2000).

Shadow Report of the Egyptian NGOs coalition on the CEDAW (December 2000), on file with author.

Second Shadow Report for the CEDAW Coalition, Egyptian Association for Community Participation Enhancement (EACPE) (2009), available at http://www2.ohchr.org/english/bodies/cedaw/docs/EACPE_E.pdf

The Shadow Report on the Status of Egyptian women in matters of personal status and forms of violence against women according to CEDAW convention, Center for Egyptian Women's Legal Assistance CEWLA, available at http://www2.ohchr.org / english/ bodies/cedaw/docs/ngos/CEWLAEgypt_45.pdf

Special Rapporteur on violence against women, its causes and consequence, *Report*, UN Commission on Human Rights, 52nd session (1996).
System-Wide Coherence, Resolution adopted by the General Assembly, 63rd Sess., Agenda Item 107, A/Res/63/311 (2 Oct 2009).
United Kingdom Law Commission, *Intestacy and Family Provision Claims on Death*, Consultation Paper No. 191 (Overview), 29 Oct 2009 available at http://www.lawcom.gov.uk/docs/cp191_overview.pdf
UN Secretary General, *Report on the Effective Implementation of International Instruments on Human Rights, including Reporting Obligations under International Instruments on Human Rights*, UN GAOR 47th Sess.

Books and Articles

Abdel Ghani, Mahmoud, *Al Tahafuth 'Ala Al Mu'ahadat Al Dawliyyah Fi Al Qanun Al Dawly Al 'Am Wal Shari'a Al Islamia* [Reservations to International Human Rights Treaties in Public International Law and the Islamic *Shari'a*] (1986).
Abdel Kader, Hatem, *Ethics in Islam* (Cairo: Al Azhar Islamic Research Academy, 2002).
Abduh, Mohammed, *Al-Islam Wal Mar'ah* [Islam and Woman] (Cairo: Al Qahira Lelthaqafa Al'Arabiya, 1975).
Aboul Komsan, Nihad, [Director Egyptian Center for Women's Rights], *Interview* (11 Nov. 2004).
——, 'Women Between Islamic Shari'a and Personal Status Laws', *Egyptian Centre for Women's Rights* http://www.ecwregypt.org/English/researches/index.htm.
Abu-Odeh, Lama, 'Modernising Muslim Family Law: The Case of Egypt', 37 *Vand. J. Transnat'l L.* 1043 (October 2004).
Abu Lughod, Lila, 'The Marriage of Islamism and Feminism in Egypt: Selective Repudiation as a Dynamic of Postcolonial Cultural Politics', in Lila Abu Lughod, (ed.), *Remaking Women. Feminism and Modernity in the Middle East* (Princeton: Princeton UP, 1998).
Afkhami, Mahnaz, "Gender Apartheid, Cultural Relativism, and Women's Human Rights in Muslim Societies", in Marjorie Agosín (ed.), *Women, Gender, and Human Rights: A Global Perspective* (Rutgers University Press, 2001).
Ahmed, Laila, *Women and Gender in Islam* (Cairo: AUC Press, 1998).
Al-Ali, Nadje, *Secularism, Gender and the State in the Middle East* (Cambridge: Cambridge UP, 2000).
Al-Hibri, Aziza, 'Islam, Law and Custom: Redefining Muslim Women's Rights', 12 *Am. U.J. Int'l L. Pol'y* 2 (1997).
Al-Siba'ie, Mostafa, *Al-Mar'a bayn al-fiqh wal qanun* [Women between Jurisprudence and Law] (Cairo, 2002).
An-Naim, Abdullahi, 'Cultural Transformation and Normative Consensus on the Best Interest of the Child', 8 *Int'l J. of L. & Family* 62 (1994).
——, 'Human Rights in the Muslim World: Socio-Political Conditions and Scriptural Imperatives', 3 *Harv. Hum. Rts. J.* 13–52 (1990).

——, 'Human Rights, Religion, and the Contingency of Universalist Projects', *Occasional Paper* no. 2, 1–32, PARC, Maxwell School of Citizenship and Public Affairs, Syracuse University (September 2000).
——, 'Religion and Global Civil Society: Inherent Incompatibility or Synergy and Interdependence?', in H. Anheier, M. Glasius, and M. Kaldor (eds.), *Global Civil Society* 200, 55–73 (Oxford: Oxford UP, 2002).
——, 'State Responsibility Under International Human Rights Law to Change Religious and Customary Law', in Rebecca J. Cook (ed.), *Human Rights of Women: National and International Perspectives* (Philadelphia: University of Pennsylvania Press, 1994), 167–188.
——, *Towards an Islamic Reformation. Civil Liberties, Human Rights and International Law* (Cairo: American University in Cairo Press, 1992.)
Akram, Susan Musarrat, 'Orientalism Revisited in Asylum and Refugee Claims', 12 *Int'l J. Ref. L.* Issue 1, 7–40 (2000).
Ali, Shaheen Sardar, *Gender and Human Rights in Islam and International Law: Equal before Allah, Unequal Before Man?* (The Hague: Kluwer Law International, 2000).
Al Qaradawy, Yusuf, *The Status of Women in Islam*, trans. Mohammed Gemē'ah (Cairo: Islamic Home of Publishing and Distribution, 1997) available at http://www.witness pioneer.org/vil/Books/Q WI/default.htm
Al-Sharmani, Mulki, 'Egyptian Family Courts: Pathway to Women's Empowerment?', *Hawwa: Journal of Women of the Middle East and the Islamic World* 7 (2009) 89–119.
——, 'Egypt's Family Courts, Route to Empowerment?', *Open Democracy* (7 September 2007), available at http://www.opendemocracy.net/article/egypt_and_family_law (last accessed 11 December 2010).
——, 'Legal Reform, Women's Empowerment, and Social Change: The Case of Egypt', *IDS Bulletin*, 41, No. 2 (2010) at 10–17.
——, *Recent Reforms in Personal Status Laws and Women's Empowerment. Family Courts in Egypt* (American University in Cairo Social Research Centre, 2007).
Anderson, J.N.D., *Islamic Law in the Modern World* (New York: New York UP, 1959).
Arabi, Oussama, 'The Dawning of the Third Millennium on Shari'a: Egypt's Law No. 1 of 2000, or Women May Divorce at Will', *Arab Law Quarterly* 6 (2001).
Arnold, Kathryn Christine, 'Are the Perpetrators of Honour Killings Getting Away With Murder? Article 340 of the Jordanian Penal Code Analysed Under the Convention on the Elimination of All Forms of Discrimination Against Women', 16 *Am. U. Int'l L. Rev.* 1343.
Arzt, Donna, 'Religious Human Rights in Muslim States of the Middle East and North Africa', *Emory Int'l L.R.* (Spring 1996) also available at http://www.law.emory.edu/EILR/volumes/spring96/arzt.html
——, 'The Application of International Human Rights Law in Islamic States', 12 *H.R. Quart.* 202–230 (1990).
Askari, Laden, 'Girls Rights Under International Law. An Argument for Establishing Gender Equality as a Jus Cogens', 8 *South. Cal. R.L. & Women's Stud.* 3 (Fall 1998).

Assaf, Georges J., 'The Application of International Human Rights Instruments by the Judiciary in Lebanon', in Eugene Cotran and Adel Omar Sheri (eds.), *The Role of the Judiciary in the Protection of Human Rights* (London: Kluwer Law International, 1997).

Badawy El-Sheikh, Ibrahim, *Nafath Iltizamat Masr al-dawliyya fi Majal Huquq al-Insan fi alNizam al-Qanuni al-Masry* [The Enforcement of Egypt's International Human Rights Obligations in the Egyptian Legal System] (Cairo: Dar El Nahda al-Arabiyya, 2003).

Badawy, Jamal A., 'Gender Equity in Islam', *World Assembly of Muslim Youth—Studies on Islam*, available at http://www.iad.org/books/GEI.html (last accessed 12/5/2005).

Badran, Margot, *Feminists, Islam and Nation: Gender and the Making of Modern Egypt* (Cairo: AUC Press, 1996).

——, 'Independent Women. More Than a Century of Feminism in Egypt' in Judith E. Tucker (ed.), *Arab Women: Old Boundaries, New Frontiers* (Washington: Indiana UP, 1993), 129–148.

Basu, Amarita, *The Challenge of Local Feminisms: Women's Movements in Global Perspective* (Boulder: Westview Press, 1995)

Bayefsky, Anne, 'General Approaches to Domestic Application of International Law', in Rebecca J. Cook (ed.), *Human Rights of Women, National and International Perspectives* (1994), 351–374.

Behrouz, Andra Nahal, 'Transforming Islamic Family Law: State Responsibility and the Role of Internal Initiative', 103 *Colum. L. Rev.* 1136 (June 2003).

Bek, Ahmed Ibrahim, and Wassel Ibrahim, *Aḥkām al-'aḥwāl al-shakhsiyya fil shari'a al-islāmiyya walqanūn* (Cairo, 2003).

Berger, Maurits, 'Conflicts Law and Public Policy in Egyptian Family Law: Islamic Law Through the Backdoor', 50 *Am. J. Comp. L.* 555 (Summer 2002).

Bernard-Maugiron, Nathalie, and Baudouin Dupret, 'From Jihan to Susanne. Twenty Years of Personal Status Law in Egypt', 19 *Recht van de Islam* (2002) 1–19.

Beyani, Chaloka, 'Towards a More Effective Guarantee of Women's Rights in the African Human Rights System', in Rebecca J. Cook (ed.), *Human Rights of Women, National and International Perspectives* (1994), 285–306.

Bielefeldt, Heiner, 'Muslim Voices in the Human Rights Debate', Vol. 17, No. 4, *Hum. Rts. Q* (November 1995) 587–617.

Brown, Nathan, *The Rule of Law in the Arab World. Courts in Egypt and the Gulf* (Cambridge: Cambridge UP, 1997).

Brownlie, Ian, and Guy S. Goodwin Gill (eds.), *Basic Documents on Human Rights* (Oxford; New York: Oxford UP, 2002).

Buergenthal, Thomas, 'To Respect and To Ensure: State Obligations and Permissible Derogations', in Louis Henkin (ed.), *The International Bill of Rights: The Covenant on Civil and Political Rights* (1981).

Bulbeck, Chilia, *Re-orienting Western Feminisms. Women's Diversity in a Post-Colonial World* (Cambridge: Cambridge UP, 1998).

Byrnes, Andrew, 'The Convention on the Elimination of All Forms of Discrimination Against Women', in Wolfgang Benedek, Esther M. Kisakye, and Gerd

Oberleitner (eds.), *Human Rights of Women. International Instruments and African Experiences* (2002) 122.

——, 'Toward More Effective Enforcement of Women's Human Rights Through the Use of International Human Rights Law and Procedures', in Rebecca J. Cook (ed.), *Human Rights of Women, National and International Perspectives* (1994), 189–227.

——, 'Using International HR Law and Procedures to Advance Women's Human Rights', in K. Askin and D. Koenig (eds.), *Women and International Human Rights Law*, vol. 2 (2000).

Charlesworth, Hilary, and Christine Chinkin, *The Boundaries of International Law. A Feminist Analysis* (Manchester: Manchester UP, 2003).

Charlesworth, Hilary, Christine Chinkin, and Shelley Wright, 'Feminist Approaches to International Law', 85 *Am. J. Int'l L.* 613 (October 1991).

Chaudhry, Zeinab, 'The Myth of Misogyny: A Reanalysis of Women's Inheritance in Islamic Law', 6 *Albany L. Rev* 511 (1997).

Cipriani, Linda, 'Gender and Persecution: Protecting Women Under International Refugee Law', 7 *Geo. Immigr. L.J.* 511 (October 1993).

Clerk, Belinda, 'The Vienna Convention's Reservations Regime and the Convention on Discrimination Against Women', 85 *Am. J. Int'l L.* 281 (April 1991).

Connors, Jane, 'The Women's Convention in the Muslim World', in Mai Yamani (ed.), *Feminism and Islam: Legal and Literary Perspectives* (New York: New York UP, 1996).

Cook, Rebecca J., 'State Accountability Under the Women's Convention', in Rebecca J. Cook (ed.), *Human Rights of Women, National and International Perspectives* (1994), 228–256.

——, 'Women's International Human Rights Law: The Way Forward', in Rebecca J. Cook (ed.), *Human Rights of Women: National and International Perspectives* (Philadelphia: University of Pennsylvania Press, 1994), 3–36.

——, 'State Responsibility for Violations of Women's Human Rights', 7 *Harv. Hum. Rts. J.* 125 (1994)

Coomaraswamy, Rhadika, 'To Bellow Like A Cow: Women, Ethnicity and the Discourse of Rights', in Rebecca J. Cook (ed.), *Human Rights of Women. National and International Perspectives* (1994), 39–57.

Coulson, Noel, *A History of Islamic Law* (Edinburgh: Edinburgh UP, 1968).

Dahl, Tove Stang, *The Muslim Family. A Study of Women's Rights in Islam* (Oslo: Scandinavian UP, 1997).

'Developments—The Family', 93 *Harv. L. Rev* 1979–1980.

Dupret, Baudoin, 'A propos de la constitutionalité de la Shari'a: Présentation et traduction de l'arrêt du 26 Mars 1994 de Haut Cour Constitutionnelle égyptienne', *Islamic Law and Society* 4 (1997).

Dupuy, P.-M., 'The Challenge of Soft Law and the International Law of the Environment', 12 *Mich. J. of Int'l L.* 420 (1991)

Duval, Soroya, 'New Veils and New Voices. Islamist Women's Groups in Egypt', in Karin Ask & Marit Tjomsland (eds.), *Women and Islamization* (1998), 45–72.

El-Alami, Dawoud, and Doreen Hinchcliffe, *Islamic Marriage and Divorce Laws of the Arab World* (London: CIMEL and Kluwer Law International, 1996).

El-Amrousy, Anwar, *Sharḥ qanūn al-aḥwāl alshakhṣiyya* [Explaining the Personal Status Law] (Cairo: *Dār el-matbū'āt al-gāmi'iyya*, 1993).
El-Bendary, Amina, 'Conditional Surrenders', *Al-Ahram Weekly* 13–19 January 2000.
El-Gabry, Abdel Met'al Mohamed, *Al Mar'a Fil Tassawor Al Islamy* (Cairo: Maktabet Wahba, 1994.)
El-Guindy, Ahmed Nasr, *al-ta'līq 'ala nuṣūṣ qanūn tanẓim ba'ḍ 'awḍā' wa igra'āt al-taqaḍī fi masā'il al-aḥwāl al-shakhṣiyya* [Commentary on the text of the Law to Organise Certain Conditions and Procedures of Matters of Personal Status] (Cairo, 2000).
El-Morr, Awad Mohammed, 'Judicial Sources for Supporting the Protection of Human Rights', in Eugene Cotran and Adel Omar Sherif (eds.), *The Role of the Judiciary in the Protection of Human Rights* (London: Kluwer Law International, 1997.)
Elsafty, Madiha, 'Gender Inequalities in the Arab World. Religion, Law or Culture?', paper presented at the Fourth Mediterranean Social and Political Research Meeting, Florence and Montecatini Terme (19–23 March 2003).
El-Sayyed, Mustapha Kamel, 'The Islamic Movement in Egypt: Social and Political Implications', in Ibrahim M. Oweis (ed.), *The Political Economy of Contemporary Egypt* (Washington: Georgetown UP, 1990), 222–239.
El-Solh, Camillia Fawzi, and Judy Mabro, 'Introduction: Islam and Muslim Women', in Camillia Fawzi El-Solh and Judy Mabro (eds.), *Muslim Women's Choices. Religious Belief and Social Reality* (Oxford: BERG, 1994), 16–19.
Engle Merry, Sally, 'Vernacularization in Action: Using Global Women's Human Rights Locally', in Sally Engle Merry and Peggy Levitt (eds.), *Special Issue of Global Networks* 9 (4), 2009.
Entelis, Joelle, 'International Human Rights: Islam's Friend or Foe? Algeria as an Example of the Compatibility of International Human Rights Regarding Women's Equality and Islamic Law', 20 *Fordham Int'l L.J.* 1252 (1997).
Essam El-Din, Gamal, 'Only Half the Story', *Al-Ahram Weekly* 13–19 March 2003.
Esposito, John L., *Women in Muslim Family Law* (Syracuse, NY: Syracuse UP, 1982).
Evatt, Elizabeth, 'Finding a Voice for Women's Rights. The Early Days of CEDAW', 34 *Geo. Wash. Int'l L. Rev.* 515 (2002).
Ezzat, Heba Raouf, 'The Silent Ayesha: An Egyptian Narrative', in Jane H. Bayes and Nayereh Tohidi (eds.), *Globalization, Gender and Religion: The Politics of Women's Rights in Catholic and Muslim Contexts* (New York: Palgrave, 2001), 231–257.
——, 'Women and the Interpretation of Islamic Sources', *Women's Issues*, available at http://www.islam21.net/pages/keyissues/key2–6.htm (last accessed 12 February 2005).
Faheem, Adham, [Deputy President of the Southern Cairo Court], *Interview* (15 November 2004).
Fairweather, Cynthia R.L., 'Obstacles to Enforcing International Human Rights Law in Domestic Courts', 4 *U.C. Davis J. Int'l L. & Pol'y* 119 (Spring 1998).
Falk, Richard, 'Cultural Foundations for the International Protection of Human

Rights', in Abdullahi An-Na'im (ed.), *Human Rights in Cross-Cultural Perspectives: A Quest for Consensus* (1992), 44–64.

Fournier, Pascale, *Muslim Marriage in Western Courts* (UK: Ashgate, 2010).

Greig, D.W., 'Reciprocity, Proportionality and the Law of Treaties', 34 *Virginia J. Int'l L.* 295 (Winter 1994).

Golia, Maria, 'Egyptian Women: Waiting for the Gender Renaissance', *The Middle East* 1 February 2007.

Guenena, Nemat, and Nadia Wassef, *Unfulfilled Promises. Women's Rights in Egypt* (1999), available at http://www.popcouncil.org/pdfs/unfulfilled_promises.pdf (last accessed 20 Dec. 2004).

Hafner-Burton, Emilie M., 'Sticks and Stones: Naming and Shaming the Human Rights Enforcement Problem', 62 *International Organization* 689–716 (Fall 2008).

Hajjar, Lisa, 'Domestic Violence and Shari'a: A Comparative Study of Muslim Societies in the Middle East, Africa and Asia', *Islamic Family Law Project*, at http://www.law.emory.edu/IFL/index2.html (last accessed 15 March 2005).

Halwa, Saeed, 'Thaghrat Shar'iyya fi qanun al-ahwal ashakhsiyya' [Legal Lacuna in the Personal Status Law], *Al-Ahram* 8 (18 February 2005.)

Hammoud, Rafiqa Selim, *Al Mar'a Al Misriya. Mushkilat Al-Hader wa Tahadiyat Al Musttaqbal* [The Egyptian Woman: Present Problems and Future Challenges] (Cairo: Dar Al-Amin, 1997).

Hannan, Shah Abdul, *Social Laws of Islam* (Bangladesh Institute of Islamic Thought, 1995, revised ed. 1997), available at http://www.witness-pioneer.org/vil/Books/SH_SL/default.htm

Haq, Farhat, 'Jihad Over Human Rights, Human Rights As Jihad. Clash of Universals', in Lynda S. Bell, Andrew J. Nathan and Ilan Peleg (eds.), *Negotiating Culture and Human Rights* (New York: Columbia UP, 2001), 242–257.

Helie-Lucas, Marie-Aimée, 'What is your tribe? Women's Struggles and the Construction of Muslimness', in Courtney Howland (ed.), *Religious Fundamentalisms and the Human Rights of Women* (New York: St. Martin's Press, 1999), 21–32.

Helmy, Hoda, *Al Mar'a Bayn Ta'aleem al Deen al Islamy wa Wad'iha Alrahen Fi Misr* (Cairo: Dar Al Qalam Lelnashr Waltawzee', 1999).

Hill, Enid, *Mahkama! Studies in the Egyptian legal system: Courts & Crimes, Law & Society* (London: Ithaca Press, 1979).

Hodkinson, Keith, *Muslim Family Law: A Sourcebook* (London: Croom, Helm Publishers 1984).

Hoq, Laboni Amena, 'The Women's Convention and its Optional Protocol: Empowering Women to Claim their Internationally Protected Rights', 32 *Colum. Hum. Rts. L. Rev.* 677 (Summer 2001).

Hossain, Sara, 'Equality in the Home: Women's Rights and Personal Laws in South Asia', in Rebecca J. Cook (ed.), *Human Rights of Women, National and International Perspectives* (1994), 465–494.

Howland, Courtney, 'The Challenge of Religious Fundamentalism to the Liberty and Equality Rights of Women: An Analysis under the United Nations Charter', 35 *Colum. J. Transnt'l L.* 271 (1997).

Ibrahim, Helal Youssef, *Mawsūʿat al-aḥwāl al-shakhṣiyya* [Encyclopaedia of Personal Status Law] (Cairo: Dar Al-Matbu'aat Al-Gaami'iya, 1994).

Jawad, Haifaa, *The Rights of Women in Islam. An Authentic Approach* (Great Britain: Palgrave, 1998).

Jenefsky, A., 'Permissibility of Egypt's Reservations to the Convention on the Elimination of All forms of Discrimination Against Women', 15 *Maryland J. of Int'l L. and Trade* 199.

Kandil, Amany, *Address at the Third Annual Conference of the Arab International Women's Forum* (8 June 2004).

Karam, Azza, 'Women, Islamisms and State', in Mahnaz Afkhami and Erika Friedl (eds.), *Muslim Women and the Politics of Participation. Implementing the Beijing Platform* (Syracuse, NY: Syracuse UP, 1997), 18–28.

Kevane, Michael, *Ratification of CEDAW*, unpublished research paper (Santa Clara University, 10 March 2003) available at http://emlab.berkeley.edu/users/webfac/bardhan/e271_sp03/mcvane.pdf.

Khafagy, Fatma, 'Traps of Empowerment', *Al-Ahram Weekly* 10–16 March 2005, available at http://weekly.ahram.org.eg/2005/733/fe1.htm.

Khan, Maimul Ahsan, *Human Rights in the Muslim World. Fundamentalism, Constitutionalism and International Politics* (North Carolina: Carolina Academic Press, 2003).

Klabbers, Jan, 'Accepting the Unacceptable? A New Nordic Approach to Reservations to Multilateral Treaties', 69 *Nordic J. Int'l L.* 179 (2000).

Leila, Reem, 'A Family Affair', *Al-Ahram Weekly* 16–22 January 2003, available at http://weekly.ahram.org.eg/2003/621/fe1.htm.

——, 'More Maternal Rights', *Al-Ahram Weekly* 10–16 March 2005, available at http://weekly.ahram.org.eg/2005/733/eg9.htm.

Liebesny, Herbert, *The Law of the Near and Middle East. Readings, Cases and Materials* (New York: Albany State University of New York Press, 1975).

Lijnzaad, Liesbeth, *Reservations to UN Human Rights Treaties. Ratify and Ruin?* (Dordrecht: TMC Asser Inst., 1995)

Maged, Amany, 'Al mar'a: ansafha al islam wa thalamaha al-muslimun' [Women: Vindicated by Islam yet Oppressed by Muslims], *Al-Ahram* 36 (6 May 2005).

Mayer, Ann Elizabeth, *Islam and Human Rights. Tradition and Politics* (London: Pinter Publishers, 1995).

——, 'Aberrant 'Islams' and Errant Daughters', in Camillia Fawzi El-Solh and Judy Mabro (eds.), *Muslim Women's Choices. Religious Belief and Social Reality* (Oxford: BERG, 1994).

Medina, Cecilia, 'Toward a More Effective Guarantee of the Enjoyment of Human Rights by Women in the Inter-American System', in Rebecca J. Cook (ed.), *Human Rights of Women, National and International Perspectives* (1994), 257–284.

Mernissi, Fatima, *Beyond the Veil: Male-Female Dynamics in Modern Muslim Society* (London: Al Saqi Books, 1985).

——, *The Veil and the Male Elite* (Cambridge: Perseus Books, 1991)

Mofty, Mohamed Ahmed and Samy Saleh El Wakil, *Al Nazharriyya Al Siyassiya Al Islamiya Fi Huquq Al Insan Al Shar'iya* [Islamic Political Theory and Human Rights] (Cairo: Akhbar Al Yom, 1990).

Moghissi, Haideh, *Feminism and Islamic Fundamentalism. The Limits of Post-modern Analysis* (London and New York: Zed Books, 1999).
Mohamed, Youssef Kamal, *Al Huquq Walwagebat Min Surat Al Nisaa'* [Rights and Duties in *Surat al-Nissaa*] (Cairo: Dar Al Qalam, 2000).
Mohamed, Zeinab, [Lawyer], *Interview* (5 November 2004).
Montesquieu, *De l'Esprit des Lois*, Book 1 Ch. 3.
Mountis, Elene G., 'Cultural Relativity and Universalism: Re-evaluating Gender Rights in a Multicultural Context', 15 *Dick. J. Int'l L.* 113 (Fall 1996).
Muslim Women's League, at http://www.mwlusa.org
Muslim Women Studies, at http://www.muslimwomenstudies.com
Muslim Women Lawyers for Human Rights, at http://www.karamah.org
Nosseir, Abdel Rahman, 'The Supreme Constitutional Court of Egypt and the Protection of Human Rights', in Eugene Cotran and Adel Omar Sheri (eds.), *The Role of the Judiciary in the Protection of Human Rights* (London: Kluwer Law International, 1997), 47–59.
Office of the High Commissioner for human rights http://www2.ohchr.org/english/bodies/chr/special/themes.htm.
Omar Sherif, Adel, 'Unshakable Tendency in the Protection of Human Rights: Adherence to International Instruments on Human Rights by the Supreme Constitutional Court of Egypt', in Eugene Cotran and Adel Omar Sherif (eds.), *The Role of the Judiciary in the Protection of Human Rights* (London: Kluwer Law International, 1997), 35–46.
Packer, Corrine, *Using Human Rights to Change Tradition. Traditional Practices Harmful to Women's Health in Sub-Saharan Africa* (Antwerp: Intersentia, 2002).
Parvin, Manoucher, 'On the Synergism of Gender and Class Exploitation: Theory and Practice Under Islamic Rule', 51 *Rev. Soc. Econ.* 201 (1993).
Paul, Joel R., 'Cultural Resistance to Global Governance', 22 *Mich. J. Int'l L.* 1 (Fall 2000).
——, 'Resisting Culture', 16 *Leiden J. Int'l L.* 919 (2003).
Peach, Lucinda Joy, 'Are Women Human? The Promise and Perils of Women's Rights as Human Rights', in Lynda S. Bell, Andrew J. Nathan and Ilan Peleg (eds.), *Negotiating Culture and Human Rights* (New York: Columbia UP, 2001), 153–196.
The Personal Status Laws, UNESCO, at http://www.unesco.org/webworld/peace_library/EGYPT/WOMEN/105.HTM
Plattner, Margaret, 'The Status of Women Under International Human Rights Law and the 1995 UN World Conference on Women, Beijing, China', 84 *Ky. L.J.* 1249 (Summer 1995/1996).
Preston, R. Christopher, and Ronald Z. Ahrens, 'United Nations Convention Documents in Light of Feminist Theory', 8 *Mich J. of I. Law* 1 (2001).
Radwan, Zeinab, *Etefaqiyat Ezalet Gami' Ashkal Al Tamyeez ded Al-Mar'a wa Aham Altahafozat Al-Masriya 'Alayha* [The Convention on the Elimination of All Forms of Discrimination Against Women and Egypt's Most Important Reservations], Paper (Cairo: Mashroo' Benaa' Alkodorat fi Magal Huquq Al-Inssan, 2002).
Redgwell, Catherine, 'Universality or Integrity? Some Reflections on Reservations to General Multilateral Treaties', *Brit. YB. Int'l L.* (1994).

Rhoodie, Eschel, *Discrimination Against Women. A Global Survey* (London: Mc Farland and Co., 1989).

Riddle, Jennifer, 'Making CEDAW Universal: A Critique of CEDAW's Reservation Regime Under Article 28 and the Effectiveness of the Reporting Process', 34 *Geo. Wash. Int'l L. Rev* (2002) 605.

Robinson Divine, Donna, 'Unveiling the Mysteries of Islam: The Art of Studying Muslim Women', 7 *J.S. Asian & Middle East Stud.* 3–19 (Winter 1983).

Romany, Celina, 'State Responsibility Goes Private: A Feminist Critique of the Public/Private Distinction in International Human Rights Law', in Rebecca J. Cook (ed.), *Human Rights of Women. National and International Perspectives* (1994), 85–115.

Roth, Kenneth, *Domestic Violence as an International Human Rights Issue*, in Rebecca J. Cook (ed.), *Human Rights of Women. National and International Perspectives* (1994), 326–339.

Ruda, J.M., 'Reservations to Treaties', 146 *Recueil de Cours III* 95–218 (1975).

Said, Edward, *Covering Islam* (New York, Vintage Books: 1997)

Sayeh, Leila, and Adriaen P. Morse 'Islam and the Treatment of Women: An Incomplete Understanding of Gradualism', *Tex. Int'l L.J.* (Spring 1995).

Schabas, William A., 'Reservations to the Convention on the Elimination of All Forms of Discrimination Against Women and the Convention on the Rights of the Child', *Wm. & Mary J. Women and Law* (1997).

——, 'Reservations to International Human Rights Treaties', 32 *Can. YB. Int'l L.* 39 (1995).

Shaham, Ron, *Family and the Courts in Modern Egypt* (Leiden: Brill, 1997).

Shaheed, Farida, 'Dossier 23–24: Constructing Identities—Culture, Women's Agency and the Muslim World', *Women Under Muslim Laws (WUML)*, available at http://www.wluml.org/node/342 (last accessed 20 November 2010).

Shaltout, Mohamed, *Al-Islam 'Aqida wa Shari'a* [Islam: Faith and Law] (Cairo: Dar Al-Qalam).

Singerman, Diane, 'Rewriting divorce in Egypt: Reclaiming Islam, Legal activism and Coalition Politics', in Robert Hefner (ed.), *Civic Pluralist Islam: Prospects and Policies for a Changing Muslim World* (forthcoming). Available at http: // www.ucis.unc.edu/programs/Middle_East/Diane%20Singerman.pdf

Sohn, Louis, ''Generally Accepted' International Rules', 61 *Wash. L. Rev.* 1073.

Southard, Jo Lynn, 'Protection of Women's Human Rights Under the Convention on the Elimination of Discrimination Against Women', 8 *Pace Int'l L. Rev.* 1 (Winter 1996).

Stark, Barbara, 'Bottom Line Feminist Theory: The Dream of A Common Language', 23 *Harv. Women's L. J.* 233 (Spring 2000).

——, 'Symposium on Integrating Responses to Domestic Violence. Domestic Violence and International Law: Good-Bye Earl (Hans, Pedro, Gen, Chou, etc.)', 47 *Loy. L. Rev.* 255 (Spring 2001).

Stopler, Gila, 'Countenancing the Oppression of Women: How Liberals Tolerate Religious and Cultural Practices that Discriminate Against Women', 12 *Colum. J. Int'l L.* 154 (2003).

Suneja, Kathleen, 'The Empowerment of Women Through International Law', in Rekha Datta and Judith Kornberg (eds.), *Women in Developing Countries.*

Assessing Strategies for Empowerment (London: Lynne Rienner Publishers; 2002).

Sutherland, Kate, 'Form Jailbird to Jailbait: Age of Consent Laws and the Construction of Teenage Sexualities', 9 *William and Mary J. of Women and the Law* 313 (2003).

Tadros, Mariz, 'Khulʿ Passes Major Test', *Al-Ahram Weekly* 19–25 December 2002.

——, 'Rooster's Wrath', *Al-Ahram Weekly* 20–26 January 2000.

——, 'The Third Option', *Al-Ahram Weekly* 31 October–6 November 2002, available at http://weekly.ahram.org.eg/2002/610/li2.htm

——, 'What Price Freedom?', *Al-Ahram Weekly* 7–13 March 2003, available at http://weekly.ahram.org.eg/2002/576/fe1.htm

Talhami, Ghada Hashem, *Egyptian Feminism in the Balance. The Mobilisation of Muslim Women in Egypt* (Florida: University Press of Florida, 1996).

Tallawy, Mervat, 'National Machinery and Foreign Policy', in Camillia Fawzi El-Solh and Judy Mabro (eds.), *Muslim Women's Choices. Religious Belief and Social Reality* (Oxford; BERG, 1994).

Tucker, Elizabeth, *In the House of the Law, Gender and Islamic Law in Ottoman Syria and Palestine* (Berkeley: University of California Press, 1998).

Tunkin, Gregory, 'Is General International Law Customary Law Only?', 4 *EJIL* 534 (1993), available at http://www.ejil.org/journal/Vol4/No4/art4.html.

Tyagi, Yogesh, 'The Conflict of Law and Policy on Reservations to Human Rights Treaties', *Brit. Y.B. Int'l L* (2001).

UN Division for the Advancement of Women, at http://www.un.org/womenwatch/daw/cedaw/reservations.htm

Vali, Nasr, 'Islam, Capitalism, Reform. Economics Versus Extremism', *Newsweek* 2 November 2009.

Venkatraman, Bharathi Anandhi, 'Islamic States and the UN Convention on the Elimination of All Forms of Discrimination Against Women: Are the Shariʾa and the Convention Compatible?', 44 *Am. U.L. Rev.* (Summer 1995).

Vesey-Fitzgerald, S.G., 'Nature and Sources of the Shariʾa', in Khadduri and Liebesny (eds.), *Law in the Middle East* 94 Vol. 1 (1978).

Wadud, Amena, *Qur'an and Woman* (Oxford: Oxford UP, 1999).

Weisburd, Arthur M., 'The Significance and Determination of Customary International Human Rights Law: The Effect of Treaties and Other Formal International Acts On the Customary Law of Human Rights', 25 *Ga. J. Int'l & Comp. L.* 99 (Fall 1995/Winter 1996).

Wing, Adrien Katherine, 'Custom, Religion and Rights: The future Legal Status of Palestinian Women', 35 *Harv. Int'l L.J.* 149 (Winter 1994).

Welchman, Lynn, 'Egypt: New Deal on Divorce', in Andrew Bainham (ed.), *The International Survey of Family Law* (The Hague, Boston, London: Martinus Nijhoff Publishers, 2004).

Women Living Under Muslim Laws, at http://wluml.org

Women Watch. The UN Internet Gateway on the Advancement and Empowerment of Women, at http://www.un.org/womenwatch/

Zahw, Ahmed El Nagdy, *Ahkam al-mirath fil shariʿa al-islamiyya* [Inheritance Law in the Islamic *Sharīʿa*] (Cairo, 2003).

Zuhur, Sherifa, 'The Mixed Impact of Feminist Struggles in Egypt During the 1990's', 5 *Middle East Rev. Int'l A.* issue 1 (March 2001), available at http://meria.idc .ac.il/journal/2001/issue1/jv5n1a6.html

INDEX

www.ingramcontent.com/pod-product-compliance
Lightning Source LLC
LaVergne TN
LVHW081351011026
849161LV00013BA/2786